Leadership in Isolation

Leadership in Isolation

FDR AND THE ORIGINS OF THE SECOND WORLD WAR

WILLIAM E. KINSELLA, JR.

G.K.HALL & CO.
70 LINCOLN STREET, BOSTON, MASS.

SCHENKMAN PUBLISHING COMPANY
Cambridge, Mass.

Copyright © 1978 by Schenkman Publishing Company, Inc.

Library of Congress Cataloging in Publication Data
Kinsella, William E
  Leadership in isolation.

  Bibliography: p.
  1. United States—Foreign relations—1933-1945.
  2. Roosevelt, Franklin Delano, Pres. U. S., 1882-1945.
  3. World War, 1939-1945—Causes. I. Title.
E806.K56 940.53′11 77-26612
ISBN 0-8161-8249-3

This publication is printed on permanent/durable acid-free paper
MANUFACTURED IN THE UNITED STATES OF AMERICA

TABLE OF CONTENTS

I

PORTENTS OF THE FUTURE

II

WINDS OF CHANGE

III

IN SEARCH OF A RESPONSE

IV

THE STRUGGLE COMMENCES: APPEASEMENT AND AGGRESSION

V

APPROACHING ENCOUNTER — INEVITABLE CLIMAX

VI

CONCLUSION

cratic principles, moral convictions, and humane sensitivities could remain a dispassionate witness of the Nazi terror regime. FDR was not an emotionless, detached, passive observer of this tragic spectacle of brutal war aggression and murder. Indeed, he was convinced that Germany under Adolf Hitler would never accept a negotiated settlement unless it included a dictated acquiescence of submission to a new world fascist dominance. Franklin Roosevelt would never accept such terms.

Franklin Roosevelt's growing sense of alarm prior to the world holocaust was strengthened by his predilection for synthesizing the world diplomatic scene into a unified, whole, and composite picture. The primary focus was consistently on Germany, but the threat of fascism emanated from several quarters, and the increasing tendency of Germany, Italy, and Japan to cooperate in extending their spheres of influence was considered by the President to be replete with extremely dangerous potentialities for the United States. An attempt will be made to assess the personal views of Franklin Roosevelt concerning Japan, and, as in the case of Germany, there will be demonstrated the consistency with which the President assayed the intentions of the Japanese militarists. He considered a confrontation between the United States and Japan in the Far East to be a distinct possibility, if not a probability, long before the outbreak of war. Germany's success in creating a new order in Europe, combined with Japan's thrust to assume control throughout the Far East and Pacific regions, would bring about an imbalance of power which would mean the inevitable economic strangulation of the United States. Benito Mussolini's decision to cast Italy's lot with that of Germany and Japan further magnified what Franklin Roosevelt perceived as a fascist bloc inimically opposed to the United States and the forces of democracy.

No attempt will be made to uncover new revelations concerning an American commitment to aid Great Britain and France in their struggle against Germany. A discussion of Franklin Roosevelt's emphatic rejection of British and French appeasement policies will be of major importance, however, in an effort to amplify the extent of the President's determined resistance to the dictator nations. The perceived weaknesses of both Great Britain and France were also important considerations in determining the necessity for eventual participation in the war by the United States. FDR's assessment of the precarious posture of these democratic allies will therefore be set forth in detail. The other member of the future Allied coalition, the Soviet Union, will receive very close scrutiny.

The unconditional surrender of the fascist leadership was implicit in Franklin Roosevelt's condemnation of the Axis triumvirate. Preoccupied with the grave threat of these powers to a world of peace and democratic order, FDR anxiously sought the aid of a regime which he believed would be able to provide an immediate restoration of the balance of power in Europe and the Far East, and an ultimate guarantee of military victory in the future struggle. He followed a most active and persistent policy in his efforts to entice the Soviet Union into the democratic coalition. The tenacity with which Franklin Roosevelt pursued this objective will be of critical importance in this analysis for it reveals the President's resolve to constrain those nations which resolutely and aggressively promoted ambitious policies of forceful territorial conquest.

The realization that an armed confrontation with the exponents of fascism was inevitable if the democracies were to survive did not arise as a vacuous assumption in the mind of the Chief Executive. Available sources upon which Franklin Roosevelt based his appraisal of the foreign policies of Germany, Italy, and Japan consistently indicated the hostility, irreconcilability, and desire for eventual war and a new world order on the part of these fascist powers. President Roosevelt had every reason to believe that the United States would be in grave danger should the Axis nations prove successful in their expansionist ambitions. He was constantly receiving extensive information on the changing European and Far Eastern situations, and the attitudes and views taken by most of his observers were not at all sanguine concerning the future and the prospects for peace. What were the Chief Executive's primary sources of information on foreign developments?

The President's Secretary's File in the Franklin D. Roosevelt Library contains the bulk of the material which was available to the President concerning foreign affairs. Herein may be found the personal letters, memoranda, and intelligence reports which formed the substance of Roosevelt's personal views during these critical crises years. The areas of investigation which offered the most extensive analyses of developments in Europe and the Far East include the Diplomatic Correspondence containers of Germany, Japan, Italy, Soviet Union, France, and Great Britain. In addition to these important diplomatic posts, the despatches pertinent to Argentina, Austria, Belgium, Brazil, Bolivia, Chile, China, Columbia, Czechoslovakia, Denmark, Ethiopa, Finland, Greece, Hungary, Iceland, Mexico, Paraguay, Peru, Rumania, Spain, and Venezuela have also yielded valuable insights into the President's perspective of this period. The Ambassadors who were particularly expansive in their evaluations of the evolving war situation and in their suggestions to Franklin Roosevelt were William Dodd (Germany); William Bullitt (Soviet Union and France); Breckinridge Long and William Phillips (Italy); Robert Bingham, Joseph Kennedy, and John Winant (United Kingdom); Joseph Davies (Soviet Union and Belgium); Herbert Pell (Portugal and Hungary); Claude Bowers (Spain and Chile); Josephus Daniels (Mexico); and Lincoln MacVeagh (Greece). Dave Morris (Belgium); John Cudahy (Poland); Jesse Straus (France); Fred Dearing (Peru); Hugh Wilson (Germany); Myron Taylor (Vatican); Nelson Johnson (China); Joseph Grew (Japan); Laurence Steinhardt (Soviet Union); and George Earle (Austria) provided glimpses of the present in their letters to the President.

There are several other areas within the President's Secretary's File which were crucial to the task of ascertaining Franklin Roosevelt's global perspective. A most valuable source of data was the collection of diplomatic despatches sent from the State Department to the White House during the years immediately preceding the outbreak of World War II. This material consists of letters and memoranda from diplomatic officers to the Secretary of State and other officials in the Department of State. Diplomatic correspondence from Tokyo, Berlin, Rome, Moscow, London, and Vienna was forwarded to the President for his evaluation. The sheer bulk of this file is partial evidence of the extensive amount of information which was available to the Chief Executive concerning the European and Far Eastern situations.

There is also contained within the President's Secretary's File valuable departmental correspondence. The Navy, War, and State Departments' folders provided much relevant material. The letters and memoranda of departmental secretaries including Secretaries of War George Dern, Harry Woodring, and Henry Stimson; Secretaries of Navy Claude Swanson, Charles Edison, and Frank Knox; and Secretary of State Cordell Hull are deposited in this file. The memoranda of the Secretary of State's assistants may also be found herein, including those of Adolph Berle, Sumner Welles, William Phillips, J. Pierrepont Moffat, and Breckinridge Long. The departmental correspondence includes important intelligence reports from the Chief of Naval Operations and other military and naval officers on Axis aggression and suspected German and Japanese espionage efforts in Latin America and the United States Pacific possessions. The Subject and Safe Files in this same classification offer important correspondence concerning the major diplomatic events and personages of this period. The President's Personal File, consisting of the Chief Executive's private correspondence, was an important source for diplomatic perspectives.

Manuscripts deposited in the Franklin D. Roosevelt Library offered vital details and insights. The papers of Henry Morgenthau, Jr., Herbert Pell, Wayne Coy, Henry Wallace, Lowell Mellett, William Hassett, R. Walton Moore, John Carmody, Leon Henderson, Louis

Wehle, Harry Hopkins, and Stephen Early were consulted for this study. The Manuscript Division of the Library of Congress was a source of other important papers including those of Norman Davis, Joseph Davies, Herbert Feis, Josephus Daniels, William Leahy, William Dodd, Jesse Jones, Robert LaFollette, Jr., Arthur Sweetzer Laurence Steinhardt, Nelson Johnson, William Allen White, Felix Frankfurter, Key Pittman, Cordell Hull, Breckinridge Long, and Francis Sayre.

The perspective from the White House in the area of foreign affairs, as is evident from the abundance of pertinent research data, was very extensive. Franklin Roosevelt, as will be demonstrated, clearly foresaw the inevitability of war. A man of peace and civility, he watched the war preparations of the fascist triumvirate with agonizing concern. He urged the democratic countries to abandon the enticing but disastrous policies of appeasement. They responded negatively, as did the American public, until the struggle clearly became one of self-preservation. This study reveals a prescient statesman whose vision of the terrifying apocalypse was proven tragically correct, yet one whose proposals for collective resistance to aggression were ignored or rebuffed by his contemporaries. Leadership in isolation was but another inevitable consequence of mankind's decision to recognize the legitimacy of force and violence in international affairs. Perhaps the civilized community of nations will learn from the past and strengthen their resolve to join wholeheartedly in efforts to promote peace throughout the world. Indeed, the future presents no other rational alternative. The destiny of the world must never again be surrendered to the proponents of lawlessness, hate, and terror.

I

Portents
of the Future

CHAPTER ONE

PORTENTS OF THE FUTURE

YEARS OF WAR: IMPRESSIONS AND CONVICTIONS

Franklin Roosevelt's schooling in world affairs began during the administration of Woodrow Wilson. He had vigorously supported the Democratic ticket during the 1912 election campaign and was subsequently appointed Assistant Secretary of the Navy. Franklin's initial years in public office coincided, ironically, with the beginnings of the first catastrophic world war. The events of this era were portents of the trials and tribulations which were to confront the future President as nations plunged into the abyss of martial engagement. The response of FDR to the threats of aggressor nations in this early formative period offers a most prophetic prelude to, and understanding of, his actions and thoughts in later years.

The Secretary of the Navy, Josephus Daniels, had been forewarned of Franklin's arrival. Elihu Root had told him that whenever a Roosevelt rides, he wishes to ride in front and to have his own way. This prognostication was descriptive of Franklin Roosevelt's sentiments on the subject of war preparedness and intervention in the European struggle. He was to become a vocal exponent of both causes during these years of war. The Assistant Secretary's speeches on the issue of war preparedness reveal a growing concern that the United States would not be able to remain isolated from events overseas. Franklin Roosevelt warned members of the United States Navy League on April 10, 1913, that war was a grave possibility, and that every effort must be made to obtain a fighting force of the highest efficiency. The themes of preparedness and defense were enunciated wtih impassioned vigor a year later.[1]

The assassination of the Austrian Archduke Franz Ferdinand in Sarajevo, Bosnia, marked the beginning of the European holocaust.

9

Events thereafter moved with uncontrolled rapidity, seemingly dictating a logic of their own beyond the manipulative grasp of monarchs and statesmen. Franklin Roosevelt's thoughts on the consequences of these events for the United States were expressed very clearly. National security, he believed, dictated the need for a defensive preparedness. In a speech delivered in Flushing, New York, on December 21, 1915, he appraised his listeners of the fact that national jealousies and national ambitions did exist, and that nations, jealous of America's wealth and influence, would be extremely eager to take such away from the United States. This could be accomplished, he continued, either by direct attack on America's shores, or by the gradual economic strangulation of the United States. Americans must take action against both possibilities, he concluded, and should embark on immediate steps to control threatened adjacent seas.[2]

The preparedness theme was discussed in two presentations before the House of Representatives' Committee on Naval Affairs. He warned that the United States was comparatively less prepared militarily than the other major world powers. He stated that the war provided an opportunity to hurry America's defensive preparations. There was always the possibility of invasion by the victorious powers even if the United States was not to become involved in the present engagement. A "mix-up" with that victorious side, he thought, just might occur, and it seemed very doubtful to him that the shock of invasion could be sustained by defensive resistance. Every effort must therefore be made to strengthen the military posture of the United States. Although an attack on American shores had not yet occurred, it might take place tomorrow. In a rather pessimistic and alarming manner, he concluded that the United States could not assume to occupy a safe position should the war end through the exhaustion of all participants.[3]

Franklin Roosevelt's thoughts may have been on the future, but he was to become increasingly worried about the probability of either a direct attack on the United States, or the elimination of America's naval presence throughout the world and the dire economic consequences that might occur due to America's ouster from the seas. In an article written for *Scribner's Magazine* in 1917, he chastised those responsible for the "Great Inertia" which FDR defined as the failure to recognize the precarious position of the United States in the present struggle. He speculated that the reasons for this feeling of security in. isolation stemmed from individualism applied to national questions, or a lack of knowledge concerning the peoples and events beyond America's borders, or a national snobbishness, or blinding prosperity, or utopian idealism. We must, he warned, visualize the nation's position in the world. Those congressmen who advocate hiding behind the Allegheny and Rocky Mountains and viewing with smug satisfaction the impregnable Atlantic and Pacific Oceans are making a serious mistake, he added. Americans can no longer view the ocean as an impregnable barrier to that power which controls its waters. In other words, he concluded, we must admit that a great campaign in the Western Hemisphere, a campaign into which millions of men could be thrown, is a military possibility for any nation or combination of nations able to drive the United States fleet off the seas. These views were reiterated in an article published in the *Ladies Home Journal* that same year. National security will be preserved, he wrote, if the nation proved strong enough to repulse hostile armed forces from landing on the seaboard, and if the navy was sufficiently strong to keep open the highway of commerce across the seas and along the coasts. America must prepare before it is too late, urged the Assistant Secretary.[4]

While these comments stress the defensive aspect of preparedness, Franklin Roosevelt believed that national security and personal sentiment would dictate United States participation in the European conflict. He began to consider military preparedness as a necessary prerequisite for direct intervention. In a memorandum to President Wilson, he conveyed his thoughts on the necessity of formal action by the United States in the war. In his letter to the President, the Assistant Secretary was discreet. He enclosed a statement dictated in 1814 by a former Secretary of State, James Monroe. Monroe had written that a war in Europe had long been found to spread its calamities into the remotest regions. The United States, said Monroe, would not be able to avoid the alternative of either submitting to the most destructive and ignominious wrongs from European belligerents, or of resisting them by an appeal to the sword. If aggression was to be halted, the United States must commit itself in the European struggle. In a letter to the American writer Winston Churchill, Franklin was more direct in expressing his thoughts. He wrote that "what the country needs more than recruits even, is a realization of a whole lot of things which it does not realize today. For instance, our relationship to the rest of the world, the meaning of getting ready for and conducting a war, and a few other little trifles of that kind."[5]

Franklin Roosevelt was not as discreet on the issue of intervention in his conversations with others as he was in the memorandum to Woodrow Wilson. Josephus Daniels was aware of his subordinate's eager desire to enter the war. Franklin chafed under what he considered to be his superior's timidity and hesitation on this issue. He boasted to his wife that he was running the real work because Josephus was bewildered by it all; very sweet but very sad, he added.

In exasperation, a brash assistant referred to Daniels as too damned slow for words and an impediment to the real progress which he, Franklin, could be making during the crisis. Eleanor recalled that there were many times when her husband wished that a final decision for intervention could be reached more quickly. Franklin Roosevelt seems to have become emotionally involved in the struggle from its very inception. He considered himself to be a participant in a climactic episode of world history. He wrote to Eleanor telling her that these were history making days, and that the greatest war in the world's history was now taking place. He believed that the war would give rise to a hundred different complications in which the United States would have a direct interest.[6]

Personal sentiment pushed Franklin Roosevelt toward intervention. He confided to Eleanor that he hoped England, France, and Russia would be able to prevent a long drawn out struggle and force peace at Berlin. He derisively remarked that his feelings had been hurt because the Emperor William had left the United States out after having declared war against everybody else. He believed that the Germans might be doing more than many suspected, and that the sympathies of most Americans were strongly against Germany. He noted with delight that England had moved against Germany, although he expressed disappointment concerning the British failure to force a decisive naval action. Aware of his innate sympathies, Franklin feared that he might do some awful unneutral thing.[7]

These sentiments against Germany may have been strengthened as the war progressed. The unrestricted German submarine campaign horrified and angered most Americans. The sinking of the Cunard liner *Lusitana* with the loss of many American lives served to solidify public opinion in opposition to Germany. The Secretary of State, William J. Bryan, of strong anti-interventionist views, submitted his resignation fearing that public opinion would force President Wilson into making a formal declaration of war. Franklin expressed unbridled disgust with Bryan's action. Germany's policies, he believed, left little room for pacifism. The sinking of the White Star liner *Arabic* further angered Franklin Roosevelt. He was certain that now, once all the facts were in, President Wilson would declare war. He personally would not wait for Germany to tell its version of the incident. This was no time to be polite. Woodrow Wilson, however, refused to act in haste, and, during a discussion with Franklin, spoke candidly of the necessity of placing Germany very clearly in the role of the aggressor. The United States must do nothing provocative, said the President. Future historians could thereby write that America entered the conflict for the sole purpose of defeating a hostile aggressor power. President Wilson's prescient words would not be forgotten by the impetuous Assistant Secretary. A great amount of patience would be demanded of a later President who, while believing in the necessity of war, was forced by the realities of democratic government to await what he considered to be the inevitable climax.[8]

Franklin Roosevelt wholeheartedly endorsed the declaration of war made by the United States against Germany on April 6, 1917. In the days that followed the entrance of the United States into the war, the Assistant Secretary pushed hard for the sending of immediate aid, in both men and materials, to Great Britain and France. In an emotionally charged speech to members of the British War Commission, Franklin Roosevelt condemned, in no uncertain terms, the failure to make good on promises made to America's allies. There had been, he charged, too many fair words, too many pledges of what was going to be done. The time had come to discuss what must be done now, he said. Days, weeks, months have gone by with very little accomplished; we must now insist on action at once. What our allies need, Roosevelt said, are definite ships and definite men on a definite day. We are in this war to stick, he admonished, and we must take stock of the little bit we are doing before it is too late. He concluded that on the basis of United States action thus far, the British and French have every right to reproachfully ask about the men and ships they had been promised. Aid to beleaguered opponents of Germany would again occupy Franklin Roosevelt's attention on the eve of America's participation in the Second World War.[9]

The Assistant Secretary's role in the high level operations of the war effort does not seem to have been a major one. He did contribute plans for an elaborate scheme to mine the English Channel and the North Sea. This would prevent German submarines from entering the Atlantic and Mediterranean areas. He wrote to Josephus Daniels saying that, if successful, the project would be the biggest single factor in winning the war. The importance of this war period for Franklin Roosevelt is not to be found, however, in war plans and administrative experiences. Impressions of future aggressor countries, specifically Germany and Japan, seem to have remained with Franklin Roosevelt. They were strengthened by the course of future events.[10]

In Roosevelt's mind, Germany was the most dangerous and treacherous opponent from the outset. He was fearful of a direct attack by that nation on the United States. He warned Eleanor that if, by any perfectly wild chance, a German submarine should bombard Eastport, she must grab the children and beat it into the woods. He stressed that he was not joking about this, and that although the chances were 500 to 1 against the possibility, the *Boche* might still do the foolish and unexpected thing. In one instance, the Assistant Secretary sent a personal note to the Office of Naval Intelligence urging close supervision of a Naval Coast Defense Reserve officer because he was suspected of personal affiliation with Germany. There was always the danger of sabotage.[11]

There were also horrifying scenes bearing witness to the awesome power of the German war machine. In the summer of 1918, Josephus Daniels sanctioned a European inspection tour by his Assistant Secretary. Franklin Roosevelt's diary entries for these months reveal his impressions of this appalling picture of destruction. Franklin agreed fully with the King of England. In an interview with Roosevelt, King George V had spoken of numerous German atrocities in Belgium and northern France. Franklin commented that as a boy in Germany he had personally witnessed the preparation of the war machine. The King likewise recounted his early schooling in Germany, and, with a twinkle in his eye, told his visitor, "You know I have a number of relations in Germany, but I can tell you frankly that in all my life I have never seen a German gentleman."[12]

Traveling on the continent of Europe, Franklin recorded his observations of the war crimes perpetrated by the "Huns." Visiting the front lines in France, he made the following diary entry:

> The little church in Cierges remained just as the Boche had left it. It had evidently been used as a hospital for litters of straw were still on the floor and various articles of Hun clothing. Every altar ornament and embroidery was gone and the houses themselves were cleaned out and more furniture broken than could possibly happen by shell fire. For instance, you could go into a small room, the walls and even the ceiling of which were completely intact, and in the corner you would find a wreck of three chairs, one leg of a table gone, and smashed china on the dresser. That kind of work was done deliberately and maliciously by the Huns.[13]

The next day, Franklin described a French hospital that had been shelled. All the windows had been blown in, and two sheds in the courtyard destroyed. A soldier on the operating table at the time of the attack had been showered with window glass, but had not been seriously injured. He wrote in his diary,

> I was told that the enemy must have known that it was a hospital. It had been used for many months, and the two big white crosses marked out on the ground must have been seen many times by Hun observation planes. The attack was made in daylight, the bomber circling above the hospital for fully ten minutes.

In a letter to his mother, he described yet anothed gruesome scene of war. American troops, wrote Franklin, had evacuated eight little girls, between the ages of eleven and thirteen, enceinte from the Germans. Men were openly crying and all would have murdered any

German in sight, he noted. In a letter to Sara the following day, referring to the Germans as Huns and Germany as Hunland, Franklin recounted tales of indiscriminate German bombing and strafing of a British hospital at Doullens.[14]

Japan was also of constant concern to Franklin Roosevelt. There were many naval officers who shared the opinion that eventually, inevitably, a confrontation between the United States and Japan in the Pacific must take place. Memoranda and letters expressive of this viewpoint often crossed the Assistant Secretary's desk. Despite Japan's entrance into the war on the side of the Entente powers, most observers impugned its motives. They charged that Japan's real objective was the acquisition of all German islands in the Pacific, and the ousting of German influence from China with Japan as the benefactor. This was the opinion expressed by Admiral Alfred T. Mahan in a letter to Franklin Roosevelt. Japan, wrote Mahan, will be at liberty to take the German islands, Pelew, Marianne, Caroline, and Samoa. The first three, he noted, flank our course to the Philippines. In the hands of Germany, whose strength is in Europe, the islands had served little strategic value. However, observed Mahan, should they pass to a Pacific power such as Japan, the islands might easily be used to reduce American influence in that region of the world. Japan's action in threatening to declare war on Germany was at best, in the eyes of the Admiral, disingenuous. He concluded that, although his own sympathies had been strongly against Germany as the state responsible for the war, the Japanese seemed to lack an understanding of fair play.[15]

Admiral Mahan's opinions confirmed what many others had expressed in their warnings to Franklin Roosevelt. A Japanese attack on the Pacific possessions of the United States was anticipated before the alignment of Japan with the Entente powers. Theodore Roosevelt had expressed his concern to Franklin saying that should Japan decide to come in against America, the attack would come suddenly. Memories of the surprise assault against Russian forces at Port Arthur by Japan had not been forgotten. In an alarming memorandum, Roosevelt was warned by Rear Admiral Bradley Fiske, Aid for Operations to the Secretary of the Navy, that Japan might decide to go to war with the United States in order to secure possession of the Philippine Islands and the Hawaiian Islands. Fiske saw the islands as outlets for Japan's surplus population. The Japanese, he observed, have a tremendous national feeling and a great deal of endurance and determination which would serve them well in a confrontation with the United States. An official of the Department of Justice detailed Japanese plans to work through the colored races in America in an effort to create friction and mistrust between these people and their government by establishing colonies of such disgruntled emigrants in Mexico for future use in sabotage and other clandestine operations.[16]

The decision of Japan to support the Entente cause did not dispel the preconceived views of that power as an aggressor nation. A report from the Office of Naval Intelligence described an elaborate spy ring constructed by Japan in the United States, Mexico, and Canada. Japanese and German agents were working closely together in subversive operations. Included in the memorandum was the statement that the opportune psychological moment to attack the United States will have arrived when the European war ends. It is not clear what Franklin Roosevelt might have thought of this rather unsubstantiated information. The general thrust of the memorandum does coincide, however, with numerous other intelligence reports which were forwarded to his office.[17]

There was evidence to strengthen the opinion that a Japanese attack would occur after the war's conclusion. The Office of Naval Intelligence described for the Assistant Secretary plans for a nation-wide terrorist campaign to be conducted by German, Russian, Mexican and Japanese terrorists in the United States. The Director of Naval Intelligence forwarded information of extensive war preparations by Japan. Eight hundred German specialists were aiding Japan in submarine construction in preparation for a war of the greatest magnitude against the United States. Japan's Monroe Doctrine necessitates the coming war, he warned. Naval Intelligence forwarded another report telling of a secret Japanese-Mexican alliance. If Japan and the United States should engage in war, then the army and navy of Mexico, under Japanese direction, would attack the United States. Japan had pledged to guarantee for Mexico control of Texas, New Mexico, California, and Arizona.[18]

These purported plans of Japan did not come to fruition. Another memorandum, however, offered to Franklin Roosevelt an extensive analysis of the long range foreign policy interests of Japan. In handwriting on the report are the comments "Splendid Report," and "It bears very careful reading as being the opinion of one of the best informed foreigners on Far Eastern affairs." The writer begins ominously with the statement that Japan is a frankly militaristic and imperialistic nation. Military achievements alone explain her now prominent position in world affairs, and her rulers are imbued with the idea of establishing their military supremacy throughout the Orient. This objective dictated Japanese absorption of China, and should such occur, Japan's position in the Pacific would be almost impregnable. American interests would never be able to expand beyond the California coast without the consent of Japan. It should be obvious that American free trade and freedom of action in the Pacific, west of the three mile limit, would be wholly dependent upon China's continued independence. A strong China was as essential to America in the Pacific as a weak China was to Japan's imperialistic ambitions. The United States, therefore, would have to support every effort which would hasten the formation of a strong democratic government in China. The author's final remarks stressed the inherent belligerence in the Japanese position. The Japanese unanimously believed that an armed conflict with the United States was inevitable, and that such a war would take place over China seemed to the observer a foregone conclusion.[19]

The advice given in this memorandum coincided with Franklin Roosevelt's personal views. There would be moments when he would give evidence of a contradictory position. Writings in which he advocated that trust and understanding be extended to Japan will be cited. Nevertheless, the suspicions of Japan's imperialistic designs, originating during this period of service in the Wilson administration, remained with Roosevelt, and were reaffirmed repeatedly in the intelligence reports that came to the Office of the President. Eleanor Roosevelt recalled many years later that her husband's concern for the security of America's island outposts in the Pacific began "way back when he was Assistant Secretary of the Navy. I think his suspicions of Japan were based on his own outlook of what he felt made the Pacific safe for us. In all the war games, Japan was always considered the enemy in the Pacific." [20]

1920: Roosevelt, The United States and Collective Security

In the years immediately following the end of the war, it would appear that Franklin Roosevelt devoted his most serious thoughts to the subject of foreign policy. During these moments of reflection, he was to articulate an approach to international affairs which would remain a constant theme throughout his presidency: the United States must abandon its isolationist posture and participate actively in the community of nations. This, and only this, would prevent a repetition of the recently witnessed holocaust.

The influence of Woodrow Wilson on Franklin D. Roosevelt was decisive. It was the former's plans for a League of Nations that provided the stimulus for Roosevelt's explicit concentration on international issues. His strong commitment to the cause of international cooperation and to the goals of Wilson were evident in the presidential campaign of 1920. The Democratic ticket was headed by Governor James Cox of Ohio. Franklin Roosevelt, the Democratic candidate for Vice-President, made the League of Nations the decisive issue. He had said, upon returning from Paris, that something nobler and higher than a mere treaty of peace must be achieved. The campaign was, for Roosevelt, an opportunity to realize the ideals of Woodrow Wilson and to bring the United States into the community of nations. During a private meeting with the ailing President Wilson, the two Democratic candidates gave their personal pledge that the League of Nations would be the paramount issue. During this emotional scene, not forgotten by Roosevelt, Wilson uttered his appreciation in a tired and almost silent voice, twice repeating, "I am very grateful." [21]

Franklin Roosevelt carried the campaign for the League to the American people. The pervasive idealism of Woodrow Wilson may have enveloped Franklin, as Eleanor asserts, in Paris, but the vice-presidential candidate was too pragmatic and realistic to have given serious consideration to thoughts of a millenium of universal peace. He would stress the necessity of the Wilson experiment because he believed that war would be inevitable in the future. In his acceptance speech after the Democratic Party's convention, he purposefully avoided any reference to the League as a panacea for the world's ills. We cannot exist as a hermit nation, he asserted. Civilization is so complex and the lives of civilized men are so interwoven that it is impossible to be in the world and not a part of it. Monastic seclusion, in order to avoid that Devil's catch-word international complications, is no longer an alternative, he said. The League of Nations' in Roosevelt's opinion, offered a practical solution of a practical situation. In concluding this speech, the candidate stressed that the peaceful forces in the world must have the machinery by which the opinion of civilization might become effective against those who seek war. Smaller peoples must be safe to work out their own destiny, and the burdensome taxation brought on by increasing armies and navies must be lifted. The League may make such possible, he told the audience. [22]

Franklin Roosevelt, in the speeches that followed, enlarged on the themes implicit in the above passage. He emphasized that the power of the United States carried with it a very grave responsibility. We are, he said, the keystone of the arch of world peace. The nations of the world have what might be called a fire department, but that fire department just now lacks a chief. An apparatus has been constructed. There is a pole for the firemen to slide down, and there are uniforms; but, there is no chief. "And what the League of Nations needs today is a chief — a man who knows how to fight fire — a man who knows how to keep fire from spreading — and that man is the United States." [23]

A sense of dutiful responsibility was not the only motive which should compel the United States to enter the League. The security of the United States and of the world likewise necessitated America's entrance into the League. Under this new law of nations, an aggressor can safely assume that all other nations will be against it, he reasoned. Would Germany have attacked Belgium and France if she knew that England, Italy, and the United States would not remain neutral? Is it right that one outlaw nation should be able to run amuck and murder or maim a brother nation without being called to account for it? The League of Nations offers assurance that never again could a monstrous world crime like that of 1914 be perpetrated. The League is the most practical way of restoring international peace and of preventing another attack on civilization. Roosevelt attacked the Republican plan for a Permanent Court of Arbitration, comparing it to a hospital, constructed at the foot of a cliff in order to care for the broken limbs of the nations who fall over the edge. The Democrats wished to erect a stout fence around the top in order to prevent the nations of the world from falling off. In Roosevelt's opinion, the League was to serve as preventive medicine for international ills.[24]

The vice-presidential candidate warned his countrymen that failure to join the League would bring disastrous consequences. The abandonment of the League would mean a revival of the old system of national jealousies, competitive armaments, and balances of power. It would mean a return to the days of imperialism and aggression, to the old attitude of contempt for smaller and weaker people, and to the cry of 1914 to the victor belongs the spoils. He cautioned that to quit now is to invite terrorism and anarchy. Rejection of the League will prepare the way for brute force, the way of Napoleon, of Caesar, and of Alexander the Great. Should there be a future war, America will be drawn in anyway, Roosevelt asserted, and it would be to our benefit to stand united against the forces of aggression. If you wish to send troops overseas, he warned, then stay out of the League. These words, in retrospect, seem unusually and remarkably prophetic.[25]

Franklin Roosevelt concluded a speech on November 1, 1920, with the admonition, "It is for you to decide Mr. Individual," and, indeed, his fellow countrymen did decide decisively. Warren Harding and Calvin Coolidge had won an impressive victory. The League of Nations had been repudiated. The Treaty of Versailles, containing the Covenant of the League, was rejected. Franklin Roosevelt would seldom again speak so candidly and boldly concerning what he considered to be the necessary role of the United States in world affairs. Isolationist sentiment and its voting strength would demand a politically astute reticence in the future. The campaign did provide the opportunity for formulating a substantive and cohesive viewpoint on foreign policy matters. The belief that the United States must assume leadership in world affairs and that America's national security demands active cooperation with nations of peace in opposition to the aggressor powers remained a constant conviction in the mind of Franklin Roosevelt. Woodrow Wilson's dream of an association of nations united for the cause of peace was not forgotten. President Roosevelt later praised Wilson for his vision of a world emancipated from the shackles of force and the arbitrament of the sword. Roosevelt recalled, "He taught — and let's never forget it — he taught that democracy could not survive in isolation. We applaud his judgment and we applaud his faith." [26]

Momentary Interlude
and Thoughts on Foreign Policy

Twelve years of tragedy and political triumph intervened in the life of Franklin D. Roosevelt. Stricken by a polio virus on August 10, 1921, he was ordered to undergo vigorous physical therapy in an attempt to ameliorate his paralytic affliction. The months that followed were spent in rest and recuperation. In 1924, he returned to the political arena by actively campaigning for the Democratic candidate for President, Al Smith. Four years later, Franklin Roosevelt was elected Governor of New York and found himself again in the center of Democratic Party politics. The primary focus of his attention throughout this period was not foreign policy. He personally believed that the Governor of a state had absolutely no right to take part officially in international questions. Nevertheless, foreign affairs and developments in overseas countries did not escape his attention.[27]

Despite the defeat that he had suffered in the 1920 election, Franklin Roosevelt still vigorously promoted the Woodrow Wilson ideal of a society of nations. Until the Presidential election of 1932, he was not deterred in this effort by those who warned that such activity might be politically damaging. William A. White refused to direct a campaign collection for the Woodrow Wilson Foundation, despite Franklin's entreaties. White informed him that any activity in behalf of Wilson's foreign policies would arouse antagonism. He bluntly told Roosevelt, "I do not like to go into a contest which I fear may be disastrous." [28]

Franklin Roosevelt did not hesitate to endorse the fundamental aim of Woodrow Wilson's foreign policy: the union of peace-loving nations in opposition to the forces of aggression. This unity, he realized, would be effective only with the participation of the United States in European affairs. His work in behalf of the Woodrow Wilson Foundation and the Walter Hines Page School of International Relations at Johns Hopkins University, and his participation in the American Peace Award contest sponsored by Edward Bok, editor of the *Ladies Home Journal,* were activities which Franklin Roosevelt believed would promote the Wilson vision. The Wilson Foundation was not merely a tribute, nor an idealistic conception. It was to be a thoroughly practical and useful stimulant in efforts to achieve international peace. The Walter Hines Page School was also for Franklin a much needed part of an educational system and, in his opinion, anything which served to make the United States more internationally minded would be so much to the good. When asked how the youth of his generation could best contribute toward a durable peace, Franklin replied that they must learn more about world conditions and the relationship of the United States to them. Prejudice, narrow mindedness, and lack of understanding concerning the role of the United States in world affairs had obstructed efforts made in the interest of peace.[29]

A proposed plan to circumvent prejudice and narrow mindedness was offered by Roosevelt in the American Peace Award contest sponsored by Edward Bok. The League of Nations debate had aroused heated passions; the phrase itself prompted emotional debate. Roosevelt therefore submitted a plan to kill the existing League and set up something in its place that would allow countless thousands, who for personal or other reasons refused to endorse America's entry into the League, an opportunity to help put the United States into a new Society of Nations, thereby "saving face, honor, and all other fool things they think have to be saved."[30]

In his plan to preserve world peace, a structure of the society of Nations was outlined by Roosevelt. There would be an Assembly composed of all nations, each with one vote, and an Executive Committee of eleven states, including the United States, Great Britain, France, Italy, and Japan as permanent members. A decision of the Executive Committee would be implemented if approved by a two-thirds vote in the Assembly. One or two recalcitrant nations could not block the will of the great majority in the settling of disputes because the votes of members alleged to have resorted to war and of members against whom action is directed shall not be counted. All disputes not settled by diplomacy would be solved by binding arbitration. The institutional structure of the new Society of Nations was not, however, the key to its success; that would depend primarily, wrote Roosevelt, on the effective participation of the United States in this experiment.[31]

While recuperating in Warm Springs, Georgia, Roosevelt wrote an article in the Mason *Daily Telegraph* in which he further stressed that the maintenance of world peace was possible only if the United States would fully commit its power to the civilized community. The world, he believed, would follow America's lead more readily than that of any other nation. This country must play the part of a man, he wrote, and lead the effort to lessen the chances of war. Roosevelt's real concern was not with the form that the civilized community would take, whether a League or Society, but with the creation of a unifying spirit that would bind peace loving nations, especially the United States, in a solid front against aggressors. There could be no other alternative. If nothing is done, he asserted, the world would witness a return to the horrible conditions of warfare in the Dark Ages, made even more horrifying by the latest technological advances in the machines of destruction. He concluded, "Are you satisfied, by the way, that America is today doing its full duty to mankind?"[32]

Franklin Roosevelt definitely was not satisfied, as is evident in an article written in 1928 for *Foreign Affairs*. The views expressed were those of Roosevelt, although in the preparation of the article he had asked his close friend Norman Davis for advice. Davis urged Roosevelt to exercise caution in advocating outright membership in the League. However, continued Davis, the United States should cooperate and give support to the League in its effort to promote world peace. It can no longer be a law unto itself. War can only be banished by mobilizing the positive moral forces to combat it, and that would require cooperation. War must be throttled at its source, and to contend that the United States could prevent war by codifying international law, reasoned Davis, thereby simply making war illegal, was to assume that negative forces could be made to prevail. War in the future will be a public war, he told Roosevelt, and America must not find itself alone in isolation.[33]

Davis' internationalist views were in complete accord with those of Roosevelt. In the article, Franklin appealed to the Wilson vision of an association of nations through which the world could avoid armed conflict and substitute reason and collective action for the age old appeal to the sword. The past nine years, he said critically, had witnessed a foreign policy of isolation and withdrawal. Many seem to feel that the United States owes nothing to mankind; they seem content to ignore the world so long as America's seacoasts remain impregnable. We Democrats, wrote Roosevelt, reject that approach to international affairs. We must support the League and the World Court, and take an active, hearty, and official part in all proceedings bearing on the general good and common ills of mankind. War cannot be outlawed by resolution alone. The League offers a common round table where threats against the peace of the world can be discussed and divergent views compromised. The increasing effectiveness of the League in the areas of international health, improvement of labor conditions, education, aid to backward peoples, international law, and world trade is clearly visible. We must, he urged, be more generous and sympathetic in suport of this great agency of peace, and every other organization that has as its goals the perpetuation of world peace. We must reject, he concluded, an isolated national existence. "It is the spirit, sir, which matters."[34]

In a column written for the *Standard* of Beacon, New York, Roosevelt was more critical of isolationism. He asserted that the United States had lost its leadership of the moral forces of mankind and had contributed nothing to the settlement of international problems. Pious resolutions such as the Kellogg-Briand Peace Pact outlawing war were excellent expressions of good will, but would be duly forgotten when these same nations got involved in some subsequent quarrel, he predicted. A problem arises too in that the Pact does not outlaw defensive war, he wrote, and no one has yet been able to get nations to define what they mean by defensive war. He concluded that America's efforts to eliminate the causes of war before those causes reached a serious climax had been wholly negligible.[35]

A subtle tone of alarm seems to permeate these critical writings of Roosevelt. In the years immediately preceding the election of 1932, events in Europe were disturbing to him. Naval disarmament proposals seemed to be floundering. A good newspaper headline, he mused, would be "Naval Disarmament Conference Highly Successful — United States to build $1,000,000 of New Ships." In Italy and Russia, Lenin, Mussolini, and Stalin appeared to him as blood brothers breaking down the safeguards of liberty and constitutional government. He thought that the year 2030 might witness the absence of the American conception of representative government throughout the world. Impressions recorded by Roosevelt after a seven day visit to France in May, 1931, to be with his ailing mother, also reveal that the future president was disturbed by the difficult economic and political conditions existing throughout Europe. We were about to enter, he believed, a period of real danger to our type of civilization. The United States and every European country will need some formal definite leadership in the future to avoid severe dislocation. Japan's occupation of Manchuria may have shaken his recently expressed trust in that nation's peaceful intentions. In an article appearing in *Asia Magazine* he had urged that the United States must think of Japan in terms of peace, not of war. He even recognized the necessity to Japan of the markets and raw materials of that part of the Chinese mainland contiguous to its island shores. In a column appearing in the Macon *Daily Telegraph* he asserted that there existed no fundamental obstacles to peaceful relations between the United States and Japan. Perhaps now, with Japanese troops on the move in Manchuria, he was not so certain about the possibility of maintaining cordial relations between the two nations. Surveying the world situation, Roosevelt entertained a bleak picture of the future.[36]

The fact that developments in international affairs were ominous may partially explain Franklin Roosevelt's refusal to address himself to the issue of foreign policy in the 1932 presidential campaign. Then, too, he had been rather outspoken in the past concerning his support of the League and the need for the United States to develop an internationalist perspective in world affairs. Wilson's program, calling for America's involvement in European affairs, was not popular. The sentiment of most appeared strongly isolationist. Finally, the immediate problem to be faced was the depression. Events occurring in far off distant lands were not as yet of much concern to many who faced unemployment and impending poverty and hunger.

Close friends of Roosevelt urged him to take the lead in breaking away from past isolationist policies. Francis Sayre, who served as Assistant Secretary of State and as High Commissioner to the Philippines under Roosevelt, wrote to the presidential candidate urging him to make some declaration on foreign policy. A ringing pronouncement is needed, wrote Sayre, showing the true slant of your mind. He suggested a single unified speech on the foreign problem. Americans are so prejudiced on this issue, he concluded, that you must carefully explain the principles underlying your views in order to make people see the inevitable logic and force of your conclusions. Roosevelt thanked him for the enthusiastic letter and for his very frank and free discussion of foreign problems. Francis Sayre was not satisfied by this noncommittal reply. He wrote Roosevelt again stressing once more that the destiny of the world depended upon what policy the administration would follow during the next eight years. He warned that immense pressure would be applied by selfish interests that stood in opposition to Roosevelt's views. Sayre was certain, however, that Franklin Roosevelt would not yield. Arthur Sweetzer, Director of the United States Information Section at the League of Nations, was more direct with the presidential aspirant urging him to ensure, in one way or another, that the United States would be represented at the League deliberations in Geneva so that it might enter those conference chambers whenever its interests should demand it.[37]

Franklin D. Roosevelt was adamant in his refusal to deal with this controversial issue. His original statement on the subject of foreign policy had been made before the Democratic Convention had convened. In a speech delivered to the New York State Grange Association on February 2, 1932, he clearly disassociated himself from the more enthusiastic supporters of international cooperation and the League of Nations. The League today, he said, is not the League conceived by Woodrow Wilson, although it might have been had the United States joined. The League had become a mere meeting place for the discussion of strictly European political difficulties, and the United States would not participate in political controversies in Europe or elsewhere. He added that American participation in the League would not serve the highest purpose of the prevention of war and a settlement of international difficulties in accordance with fundamental American ideals.[38]

Norman Davis was thoroughly disgusted with Franklin Roosevelt's comments on the League. Davis observed that when a man wanted the nomination so badly that he was willing to forego every sense of loyalty and to undervalue principle and sincerity it was a hopeless case. Roosevelt's speech, however, must be considered politically astute. It laid to rest an issue that could have posed problems for his candidacy. Was Roosevelt sincere in this speech? He had confided to Louis Wehle on July 26, 1932, that he believed the United States should join the League of Nations to help restore world order. Wehle's response was immediate and negative: the League was beyond repair.[39]

Franklin Roosevelt probably accepted Wehle's realistic assessment for he would make no attempt to revive this volatile issue. Furthermore, Roosevelt was cautioned to steer clear of any involvement in European affairs. He had considered taking a trip to Europe. Norman Davis suggested that if he should go, the visit must be for rest, information, and personal contacts, but not for the purpose of entering into any formal negotiations. Felix Frankfurter suggested that he not go at all. He believed that a trip abroad would be a very serious mistake. Some would say, charged Frankfurter, that those clever devils in Europe had hornswoggled you. There would be references to the secret diplomacy of European conversations. It will be extremely difficult, said Frankfurter, to convert Americans to necessary action in the international field. A European trip would further complicate an already formidable task. Frankfurter's logic prevailed. Roosevelt agreed: "You are absolutely right about the trip. It is already out of my mind."[40]

The avoidance of a troublesome debate on foreign policy during the election campaign was politically astute. Franklin Roosevelt was elected President, defeating his Republican rival Herbert Hoover by a wide margin. Events in Europe and the Far East, however, would soon demand the President-elect's constant attention. Never again would he be able to ignore developments in international affairs. Ominous signs were appearing overseas. The voices of bellicose nationalism were loudly trumpeting the call to the sword.

In retrospect, the portents of the future are discernible in the personal experiences and expressed viewpoints of Franklin Roosevelt. Impressions of Germany, gained from memories of a bombed hospital at Doullens, a destroyed church in Cierges, and the faces of young French girls removed enceinte from the front line areas may have remained with the President as he witnessed in future years the construction of a new order under German auspices. The warnings of Japanese aggression in the Pacific, of a possible Japanese attack on American possessions, and of that nation's imperialistic ambitions in China and the Orient, repeatedly expressed to the Assistant Secretary by high ranking naval officers, were not dismissed by Roosevelt as he viewed Japanese expansion in the thirties. The personal sentiment he expressed in favor of the Entente cause and of Great Britain, France, and Russia in their struggle against Germany would once more reappear to be phrased in even stronger terms. The Wilson ideal, described so eloquently in the 1920 election, did not fade from his vision. The United States in the future would be the keystone of the arch of world peace. The search for a unifying spirit that would bind peace loving nations together in opposition to the forces of aggression would continue. The failure to make visible any manifestation of that spirit did bring to the fore, as Roosevelt had prophesized, another Napoleon, another Caesar, another Alexander the Great. Finally, Franklin Roosevelt's attempts to undermine what he termed the Great Inertia, or false security through isolation, would persist, but in a tone of subdued reticence. Fully cognizant of the strong isolationist feelings shared by many Americans, he would move with patience and caution in his advocacy that the United States must embark on a more activist foreign policy. When national security seemed to him to be gravely threatened, then he would speak again without restraint of the need to send definite ships and definite men on a definite day. This formative period, prior to his accession to the Presidency, was for Franklin D. Roosevelt a microcosm of the future.

II

Winds of Change

CHAPTER TWO

WINDS OF CHANGE

FRUSTRATED SEARCH FOR ENTENTE

Franklin Roosevelt had tactfully ignored foreign policy issues in the campaign for the Presidency. He would soon, however, be absorbed in European and Far Eastern developments. Anxiety, frustration, and fearsome concern mark his response to the climactic changes that occur overseas during the first three years of his administration. Attempts to solve important international problems result in desultory and acrimonious debate. The World Economic Conference collapses amidst mutual recrimination. The Geneva Disarmament Conference adjourns without result; an apparent exercise in wishful futility. Adolf Hitler's accession to the Chancellorship in Germany signals the beginning of an awesome chain of events which culminates in that country's domination of Europe. Japan, having entrenched itself in China with the creation of the puppet state of Manchukuo, proceeds to gain paramount influence in that country. Armed force serves as the cutting edge of Japanese diplomacy. The Japanese navy begins rapid expansion and modernization under the guise of national security. Preparatory discussions in Great Britain on the continuation of the Washington and London naval limitation treaties conclude with an official termination of those treaties by Japan. Italy's invasion of Ethiopia appears to be only a prelude to fascist aggression elsewhere. Franklin Roosevelt was fully informed concerning these developments and thoroughly alarmed. In his Inaugural Address he had pledged this country to the policy of the good neighbor. The policy of the good neighbor quickly disappeared in Europe and the Far East. In the annual message to Congress in 1933, Roosevelt candidly admitted that it was impossble to present a picture of optimism regarding world affairs. One year later he described international relationships

29

as floundering on old jealousies, revived passions, and new strivings for armament and power. In a speech delivered at the San Diego Exposition in October, 1935, he warned that the threat of war was a real and potent danger to the future of civilization. Basic ideals and principles cherished by the United States were being challenged. He concluded with the hope that in future years nation would follow nation by deed and word in their adherence to the good neighbor ideal of the Americas.[1]

It soon became apparent that the deeds of nations and the words of their leaders did not reveal an adherence to the ideal of the good neighbor. Franklin Roosevelt was forcefully blunt while discussing foreign affairs before Congress in January, 1936. He asserted that a point had been reached where the people of the Americas must take cognizance of growing ill-will, marked trends of aggression, increasing armaments, and shortened tempers. Peoples were following blindly and fervently the lead of those who espoused the twin spirits of autocracy and aggression. Nations that had subscribed to the law of the sword possessed the fantastic conception that they alone were chosen to fulfill a mission and that all others must be subject to them. World peace and good will, he continued, were blocked by only 10 or 15 percent of the world's population. Roosevelt on this occasion seemed to have spoken very pointedly and in a tone of subtle outrage and indignation. What was the basis of the anxiety and anger expressed in this and other speeches? What did President Roosevelt know about the ambitions of Germany, Japan, and Italy at this early date? Finally, was his alarm intensified by the disunity of those nations representative of the forces of peace?[2]

This ominous state of world affairs was perceived by very few in the first days of the Roosevelt Administration. Franklin Roosevelt was perhaps asking the very same questions directed to him by Senator Key Pittman. The Senator asserted that it was distressing to find that there was no one who knew what the foreign policy of our Government might be in the future. Are we going to participate in European affairs, Pittman queried, or are we going to keep out of them? Are we going to enforce treaties or are we going to abandon them?[3]

The answers to these questions would seem to depend on the degree of cooperation in world affairs that could be elicited from Great Britain and France. Norman Davis, in Geneva for the Disarmament Conference, had urged such a policy. Referring to the increasing belligerence of Japan, Davis wrote to Roosevelt saying that the most practical procedure would be for the United States to talk the situation over very frankly with England and France with a view to maintaining a similar policy. The first efforts of the newly elected President were directed toward achieving a cordial working relationship with statesmen of both countries. Initial contact with the leaders of the two countries came through visits of William Bullitt. Bullitt, recommended to Roosevelt by Louis Wehle, sailed inconspicuously as the President-elect's personal and secret representative on a "look-see" mission to Europe. Discussions did take place with outgoing French Premier Joseph Paul-Boncour and British Prime Minister Ramsay MacDonald. Topics ranged from a common front against Japan in the Pacific, to debts and mutual cooperation. Bullitt informed the British Prime Minister that the President desired the most intimate collaboration between England and the United States in all fields of world affairs. He reported to Roosevelt that MacDonald also desired to cooperate in every way. Boncour, noted Bullitt, had been moved by the President's expressions of good will toward France. Marked cordiality characterized these initial discussions.[4]

Prime Minister MacDonald expressed his sentiments directly to Roosevelt. He hoped that relations between Great Britain and the United States would achieve a very great measure of cooperation in all the international conferences. Roosevelt too thought it would not be difficult to achieve a personal relationship of intimate friendship. In April, 1933, the British Prime Minister visited Washington for private talks with the President. When asked what the topic for discussion would be, Roosevelt humorously replied, "Well, ships and kings and sealing wax and things like that." He revealed the true purpose behind the meetings to a close friend in London, Arthur Murray. Roosevelt believed that such a trip would greatly help public opinion. The President was sure that he and MacDonald believed in realistic action on broader lines than the isolationists would be willing to concede. MacDonald was more candid in describing the meetings. We understand each other, he said, elbow to elbow; we have gotten above mere "market haggling and foggling." It is our moral responsibility to come to an agreement. He then assured reporters that there had been no alliances, and no entanglements. In concluding, however, MacDonald stated philosophically that no man can live to himself alone, and the man who is strongest and most independent is the one who has stretched out his hand to somebody else and grasped it.[5]

Relations with France also continued to develop satisfactorily from the viewpoint of the President. In two discussions with the French Ambassador, Paul Claudel, Roosevelt expressed his sincere interest in cooperating closely with France in world affairs. Claudel's description of the meeting with the President is revealing. The French Ambassador compared Roosevelt's thoughts to those of Woodrow Wilson. Roosevelt was quoted as saying that the forces of conservation, stability, and conciliation must join in opposition to the forces of greed and destruction. Great Britain, France, and the United States must conclude a general rapprochement. The new French Premier Edouard Herriot visited the United States at the same time as Mac-Donald and seems to have shared in the renewed spirit of harmony.[6]

This exuberant cordiality shared by the leaders of Great Britain, France, and the United States unfortunately was not long lasting. The problems posed by the depression placed a severe strain on the recently nurtured friendship. The World Monetary and Economic Conference meeting in London in June and July, 1933, proved to be a disappointment to all participants. The initial test of the embryonic rapprochement of the three major powers resulted in dismal failure. The conference had as its purpose the alleviation of the world depression through the concerted action of the dominant nations. Franklin Roosevelt had insisted that the rancourous subject of war debt not be a topic for discussion at the conference; a personal request to this effect was sent to Ramsay MacDonald. The British Prime Minister proceeded to discuss such in his opening address to the conferees. Robert Bingham, American Ambassador to Great Britain, reported to Roosevelt that this must be regarded as a breach of faith. Bingham's remarks anticipate the disillusionment that would soon be shared by all. Secretary of State Cordell Hull, Chairman of the American delegation, cabled to Roosevelt a plan to realize one of the conference's foremost objectives which was to achieve eventual currency stabilization through a gradual return to the gold standard by all powers. Franklin Roosevelt rejected this compromise solution as a purely artificial and temporary experiment affecting the monetary exchange of a few nations. The price of a nation's currency in changing terms of the currencies of other nations is not as important, asserted the President, as the sound internal economic system of a nation which could be achieved by domestic currency manipulation.[7]

The depressing effect of this bombshell message of the President to the conference was clearly visible, and adjournment followed on July 27, 1933. Ramsey MacDonald, citing the lack of cooperation from the United States, described the conference as a failure, and his own mood as one of despair. The conference demonstrated that there was no coordinated leadership among the European nations. Herbert Feis, Economic Adviser to the State Department, and a member of the United States delegation, recorded in his diary that the French sensed that this was a diplomatic fiasco, and that the British Prime Minister seemed much displeased. Cordell Hull was most perceptive in his comments on the events in London. The entire affair, wrote Hull, had played into the hands of Germany, Japan, and Italy. The United States, Britain, and France had engaged in bitter recrimination. The dictator nations could now proceed in the hope that disunity would prevail in British, French, and American relations. The World Economic Conference, concluded the Secretary of State, was simply another "might-have-been" in European history.[8]

Germany: The War Fulcrum

Franklin Roosevelt had every reason to be concerned about the breakup of unity that had occurred at the London Economic Conference. Reports of events in Germany throughout 1933 were especially disconcerting. William Bullitt's prediction of Adolf Hitler's demise had been totally inaccurate. He had informed Roosevelt in December, 1932, that Hitler was finished as a possible dictator, and that German President Paul von Hindenburg had absolutely refused to have Hitler as Chancellor. The German Government, said Bullitt, was no longer afraid of the Nazi movement. Adolf Hitler was named German Chancellor on January 30, 1933.[9]

Rexford Tugwell, a close advisor to the President, has described Franklin Roosevelt's first impressions of Adolf Hitler. He viewed him, wrote Tugwell, with a curious mixture of detestation and dread. In caricature, Roosevelt saw the Führer as insensitive, overbearing, gross, unsportsmanlike, and aggressively German. The President was implacably opposed to all that Hitler represented. He foresaw, asserts Tugwell, that an encounter with Germany might be inevitable. The probable possibility of war was accepted by the President without hesitation.[10]

Tugwell's description of Roosevelt's views, although written in retrospect, seems credible. There were few exceptions to the unpleasant reports concerning Germany from overseas observers. John Cudahy, the Ambassador to Poland, was practically alone in his optimism. He described as entirely baseless the rumors that Germany was training large bodies of troops for war. Cudahy was sure that there was nothing essentially belligerent or alarming about these activities. The Germans, he wrote, simply love display and pageantry. This blatant exhibition of militarism was merely an expression of a unique German gregarious instinct, much like that of our Elks, Eagles, and Woodmen.[11]

The assumptions in Cudahy's letter are contradicted by descriptions contained in almost all other correspondence to the President. William Dodd, Ambassador to Germany, wrote lengthy accounts of the pessimistic trend of events. The Ambassador's letters were read with growing trepidation by Franklin Roosevelt.[12]

Ambassador Dodd was initially uncertain about the course that Germany would pursue. It was impossible to predict, he wrote to the President, whether the new regime was going to follow a more

liberal or a more ruthless direction. He described the German statesman as quite adolescent in their analyses of international problems.
They had not learned the give and take of group compromises prevalent among the English and American leaders. A month later, although concerned about mounting evidence that armaments and
training men for war were major German interests, Dodd was still
willing to give men a chance to try their schemes. A people had a
right to govern itself, and others must exercise patience even when
cruelties and injustices are done, he cautioned the President. Dodd
expressed his belief on October 13, 1933, that all liberal Germany
was with America, and that more than half of Germany was at heart
liberal. He noted two weeks later, however, that liberal and intellectual Germany did not dare speak out against the Hitler regime.
Elections being conducted at that time were described by Dodd as
a farce.[13]

If Germany was firmly controlled by the new regime, what was the
character of its leadership? Ambassador Dodd described it in detail
for the President. Hitler he pictured as romantic minded and a strict
imitator of Mussolini. His support came from the partly unemployed
and the wholly indigent, wrote Dodd. Hitler believed that a people
survived by fighting and died through peaceful policies. In the back of
his mind, asserted Dodd, was the old German idea of dominating
Europe through war. Hitler's influence was, and would continue to
be, belligerent. Joseph Goebbels, Hitler's first lieutenant, was an even
less attractive figure, wrote Dodd, whose mastership of propaganda was
aimed at stirring up animosities and hatreds whenever there was an
opportunity. He was more clever and belligerent than Hitler. The
third member of the triumvirate, Hermann Goering, was intensely
opposed to all democratic and socialist groups. Dodd concluded by
telling Roosevelt that this was a unique triumvirate: Hitler, less educated, more romantic, with a semi-criminal record; Goebbels and
Goering, both Doctors of Philosophy, animated by intense class
and foreign hatreds, and willing to resort to the most ruthless methods. In a letter written to Roosevelt in December, 1933, Dodd warned
that if negotiations for peace failed, nations would follow the old road
to war. Based on Dodd's reports of 1933, the latter course may have
appeared most likely to the President.[14]

Reflections of developments in Germany were also forwarded to
Roosevelt by George H. Earle, Minister to Austria. In a letter of
November 27, 1933, Earle offered a description of the German
Chancellor which reaffirmed the observations made by Ambassador
Dodd. Early portrayed Hitler as a paranoic with a gift of eloquence
half-way between Bryan and Billy Sunday. The future of Europe
centers on this man, he wrote, and what a paranoiac will do when

Germany is adequately armed is impossible to predict. At this moment, wrote Earle, he has made the militaristic spirit the most intense in German history, and there were already indications that the first country destined to fall to the German Army will be Austria. Hitler is an Austrian, said Earle, and more than anything else he wishes to incorporate Austria as part of the German Reich. A memorandum on the Austrian situation was forwarded to the President, and the views of the writer buttressed Earle's observations. The reporter in this memorandum described Vienna as but a stepping stone for Germany's conquest of the entire Danubian basin. The six states therein contain sixty million people, and five of the nations were composed of important German minorities. The observer concluded that if Hitler decided to absorb Austria it could be no half way house for him, "for the attempt to seize Vienna will either end in creating a Reich of Napoleonic grandeur or else bring on a disaster for the entire Nazi regime." [15]

Perhaps the most prophetic analysis of the new regime in Germany was sent to Roosevelt by a close friend, Samuel R. Fuller. Fuller, Director of the American Bemberg Corporation, had numerous business contacts in Europe, and through them he continually obtained information of vital interest to the President. This particular report of May 11, 1933, was considered important enough by Roosevelt to send to officials in the State Department. Fuller portrayed Hitler as a successful dictator who was fully organized, absolutely self-confident, and in full power. The Germans view him almost as a God, and trust him implicitly. His regime feeds on intense nationalism and pride of race, and it seems probable that war will be the end result. In summary, Fuller warned "that Germany, a nation which loves to be led, is again a marching nation, and so a danger." [16]

Samuel Fuller made reference to another policy being pursued by the government in Germany and one which was particularly distressing: the persecution of the Jews. Hitler intends to keep the Jews out for good, and even more ominously, observed Fuller, it does not seem that he is punishing them temporarily to make them be good. Dr. Hjalmar Schacht, soon to be appointed German Minister of Economics, had described the prohibition against the Jews as a campaign of purification. Schacht told Fuller that if he himself were a Jew, he would be concerned. [17]

Franklin Roosevelt was aware of the intensifying campaign against the Jews. In a press conference on March 24, 1933, a reporter asked the President if he had received reports of the persecution of Jews in Germany. Roosevelt replied that many such reports had come in, and that they had been forwarded to the State Department. William Phillips, Undersecretary of State, sent a memorandum concerning the proposed boycott of Jews in Germany to the President. In April,

Governor I C. Blackwood of South Carolina depicted the Jewish plight in Germany as a most deplorable situation. Roosevelt responded, saying that the matter had been under very serious consideration for some time. In May, 1933, Irving Lehman wrote of his concern for the Jews. The President replied that his personal feelings concerning this issue had been made known to Dr. Schacht, and that the German Government knew just how he felt about such things. Roosevelt believed that any notes of formal protest might result in reprisals in Germany. Lehman wrote again that same month and described the Jewish persecutions as being even worse than was generally realized.[18]

Felix Frankfurter voiced his disgust with Hitler's anti-semitic program in several discussions with Franklin Roosevelt. In April, 1933, Frankfurter forwarded to the President a memorandum on the problems facing German refugees. In May Frankfurter confided to Cordell Hull that he had urged the President to find an effective means whereby the government might publicly manifest its disapprobation of the breach of civilized standards by the Hitler regime. Failure to do so, he reasoned, would give the impression that the United States condoned these most baleful aspects of Hitlerism. Then, in a letter dated October 17, 1933, Frankfurter offered to the President his personal views of the violence and madness now dominating Germany. Developments in Germany, he wrote, make it abundantly clear that the significance of Hitlerism far transcends ferocious anti-semitism and fanatical racism. The attack against the Jews, he said, was merely an index to the gospel of force and materialism that explains the present rulers of Germany. He warned Roosevelt that the forces of violence and chauvinism of the Hitler regime would be accelerated and intensified, and that the air was charged with the kind of feeling that preceded 1914. He suggested that the President might become the rallying center of the world's sanity by speaking to the German peoples, now living in darkness, and saying some plain things that have to be said. The fear of reprisals against Jews in Germany, as Roosevelt had written to Lehman, made it impossible for the President to acquiesce in this last suggestion.[19]

Franklin Roosevelt's thoughts concerning Germany, if based on the numerous reports cited above, were certainly reaffirmed by developments occurring at the Geneva Disarmament Conference. Discussions on the limitation of armaments had been taking place for a full year prior to the Presidential Inauguration, yet there were few signs of progress. The President told reporters on March 17, 1933, that the question of disarmament was one of the principal keys to the world situation. He pledged to use every possible means to achieve success at the Disarmament Conference, and promised that every effort would be made to prevent the conference from either blowing up or arriving at some patch-work solution. Three days before the press conference, Roosevelt had appointed Norman Davis to head the United States delegation at Geneva. The President planned to vigorously push for disarmament.[20]

In March, 1933, Prime Minister Ramsay MacDonald presented a disarmament proposal to the participants at Geneva. The Mac-Donald Plan received full support from the President. He considered it to be an initial step in setting forth positive limits to armaments and military forces. The plan envisaged the possibility of collective action against an aggressor nation, and this too seems to have been warmly endorsed by Roosevelt. He did stress, however, that the United States was in no way limiting its right to determine a specific course of action once all the facts had been brought out.[21]

Roosevelt appeared sanguine about the possibility that the conference might succeed. Norman Davis, writing from Geneva, had assured the President that he was hopeful of real accomplishment in disarmament. Franklin Roosevelt, optimistic and perhaps somewhat buoyant in this early stage of the discussions, decided to place the moral weight of the United States solidly behind the efforts being made at Geneva toward universal disarmament. In early May, the President had discussed with Felix Frankfurter the idea of issuing a personal appeal to the conference participants urging them to persevere and to succeed in their task. Frankfurter encouraged Roosevelt to do so, for he believed that such an appeal would touch the imagination and hopes of men everywhere. There is every reason to believe, wrote Frankfurter, that the peoples of Europe would respond favorably, even though their governments might be timid and lethargic. Today, with all of Europe at the edge of an abyss, this daring action would tap new forces for peace. The President believed that the time was ripe for a dramatic declaration.[22]

The historic announcement came on May 16, 1933. In a message to the conferees at Geneva, Roosevelt declared that the time had come to sweep away petty obstacles to disarmament, and to achieve the primary aim of the conference which was the complete elimination of all offensive weapons. The MacDonald Plan, he said, was a first definite step toward that goal. Nations must pledge that they will not increase their existing armaments over treaty limitations. Finally, proclaimed the President, all nations of the world should enter into a solemn and definite pact of non-aggression. When asked during a press conference why nations that had failed to uphold the Kellogg-Briand peace pact might be persuaded to faithfully adhere to the pact of non-aggression, Roosevelt replied that it was simply his general hope that nations would respect their treaties.[23]

There appears to be, at least superficially, an apparent naivete in this declaration. Pious platitudes had failed to restrain Japan, and from information being sent from Berlin, it would seem that such hollow rhetoric would have no effect on Germany. What then was the President's motive in this pronouncement? Included in the message sent to Geneva was the caveat that nations which obstructed or ultimately blocked a disarmament agreement must bear full responsibility for the failure of the conference. The President publicly declared that these words were directed to the whole world, not specifically to Germany or Japan. Privately, on May 6, 1933, he intimated as strongly as possible to Hjalmar Schacht that he considered Germany to be the only possible obstacle to a disarmament treaty. Hitler's speech of May 17, 1933, may have given Roosevelt a brief moment of optimistic expectations. The German Chancellor promised to disband his nation's entire military establishment and destroy all arms if Germany's neighbors did likewise. The President commented to reporters that he was encouraged by this response, and was certain that if the intent as expressed could be translated into similar action, then rapid progress could be made at Geneva.[24]

Norman Davis was instructed, however, to deliver a momentous policy statement which would appear to have been enunciated in the belief that Germany's intentions would not find their corollary actions. Davis' speech at Geneva, as noted by Cordell Hull, marked a radical change, if only briefly, in United States foreign policy. Speaking on May 22, 1933, Davis reiterated the President's desire for universal disarmament, but added that the United States would be willing to consult with other nations in case of a threat to peace, and would refrain from any action tending to defeat a collective effort to restore peace. Roosevelt retreated from this endorsement of a scheme for collective security in an abrupt manner for a variety of compelling reasons, both foreign and domestic. Davis' speech, however, does reveal the President's preoccupation with the perplexing problem of how to confront the anticipated aggressive actions of Germany and, as will be seen, Japan.[25]

Germany's withdrawal from the Disarmament Conference and the League of Nations on October 14, 1933, reaffirmed Roosevelt's growing distrust of Hitler's ambitions. The President had expressed his conviction throughout the conference that Germany was primarily responsible for the delays in the negotiations at Geneva. A close friend, Owen Johnson, had written him saying that the full racial megalomania of Hitler's program was realized by some Frenchmen, and that they were most reluctant to disarm. The President seemed to agree with Johnson's observations and the legitimacy of France's refusal to disarm. During a press conference on August 25, 1933, Roosevelt stated that everyone knew that the Germans were drilling, that school children were drilling, and that they had been secretly manufacturing guns. French reluctance to go along with disarmament was, for that reason, quite understandable. Five days later, he wrote the British Prime Minister, noting his personal concern that Germany's rush for arms was infinitely more dangerous than all other European developments. England and the United States, said Roosevelt, must think along parallel lines. He pleaded with Mac-Donald, "Do, please, for the sake of peace, do all you can."[26]

Gradually it became evident to the President that the exit of Germany was imminent. He wrote to Norman Davis in a tone of resigned alacrity, pledging that if he, Davis, could pull off disarmament, then a burial in Arlington National Cemetery was assured. Roosevelt, believing that a successful conclusion of the conference was impossible, was determined to place all blame on Germany. He wrote to Dodd of his hope that France and England, indeed all of Europe, would clearly "put it up" to Germany at the Disarmament Conference. He tersely noted that world problems were getting worse instead of better, especially when "8 percent of the population of the entire world, i.e. Germany and Japan, is able, because of imperialistic attitude, to prevent peaceful guarantees and armament reductions on the part of the other 92 percent of the world."[27]

The year 1934 saw no improvement in the international situation. Ominous reports of Germany's aggressive aims continued to come to the White House. Arthur Sweetzer, Director of the League of Nations Secretariat, was one of the few correspondents of the President who still believed that Woodrow Wilson's vision of a world at peace seemed a possibility. There would be problems, he cautioned the President, such as Germany's contentions with France over the Saar, but the future was not that dismal. Roosevelt perhaps found this information at least refreshing for he thanked Sweetzer for his analysis of the long term developments in European diplomacy and especially for the note of optimism he had conveyed in his letter.[28]

There were very few, however, who agreed with the hopeful prescience of Arthur Sweetzer. Ambassador Dodd, writing from Berlin, gave no cause for optimism. In a letter to the President on August 15, 1934, Dodd wrote that more men have been trained, uniformed, and armed in Germany now than in 1914, and that this military might was designed for war, not peace with Austria as the most likely spot for an initial confrontation. The Ambassador said also that the campaign against the Jews had not been relaxed, and quoted for Roosevelt Goebbel's declaration that the Jews were the syphilis of all European peoples. The President admitted to Dodd that his letter had confirmed his personal fear that the drift in Germany was definitely downward, and that war seemed possible in the next six months or a year. R. Walton Moore, the Assistant Secretary of State, sent to Roosevelt another letter from Ambassador Dodd which was very pessimistic. Dodd had written privately to Moore telling him that once Germany was united, she would march against France. In almost every city people were marching. Preparations for war, said Dodd, were visible everywhere, and there had been reports that poison gas and explosives were being produced in great quantities.[29]

Similar viewpoints were forwarded to the President from other diplomatic posts, and all conveyed the impression that Germany contemplated aggressive expansion. The American Minister to the Baltic countries told Roosevelt that a Nazi movement in these nations had been surreptitiously undertaken among the resident minority of German extraction. There was genuine fear that this movement was in anticipation of an expected thrust eastward by Germany. Robert Bingham in Great Britain described for the President the views of Sir Robert Vansittart, Under Secretary of State for Foreign Affairs. Vansittart feared Germany's potential for war. He had heard that they were training their children from the age of two years for war, and inculcating their youth with the idea that it was their mission to conquer and control the world. Lincoln MacVeagh, Minister to Greece, wrote of the country's fears of inflammatory action by Germany, especially now that President Paul von Hindenburg had died, and Hitler had assumed complete control of the government. John Montgomery, Minister to Hungary, described for Roosevelt the alarm expressed by many Hungarians concerning a possible move by the German Army. The American Consul in Berlin was most direct. Hitler's regime must collapse and be replaced by a Government with which the United States could deal in the ordinary way.[30]

Personal friends of the President gave their observations on Germany. Felix Frankfurter warned that the Nazis were trying to promote mischief all over the world. Leonard Elmhirst, in Germany for an International Conference of Agricultural Economists, wrote to Roosevelt of his shock upon realizing the inborn faith of so many Germans in military training and conscription as a vital part of any sound education program. Elmhirst said that he was alarmed by the fact that among the older Germans there existed a taken-for-granted conviction that war was a legitimate method in statecraft and must be regarded as inevitable in the future. Herbert Pell toured Europe in 1934, and was asked by the President to send back his observations. Pell had difficulty in describing conditions in Germany, telling Roosevelt that the Berlin situation was simply beyond words. Pell thought the situation to be even more dangerous than that on the eve of the world war.[31]

Franklin Roosevelt discussed the German situation during a press conference in September, 1934, and his words reflect the same fears of Germany which his correspondents had expressed to him. Roosevelt described the German preparation for war. Factory workers had gas masks at their side. School children were learning the particular smells of poisonous gases. Bomb shelters were being built everywhere, and with the aid of a government tax deduction. Roosevelt told reporters of the little German boy who prayed each night that God would permit him to die with a French bullet in his heart. The President intimated that this war psychosis was being deliberately stirred up by the German Government in anticipation of an eventual move against France. There is no doubt that these remarks reflect Roosevelt's personal feelings. He had developed by this time a marked distaste for the German experiment under Hitler. Eleanor recalled her husband's rebuke to a columnist who had visited Europe, and had returned with glowing reports of 'naziism'. Franklin, she said, knew that he was either completely insincere, or had a warped and twisted mind. The columnist's writing from then on were given no consideration.[32]

Franklin Roosevelt warily anticipated some precipitate action by Germany in 1935. Reports to this date had been too ominous and foreboding to discount the possibility of a war initiated by that nation. The German Chancellor's foresight in avoiding just such a calamitous act, however, did not allay the President's fears. In a few dramatic diplomatic moves, Germany in this year was to take its place alongside the major world powers; the strictures of the Treaty of Versailles were soon to be discarded. The President, dismayed and angry, would search for a response.

The first indication that this was a year of movement for Germany came peacefully on January 13, 1935. A plebiscite in the Saar Basin ended that area's anomalous status. The inhabitants of the Saar voted overwhelmingly to join with Germany. Franklin Roosevelt's appraisal of this event might not have been much different than that of Breckinridge Long. The Ambassador to Italy described the Saar plebiscite as a big drink of Schnaps to the Germans and said that Hitler would be emboldened now to pursue his Pan-Germanic ideas into the fields of former German territories and Austria. Germany is still suspected like a wolf, he confided to the President, and her intentions are about as peaceful as were those of Attila. Hitler announced the formation of the German Air Force, the Luftwaffe, on March 9, 1935, and a week later initiated an action which he believed would safeguard peace for the Reich and all of Europe. The Chancellor proclaimed universal military service for all Germans, and an increase in the size of the German Army to approximately 500,000 men. There was no immediate response to this action by the President. During a press conference on March 20, 1935, however, he said, perhaps wistfully, that it was still his hope that the principle of the good neighbor would be extended to Europe and would contribute to the peaceful solution of problems, including the reduction of armaments.[33]

Limitations on the size of the German Army were thus disposed of without protest; limitations on the size of the German Navy were removed by the willing acquiescence of Great Britain. The Anglo-German Naval Agreement was signed by Germany on June 18, 1935. This empowered Germany to build a submarine force equal to that of Great Britain. Roosevelt correctly appraised the import of Hitler's actions in ending previous armament limitations. The President, writing to Ambassador Dodd, said that the Führer's policy was succeeding admirably; Germany had obtained a passive acceptance of its rearmament by land and sea.[34]

These policies of Germany were disturbing, and they appeared even more so in light of information sent to the White House throughout this year. Ambassador Dodd's letters were, as usual, especially alarming. In May, he wrote the President that practically every young German, including some women, wears a butcher knife at his side with the inscription 'Blut und Ehre' on the sharp blade. Dueling is common. Children, ages eight to twelve, are taught two or three times a week to throw bombs, and from twelve to eighteen they practice with rifles. Anyone who resists the government, or talks pacifism or democracy, is imprisoned. Germany can have no other objective than that of conquest, he concluded, and a marching nation of 67,-million people, with the most complete military machine in the world, must move somewhere. In July Dodd wrote the President again and reiterated his conviction that Germany had never been so warlike.[35]

Other informants of the President were as alarmed as Ambassador Dodd, Robert Bingham spoke of the possibility that Germany may have recourse to war if her world trade problems could not be solved. Edward House wrote to Roosevelt saying that war was much more probable now that Germany intended to rearm. Hitler's madness, confessed House, was impossible to understand. Lincoln MacVeagh, writing from Greece, described the growing anxiety of many in the Balkans, the tinder box of Europe, because of Germany's belligerence. John Cudahy warned Roosevelt that Germany's policies will either culminate in war, or the present government would be overthrown. Hitler, he said, plans to complete his military preparations by 1938, and any eventuality might then occur. General John J. Pershing told the President that he believed Germany would be militarily prepared for any action well within the ten year period in which she pledged to keep the peace. Charles H. Sherrill, after an interview with Hitler, informed the President that Germany would march as soon as its army was ready, probably in the direction of the Soviet Union. Samuel Fuller offered his analysis of European trends to Roosevelt. He described Germany as a day-to-day menace to the peace of all nations. The German people possess great virility and fervor for collective obedience to their Government, he observed. A united Germany under Hitler must be considered the most dangerous of all the world powers.[36]

Franklin Roosevelt shared these views. Publicly, he remained tactfully silent about events occurring in Germany. In a subtle way he did intimate an official disapproval of Hitler's regime. William Phillips had prepared a congratulatory message to the German Chancellor in celebration of Germany's national holiday. The note, consisting of fourteen words, was terse and cool. When asked if he wanted the greeting warmed up, the President jotted the notation, "No message," on the prepared text. In his private correspondence, Roosevelt elaborated plans for a less passive response to the threat of an aggressive militarist Germany. He had discussed with the Secretary of the Treasury, Henry Morgenthau, as early as March, 1935, a proposal that envisaged a direct confrontation with Germany. The nations of England, France, Italy, Belgium, Holland, Poland and possibly Russia should get together and agree on a ten year disarmament pact which would eliminate all methods of warfare other than what a soldier could carry on his back and in his hand. Having signed the pact, the aforementioned nations would then present it to Germany for acceptance. If Germany refused, said Roosevelt, these countries would establish a two-way blockade around her, not permitting anything to enter or leave Germany. Should such a plan fail, he told Morgenthau, chances are we will have a world war.[37]

The President gave more than a passing thought to this plan. In a letter to Edward House on April 10, 1935, he proposed that France, Italy, England and the Little Entente countries should establish a complete blockade of Germany. The Polish, Czecho-Slovak, Austrian, Swiss, French, Belgium, Dutch and Danish borders would be blocked. Access to German ports would be taken care of by British naval operations. The United States would then participate in what was a blockade of Germany, not a boycott or sanction, he reasoned. Congressional action would not be needed, thought the President, because recognition of a blockade would fall under the Executive's power.[38]

These proposals never got beyond the musings of the President. Numerous reasons account for his reticence in these matters. Foremost among them must be domestic political pressures and the appeasement policies of Great Britain and France. Roosevelt was

angry over the prevalent attitude in most countries. He wrote the
Ambassador in Moscow, William Bullitt, that no European capital
cares a "continental damn" what the United States thinks or does
and that he thought they were very unwise in this attitude. In the
same letter, he ridiculed the British Ambassador, Sir Stafford Cripps,
for holding the view that the German people would not back Hitler
in a war. The President compared Cripps to Lord Chancellor Vis-
count Haldane who in 1915 withdrew from political activity because
of his pro-German sentiments. Roosevelt was no Haldane. He
wanted to initiate action against Germany at this very moment. The
time was not yet propitious, and the European statesmen were not
yet willing for such a confrontation.[39]

Japan: Ultimate Intentions Revealed

Franklin Roosevelt's eagerness to confront the increasing menace
of Germany might have been prompted by developments in another
far corner of the world. If events were permitted to drift and take
their own course, it seemed possible that the United States might
one day face two hostile powers, Germany and Japan. Japanese
actions were of concern to the President throughout the first three
years of his administration. Before assuming office, he had endorsed
the policy of non-recognition of Japan's acquisitions in China that
had been enunciated by Herbert Hoover and his Secretary of State,
Henry Stimson. Roosevelt adhered firmly to Stimson's conviction
that the sovereignty of the Republic of China was to be maintained,
and that Japanese aggression was to be condemned. Friends had
cautioned the President-elect that this rigid moralistic stance toward
Japan would create difficulties in American-Japanese relations and
perhaps lead to war. Rexford Tugwell, Raymond Moley, and Louis
Wehle had warned Roosevelt of the dangers of implacably opposing
Japanese ambitions, but their criticisms of Stimson seemed to have
had no effect on the President. In a discussion at Hyde Park with
Roosevelt on January 9, 1933, Stimson found that Hoover's suc-
cessor fully understood and approved of his Manchurian policy.
Roosevelt promised in this meeting to do nothing that would weaken
Stimson's stand against Japanese aggression. It was Stimson's impression that they were in complete accord on foreign policy issues.
An official press statement issued by the President-elect was heart-
ening to Stimson. Roosevelt declared on January 18, 1933, that
American foreign policy must uphold the sanctity of treaties, and that
this was the cornerstone on which all relations between nations must
rest. Throughout his Presidency, he refused to retreat from this
announced policy of opposition to Japanese expansion.[40]

The President's antipathy toward Japan stemmed from many factors. His grandfather, Warren Delano, had engaged in trade with China, and Roosevelt's sympathies were with that country. The militaristic belligerence displayed by Japan toward China was becoming all too familiar to Franklin Roosevelt. In the years of war, as Assistant Secretary of the Navy, he had been repeatedly warned of Japan's ultimate ambitions, both in China and possibly in the United States. His critical views might have waned with Japan's adherence to agreements negotiated at the Washington Conference in 1921 and 1922 for the limitation of naval armaments. Japan's signing of the Kellogg-Briand Pact to outlaw war seemed to be a portent of a future of peace. The acceptance by Japan of the London Naval Conference accords of 1930 also gave evidence of an enlightened policy of conciliation.[41]

Japan's invasion of Manchuria in September, 1931, and the establishment of the puppet state of Manchukuo brought an end to an era of accord and good will. Japan officially withdrew from the League of Nations on March 27, 1933. In the same month, Franklin Roosevelt assumed office. Japan's actions in the preceding three years formed the basis of his personal detestation of a power which he believed had thrown aside every international law that had in the past been subscribed to in good faith. If it should come to war, he was prepared to make that fateful decision.[42]

These initial impressions of Japan were shared by most diplomatic observers who had access to the President. Norman Davis told Roosevelt on January 10, 1933, that the general feeling at Geneva was one of pessimism. Prospects for a solution of the Far Eastern controversy through conciliation, said Davis, have been practically abandoned. It appeared that Japan's gains in Manchuria would be permanent.[43]

Japan's predatory ambitions were emphasized repeatedly to the President by Stanley K. Hornbeck, the Chief of the Far Eastern Affairs Division in the State Department. In a memorandum of April 3, 1933, Hornbeck responded to Roosevelt's inquiry concerning Japanese mandates in the Pacific by stating that Japan fully intended to keep the islands. They were regarded as Japanese territories, said Hornbeck. A month later Hornbeck wrote a lengthy account of the Manchurian situation which the Undersecretary of State forwarded to the President immediately. Hornbeck was vivid and blunt in his comments. The Japanese objective, he wrote, is the amputation of Manchuria and the dismemberment of China. War has become an instrument of national policy for Japan, he asserted. There is absolutely no truth to the claim of the Japanese Army that it is engaged on Chinese soil in defense of the lives and property of their nationals. He portrayed Japan's action as simple naked aggression.[44]

The Chief of the Far Eastern Division was quick to contradict Japanese assertions that the deterioration in United States-Japan relations was due to a lack of understanding by Americans of Japan's peacemaking role in the Far East, or to pro-Chinese sympathies in his own country. These explanations had been sent to Roosevelt by Otohio Matsukata in defense of Japanese action in China. In this letter, Matsukata also defended the military's acts of violence in Japan as reflecting the desire of army and navy officers for clean and efficient government. The assassination of Premier Tsuyoshi Inukai in May, 1932, was depicted by Matsukata as a necessary prerequisite in the struggle against corruption and ineptitude. Franklin Roosevelt's views of Matsukata's logic were not recorded. The President did receive Hornbeck's analysis of the Matsukata letter. Japan, countered Hornbeck, has been persistently aggressive and bellicose. Japanese misbehavior in international affairs has been deliberately planned and efficiently carried out. Japan's leaders, he wrote, seem to show no concern for the numerous treaty commitments which they have broken. While Japan laments the absence of close relations with the United States, said Hornbeck, never once have Japanese leaders offered to make concessions to the United States. It is time for Japan to do something definite to improve diplomatic ties. There is no reason whatsoever, he concluded, for Americans to send Japan flowers, or pay her compliments as a peace offering.[45]

In April, 1934, Stanley Hornbeck offered an extensive analysis of the difficulties in American-Japanese relations, and then suggested possible strategies to be pursued in the future by the United States. We must not recognize Manchukuo, he urged, because it exists solely by virtue of the presence in Manchuria of 100,000 Japanese soldiers; it is by no means a sovereign or independent entity. We must oppose any proportionate strengthening of Japan's naval armament and weakening of that of the United States. If Japan should propose a non-aggression pact, which Hornbeck considered unlikely, the government must respond in a doubtful manner. In brief, he wrote, there is little that needs to be done and little that can safely be done by the United States to improve relations with Japan. The United States has taken nothing from Japan and owes Japan nothing. We have at no time threatened Japan. All of the threatening has come from the Japanese side. There were no notations on this document by the President to indicate approval or disapproval. It does appear, however, that Hornbeck's analyses may have been in accord with the President, for he has in this memorandum set forth the basic policy pursued by the Roosevelt Administration in its relations with Japan.[46]

The American Ambassador to Japan, Joseph Grew, was also critical of Japanese foreign policy during these years. Ambassador Grew
sent an alarming despatch to Cordell Hull in May, 1933. The Secretary of State, in agreement with Stanley Hornbeck's appraisal of the
despatch as one of the most important to come in for a long time,
delivered it to Roosevelt for his perusal. Grew's observations were
not reassuring. Japan, he wrote, could not be considered a small and
weak country. The Japanese Empire, without Manchukuo, is considerably greater than France or Germany and much more than that
of either Spain or Italy. If Manchukuo is included, then Japan's size
is even greater than France, Germany, Spain, Switzerland, Belgium,
Netherlands and Denmark combined, and its total population of
around 120 millions is equal to that of the United States. Grew described the Japanese people as extremely nationalistic, war-loving,
aggressive and unscrupulous. Their national morale and espirit de
corps reflects a spirit not equalled since the time that the Mongol
hordes and Genghis Khan conquered Asia. Japan's military machine
was appraised by Grew as the most complete, well-balanced, coordinated and powerful in the world. Its strength, he wrote, would shock
many people; it is immeasurably stronger than any other power.
Although its aggressive action does not seem to be designed for areas
outside the Far East, he concluded, its fighting potential is such that
Japan bears careful watching, especially since many Japanese consider the United States to be their major obstacle to expansion in the
Far East. An attached memorandum by the Military Attaché, R. S.
Bratton, described the Japanese resentment of America as deep and
bitter. He wrote that Japan was embarked upon acts which make her a
dangerous friend and a formidable enemy.[47]

Undersecretary of State William Phillips sent to the President another of Grew's despatches in January, 1934. The Ambassador reported the views of General Pabst, the Netherlands Minister to Japan,
regarding anticipated Japanese expansion. Grew described General
Pabst as a man not prone to find sensation where none exists. He is
an intelligent and conservative observer, whose phlegmatic hard-
headedness and common sense strengthen the import of his observations, said Grew. General Pabst had informed him that the Pan-
Asiatic movement in Japan was exceptionally strong. The Japanese
Minister for Foreign Affairs, Koki Hirota, was a staunch supporter of
the movement, said Pabst. The Netherlands Minister believed that
Japan wished to dominate an Asiatic League of Nations which would
include Manchukuo, Siberia, China, French Cochin-China, Siam, the
Straits Settlements, the Philippines and the Dutch East Indies. The year
1935 had been selected by the Japanese military for the start of radical action to construct this new order. Pabst did not think that the

Japanese army or navy could be restrained in attempting to realize these ambitions; questions of economic or financial loss would carry no weight in military circles. Ambassador Grew apparently agreed for he concluded the despatch with the comment that the United States must approach the year 1935 in all wakefulness. William Phillips, in a note accompanying this memorandum, wrote to Roosevelt remarking, "It is of interest to note how closely General Pabst's opinions coincide with our own." [48]

One year later, Ambassador Grew sent to Cordell Hull a memorandum entitled "The Importance of American Naval Preparedness in Connection with the Situation in the Far East." It is evident at this time that General Pabst's views were fully shared by the American Ambassador. Hull, describing Grew's thoughts as being in accord with his own and of especial interest and value, forwarded them to Roosevelt. Grew had written that the bluster, chauvinism, and xenophobia engendered by organized national propaganda in Japan had created a belief that it was Japan's destiny to subjugate and rule the world. A swashbuckling temper was evident in that nation's drive to create a 'Pax Japanica East Asia'. Voices of restraint in Japan were inarticulate and largely impotent, reported the American Ambassador. The United States, wrote Grew, must avoid any semblance of a pacifist response to Japanese belligerence. Although he suggested that the United States might pursue a more flexible policy toward Japan in the future, Hull told Roosevelt that the United States attitude had always been one of cooperation. The Secretary of State added that conciliatory actions by the United States had produced no corresponding compromising tone from Japan.[49]

The President had other sources of information concerning Japan which were in agreement with the analyses offered by the most knowledgeable diplomatic observers. President Lin Sen of China described the Japanese advance into China. He wrote that cities were being destroyed, and men, women, and children were being slaughtered. Ambassador Long reported from Italy the substance of an interview he had with T. V. Soong, the brother-in-law of Chiang Kai-shek. Soong was convinced that Japan contemplated the complete absorption of China and the maritime provinces of Russia. Thereafter, he was certain that Japanese ambitions were to dominate the world. Arthur Sweetzer believed that the Pacific area would be especially volatile, and would be profoundly disturbed should Japan terminate the Washington and London Naval Treaties. The Acting Secretary of the Navy, Henry Roosevelt, warned that Japan's military preparations were proceeding at a very great pace. Norman Davis suggested to Roosevelt that any pact of non-aggression with Japan would be illogical in view of the fact that Japanese forces continued to penetrate China and do things in flagrant violation of treaties. Grenville Emmet, American Minister to the Netherlands, sent to the President an assessment of Japanese ambitions by the Dutch Prime Minister, Dr. Colijn. The latter expressed the same views as had General Pabst. Arthur Holcombe, a Harvard political scientist in Nanking, informed Roosevelt that the Japanese powers-that-be believe that they have a right to do in China what the Manchus and Mongols had done before them. Japan, said Holcombe, intended to absorb the whole of China.[50]

Official declarations of Japanese foreign policy gave the President cause for concern. Eiji Amau, the Japanese Foreign Office spokesman, announced on April 17, 1934, that Japan would exert its utmost effort in carrying out her mission in East Asia. Japan, he said, opposes resolutely all attempts by other countries to aid China in its resistance to Japan. Offers of aid to China would be deemed of political significance, stated Amau. Franklin Roosevelt probably did not have to stretch his imagination to envisage what Amau described as Japan's special mission in East Asia.[51]

What were the President's personal impressions of developments in Japanese foreign policy? In April, 1933, he expressed his concern about the "Junker crowd" in Japan to Colonel House. Emperor Hirohito had written to Roosevelt in May, 1933, promising that his government would give earnest consideration to his proposals for peace. It is evident that, in the mind of the President, Hirohito's pledge had meant very little. Roosevelt wrote to Reverend Malcolm Peabody on August 19, 1933, saying that the whole scheme of things in Tokyo did not make for an assurance of non-aggression in the future. In May, 1934, he gave to Henry Stimson a very detailed and candid appraisal of the direction in which he believed Japan would move to assert its military dominance over Asia and the Pacific. The President told Stimson that a Japanese friend at Harvard had described in 1902 a one hundred year plan for the expansion of Japan. Roosevelt had been told that China, Korea, Manchuria, Mongolia, Australia, New Zealand, and all the islands of the Pacific, including Hawaii, were to be absorbed. Japan's ultimate goal, the President was told, was a rather fatherly control of all the yellow races. Did he, Roosevelt, believe that these revelations were credible? He remarked to Stimson that in many particulars this plan had been confirmed by subsequent events.[52]

A month after the interview with Stimson, the Roosevelt Administration received an interesting proposal from Hiroshi Saito, the Japanese Ambassador to the United States. Ambassador Saito set forth a plan whereby the United States would recognize the legitimacy of Japanese hegemony in the western Pacific regions. This Japanese Monroe Doctrine for the Far East, said Saito, would enable Japan to establish a reign of law and order in regions that were geographically adjacent to her. In exchange, Japan would recognize American predominance in the eastern Pacific regions. Hull's response was vigorously negative. The Secretary of State implied that the Japanese request to construct a peace in Eastern Asia would amount to a Japanese overlordship of the Orient. He angrily told Saito that there were only two countries responsible for bellicose talk of armaments and military expansion, Germany and Japan. Hull was determined that the United States would not aid the forces of aggression through the contrivance proposal by the Japanese government.

A copy of these conversations was sent to Roosevelt. In an accompanying note, Hull warned that Saito might attempt to gain acceptance of the plan by negotiating directly with the President. Hull urged Roosevelt not to enter into any revived Lansing-Ishii Agreement. Franklin Roosevelt had no intention of doing so. "If Saito comes to see me," said the President to Hull, "I want you to be there."[53]

The President's opposition to the Japanese bid for dominance in the Far East stiffened as he received reports from representatives attending discussions in London for a future naval conference. Japan had made known its intention to terminate the Washington Naval Treaty in 1934, and the London Naval Treaty which was to expire on December 31, 1936. Delegates of the major naval powers began discussions in October, 1934, in an attempt to arrive at some form of continued naval armament limitation. Roosevelt, when asked by a reporter if the United States would strongly oppose Japan's demands at London, replied that the American position was to carry out the objectives that had been sought since 1922 in the limitation of naval armaments. In private, however, the President was certain that Japan would take an impossible position. He believed that the conference would fail because of Japan's demands for treaty revision. Norman Davis, the Chief of the American Delegation to London, told Roosevelt that until the Japanese look upon treaties in the same way as the American Government, it would be unwise to enter into any further treaties with them. The London discussions seemed destined to collapse.[54]

The President's proposals to the conference were ambitious in their aims. He suggested a total tonnage reduction of twenty percent below existing treaty tonnage; if not twenty, then a fifteen, ten or five percent reduction. Norman Davis soon appraised the President that Japan desired neither reduction nor limitation. In a letter to Roosevelt on October 31, 1934, Davis reviewed comments made to him by the Japanese Ambassador to Great Britain, Tsuneo Matsudaira. Matsudaira had intimated to Davis that the military authorities had gotten completely out of hand in Japan, and that a feeling of national resentment concerning previous naval limitation treaties now forced their termination. Davis told the President that Japan's avowed policy was evidently one of war. They are acting independently and in disregard of treaty rights and interests of other powers, he reported.

Roosevelt, in reply, expressed his admiration of Davis' patience in the face of the Japanese position. In December, 1934, the talks recessed briefly, and Roosevelt publicly expressed his disappointment at the outcome of the preliminary discussions. When asked if next year would bring better negotiations, the President replied, "I hope so. I hope so." [55]

The months that followed, however, were completely unproductive. Norman Davis described for Roosevelt the results of one year of negotiations by stating simply that as of December 20, 1935, he saw no more promise of agreement than there was at the beginning of the negotiations. Cordell Hull told the President that in his opinion there was very little use in continuing the discussions in London in the face of the fixed attitude of the Japanese Government. The expected conclusion to three years of interminable debate came on January 15, 1936, when the Chairman of the Japanese delegation, Osami Nagamo, announced Japan's withdrawal from the conference. [56]

Franklin Roosevelt told a reporter on January 17, 1936, that there was little he could add to the official statements coming from London concerning the Japanese action. Said the President, "It is quite clear". Roosevelt was laconic and restrained. He had received further reports of Japanese attempts to control all of north China. In private, he openly expressed his anger and frustration in his attempts to contain Japan. He gave serious consideration to plans that provided for a cessation of trade with Japan as a means of putting pressure on the present militaristic government. He proposed to Henry Morgenthau a naval blockade of Japan by the United States, France, and England. The President's eagerness to constrain Germany was matched by his desire to permanently contain Japan. Others however urged caution. Hornbeck feared that any ill-advised opposition might easily carry the Japanese over the breakwater of reason and into a war regardless of the prospects for success. Ambassador Grew, citing Japan's over-population, lack of natural resources, and scarcity of arable land, believed that a sympathetic, cooperative and helpful attitude toward Japan might bring about an improvement in the diplomatic relations between the United States and Japan. Perhaps reflecting on the substance of these memoranda, the domestic political scene, and the conciliatory policies of the major powers, the President decided once again that the time was not propitious for attempts to organize a bolder course of action against Japan. [57]

Italy: The End of Ambivalence

Franklin Roosevelt was also giving serious consideration to another overseas development. In early October, 1935, Italy commenced the invasion of Ethiopia. This brazen act of aggression was no doubt shocking to the President, especially after the three years of cordial relations between the United States and Italy. Benito Mussolini's experiment had been described in glowing terms by the American Ambassador in Rome, Breckinridge Long. The Italian dictator, reported Long in numerous despatches, had unified Italy, restored prosperity, and, most important, could be counted upon to have a restraining influence on Hitler.

These views might have been shared initially by the President. His first contact with Mussolini was a very pleasant one. In April, 1933, the Chief Executive had received from Mussolini a personal gift consisting of the manuscripts of Virgil and Horace from the Laurenziano Library in Florence. Roosevelt sent a note of appreciation the following month, and referred to the manuscripts as symbols of the great spirit and understanding of the Italian people and their leader.[58]

The warmth evident in this exchange of greetings was apparently real. Ambassador Long, in a letter to Roosevelt, reported that during his introductory interview with Mussolini, the Italian leader had expressed his personal admiration of the President, who he believed was doing a great work and would soon defeat the Depression. Mussolini, said Long, was a man of comparatively short stature with a very soft, well modulated voice and an air of quiet and dignified elegance. Long concluded that he had been shown extreme courtesy which he saw as an indication of the very high opinion in which the Italian people held the President. Roosevelt replied saying that he was much interested and deeply impressed by what Mussolini had accomplished and by his honest purpose of restoring Italy and seeking to prevent general European trouble.[59]

Italy's foreign policy may have been viewed favorably by the President. Mussolini had provided impetus for the formation of the Four Power Pact signed in Rome on June 6, 1933. Ambassador Long believed that the unity then displayed by Great Britain, France, Germany and Italy would insure peace. Franklin Roosevelt publicly expressed his satisfaction concerning the pact. Long reported that the Italian people were optimistic about the pledged unity, and that they had celebrated the signing of the pact with a regular orgy of enthusiastic self-appreciation.[60]

Italy's presence at the Geneva Disarmament Conference was welcomed by Ambassador Long and the President. Long reported that Mussolini would not only go along with disarmament, but would do everything possible to get the Germans and the Japanese into line. Roosevelt believed that the Italian leader could force through an agreement at the Disarmament Conference, and that he, Mussolini, could accomplish more than anyone else in achieving this objective.

Ambassador Long praised the Duce for sincerely desiring disarmament. The Italian Government had already diminished appropriations for both its army and navy, said Long.[61]

Despite the failure of the Geneva Disarmament Conference, Ambassador Long continued to stress the importance of Italy as a bulwark against German aggression. He described Mussolini for the President as not only Europe's best political salesman, but an outstanding international strategist and political evangelist who had already sold to the Austrians the Fascist idea as a method of escape from Nazi Germany. In what must have appeared to Roosevelt as a most perplexing statement, Long wrote that Mussolini's ideology held out the prospect of satisfying the Nazi psychology with the substance of socialistic doctrine without the baneful influence of Marxist philosophy. One year later Ambassador Long reported that Italy was preparing to challenge Germany directly, this time with military arms and not simply Fascist ideology. Long told Roosevelt on February 3, 1935, that Mussolini expected war with Germany in a very short time. The Ambassador, believing that war was coming soon, suggested that the President send gas masks to all diplomatic and consular officers in Europe. A few days later, Long informed Roosevelt of an Italo-French accord which he depicted as amounting to an alliance against Germany. According to the analyses of Ambassador Long, only the Stresa Conference had postponed the evil day of reckoning with Germany. This meeting of French, British, and Italian representatives had met in April, 1935 to consider Hitler's rearmament program. They issued a rather innocuous declaration pledging to reaffirm their earnest desire to sustain peace. Long believed that the Stresa Conference had brushed away the war clouds and flattened over the troubled waters.[62]

Franklin Roosevelt might have been pleased by his Ambassador's description of Italian foreign policy, but it seems doubtful that he would have approved of the fascist ideology of Mussolini. This too, however, seemed to have the endorsement of Breckinridge Long. The Fascisti were described by Long in a letter to the President as dapper, well dressed, and straight in their posture. They lend an atmosphere of individuality and importance to their surroundings, said Long. Fascist efficiency also impressed the Ambassador. The trains, he wrote, were punctual, well-equipped, and fast. The fascist experiment, he told Roosevelt, had produced clean and well paved streets, improved sanitary conditions, country farms that seemed to have been manicured every morning, and a well dressed and happy populace.[63]

These accomplishments of Mussolini, and the assumed intentions of his initial foreign policies, were quickly forgotten by the President as reports of a possible Italian invasion of Ethiopia became more and more frequent. The Ambassador in Rome said in February, 1935, that Italians were busily engaged in preparing detailed maps of all Ethiopia. Milanese factories, wrote Long, were working day and night producing tanks, airplanes, bombs, trucks, and machine guns. The President, fully apprised of the extent of Italian war preparations, made a personal appeal to Mussolini to avoid an armed conflict. The Italian leader refused. Italy, he said, could not draw back now and destroy its prestige; besides, a million men had been mobilized and two billion lire had been spent on this war effort. Roosevelt did not accept these excuses. He told Cordell Hull that in any future message to Mussolini it should be stressed that Italian prestige would be enhanced by cancelling all military preparations and submitting the whole question to peaceful settlement by arbitration.[64]

Roosevelt's hopes did not materialize. In September, 1935, Ambassador Long told the President that the Italians had worked themselves into a state of self-adoration and self-consciousness which leads them to believe that they can meet any power in battle with success. Long then offered a detailed analysis of Italian ambitions. They will be troublemakers in Africa, he wrote, and will attempt to connect Libya and Ethiopia, and may even move on to the eastern side of the Red Sea. Long described the attitude of Mussolini and the Italian people regarding this operation as being deliberate, determined, obdurate, ruthless, and almost vicious. Should they be successful here, he warned, they would surely move on to other fields. Italy, Long wrote, had not a leg to stand on, either moral or legal, in her invasion of Ethiopia.[65]

Franklin Roosevelt was alarmed and frustrated by his failure to constrain the aggressive ambitions of Germany, Japan, and Italy. In reviewing developments in foreign affairs during the first three years of his administration, it must have been evident to him that the future held forth ominous potentialities. He had sufficient reason to believe that Germany's territorial ambitions were quite extensive and that, given the ideology of hate and violence espoused by Hitler, any program of aggrandizement would be achieved by war. Japan's systematic policy of aggression in China and the bellicose warnings of an inevitable confrontation with the United States in the Far East, should there occur any resistance to Japanese expansion, may have strengthened the President's belief that Japan's war policy envisaged absolute dominance over Asia and the Pacific. The one hundred year program to create the Japanese Empire, which had been described to him in 1902, seemed under way and gaining momentum. Italy's invasion of Ethiopia appeared as a logical climax to three years of discord and lawlessness in international affairs. He foresaw that Mussolini's success would serve as a stimulant to those nations which yearned to extend their power and control over weaker neighbors.

III

In Search
of a Response

CHAPTER THREE

IN SEARCH OF A RESPONSE

CONDEMNATION OF APPEASEMENT

During a press conference on November 6, 1935, Franklin Roosevelt told a reporter that foreign affairs were of far greater concern to him than was the domestic situation. Stephen Early, the President's Press Secretary, immediately suggested another topic for conversation. There is no evidence that Mr. Early was trying to circumvent what might have developed into a prolonged discussion of a troublesome issue months before the 1936 election campaign. An extemporaneous elaboration on the perplexing problem of foreign affairs by the President, however, would probably have been especially distressing. Press Secretary Early may have realized that Roosevelt's portrayal of the growing crisis situation and the threat it posed to the nation's security would have suggested that the only solution to the challenge of the aggressors was to be found in some form of United States participation in, even leadership of, collective punitive action.[1]

This was the view of the President, and it was based on the assumption that a war in Europe and the Far East was probable in the near future and that such a conflict could have alarming repercussions for the United States. It would be an understatement to assert that Franklin Roosevelt disagreed with the prognoses of his Ambassador to Belgium, Dave Hennen Morris. Morris had written the President on December 26, 1935, and consoled him with the following words: "Do not have any doubts about the future: it is safe in the laps of the Gods." Roosevelt thought otherwise as is amply documented in his private correspondence. In a letter to Ambassador Long on March 9, 1935, he described these years as the most hair trigger times the world had gone through in his lifetime, even more so than June and July, 1914. In August, Roosevelt confided to Ambassador Dodd that

57

last year he had been fairly optimistic, but recently any reasons for a sanguine outlook had disappeared. In that same month, he told Senator Josiah Bailey of North Carolina that the world situation was much more disturbing than the domestic, and that he hoped there would be no overseas explosion before October, 1935. In another letter to Ambassador Long, Roosevelt admitted that both Long and Dodd had been more accurate in their pessimism than all other observers in Europe.[2]

What might be the response of the United States to the approaching probability of war? The President was not sure, but he did know that some initiatives had to be made to halt the rising tide of aggression. In March, 1935, he informed Ray Stannard Baker that the time for a new stimulation of united American action in foreign affairs was close at hand, and that within a year he would propose such a stimulant. It came subtly on January 3, 1936, in the President's annual message to Congress. The contents of this speech, already alluded to, were intended to awaken the American public and the forces of peace to the serious threat posed by those nations that had subscribed to the law of the sword. A corollary aim of Roosevelt in delivering these remarks was to alert democratic statesmen everywhere to the fact that he, the President of the United States, was personally alarmed by developments in Germany, Japan, and Italy. The time had come for united action against the ten or fifteen percent of the world's populace which blocked the construction of peace by the civilized powers of the world. Three days after the speech, Roosevelt told Ambassador Dodd that recent information from Germany had confirmed his own feelings of disquiet in regard to European and Asiatic affairs, and, with these thoughts in mind, he had delivered a serious and very clear message to Congress. In that same month he wrote Norman Davis, explaining that although he had expected a great deal of bitterness in Japan, Germany, and Italy because of his comments, the speech had to be made in order to solidify the forces of non-aggression. The question that remained in the President's mind was whether or not Great Britain, France, and the Soviet Union would respond in energetic earnestness to what was in fact not a proposed solution, but a suggested tone of stiffening opposition to the aggressor nations. He had many reasons to be pessimistic in his expectations.[3]

Franklin Roosevelt's efforts to bring about closer ties between the United States and Great Britain had not proven productive. The collapse of the World Economic Conference had dampened the hopes of many who had anticipated the creation of a working partnership between the British and Americans. The President's opinion of British foreign policy was also growing more critical throughout the early years of his administration. His personal representatives overseas initially informed him that the British were eager to cooperate with the United States because of ominous portents in international affairs. Ambassador Long had written the President telling him of a discussion with Arthur Henderson, British representative to the Geneva Disarmament Conference. Henderson had implied that a united front against Japan would be warranted if that nation persisted in blocking disarmament. Ambassador Bingham in London informed Roosevelt that the British attitude of mind now favored conciliation. One year later, Bingham was certain that the time for dealing with the British was very propitious. All thoughtful people with whom he had contact, wrote Bingham, realized that the hope for peace in the world rested in cooperation between Great Britain and the United States. Developments in Europe and the Far East, he said, had thoroughly alarmed the English, and they now eagerly desired to deal with the United States on a basis of intimacy.[4]

Yet, as the Geneva Disarmament Conference moved forward ever more sluggishly and the London Naval discussions bogged down because of Japan's intransigence, it became evident that the views of Prime Minister Ramsay MacDonald and Foreign Secretary Sir John Simon concerning Germany and Japan indicated a willingness to compromise which was not shared by Roosevelt. In April, 1934, Sir Ronald Lindsay, the British Ambassador to the United States, declared to William Phillips that Great Britain was opposed to any concerted action in the Far Eastern situation. Cordell Hull immediately forwarded to the President an account of this conversation. Ambassador Bingham wrote Roosevelt in May saying that Great Britain was not willing to adopt any Anglo-American policy that might be interpreted as coercion in Japan.[5]

The President began to have his doubts about the British attitude. In a letter to Nicholas Butler, President of Columbia University, Roosevelt candidly admitted that he was no longer certain of the cooperation which had been expected from Great Britain, and that efforts to achieve this cooperation for peace were producing results much like the sowing of seed in exceedingly rocky ground. Norman Davis had described MacDonald's policy toward Japan as one of counseling patience in the hope that cooperation would be forthcoming. Roosevelt responded angrily saying that if Great Britain was even suspected of preferring to play with Japan instead of the United States then he would be compelled to approach public sentiment in Canada, Australia, New Zealand, and South Africa in a definite effort to inform the Dominions that their future security was tied to that of America. He told Norman Davis to inject this thought into the minds of British leaders in the most diplomatic way. During the final days of 1934, there was some stiffening in the

British attitude toward Japan. Davis perceived a distinct crystalli-
zation of opinion against Japan, which, he told the President, was
really encouraging. Roosevelt, in a letter to Henry Stimson, expressed the opinion that real progress was being made with British
friends. This renewed optimism was short-lived. Norman Davis,
writing to the President on December 14, 1934, seemed to have reluctantly concluded that the British would not firmly oppose Japan.
MacDonald, said Davis, was singing his old song about being fearful
of arousing the wrath of Japanese militarists. He added that the
leaders in London were concerned about a possible German-Japanese
alliance, the threat of a naval arms race, and pressure from industrial-
ists to expand trade with Japan.[6]

Great Britain's relations with Germany also alarmed Roosevelt.
The Anglo-German Naval Treaty of June, 1935, seemed to indicate
the beginning of an appeasement policy which the President vigorously opposed. Ambassador Bingham explained the British position
to Roosevelt, saying that the MacDonald cabinet had not wished
to miss this opportunity for an agreement with Germany. The President did not accept British logic on this issue. In his reply to the
Ambassador, he expressed the opinion that the British had made a
serious mistake in coming to terms with Germany. They will find,
he continued, real resentment on the continent, and much trouble
for themselves in the days to come. Roosevelt foresaw that there was
nothing which would prevent the Germans from violating this treaty,
and he expected them to do so after witnessing their abandonment
of other treaties in the past. The President's appraisal of this treaty
was similar to that drawn by Ambassador Dodd in Berlin. In a letter
to Roosevelt, Dodd complained that this was the first time that England had sided with a threatening imperialist power rather than guide
weaker powers against the threatening one. In a conversation with
Henry Morgenthau, the President disclosed that he believed there
existed a more devious aspect to the emerging accord between Germany and Great Britain. He surmised that there might be an offensive-defensive treaty linking the two powers in their efforts to dominate Europe, and that the British had made known only that part
of the agreement that had to do with the German Navy. He speculated that Japan and England had signed a similar treaty to share
complete control of the high seas. What effect would British action
have on that nation's relations with the United States? Roosevelt
suggested to Ambassador Bingham that it was a mistake to make
any advances to the British Government, and that practical results
would be forthcoming only when they make the advances themselves. The British were funny people, he continued, and while always polite tended to exhibit a national selfishness which made mutual

hopefulness very difficult to accomplish. In the early months of 1936, more information came to the President's desk which tended to support his cynicism. The British, wrote Norman Davis, will not overlook the possibility of exercising moral influence over Germany to bring about an appeasement of their differences, and will move in a constructive way to satisfy that nation's demands. The thrust of British foreign policy greatly disturbed Franklin Roosevelt. A united front in opposition to the forces of aggression seems at this point to have been only a chimera of wishful imagination.[7]

The other power which was to serve as a cornerstone in the structure of peace as conceived by Franklin Roosevelt was France, and reports concerning the French situation were exceedingly pessimistic. Early in his administration, Roosevelt expressed dismay over the chaotic state of French politics. In a press conference he described the French as easily upset, "awfully upsettable," by rumors. He thought that the parliamentary situation in France was one of the most difficult to control in the world. No human being can tell from one day to another, he told a reporter, what the Chamber of Deputies was going to do. Our troubles with Congress, he concluded, were nothing compared to the French. Ambassador Long in Italy had told the President that there existed intense dissatisfaction with the Government in France. There was widespread discontent with the parliamentary system, said Long, and the idea of a fascist dictatorship had ardent supporters throughout France. He described the French as too excitable and emotional to be committed to any one form of government, and with the rapid spread of srikes and rioting in Paris, he believed that revolution could take place in the near future. Ambassador Jesse Straus in Paris agreed that a dictatorship might be imposed on France, but he thought this solution an unlikely one for the simple reason that there was no one single strong man of youth and vigor to take the helm. Nothing occurred in the intervening years to alter these extremely discouraging views of France's domestic situation. Ambassador Straus wrote a letter to the President on January 20, 1936, in which he described, in an exceedingly disparaging tone, the French domestic scene. If rumor and innuendo are to be believed, he wrote, then there is little intellectual or moral honesty among politicians in France. Italian, Russian, German, and Japanese money was flowing into France for political purposes. Corruption and bribery appeared to be a matter of daily routine. The Chamber of Deputies, he said, was a poor looking and bad acting national assembly whose members behave like a lot of naughty children in a nursery. It is, continued Straus, a dirty picture and it does not make likely a very brilliant future for France. The French economy was also plagued with seemingly insoluble problems. Business was rotten, prices were high, and the franc was overvalued, wrote Straus. Franklin Roosevelt was further depressed by his Ambassador's description of the French military. In Straus' opinion, the French air force was insignificant, poorly equipped, and unprepared with modern machines compared to Germany. In conclusion Ambassador Straus described the atmosphere in France as doleful: all were looking for a miracle but there were no miracle men, only political hacks. Did Roosevelt consider Straus' views credible and accurate? He confessed in a reply to his Ambassador that he had entertained the same observations of France, and the same doubts about the future of that country. The optimistic views he once had concerning France's ability to come out of this crisis successfully, now appeared to him to be of little foundation. The President said that he was very much disturbed by the constant changes in the ministries in France. In a collective front against the aggressors, France appeared to Roosevelt as a very weak link.[8]

Russia: Prospective Alliance Partner

Great Britain and France were not the only nations considered by the President to be potential bulwarks against expansion by Germany and Japan. The Soviet Union was of critical importance to Franklin Roosevelt as he contemplated the possible alignment of powers if the situation in Europe and the Far East should deteriorate further. Prior to assuming the office of President, he had given serious consideration to the desirability of resuming diplomatic relations with that country. In May, 1932, he discussed this topic with Adolph Berle, Raymond Moley, Rexford Tugwell, and Sam Rosenman at Hyde Park. The consensus of opinion was that recognition of the Soviet Union was a necessity for economic reasons. Adolph Berle told Roosevelt that the Soviet Union was deficient in practicaly all products which the United States manufactured, and American business could certainly use the Russian markets. Farmers too, thought Berle, could dispose of their surpluses in the Soviet Union. He further advised Roosevelt that Russian foreign propaganda in favor of communism had apparently died in their preoccupation over the success of the five year plan. Purely doctrinaire ideas, said Berle, such as the belief that communism automatically outlaws a nation, should be discarded. In Berle's opinion, the American and Russian systems would, in approximately twenty years, look very much alike. There was no great difference, thought Berle, between having all industry run by a committee of commissars or by a small group of directors. There were determinants other than economic considerations, however, behind FDR's pursuit of a rapproachement with Russia. Overseas develop-

ments were also of major concern to the President as he contemplated
the establishment of diplomatic relations with the Soviet Union.[9]

Franklin Roosevelt necessarily viewed world affairs with extremely myopic vision. His attention was riveted on Germany and
Japan. There would be difficult periods in the history of American-
Soviet relations, but the threat of fascist aggression was, for Roosevelt, sufficient reason to minimize the more perceptive analyses of
Soviet foreign policy and its ultimate aims. He was determined never
to endanger the rapprochement that was affected in 1933 between
the United States and the Soviet Union. He was to persistently seek
a cordial partnership with that nation, and he would promote every
effort which might result in closer ties with the Soviet Union.

Sumner Welles recalled that beginning in 1933 Franklin Roosevelt
made the resumption of relations with Russia a cardinal principle of
his foreign policy. Secretary of State Cordell Hull has given insight
into the rationale behind the President's logic in pursuing this course
of action. The President and Hull envisaged the possibility that the
Soviet Union could help to stabilize the situation in Europe and
Asia. Russia was to join a common moral front with Great Britain,
France, and the United States in opposition to the aggressor nations.
Secretary Hull was convinced that only such a union could recall
the jingoist countries to their senses. The serious deterioration in
the prospects for world peace was uppermost in the President's
mind as he prepared his approach to Russia. He sincerely believed
that no stability could be achieved so long as the United States failed
to recognize the existence of a nation of such potential. There can
be little doubt that, from the perspective of the anticipated future,
the world balance of power was the most serious underlying consideration which would guide him in all dealings with the Soviet
Union.[10]

Rumors of the impending recognition of Russia were prevalent
throughout 1933. The President was very eager to begin discussions
with Soviet representatives on this topic. His impressions of Soviet
foreign policy during these months were favorable ones. In April,
1933, Roosevelt asked William Phillips to forward to him the statement on aggression which had been issued by the Soviet Foreign
Minister, Maxim Litvinov, at the Geneva Disarmament Conference.
Litvinov had defined an aggressor nation as one which declared war
against another state, invaded without declaring war, bombarded the
territory of another state, or established a naval blockade of a nation.
The President may have agreed with Litvinov's declaration, especially
his added suggestion that penalties should be applied to an aggressor
country because no considerations whatsoever of a political, strategi-
cal or economic nature could justify an act of aggression. In May,

1933, the Russian Government responded earnestly to the President's appeal for a universal pact of non-aggression, stating that the Soviet Union would cooperate with nations interested in the realization of such a policy. American delegates to the London Economic Conference conferred with Soviet representatives, and one topic of conversation was the question of American and Russian recognition. Cordell Hull was impressed by Litvinov, whom he considered to be a thoroughly capable diplomat and international statesman. William Bullitt, also in London at this time, and a confidant of the President on this issue, informed Roosevelt that T.V. Soong of China was pushing for United States recognition of the Soviet Union in order to restrain Japan, an action also suggested by Bullitt. He further noted that Litvinov had pledged to aid China in the struggle against their common enemy. In this letter to the President, Bullitt admitted that he had told the Soviet foreign minister not to be surprised if Roosevelt did recognize Russia.[11]

Franklin Roosevelt initiated conversations which would lead to recognition by writing a personal letter to Mikhail Kalinin, President of the Soviet Union. In this note of October 10, 1933, he expressed his belief that frank and friendly conversations could solve whatever difficulties might stand in the way of ending the abnormal relations between the two countries. Kalinin in his reply stressed what was perhaps the most important consideration in Roosevelt's mind. He noted that a continuance of a policy of non-recognition would increase the element of disquiet, complicate the process of consolidating world peace, and encourage forces tending to disturb the peace. Felix Frankfurter, in a letter to the President on October 29, 1933, was more explicit than Kalinin had been concerning the direct effect of the proposed re-establishing of diplomatic relations. He warned Roosevelt that Germany and Japan were moving on convergent lines and, given this new constellation of great powers, the termination of hostile and anomalous relations between Russia and the United States would be of momentous significance to the world's peace. Josephus Daniels reminded the President of Thomas Jefferson's characterization of the American and Russian nations as essentially pacific powers whose common cause it was to maintain the rights of peaceable countries.[12]

Formal diplomatic relations between the United States and the Soviet Union were established on November 16, 1933. In an exchange of notes, Maxim Litvinov and Franklin Roosevelt pledged that their countries would cooperate for their mutual benefit and for the preservation of the peace of the world. Litvinov promised that Americans would enjoy freedom of conscience and religious liberty in the Soviet Union; that his Government would not interfere in the internal affairs of the United States; and that it would refrain from any agitation or propaganda which would violate the territorial integrity of the United States, or bring about change by force in its political or social order. These assurances had been sought most earnestly by Robert Kelley, the Chief of the Division of East European Affairs in the State Department, Cordell Hull, and William Bullitt. There were other important prerequisites to recognition which were not a part of this diplomatic exchange, however, despite the entreaties of the above mentioned personages. The issue of debts was not resolved. Robert Kelley had computed the total debt owed by Russia to the United States at $336,691,771.03. The President and Litvinov simply agreed to further discuss a debt solution of amounts between $75,000,000 and $150,000,000 after the resumption of relations. Failure to press forward on this issue made possible interminable haggling by the Soviet authorities as they refused to make any payments on debts owed to the American government.[13]

It is doubtful that Roosevelt really concerned himself with these incidental aspects of recognition. Public opinion was reassured, perhaps, by the promises made by Litvinov, but such assurances were easily evaded and not at all enforceable. Certainly, protracted negotiations might have solved the debt problem. The President admitted that these issues were not of paramount importance. The only weakness he could find in the agreement on recognition was found in the title page of the documents. Commissar had been spelled with one 's' instead of two. The important thing, he told reporters, was that relations had been resumed. Speaking to an audience in Savannah, Georgia, two days after recognition, the President declared that the most compelling reason to establish relations was the desire of both nations for peace and for the strengthening of the peaceful purpose of the civilized world. In private conversations with Litvinov, Roosevelt was more precise. Recognition made possible the showing of a united front on the part of the whole civilized world against the unruly ambitions of Germany and Japan. Franklin Roosevelt was certain that the relations now linking his country and Russia would grow more intimate with each passing year.[14]

Initial contacts were marked by glowing cordiality. William Bullitt, appointed Ambassador to the Soviet Union, arrived in Moscow on December 11, 1933. He sent to the President on January 1, 1934, an account of his first impressions at his new diplomatic post. Bullitt described for Roosevelt the respect and admiration that the Russian leaders had expressed for the American President. Kalinin had depicted Roosevelt as a man who really cared about the welfare of the laboring men and the farmers, and said that everyone in Russia considered him to be completely out of the class of the leaders of capitalist states. Joseph Stalin echoed Kalinin's adulations, describing the President as one of the most popular men in the Soviet Union, in spite of being the leader of a capitalist nation. Roosevelt was probably impressed by Bullitt's description of the Soviet leadership. They were, he wrote, intelligent, sophisticated, and vigorous human beings. Bullitt found Stalin especially fascinating. He was described as rather short, of ordinary physique, wiry rather than powerful, with unusually long nostrils, and a mustache that covered his mouth in such a way that when he laughed his lips curled in a curiously canine manner. Lenin was a great man, wrote Bullitt, but Stalin seemed a wiry gipsy wtih roots and emotions beyond the Ambassador's experience. He was, however, a real statesman who, like Lenin and Roosevelt, said Bullitt, could treat the most serious things with a joke and a twinkle in his eye. Stalin had been exceptionally polite to Bullitt, promising him anything that he might want in the Soviet Union. All of these incidents could not have gone unnoticed by the President.

In this same letter, it was evident that the Russian leaders were emphasizing another subject which was of importance to Roosevelt. This was the threat of Japanese aggression. They repeatedly stressed the probability of an attack by Japan on the Soviet Union. Litvinov, said Bullitt, was most concerned about the preservation of peace in the Far East. Soviet diplomats were active in trying to secure their western frontiers because of the anticipated attack in the spring, he continued, and were considering negotiating a defensive alliance with France and entering the League of Nations. Bullitt assured Stalin that Roosevelt's primary aim was to prevent war in the Far East so that the Soviet Government might work out its great experiment in peace. Perhaps it was in this context that Marshal Kliment Voroshilov, Supreme Commander of the Army and Navy, had requested of Bullitt a full staff of American military, naval and air attachés in Moscow. The Ambassador told Roosevelt that this seemed a good idea which might be very useful in the future. In this first encounter with the Soviet leadership, it would seem that all of the President's expectations had been fulfilled. The future appeared to hold forth intimate collaboration. In his reply to Bullitt's letter, Roosevelt instructed his Ambassador to prohibit spying of any kind, by either diplomatic or military officials of the United States, and he urged all members of his staff to cultivate the frankest and most direct relations with members of the Soviet Government.[15]

It seems probable that Japan was the initial key to an understanding of Russian-American relations from the perspective of the President. Stanley Hornbeck had submitted a memorandum in January, 1934, on the course of action which the United States should follow in the Russo-Japanese conflict. It is impossible to determine whether or not Franklin Roosevelt accepted Hornbeck's suggestions as the bases on which he was to construct a fundamental approach to the Soviet Union, but it is evident that the advice given by this Far Eastern specialist does describe the President's attitude toward relations with Russia throughout his years in office. The German threat strengthened Hornbeck's logic. In this memorandum heavy emphasis was placed on the danger to peace because of the Japanese thirst for imperialist expansion. In Hornbeck's opinion, Japan was clearly "on the make"; the people were virile, and eager to fight to increase the wealth, power, and prestige of their country. Moreover, he continued, Japan was a clear and present danger to the United States. In several respects, he wrote, the differences between the two countries were irreconcilable, and Japan must therefore be viewed as a potential military adversary. Japan will become even more of a menace, he warned, if it should be victorious in a war against Russia or China. The American Government, he concluded, must help the Soviet Union and China toward internal improvement by peaceful processes, and should discreetly let it appear that the sympathies of the United States are with Russia if Japanese aggression against that country seems imminent. In Hornbeck's opinion, the United States had little or nothing to fear from China or the Soviet Union, but much to fear from Japan.[16]

Franklin Roosevelt did view the Soviet Union as a bulwark to Japan and Germany. He had reason to be impressed with the potential might of Russia and the vital role it might play in the future. William Bullitt offered a very optimistic account of conditions in the Soviet Union, and his observations were forwarded to the President. Bullitt wrote that the speed of change since 1914 had been incredible. Russia was then a swamp of illiterate peasants and in the immediate postwar period a mass of starving children, men, and women. Today, he continued, they face the future with confidence. The dictatorship is secure and the bureaucracy is strong. The regime has undertaken educational reforms, and has placed great emphasis on scientific research, art, theatre, and ballet. The Soviet youth is alive and enthusiastic; the young feel that an earthly paradise lies but a few years ahead. The President may have also been impressed by Bullitt's observations concerning Soviet foreign policy. Russia's officials had told him that extension of their domains would come by voluntary agglomeration and not by conquest. The Red Army, said Bullitt, was pushing for close cooperation with the United States. Its officers no longer fear defeat by Japan, noted the Ambassador.[17]

Roosevelt was reassured by continued reports of Russia's willingness to constrain Japanese aggressiveness. Maxim Litvinov had characterized the Amau statement in almost the same terms as used by Cordell Hull, and they no doubt coincided with those of the President. Litvinov called the proclamation an announcement of a protectorate over China, and he urged nations to jointly protest the heavyhandedness of the Japanese in this instance. There was mounting evidence to support the fact that the Red Army was superior to that of the Japanese, and, if provoked, could be counted upon to defeat Japan. Bullitt could report by the spring of 1935 that neither Germany nor Japan would dare to attack the Soviet Union. If the President was thinking in terms of a collective front against the aggressors, then it is reasonable to assume that Russia would have to occupy a most important position in any future alignment of powers.[18]

There were obstacles to the growing rapport of the two countries, but Franklin Roosevelt refused to jeopardize the ties established with Russia. The debt controversy became heated in the months following recognition. Litvinov and Bullitt engaged in spirited arguments over this issue. Bullitt morosely informed the President in April, 1934, that the honeymoon atmosphere had evaporated, and that Russia's underlying hostility to all capitalist countries had come through the veneer of intimate friendship. Roosevelt appears not to have been disturbed by his Ambassador's growing disenchantment. In a letter to Bullitt the President admitted that he had gotten a lot of chuckles out of the scraps between his Ambassador and Litvinov. On the specific issue of debts, Roosevelt had always been ready to accept a compromise solution. R. Walton Moore informed Bullitt that the President was inclined to go very far in modifying the original debt proposals, and was most anxious that an agreement be reached. He would, said Moore, take a very liberal view of any proposals extracted from Litvinov. The debt controversy was not solved, but Roosevelt's willingness to refrain from criticizing the dilatory bargaining methods of the Russian leadership prevented a more serious confrontation over what he considered to be a very minor issue.[19]

There were other disturbing reports coming from Moscow. In the spring months of 1935, William Bullitt described the beginnings of a reign of terror which would culminate in the terrible purge trials a few years later. The terror, Bullitt told Roosevelt, was always present but lately it had risen to such a pitch that the least of the Muscovites, as well as the greatest, live in constant fear. Exiles are frequent, he added, and no one dares to have any contacts with foreigners. The Ambassador acknowledged that it had been extraordinarily difficult to preserve a sweet and loving exterior under these circumstances. A few weeks later, Hull forwarded to the President an account by Bullitt of the murder of Sergei Kirov, a Leningrad Party leader, and the spreading wave of arrests and exiles of innocent human beings.

Stalin was portrayed by the Ambassador as enraged over the murder of Kirov and intent on punishing all those involved in the assassination. Franklin Roosevelt was very dispassionate in his reply to Bullitt's account of the incident: "That was a fascinating story," said the President, "Do write me often."[20]

Diplomatic officials seriously considered and suggested a formal severing of diplomatic ties with Russia during the months of July and August, 1935. The occasion for this confrontation was the convocation of the Third International Congress in Moscow, and the attendance at the sessions of representatives of the American Communist Party, including its leader, Earl Browder. This seemed to many to be a violation of Litvinov's pledge of 1933 that his government would not foster or support any revolutionary activities or propaganda aiming at the overthrow of the United States Government. Bullitt knew the President would roar with laughter at the thought of breaking relations over a mere technical violation of Litvinov's promise but he suggested that if the violation proved to be gross and insulting then it might be necessary to sever relations. If the United States takes no action, he said, the Soviet Government would be convinced that it could break its pledges with impunity. In a letter to R. Walton Moore, which was sent to Roosevelt, Bullitt described some Bolsheviks as very eager to attack publicly their capitalist enemy, the United States. In a memorandum to the President, Moore asserted that it was very clear that Litvinov's pledge had been completely violated Cordell Hull, angry over Litvinov's and Stalin's denial that they even knew of the Comintern meeting, issued two statements condemning the congress as a flagrant violation of the recognition agreements which the American people resented most strongly. In Hull's estimation, the Comintern sessions had struck a severe blow at the fabric of friendly relations between the two countries. Franklin Roosevelt, however, remained impervious to the criticisms of Soviet conduct. R. Walton Moore and Cordell Hull informed Bullitt that the President had decided it was best to do nothing further at the moment than to issue a protest statement. He had not been swayed by any individual, said Moore, but had acted very independently. When questioned at a press conference as to what he thought of the Soviet Government's disregarding of promises they had made, as had been asserted by news reporters in Moscow, he replied, "Depends on who wrote the press despatches."[21]

The President's determination to avoid a crisis with the Soviet Union, his decision to continue to cultivate the friendship of its leaders, and his insistence on the necessity of dealing with the Russian leadership with circumspection and patience, may serve to explain his ignorance of the aims of Soviet foreign policy as set forth for him

by William Bullitt. There are absolutely no letters from Roosevelt
to Bullitt discussing Russian foreign policy in-depth. Perhaps he
failed to take notice of these important passages, for there are repeated references to this topic in Bullitt's letters to the President.
Actions undertaken by the Soviet Union during this period might
lead the casual observer to believe that Russia was seriously attempting to form a collective response to the threat of Germany and
Japan. Bullitt was more perceptive. In September, 1934, the Soviet
Union entered the League of Nations. The American Ambassador
in Moscow said bluntly that the Russians hated entering the League
and did so only as a preliminary step to a defensive agreement with
the French. A pact of mutual assistance was signed by France and
the Soviet Union on May 2, 1935. Bullitt's analysis was correct. He
told the President that Russia had demanded that France put up or
shut up, or she would turn to Germany. The next day he repeated his
appraisal of the pact, telling Roosevelt that Russia had been the
single beneficiary of the agreement, and that now both France and
Germany would be compelled to bid high for Soviet assistance. Bullitt also clarified for Roosevelt the true meaning of the popular front
policy announced at the Seventh Congress of the Comintern. He
saw clearly, and so informed the President, that the cooperation of
communists with socialists and bourgeois democrats was predicated
on the assumption that the communists would come back from the
ride with the socialists and democrats inside. The President did not
discuss these issues with his Ambassador. His thoughts at the moment
may have been similar to those expressed by William Dodd. The
Ambassador in Berlin cautioned Roosevelt to avoid breaks with
Russia. We would have such horrors with Japan attacking Vladi-
vostok and Germany breaking into Leningrad, said Dodd, that one
could hardly imagine the consequences. The aggressor nations had
been identified by the President, and like Ambassador Dodd, he did
not consider the Soviet Union to be in that category.[22]

Europe and Asia: Aggression Ascendant

Surveying the European and Asian diplomatic scene in 1935,
Franklin Roosevelt anticipated the future with a profound sense of
pessimism. Clearly discernible were the ambitions and aggressive
designs of Germany, Japan, and Italy. Nowhere, however, did there
appear a willingness on the part of other nations to unite in the face
of what the President considered to be a very grave situation. Great
Britain had chosen the path of appeasement and compromise. France
appeared too weak to formulate and implement a consistent foreign
policy of any kind. The Soviet Union, although reflecting a vocal

disposition to oppose Germany and Japan, was becoming a pugnacious and irritating associate.

The domestic situation, as it related to foreign affairs, could give the President no cause for optimism. Isolationist sentiment was strong in the first three years of his Administration. Republican Senators William Borah of Idaho, Arthur Vandenberg of Michigan, Hiram Johnson of California, Gerald Nye of North Dakota, and Democrats such as Bennett Clark of Missouri and Homer T. Bone of Washington were opposed to internationalist policies of involvement in world affairs. Roosevelt needed their support to assure passage of New Deal measures of recovery and reform. The Nye Committee, established in 1934 to investigate the armament industry and its role in pressuring the United States into World War I, was instrumental in convincing Americans to never again sacrifice their lives overseas for munitions makers and war profiteers.

The strength of isolationism in the United States was revealed by two events in 1935. In January the Senate failed to muster a two-thirds majority necessary for adoption of resolutions of adherence to the World Court. Franklin Roosevelt had pressed for the entrance of the United States into the World Court, calling it an opportunity to throw America's weight into the scale in favor of peace. In private, the President expressed his resentment concerning the defeat of the proposed resolutions. He confided to Senator Joseph Robinson of Arkansas that the thirty-six gentlemen who had voted against the principle of a World Court would be doing a lot of apologizing when they got to Heaven, if indeed God was against war. In a letter to Henry Stimson, he expressed a tone of bitterness saying that at least he now knew his enemies, and that neither they nor his objectives would be forgotten in the future. When asked about the defeat of the World Court proposal by reporters, Roosevelt replied assertively that he, not Congress, would exercise control over all phases of foreign policy other than appropriations and treaties.[23]

He had to modify this statement on August 31, 1935, when Congress passed the First Neutrality Law. The legislation stated that when the President declared that a state of war existed between two or more countries, it would then be unlawful to export arms, ammunitions and implements of war to the belligerent countries. American vessels were forbidden to carry arms to belligerents. The President could also warn American citizens that they traveled at their own risk on the vessels of those nations engaged in war. Roosevelt was not pleased by the arbitrary embargo provisions in this legislation. He would have preferred a discretionary arms embargo which could be used to halt the aggressor without inflicting hardship on that country fighting a defensive war. In giving his approval of this legislation, he warned that the wholly inflexible embargo provisions might drag the United States into war instead of keeping it out. In his private letters, Roosevelt expressed his criticism more forcefully. What would occur, he asked Ambassador Dodd, if a European power should invade a country in South America? The neutrality law as passed, he asserted, would unfortunately aid the European aggressor. He confided to Colonel House that the United States would not stand idly by while the civilization of Europe was destroyed. In the months ahead, the President would attempt to encourage a collective response to aggression despite the constraints which isolationist sentiment and neutralaity legislation exercised on his policies.[24]

The Italian invasion of Ethiopia on October 3, 1935, was initiated despite the entreaties of Franklin Roosevelt. Benito Mussolini had committed the might of the Italian armed forces against the backward, impoverished, and defenseless nation of Emperor Haile Selassie. The Roosevelt Administration viewed the act as one of naked aggression. Ambassador Long's telegrams had given the President a vivid description of the intensity of the nationalistic war fervor prevalent in Italy. The military campaign in Ethiopia demonstrated the consequences of that unleashed martial spirit. Roosevelt's response to this conflict reflects an energetic attempt to restrain Italy and provide leadership to those European nations floundering in the mire of appeasement.

Warnings of the impending invasion prompted the President to issue on August 1, 1935, a formal note expressing the hope that an amicable solution would be found and that peace would be maintained. War preparations continued unabated, however, and the League of Nations proved incapable of halting the conflict. Mussolini's forces began to march in the early days of October. Roosevelt, realizing that the neutrality law would have a debilitating effect on Italy and not Ethiopia, was eager to implement the statute. He had told a reporter, perhaps with some satisfaction, that the United States response to the war would be one of simply following legislation. The President strained to do just that at the earliest possible moment. He informed Cordell Hull on October 3, 1935, that the neutrality law should be invoked whenever any official information of the Italian invasion was forthcoming, even if there was no formal declaration of war. Two days later, according to the provisions of the Neutrality Act, the President prohibited the export of arms, ammunition, and implements of war to the belligerent countries, forbade the transportation of such articles by United States vessels to the nations at war, proclaimed that all persons engaged in the manufacturing, exporting, or importing of said articles must be licensed and registered, and stated that citizens traveling on belligerent vessels

would do so at their own risk. He added that any American citizen
who voluntarily engaged in transactions of any character with either
of the belligerents did so at his own risk. This last warning did go
beyond the formal limitations contained in the Neutrality Law.
Roosevelt was attempting to assert a moral embargo of all trade with
Italy and Ethiopia, not simply arms, ammunition, and implements
of war. Cordell Hull reaffirmed the broadened scope of the embargo
stating that the policy of the United States was not intended to encourage transactions with belligerents. Several weeks later, the
President and his Secretary of State warned against profiteering in
war materials.[25]

Franklin Roosevelt had wanted to go beyond these prohibitions
to discourage trade with Italy. He had suggested to Cordell Hull
that the names of those trading with belligerents should be published,
and that consideration should be given to prohibiting such items as
processed copper and steel. The Secretary of State replied in disapproval of these proposals, telling the President that a cooperative
attitude with the public would probably have more beneficial results.
During a press conference, Roosevelt gave an indication of how he
would construe the embargo provisions. He told his listeners that
the Endicott Johnson Shoe Company had wanted to ship heavy shoes
to Italy, "not ladies slippers," which could be worn by Italian troops.
The President said he would not fill the order. In general, Roosevelt
was pleased with the efforts of his Administration to restrain Italy.
The day after the press conference he told Henry Morgenthau that
he had been tickled to death to issue the Neutrality Proclamation
ahead of the League. He had seized the initiative in an effort to
spark a response.[26]

The fervor of the Administration's vigorous attempts to deny Italy
vital war materials was revealed once again on November 15, 1935.
Hull issued a formal statement proclaiming that the exportation of
abnormal quantities of oil, copper, trucks, tractors, scrap iron, and
scrap steel was directly contrary to the policy of the United States
Government. This prompted an angry encounter between the Italian
Ambassador, Augusto Rosso, and Cordell Hull. In a meeting on
November 22, 1935, Rosso charged the Administration with pursuing
a very discriminatory policy. The Secretary of State responded in a
tone of moral indignation to all of Rosso's complaints. Was it not
Mussolini who had gone to war despite the pleas of the President?
Was it not Italy's action that was destined to create awful repercus-
sions in remote parts of the world? Was it not Italy that chose to
pursue a course of military aggression, and in this course violated
three or four treaties by invading Ethiopia? The United States
Government, said Hull, was attempting to insure that neither Italy

nor Ethiopia could secure war materials from America. He abruptly concluded that the charge of discrimination did not apply. The President referred to the interview as a classic, and praised his Secretary of State for pointing out the very untenable position in which Italy had deliberately placed itself.[27]

Despite Roosevelt's desire to impede Italy's advance in Ethiopia, it proceeded with mechanized swiftness. In the summer months there had been vague hopes that disease might slow the Italian plans in Africa. There had been rumors in November, 1935, that Italy could last only three more months. In truth, the road to Addis Ababa was neither long nor difficult for the Italianas. The pitiable quality of the Ethiopian army was known to Roosevelt. He had been sent an Ethiopian mobilization order containing the following statement:

> When this order is received all men and all boys able to carry a spear will go to Addis Ababa. Every married man will bring his wife to cook and wash for him. Women with babies, the blind, and those too aged or infirm to carry a spear are excused. Anyone found at home after receiving this order will be hanged.

In a letter to the President, Hubbard Wynant, an American official in Ethiopia, described the horrors of the Italian advance. Children had been blinded by incendiary bombs, he said, their faces and their bodies burnt and pitted by flying chemicals as Italian planes deliberately bombed a hospital. Wynant plaintively queried the President, "What had happened to the world outside that I a white man should be sewing up dark bodies or cutting off dark limbs which had been mangled and hurt by other white men? Was this a true example of the great white civilization of which we had been taught to be so proud?" Roosevelt was perhaps moved by Wynant's letter, for in a note to Robert Skinner, Ambassador to Turkey, he complained about the display of world ethics in the past weeks. He told Ambassador Skinner that since these methods had been applied in Ethiopia, they might be applied to Turkey later.[28]

Franklin Roosevelt agreed with the American Minister to Ethiopia Cornelius Engert, as they both reflected on the ease with which Italy was terminating the sovereignty of a once independent nation. Engert described the world as having clearly arrived at some sort of parting of the ways. The forces which make for war, he wrote, seem today to be in the ascendant, and western civilization may be in danger of collapse. Engert concluded with the admonition that pious professions of peaceful policies had not been able to prevent the unilateral repudiation of solemn treaties and the resort to violence. There was really very little more that the President could have done in his efforts to halt Mussolini and promote a collective resistance to Italian aggression. A second Neutrality Act was adopted on February 29, 1936, which renewed many of the provisions of the 1935 statute. One noted addition to the 1936 Neutrality Law, which further limited the President's discretionary power, was the requirement that he must extend the embargo provisions to any power which entered a war. Previously, he had been authorized to do this if he deemed it advisable. He renewed his appeal against profiteering in the war between Italy and Ethiopia on the same day that he signed the new neutrality legislation, and extended the neutrality provisions to both nations.[29]

Italy was in full control of Ethiopia, however, by the spring month of May. The League of Nations had failed to impose sanctions on vital raw materials such as oil. France and England, as will be discussed later, pursued policies designed to ease the Italian absorption of Ethiopia. What would be the response of the United States to this subjugation by force of arms? When asked this question during a press conference, Roosevelt gave no answer. Ambassador Long urged him to recognize the Italian conquest in Ethiopia, and to acknowledge the King of Italy as the Emperor of Ethiopia. The President refused to follow his Ambassador's advice. The embargo was lifted on June 20, 1936, but there would be no effort to legitimize Mussolini's act of lawlessness. Cordell Hull believed that Mussolini's success made probable a major war in the future. Lincoln MacVeagh, writing from Greece, told the President that many were expressing grave doubts as to the limits of Italy's imperial ambitions, and that there existed a very general fear that some spark, probably in Central Europe, could set off the whole fireworks as soon as Germany was prepared. The President shared these views.[30]

There was always the possibility, from Roosevelt's perspective, that such a spark might come from action initiated by Germany. In early February, 1936, Norman Davis described for the President the crisis atmosphere prevailing in Europe. All of the political leaders in Europe, he wrote, are thinking of how best to prepare for the war which they think Germany is going to force upon them. It was feared that Italy's success in Ethiopia would serve as a catalyst for aggressive acts by other nations. Roosevelt, in a letter to Ambassador Long, said that he was watching the daily news from Europe with the feeling each day that the next would bring a major explosion. The President added that he did not share the optimistic view that each recurring crisis would iron itself out and that nothing really serious would happen. This foreboding mood of fearsome anticipation was heightened when, on March 7, 1936, German troops moved into the once demilitarized Rhineland.[31]

Franklin Roosevelt referred to the German move as another bombshell. In a memorandum to the President, Cordell Hull labeled the action as a violation of the Treaty of Versailles and the Locarno Pacts. The technicalities of treaty violation were not foremost in the President's mind at the moment. The question that remained unanswered was what might be the reaction of the other European powers to the German initiative. War seemed a possibility. Experts had told Roosevelt that there would be no war, but he confided to Ambassador Dodd that similar experts had predicted there would be no war in July, 1914. Today, he continued, the President had his tongue in cheek, and would be ready just like a Fire Department for any eventuality.[32]

The quiescent response of France and the other major European nations eased the immediate threat of war, but did not calm Roosevelt's anxieties about the future. He was critical of what he termed this thoroughly disgusting spectacle of German militarism. John Cudahy, Ambassador to Poland, made known his observations on the significance of this treaty violation. Cudahy's analysis for the President was not a reassuring one. Hitler, said the Ambassador, had ignored the principle of the sanctity of treaties, and he had done so with impunity. In our past history, he told the President, vigilantes would have hung such outlaws. The European powers and the League of Nations, he said, did not have the resolve to chastize Germany, and in the future it would seem that any hope for collective action against aggression would be illusory. He concluded by warning the President that if Hitler was not overthrown, then war in Europe was as certain as the rising sun. Perhaps a year, two years, or five years, but that another contest with Germany was inevitable was recognized by even the most conservative diplomats. William Dodd wrote to Cordell Hull from Berlin asking that the despatch be shown to the President, and offered his views of the implications of Germany and Italy's most recent actions. In Dodd's estimation, it was clearly dictator Europe against western Europe. The German people were now solidly united. Hitler's plan, according to Dodd, was to extend Germany's power to the Danube zone all the way to the Black Sea. Germany in exchange would support Italy's quest for a renewed Roman Empire.[33]

Ambassador Dodd's prophetic prediction that the agagressor powers of Germany and Italy would unite in their quest for European dominance may have appeared to Roosevelt as entirely accurate, especially in view of the developing situation in Spain. The crisis atmosphere of the spring months had barely subsided when on July 17, 1936, civil war erupted in that country. The American Ambassador to Spain, Claude Bowers, provided the President with detailed accounts of what he would repeatedly describe as a war against democracy and free government. Bowers' sympathies were clearly on the side of the Republican administration of President Manuel Azana, and were in violent opposition to the rebel forces under General Francisco Franco.

Premier Azana was described by Bowers in letters to Roosevelt as a republican and democrat who had no sympathies with subversive doctrines. He was the most enlightened and constructive statesman produced by Spain in fifty years, wrote Bowers, and his educational and agrarian reforms were in the best interests of the vast majority of Spanish citizens. The Ambassador saw no reason to fear the predominance of leftist elements in the Republican government. Communists, socialists, syndicalists and anarchists were all engaged in the struggle against a fascist rebellion, said Bowers. He criticized the lawlessness of anarchist and socialist groups, but told the President that he expected them to find common cause if given strong leadership. In Bowers' opinion, Prime Minister Largo Caballero was the individual who could bring unity to the republican forces. A noted leader of the Socialist Party, Caballero was depicted as a man of impeccable honesty and irreproachable moral standards. In contrast, the rebel movement was described as reactionary and anti-democratic. If Franco should be successful, warned Bowers, he would create a military dictatorship, end parliamentary government and all agrarian reforms, suspend all constitutional guarantees of freedom of speech, liberty, and the press, make it a crime for workers to strike, and restore the land to absentee landlords.[34]

Bowers' Republican sentiments were strengthened when he observed increasing evidence of Italian and German support of Franco's rebels. He told Roosevelt that the German and Italian Ambassadors had been openly and brazenly against the Azana Government from the beginning of the civil war. Bowers discerned more than sympathetic interest in this affair by the two countries. Italy, he reported in September, 1936, was sending material to the rebels all the time. The Big Bad Man with a Gun, Inflated Chest, and Loud Voice was active in Spain, charged Bowers. The President received two memoranda by Bowers in October asserting that the fascist powers were sending arms, ammunition, tanks, airplanes, and men to fight against the Loyalists. In the Ambassador's opinion, the conflict had become an international fascist conspiracy to destroy the democracy of Spain. In the month of December, Ambassador Bowers informed Roosevelt that 6,000 German soldiers and 2,500 Italian troops had just arrived, and that the Baleric Islands had been converted into an Italian colony. He reiterated his belief that this was without doubt a fascist war on democracy in Europe.[35]

Events in these winter months served to strengthen Ambassador Bowers' conviction that there was an emerging alignment of the aggressor nations in opposition to the forces of peace. The Italian Foreign Minister, Count Galeazzo Ciano, visited Germany on October

25, 1936, and an official communique described the discussions with Hitler as friendly and cordial, and stressed that both countries had come to a concurrence of views in international affairs. Franklin Roosevelt was not surprised by this action. Ambassador Dodd had warned on October 19, 1936, that Hitler and Mussolini intended to control all of Europe. Events in Spain seemed to indicate that their ambitions, in Dodd's opinion, would not create dissension between the two powers, but would in fact strengthen their unity and purpose. The communique was a terse statement of an evident fact.[36]

One month after the German-Italian communique had been released, Germany and Japan signed an agreement which was directed against the activities of the Communist International. The Anti-Comintern Pact of November 25, 1936, pledged the contracting parties to cooperate for defense against communist subversion. Franklin Roosevelt had expected this development. In May, 1935, Ambassador Dodd informed the President that Berlin and Tokyo had opened long distance conversations, and that the Japanese Naval Attaché in Germany was almost an understudy of Goering. Dodd believed that a German-Japanese alliance had already been concluded, and he seemed to think that there was a fixed purpose to the cordiality that marked the relations between the two countries. The Ambassador further informed Roosevelt in October, 1935, that military specialists were being exchanged by Germany and Japan. He reported that the Russian Ambassador to Berlin was fairly certain that a German-Japanese alliance definitely existed. The signing of the Anti-Comintern Pact was final confirmation of what the President perceived as ever increasing intimacy among the fascist regimes. In the words of Cordell Hull, the designs of the dictators seemed to be taking shape.[37]

Franklin Roosevelt was alarmed by the rising tide of aggression in this year, 1936. Despite the fact that an election was to be held in November, he was compelled to discuss the disturbing conditions overseas. The President's most forceful comments came at Chautauqua, New York on August 14, 1936. He warned his audience that acts of belligerence might someday draw even the United States into war. We desire to remain out of any conflict, he added, but it was impossible to provide for every contingency in the vast unchartered area of international relations. He pledged that any nation which provoked war would forfeit the sympathy of the American Government. What the President did not discuss in this speech was the possible method by which aggression was to be halted by the democracies. He was simply asking his audience to think about what the future might portend for the United States. He had failed to discern either the desire or capability on the part of Great Britain and France to resist Germany, Japan, or Italy, and this may account for the omission of any reference to a program of collective resistance. Isolationist voting strength also dictated a tactful silence on the topic of international cooperation. His resounding victory at the polls made possible a more candid emphasis on the need for collective security. In the month after the election, Roosevelt addressed the Inter-American Conference for the Maintenance of Peace at Buenos Aires, and the tone of his speech reveals an intensifying animosity toward fascist methods. No doubt referring to Germany, Japan, and Italy, he described the conference as one convened not to form alliances, or to divide the spoils of war, or to partition countries, or to deal with human beings as though they were pawns in a game of chance, but to assure a continuance of peace. In the future, he would express his contempt for the advocates of war in stronger terms, and would press more openly for a collective response to aggression.[38]

The new year dawned with the now familiar sounds of war. In Spain, Germany and Italy abandoned even the pretext of non-intervention. Ambassador Bowers' letters to the President were replete with references to a worldwide fascist conspiracy for which Spain was simply a testing ground. In February, 1937, he described the conflict as clearly a war against the Spanish Government by the Italians and Germans assisted by Spanish insurgents. He reiterated in March his conviction that this was the beginning of a conspiracy of the fascist powers to destroy democracy in Europe; the Sublimated Gun-Men and Gangsters of Rome and Berlin had just begun their conquests. Bowers later warned Franklin Roosevelt that with every surrender, beginning long ago with China, followed by Abyssinia and then Spain, the fascist powers, with vanity inflamed, will turn without delay to some other country such as Czechoslovakia, and with every surrender the prospects of a European war will grow darker. The pitiful policy of retreating before the gestures of bullies, he told the President, will simply make stronger the Fascist Internationale. It appeared to the Ambassador that Germany and Italy were now as one. Unbridled in their ambitions, the Duce and Führer had unharnessed their machines of war. The Spanish interlude was but a prelude to other undeclared wars against the democracies in Europe.[39]

Franklin Roosevelt could not have failed to note with interest the views of his Ambassador. The President's sympathies were clearly with the Republican Government, but there was very little that could be done to bring this affair to a conclusion. The policies of Great Britain and France were such as to discourage any attempt to halt aggression in Spain. The United States pursued a passive role from the inception of the struggle. Cordell Hull had set forth the policy of the United States Government in August, 1936, as one of scrupulous non-interference in Spain. An embargo prohibiting the export of arms, ammunition, and implements of war was applied to Spain by the terms of the May 1, 1937 Neutrality Act. Roosevelt personally doubted the wisdom of the embargo, and later regretted what he had always considered to be a grave mistake. The embargo was lifted on April 1, 1939, but in the meantime German and Italian aggression had proceeded with impunity.[40]

The European malestrom was not the only concern of Franklin Roosevelt as he looked to the future. Developments in the Far East were also attracting his attention. American and Japanese relations had not improved, and the intensifying hostility between the two countries began to assume dangerous proportions in this new year. Abortive attempts to agree on naval limitation in 1936 ushered in an age of discord and confrontation as Japan sought to construct its New Order in East Asia. The embroilment of Japan in China began with the China Incident of July 7, 1937, and to many observers, including Franklin Roosevelt, this marked the real beginning of Japan's attempt to realize its imperial ambitions in the Far East.

In the months preceding the beginning of the Sino-Japanese war, Roosevelt considered proposing a plan to Japan for the neutralization of all islands in the Pacific, exclusive of Hawaii, Australia, and New Zealand. Norman Davis, with whom the President had discussed these proposals, pressed Roosevelt to abandon them. He doubted that the Japanese would follow any program for insuring peace in the Pacific. A nation which had flagrantly violated existing treaties could not be trusted, said Davis. Did the President believe that Japan would abide by this neutralization scheme? The course of events in Japan gave little cause for optimism. In February, 1936, moderate leaders of the Japanese government were executed by what one observer described to the President as a reactionary, radical, fascist group comprised of younger officers of the Japanese army and navy. Roosevelt was informed that the military organization was becoming completely dominant in the affairs of state. This development did not augur well for peace in Asia. A memorandum that he sent to the Chief of Naval Operations on August 10, 1936, reveals the extent of Roosevelt's distrust of the Japanese. The President suggested that any Japanese residents in Hawaii who were observed greeting ships from Japan, or who appeared to have connections with the officers or enlisted men, should be secretly identified and his or her name placed on a special list of those who would be the first to be placed in a concentration camp in the event of trouble. The neutralization proposal was perhaps of momentary consideration, but Roosevelt's inherent fear and distrust of Japan was too great to have warranted a belief in its successful implementation. Japan's continued advance in China quickly forced the abandonment of any thoughts of compromise or peace negotiations. The time for a firm stand against aggression was fast approaching.[41]

Several days after the encounter between Japanese and Chinese troops at the Marco Polo Bridge near Peiping, Cordell Hull issued a statement on the position of the United States in this conflict after consulting with the President. In comparison to the restraint exercised during the Spanish Civil War, this pronouncement seemed to indicate that a more activist policy by the Roosevelt Administration would be pursued in an effort to halt the rising tide of aggression. Hull suggested that nations must pursue policies of national and international self-restraint, faithfully observe international agreements, and abandon the recourse to war. Japan had no intention of respecting the moral platitudes of Cordell Hull.[42]

Franklin Roosevelt was thoroughly informed concerning the strength and purpose of the Japanese drive into China. Ambassador Joseph Grew wrote in August that Japan was confident that it would achieve an overwhelming military victory within a few months. Japanese military officials were certain that their mechanized army and air forces could attain their objectives. Admiral William Leahy, Chief of Naval Operations, forwarded to Roosevelt the reports of military officers who were in touch with the situation in China. One memorandum predicted that Japan would eventually win out due to its vastly superior military machine, and that the bombing of defenseless towns and villages was part of a concerted effort by Japan to shorten the war by forcing a terrified populace to demand peace. Admiral Leahy also relayed to the President several messages from Admiral Harry Yarnell, Commander of the United States Asiatic Fleet. Yarnell believed that Japan's military success in the Chinese venture was practically assured, and that it would bring about a complete unbalance of forces in the Far East and the world. The destiny of civilization and the white race was at stake, added the Admiral. How firm was Japan's resolve to prosecute the war? One military attaché, in a despatch that was sent to Roosevelt, said that Japanese public opinion was solidly behind the armed services. They were spiritually prepared for any eventuality, he noted, including the spread of hostilities to the west.[43]

Japan's thrust into China was not viewed by Franklin Roosevelt as an isolated act of aggression by an overzealous nationalistic peoples. It was considered to be part of a much larger scheme undertaken by Japan to secure a position of dominance throughout the Far East. The President carefully watched Japanese activities in the Pacific regions. He directed Admiral Leahy in August, 1937 to gather intelligence information on Japanese vessels located in the Bering Sea. It seemed a little farfetched to Roosevelt to presume that these vessels were conducting operations solely for instructing students and studying migration and the availability of salmon and crabs. It was possible, thought the President, that behind the whole thing was a definite effort to study at close range a base of operations in the event of war. His suspicions of Japan were also heightened by the analyses of Japanese espionage activities which were submitted to him by military officials. A memorandum by Brigadier General Charles Barnett, Chief of the Bureau of Insular Affairs, gave to Roosevelt detailed information on the Japanese penetration of the Philippine Islands and, in the words of the author, an educated guess concerning Japan's ultimate aims. Barnett predicted that Japan would attempt to dominate the Philippines economically and politically. Economic penetration of the islands by Japan was already in process, he informed the President. The efforts of Japan to control this area, said Barnett, appeared to be part of a Japanese drive to attain hegemony in the Far East. Secretary of War, Harry Woodring, informed Roosevelt of extensive Japanese espionage in South America. Japanese ships were believed to be engaged in a continuous operation of observing, hydrographic sounding, and transmission of information of a military character, he told the President. Woodring added that in Panama and in the Central American region there was now operating a well organized and thoroughly trained espionage organization. Their activities, he concluded, constituted an inherent potential danger to the Panama Canal.[44]

Franklin Roosevelt's Proposed Response

It was in the context of these dire assessments of Japan's ultimate intentions that Franklin Roosevelt began to think in terms of a response to aggression. He had not invoked the Neutrality Act concerning the Sino-Japanese war perhaps because it was apparent to him that this struggle was of such proportions that the United States could not assume a posture of true neutrality. Technically he claimed that a declaration of war had not been formally issued by either of the participants. He did forbid the transporting of arms, ammunition, and implements of war by American merchant ships to either China or Japan on September 14, 1937. Roosevelt fully realized at this point, however, that some alternative to the traditional isolationist neutrality policy of the United States must be devised and implemented. The forces of aggression were being permitted to construct a world order in their own image and without any opposition whatsoever from the democratic powers. The time had arrived for a concerted rebuttal.[45]

One possible response contemplated by the President was a world peace conference. The origin of this idea, which was formally proposed by Under Secretary of State Sumner Welles in October, 1937, dates back to initiatives made by Roosevelt in 1936. FDR had requested Ambassador Dodd in August, 1936, to give his opinion of Hitler's probable response to a peace proposal concerning arms limitations. The Ambassador had replied negatively, stating that he doubted the efficacy of any peace initiatives. Joseph Davies, soon to be appointed Ambassador to Russia, was asked to sound out foreign potentates concerning a possible peace proposal during a private interview with Roosevelt in that same month. Henry Morgenthau recalled in January, 1937 that Roosevelt took a very simplistic view of the world's problems. The President, he wrote, pictured himself as a consultant for the various nations of the world, prescribing for their ailments and making studies of their illnesses. Roosevelt had elaborated on a scheme whereby the nations of the world would disarm, and an international cartel would then relocate and find employment for those workers who had once earned their livelihood by toiling in the munitions industries. An assemblage of the leading nations of the world might afford an opportunity to discuss such ideas. The proposal for a peace conference was discussed on several occasions in the months that followed, but the pessimistic comments concerning prospects for success in this endeavor apparently convinced Roosevelt that a simple and direct neighborly talk between and among the world's foremost leaders would not halt the expansionist policies of Germany, Japan, and Italy. The events of this year had convinced the President that a peaceful solution of the difficult problems in Europe and the Far East seemed highly unlikely.[46]

There were important considerations other than the imbroglio in Japan which would compel Franklin Roosevelt to adopt a much tougher stand against those nations that he had clearly marked as the aggressors. Information coming to the President concerning expected developments in German foreign policy was discouraging. The military occupation of the Rhineland had scarcely been completed when alarming reports of probable future aggressive action by Germany began to come to Roosevelt's desk. Emil Ludwig predicted for the President in August, 1936 that Germany's militant character, longing for revenge, inferiority complex, and race theory would eventually make inevitable the pursuit of war by that nation. William Dodd forecast in September a German thrust toward Austria, Czechoslovakia, Hungary, and Romania. A month later, Samuel Fuller told the President that the militarists in Germany, convinced that negotiations were useless, were ready for action. William Bullitt was certain that Czechoslovakia was the next item on Hitler's menu. Nigel Law, an English friend of Roosevelt, told him that it was useless to negotiate with such people as the leaders of Germany.[47]

The next year did not witness any change in the views of the President's correspondents. William Bullitt offered what was becoming a consensus opinion. The deluge, Bullitt told Roosevelt, is approaching. Germany will not accept peace except at the price of domination of Eastern and Central Europe and the Balkans. The President by this time had no doubts that Germany was the pivotal nation in determining whether there would be war or peace in Europe. Reflecting on the information he was receiving daily, the most likely course would be war. During the spring months there were rumors that Austria would soon be annexed by Germany. Bullitt depicted the Austrian position as that of an apple left hanging on the bough to be plucked at an appropriate moment by Hitler. Roosevelt hoped that it would have the effect of a green apple. William Dodd noted the constant and increasing pressure exerted by the German Government towards the Nazification of Austria. Norman Davis sent to the President a summary of conversations between the British diplomat, Philip Kerr, and several German leaders. Herein, Hermann Goering had remarked that six million Austrians, four million Germans in Czechoslovakia, and the populace of Danzig were all organic parts of Germany. William Dodd quoted Hans Dieckhoff, the German Ambassador to Washington, as saying that Germany must control or annex all the Balkan-Danube states. Dodd had replied that perhaps the United States should annex Canada and Mexico. Dodd told the President that Dieckhoff had not seen the meaning of that last remark. Herbert Pell, the Ambassador to Portugal, warned Roosevelt in September, 1937 that the fascist movement was approaching the status of a new religion: a faith that would produce fanatics, hypocrites, martyrs, and human sacrifices.[48]

The spread of this gospel of force to Italy was also of concern to the President. Mussolini's tirades were becoming more strident. Buoyed by the Ethiopian conquest, the Italian leader and the government controlled press spoke in bellicose terms of a return to the glories of Rome. Lincoln MacVeagh had commented to Roosevelt that living near Mussolini was like living on Vesuvius. War-talk and fear-talk, he added, entered every conversation. William Phillips, Ambassador to Italy, was not quite as alarmist in his initial letters to the President. He believed that Mussolini would moderate his actions, and that his persistent rattling of the sword was necessary for domestic consumption. The President's reply was less sanguine as he cautioned Phillips that the disease of war was spreading and would probably prove fatal in the next five years. What caused Roosevelt most anxiety perhaps were the continuing reports of the growing intimacy of Germany and Italy. American diplomats in Rome were in agreement concerning the union of the two countries, and there were indications, also known to Roosevelt, that coordination of the Italian and German armies was being planned at the highest military levels.[49]

In this atmosphere of precipitate crisis, Franklin Roosevelt decided to make an important address on the subject of foreign affairs. The speech was given in Chicago, a city carefully selected by the President because of the strength of isolationist sentiment in that area. The remarks delivered by Roosevelt on October 5, 1937 were deliberate, provoking, and subtly terrifying. He began by describing the present world situation as one of international lawlessness. Law, order, and justice were being swept away and innocent peoples were being cruelly sacrificed. He then pursued a most important theme of this speceh. These developments, he asserted, posed a direct threat to the United States. War was contagious, he warned, and it could easily engulf states and peoples remote from the original hostilities. It would be dangerous to assume, he added, that America could escape the war that now threatened mankind or that the Western Hemisphere would not be attacked. Neither isolation nor neutrality assured an escape. What could be done to halt the epidemic of world lawlessness? Franklin Roosevelt offered a solution to stop the aggressors that he had deliberated for years in the utterance of the word quarantine. The ten percent who were threatening the security of peace-loving nations should be quarantined to protect the health of the civilized community.[50]

The draft for this speech had been prepared in the State Department by Cordell Hull and Norman Davis. The quarantine statement, however, was an insertion made entirely by the President. His dramatized delivery of this portion of the speech surprised many diplomatic officials. What precisely did Franklin Roosevelt envisage when he uttered these words? He attempted to ignore an initial question on October 6, 1937 concerning his quarantine remarks in Chicago, but reporters persisted in their efforts to find out what the President actually had in mind. Was there to be a peace conference? No, Roosevelt replied. Was anything definite contemplated? No, just the speech itself, he answered. Would economic sanctions be applied? They are out the window, he said tersely. Perhaps all were perplexed when he then denied that his remarks were solely a form of moral coercion, and stated that they were meant to be applied in the practical sphere.[51]

Franklin Roosevelt earnestly hoped in his private thoughts that an economic boycott of Japan, and later of Germany, would be forthcoming in the near future. He had discussed plans for such an embargo in earlier years, and he still believed that this form of sanction would be the most successful in stopping the aggressors without the direct involvement of the United States in war. Admiral Yarnell had warned on October 8, 1937 that the United States might soon become involved in a war against Japan because of that nation's policy of force and its total disregard of treaties. Yarnell went on to suggest that the American Government should conduct an economic war of strangulation by blocking shipments of iron, coal, oil, copper, wool, rubber, aluminum, and tin which were being sent to Japan. Franklin Roosevelt received Yarnell's message on November 8, 1937 and two days later he discussed the feasibility of the proposed blockade with Admiral William Leahy. The President was enthusiastic. Yarnell, he said, had made a lot of sense. He asked Leahy how quickly oil burning merchant ships could be converted so that they could remain at sea for an extended period, could carry eight or ten planes for flight over a wide area, could ward off small air attacks, and sink less powerful merchant ships. This economic blockade was for Roosevelt the ultimate solution, and it would seem to have been planned for application initially against Japan.[52]

It is important to distinguish between what the President most anxiously desired to achieve and what he expected to achieve by the Chicago quarantine address. Perhaps most important was his expectation that these remarks should serve as a tonic toward a realistic appraisal of the grave threat to the security of free peoples and their governments. The word quarantine was chosen because it could be broadly understood and was graphic in its applications. This was the first of many efforts to educate public opinion. Unfortunately, the general response to the President's views was negative. He had planned to make a second major address on foreign affairs after noticing the appreciable lack of enthusiasm, but political tact and an awareness that other European nations would not follow America's leadership in any collective action at this moment, forced him into silence. He was personally convinced, however, of the necessity of concerted international action against the bandit nations. A close friend of the President recalled that after 1937 a hundred isolationist speech writers could never have changed his views on foreign affairs.[53]

A very important audience in Franklin Roosevelt's estimation was to be found overseas. It seems doubtful that he could have expected Great Britain and France to respond to his suggestion for a quarantine. The President was trying to awaken the statesmen of Europe, in addition to the domestic isolationists, to the dangers of continued appeasement. In the past, neither Great Britain nor France had displayed any real determination to oppose Germany, Japan, or Italy. The general direction of British and French foreign policy had not changed. In Ethiopia the two nations appeared eager to placate

Mussolini. Roosevelt was especially dismayed concerning the agreement between French Premier Pierre Laval and British Secretary of State for Foreign Affairs, Sir Samuel Hoare. This proposal of December, 1935 provided for the cession to Italy of most of the territory that it had demanded in Ethiopia. William Dodd accused both men of defeating the first real movement by the League of Nations to halt war. Ambassador Dodd was critical of the French in particular. He told the President that they had promised support to Mussolini in his ambition to annex Ethiopia. England and France, he concluded, had entered a definite decline. Mussolini, said Lincoln MacVeagh, had bluffed England out on the Abyssinian question. Roosevelt was more succinct than the Ambassador to Greece stating that his British friends had come up a sad cropper in the Hoare-Laval proposal. Felix Frankfurter thought the plan had proven so embarrassing to the authors that public reaction would stiffen the will to resist. The President disagreed. William Bullitt had told him of a British plan to throw the entire onus of appeasement on the United States. British and French timidity had contrasted sharply with Roosevelt's desire to impede Italy's advance.[54]

In the Spanish Civil War, Great Britain and France had adopted a non-interventionist course. Ambassador Bowers was harshly critical of their inaction, accusing the leaders of both countries of deliberately and dishonestly closing their eyes to what was going on in Spain. The prestige of Britain and France, said Bowers, had fallen. The cringing and apologetic attitude of both countries was disgusting. He advised the President not to intervene diplomatically in the struggle for the British and French seemed especially eager to have someone pull their chestnuts out of the fire after they had made a miserable mess of non-intervention. Roosevelt appeared disenchanted once more with his erstwhile allies. He told Cordell Hull that it seemed a ridiculous situation to him for France and Great Britain to claim solemnly that they had no proof of Italian or German participation in the Spanish war.[55]

There were other memoranda reaching the President's desk which could not have served to strengthen American and British relations. During his campaign for the Presidency in 1936, Franklin Roosevelt had been alerted by Ambassador Dodd to a scheme engineered by prominent Englishmen, including Lord Beaverbrook. Dodd said that large amounts of money from London were being sent to William R. Hearst to finance a press campaign against Roosevelt's re-election. R. W. Moore later informed the President that the Hearst-Beaverbrook connection mentioned by Dodd did indeed exist. Equally disturbing to Roosevelt may have been Robert Bingham's information concerning a pro-German cabal led by Lord Lothian and actively

fostered by the Waldorf Astors. The Ambassador to London described Prime Minister Stanley Baldwin's administration as fumbling
with no definite and capable leadership. Ironically, the monarchic
crisis that began with the death of George V in 1936 and the accession to the throne of his son Edward VIII was not viewed as having
had a debilitating effect on Great Britain. Edward's decision to forsake the crown and wed Mrs. Wallis Simpson was interpreted by
Ambassador Bingham as a fortunate turn of events. Bingham charged
that the Duke of Windsor had been surrounded by pro-German
advisors and that Mrs. Simpson was suspected by many of being in
German pay. The coronation of King George VI, who was considered by Bingham to be most stable and reliable, seemed a portent
of closer and more intimate cooperation between the United States
and Great Britain. Bingham noted the changed attitude of the British
in a letter to Roosevelt. Parliamentary committees, he said, were
studying methods of cooperation with the United States, and many
such groups were planning to visit America soon. British army and
navy officers had also received official orders to cultivate closer ties
with their American counterparts. This progressive and almost be-
wildering friendliness, he concluded, could not pass unnoticed.[56]

Franklin Roosevelt was momentarily favorably impressed by developments in Great Britain for in the early months of 1937 he took
steps to inaugurate a more cordial relationship with that country.
When asked by a reporter on April 15, 1937 if the United States
should have an offensive and defensive alliance with Great Britain
and France to guarantee a new *Pax Romana,* Roosevelt answered
that he would make that the policy of the nation if a majority of the
Senate would support him in this endeavor. The President attempted
to construct this new partnership in June, 1937. Norman Davis served
as the intermediary between Roosevelt and the new British Prime
Minister Neville Chamberlain. Davis suggested on behalf of the
President that a meeting of the two heads of state would be most
useful in laying the foundation for Anglo-American cooperation.
Chamberlain, however, refused the President's invitation. He replied
on July 8, 1937 that the time was not ripe. Roosevelt sent his personal regrets to the British Prime Minister concerning the failure to
agree on the proposed meeting.[57]

The tone of this note was formal and courteous. The Chief
Executive was not pleased, however, by Chamberlain's response, and
his frustration and anger became visible during a press conference
in July of that year. Roosevelt was asked if he planned to take the
lead in calling an international conference. He responded testily that
although there were many in Europe who were looking for someone
to come forward with a hat and a rabbit in it, he had neither hat nor

rabbit. During this month, the President received a report asserting that the British led by their Prime Minister were unanimous in the position that Germany must be appeased, that the Franco-Soviet Pact had justified Germany's rearmament, that the German minority in Czechoslovakia was being cruelly treated, and that some relief must be given to Germany in this general situation. Roosevelt commented to his Secretary of State that the British Tories appeared to be unchanged Tories who, in spite of the denial of their Foreign Secretary Anthony Eden, still wanted peace at a great price. Franklin Roosevelt did not expect the British to embark eagerly on a program of collective resistance as described in the quarantine speech. Whenever a suggestion is made to the British by the American government, he told a reporter, they get 90 percent and we get 10 percent; if they make the suggestion it comes out nearer 50-50. Why should we be doing the suggesting, he asked rhetorically. The Chicago address marked an attempt to awaken British public opinion as well as that in the United States. The President would in the future wait patiently for a British initiative.[58]

France presented a discouraging image of weakness, corruption, and lack of will to resist the aggressors. Bullitt told the President that what the French needed was a man who had both intelligence and character, but that unfortunately such a man was utterly invisible at the present moment. The French were not expected to embrace a program of sanctions. The quarantine address seems to have been an effort to strengthen their resolve. William Bullitt depicted the French attitude as one of complete hopelessness. They accept the drift to war, he said, but offer nothing to counter it. Moreover, Bullitt cautioned the President, the French wish to drag the United States into the coming struggle. First, however, they will attempt to seek a compromise with Germany, he told Roosevelt. American representatives will have to make it clear to the French, said Bullitt, that God helps those who help themselves. Franklin Roosevelt probably agreed with his Ambassador in Paris. Throughout the months of 1937, there were no signs that the French would change their policy of conciliation with Germany. Yvon Delbos, the French Foreign Minister, had told Bullitt that France could do nothing to prevent Germany's annexation of Austria and Czechoslovakia. The ouster of Leon Blum as Premier in June, 1937 and the accession of Camille Chautemps to that office seemed to indicate no change in this consistent policy of appeasement.[59]

These impressions of British and French foreign policy and domestic criticism of the Chicago address were the primary determinants in influencing Franklin Roosevelt's proposals for United States participation in the Brussels Conference. The meeting in Brussels was convened by the League of Nations in an attempt to halt the intensifying Sino-Japanese conflict. The conference met a month after the President's quarantine address and many European diplomats expected America to assume a role of leadership in a campaign of sanctions against Japan. Roosevelt, however, refused to be pushed into the forefront of such a campaign because he believed that other nations would not follow the initiative of the United States against Japan or would follow very reluctantly. Norman Davis, an ardent Anglophile, was selected to head the American delegation. Some feared that Davis' pro-English bias might force him to play the part of Walter Hines Page, the American Ambassador to Great Britain prior to World War I who had been eager to abandon neutrality and enter the conflict. The President, however, placed tight constraints on Davis' diplomatic activities. Roosevelt outlined the American position during an interview with Davis on October 19, 1937. The United States could not participate in joint action with the League of Nations, nor would it lead any future action against Japan, or be forced into any action by Great Britain. If proposals should be forthcoming at Brussels, he instructed Davis, they must reflect the unanimous action of the nations meeting there, and later of all nations whether in or out of the League. Cordell Hull similarly cautioned Davis not to initiate any unilateral action, and to constantly keep in mind that public opinion in the United States did not wish to get involved in war. Davis, in his opening address to the conference, stressed that all nations of the world must realize the grave repercussions of this Far Eastern conflict.[60]

The Brussels Conference was a desultory failure. Pierrepont Moffat, a member of the American delegation, recalled that eight out of ten persons in attendance had uppermost in their minds how to close the conference. More important to Roosevelt were the activities of the British and French delegations. The British representatives attempted to push the United States to the front by repeatedly stressing that Brussels was America's conference and that the Far East was an American problem. France seemed interested only in preserving its Far Eastern possessions. Foreign Minister Delbos, emphasizing the connection between the Sino-Japanese war and French Indo-China suggested that the United States and Great Britain might wish to guarantee the territorial integrity of Indo-China. Delbos noted that any supplies going to China would have to be routed through this French territory. This seemed ironic to Roosevelt for France had refused to permit shipments to China. The President described the French as behaving like scared rabbits. This remark prompted a harsh reply from Premier Chautemps who accused the President of speechmaking while having no real intention of undertaking any activist policies. In this atmosphere of mutual recrimination, suspicion, and mistrust, the Brussels Conference adjourned. No unity of action against Japan had been forthcoming. Franklin Roosevelt had hoped that the sessions could be extended for a lengthy period in an effort to mobilize public opinion against Japan. In this objective too, he had been frustrated. He pledged, however, to continue his efforts in positive search of peace.[61]

The year 1937 concluded with two alarming occurrences which were of much concern to Franklin Roosevelt. The growing intimacy of Germany, Japan, and Italy became even more manifest on November 6, 1937, when Italy joined the Anti-Comintern Pact. The three powers agreed to adopt a policy of close cooperation in establishing a new order in Greater East Asia where Japan's dominance was to be recognized, and in Europe where Germany and Italy were to assume ultimate control. Roosevelt assumed that there existed secret clauses which further delimited their respective spheres of influence. Germany, he believed, had received Austria, Czechoslovakia, Hungary, Poland, and Lithuania. Italy was to control the Mediterranean, including Spain, Egypt, Greece, Turkey, and various French and British colonies. Japan was to be given the right to use a free hand in China. Ambassador Grew interpreted the agreement as a combination of those states which were bent upon upsetting the status quo. William Phillips, writing from Rome, thought that the pact was another indication of the tendency to crystallize a fascist bloc in opposition to the democratic powers. The Italian press, wrote Phillips, was emphasizing that there now existed a combined naval strength of two million tons of warships and an army of over two hundred million men. Ambassador Dodd used these same figures in a despatch to Hull describing Germany's account of the import of the Three Power Pact. Roosevelt confided to Ambassador Biddle in Warsaw that the German-Italian-Japanese combination was proving successful whether it represented bluff, power, or a real accomplishment of unity. The significance of this alignment lay in the future, but it is apparent that to many observers, including Franklin Roosevelt, the aggressor powers had consummated a collaborative relationship. The timidity in evidence at Brussels stood in stark contrast to the Three Power Pact.[62]

The haughty belligerence which this union of Japan, Germany, and Italy seemed to generate was demonstrated on December 12, 1937, when the American gunship *Panay* was bombed and sunk in the Yangtze River by Japanese planes. Roosevelt and Hull believed the attack to have been a deliberate one. The President angrily demanded from Japan full expressions of regret, compensation for damages, and guarantees against a repetition of any similar incidents in the future. Regrets, indemnities, and the requested assurances were offered by Japan on December 23, 1937 and this incident was thereby settled. William Leahy had suggested to Roosevelt that he send a fleet off the coast of China to demonstrate the seriousness of this provocative act. The President, recalled Leahy, was not prepared to take this extreme action at that time. He had been actively pursuing, however, a means to constrain Japan in the future. The hesitancy displayed by Great Britain and France, and the increased threat of precipitate action by Germany, Japan and Italy had strengthened the President's resolve to entice the Soviet Union into the democratic peace front. Franklin Roosevelt would avoid a direct encounter with Japan until such time that he could be assured of Russia's support.[63]

Nurturing a Relationship: The Soviet Union

Attempts to nurture a collaborative relationship with the Soviet Union had continued under the President's direction throughout these years. The difficulties which had surfaced in 1935 had not impeded his personal efforts to lay the basis for a future alliance with that nation. Franklin Roosevelt seems to have ignored a most perceptive analysis of the aims of Soviet foreign policy, and of the methods by which the leadership of Russia maintained its regime of terror. William Bullitt had warned against placing any trust or confidence in the Soviet Union. The sole aim of the communist movement was the spread of world revolution, wrote Bullitt. Faith in communism and its ultimate goal was thought to be superior to all restraints of justice, truth, honor, kindness, and human decency. He observed that to lie or murder millions for this cause was considered a virtue. Russia was a police state, said Bullitt bluntly, and as a nation it had never emerged from barbarian status nor created a civilization. He believed that to speak of the Russians as Asiatics was unfair to the Asiatics. In conclusion, he offered the following suggestions for dealing with the Soviet Union. Never cherish for a moment the illusion that it would be possible to establish friendly relations with the Soviet Government. In any approach to the Soviet leaders, always speak with sheer honesty for they know very little about it. William Bullitt left the Soviet Union in the summer of 1936. His personal hatred for a regime of brutal suppression, where murder was considered legitimate when in the interests of the Communist Party, served to give his diplomatic despatches the appearance of involvement prejudicial to objectivity. In retrospect, Ambassador Bullitt's insights into the nature of the Soviet system and the intricacies of its foreign policies would have been of value to the President in later years.[64]

There were other reports coming from the American Embassy in Moscow which set forth disconcerting evidence that supported Bullitt's description of the Soviet regime. Loy Henderson described the first of several major purge trials which ushered in a reign of terror and executions. In August, 1936, several prominent party members of the alleged Trotskyite-Zinovievite Terrorist Centre Group were brought to trial. They were accused of plotting to kill Stalin and other high government officials. Henderson commented that the trial had been beautifully staged with the prosecutor, Andrei Vyshinsky, playing the role of Lionel Barrymore as criminal lawyer. The accused, he continued, never argued with Vyshinsky, and tried at all times to give the expected reply to his questions. Vyshinsky was depicted as a circus director putting a group of well trained seals through a series of difficult acts. Confessions were simply carefully memorized orations. Henderson personally doubted the authenticity of any of the accusations against the accused. He concluded this memorandum, which was forwarded to the President, with the comment that the execution, within a twenty-four hour period, of every man who had had been charged in the conspiracy had ushered in a wave of fear which was sweeping the country. Roosevelt never understood the machinations of Joseph Stalin. The President admitted to a close friend, "I just can't make it out. Why would they want to get rid of people in their own party; it just doesn't make any sense." [65]

The appointment of Joseph Davies as Ambassador to the Soviet Union, and his arrival in Russia on January 19, 1937, marked the end of any attempt to report accurately and critically on the developments in that country. Ambassador Davies' despatches reflect a blinding bias in favor of what he considered to be a noble experiment. The selection of Davies angered many members of the American Embassy staff in Moscow, and serious consideration was given to a mass resignation from the service. William Bullitt foresaw clearly that Joseph Davies could not handle the Russian situation in a serious manner. Charles Bohlen of the Embassy staff described Davies as being sublimely ignorant of the most elementary realities of the Soviet system and its ideology. George Kennan remarked that if Franklin Roosevelt had wished to slap down the diplomatic officers serving in Moscow he could have done it in no better manner than by Davies' appointment. Kennan viewed the Davies' Ambassadorship as a political plum which had been handed out in return for campaign contributions. It may have been that Davies' ardent pro-Soviet line was precisely what Franklin Roosevelt desired at this moment. He could be relied upon to push vigorously for American-Russian unity against the aggressor. [66]

Ambassador Davies was favorably impressed by what he discovered in the Soviet Union. He wrote a letter to Franklin Roosevelt on January 25, 1937, and described the Constitutional Convention which he had attended in Moscow. He noted that the spontaneous singing of the international communist anthem at the conclusion had been quite moving in its sincerity and earnestness. He assured Roosevelt that the Soviet Constitution contained protective guarantees of freedom of speech, the right of assembly and other basic freedoms. Everyone, said Davies, was comfortable and warmly clothed, and the streets were active and bustling. In other personal letters to the President and his secretaries, Ambassador Davies spoke with admiration of Soviet economic advancement. He reported that they had painted on a ten-league canvas, in terms of industrial growth, with a brush of comet's hair. Moreover, he informed the President, the communist principle had been completely abandoned. This was a socialistic enterprise based upon capitalist principles of profit and self-interest. The original communist idea of a classless society had been radically modified, if not destroyed, said Davies. Classes did thrive, as did family life, love of parents, and nationalism. The Russians were doing a big job, he told Marvin McIntyre, and were making tremendous economic strides. Mrs. Marjorie Davies urged the President's wife to visit the Soviet Union where, according to Mrs. Davies, the ability of women was recognized. She observed that they worked side by side with men in executive positions and in manual labor.[67]

The Ambassador wrote to Stephen Early noting that the Soviet leaders had a very great admiration for the President, and that they had kept in constant touch with Roosevelt's reform program. Davies added that many considered him to be the world's greatest figure in government. Joseph Stalin was praised by Ambassador Davies as a decent and clean living man with sufficient resiliency in his makeup to stamp him as a politician and a great leader. In this atmosphere of mutual admiration, Joseph Davies attempted to eliminate the past problems which had blocked the development of true cordiality. The debt issue was for Davies one such insignificant issue. A month after he had arrived in the Soviet Union, Davies expressed to Russian officials his conviction that the amount of money owed to the United States was relatively a flyspeck on the wall. The most important consideration, he said, must be that war was a grave possibility, and since there was no body of democratic public opinion in the world such as that of the United States which might be available to them in such a contingency, it would seem propitious to stabilize American-Russian relations. Ambassador Davies' task was to give impetus to Roosevelt's initiative for unity of the two powers.[68]

Several months after Davies' arrival, two major purge trials were staged in Moscow. Diplomatic professionals such as George Kennan,

Charles Bohlen, Loy Henderson, and Alexander Kirk were much distressed by the ruthless measures used by the Soviet regime to repress all opposition, real or imagined, to Stalin. In January, 1937, the trial of Communist Party members accused of participating in an Anti-Soviet Trotskyite Centre conspiracy began in the capital city. The charges were familiar ones such as spying on behalf of Germany, Japan, and Leon Trotsky, sabotaging industry, and conducting terrorist operations. The purging of the army began in June, 1937, and mass executions followed in the wake of numerous arrests and interrogations. Objective observers seriously doubted the guilt of the defendants in these trials, and questioned the motives behind this drastic action. The imposition of similar terror controls in Germany under Adolf Hitler had aroused the ire and wrath of the President and his Administration. Joseph Davies was not able to perceive the similarities in the two systems of government. He informed Franklin Roosevelt that Joseph Stalin was acting in a resolute and forthright manner to crush conspiracies directed against his government. Davies was somewhat dismayed by the horrifying oriental ruthlessness and cruelty which he observed, but, as he told the President, the government had clearly established its case against the terrorists, saboteurs, and erstwhile assassins. Ambassador Davies wrote to Marvin McIntyre and informed him that a counter-revolution was in progress and that it was directed toward the overthrow of the regime. Davies told the President that Stalin was striking fast and hard in an effort to clean up treason in preparation for the coming struggle wtih Germany and Japan. The Ambassador asserted that the army officers who were purged were collaborating with Germany. He spoke to Roosevelt in phrases reflecting subtle admiration for Stalin's resolute decisiveness in ferreting out the opposition. They don't coddle a nettle, they crush it, said the Ambassador. He expressed, in a letter to Secretary McIntyre, the conviction that the regime was going to make all men free even though they had to put every damn man in prison or shoot him to do it. If Ambassador Davies' rationale of the purge trials was accepted by the President, then this blood-letting in Russia may have appeared to be justified and necessary. It was perhaps viewed as a preliminary consolidation of power prior to war with Germany and Japan, and as the expected action of a man whose authority was threatened by elements aiming to weaken the Soviet Union and to eliminate Joseph Stalin.[69]

Franklin Roosevelt had very competent sources of information concerning the Soviet Union in the Division of Eastern European

Affairs of the State Department. This department, however, was abolished in the summer months of 1937, with a suddenness more characteristic of Soviet politics than of American administrative procedure, recalled George Kennan. Knowledgeable persons were certain that the decision for abolishing the division emanated from the White House. Perhaps the President viewed criticism of the Soviet regime as harmful to the development of American-Russian cordiality. Whatever the reason, the Division of Eastern European Affairs was merged with the Western European Affairs Division and placed under the control of Pierrepont Moffat, a man who had no special interest in the Soviet Union. William Bullitt was probably correct when he warned Cordell Hull that too many individuals were so worried about the activities of Hitler, Mussolini, and the Japanese that they were inclined to ignore the enormous strength of the world communist movement. Bullitt described Robert Kelley's extinct division as the most efficient agency for the appraisal of the situation in Russia. The Secretary of State thanked the former Ambassador for his letter, and urged him to call attention in the future to any similar weaknesses or omissions in the State Department. The merger decision was never rescinded.[70]

Franklin Roosevelt's desire to pursue a policy of conciliation with Russia was based on his perception of that nation's presumed opposition to Germany, Japan, and Italy. Soviet foreign policy had appeared to him to have been directed against the forces of aggression. In Spain, Ambassador Bowers spoke with approval of the efforts of the communists and Soviet military advisors to halt Germany and Italy. In contrast to the timidity of France and Great Britain, thought Bowers, the Russians were eager to help save the Republican regime. The Soviet Union was clearly, from Bowers' perspective, on the side of the democracies in Europe. The President was also continually informed of Soviet Foreign Minister Maxim Litvinov's increasing criticism of the failure of the democracies to halt the tide of fascism. Litvinov's utterances warning against the dire consequences which would take place if the fascists should prove victorious, were applauded by the President. Roosevelt had also been impressed by the resolve of the Soviet leadership to constrain Japan. All diplomatic despatches indicated that Russia was the stronger of the two powers, and that the Red Army officers were most confident of their military strength. Ambassador Grew and Davies agreed that the Soviet position was one of decisive superiority. Russian diplomats, reported Joseph Grew, reflected a spirit of frank unwillingness to yield an inch unless the Japanese submitted to Soviet demands. Henry Morgenthau had emphasized to the President that the Soviet Union had taken a very aggressive role against Japan and Germany, and that the clash between these rival powers went completely around the world. This may have been Roosevelt's personal view as he surveyed the world scene. He was determined to give concrete aid to all opponents of fascist aggression. The future coalition against Germany, Italy, and Japan would be successful only if the Soviet Union joined the democratic nations in opposition to the fascist triumvirate. The President would seize every opportunity to demonstrate to Joseph Stalin his sincerity in attempting to construct a far-reaching rapprochement.[71]

Franklin Roosevelt was apprehensive about the possibility of a combined German-Japanese attack on the Soviet Union. He initiated steps to aid Russia in preparation for this eventuality. He personally attempted throughout the months of 1937 to persuade the Department of the Navy to inaugurate a battleship building program in the United States on behalf of Russia. Roosevelt discussed this project with Admiral Leahy. Leahy noted in his diary account of the meeting on January 2, 1937 that it appeared desirable from an international point of view to permit Russia to build battleships in America. Ambassador Troyanovsky was encouraged by the President to approach proper authorities and urge this program of naval expansion for his country. Cordell Hull and Joseph Green, Chief of the Office of Arms and Munitions Control in the State Department, notified several private companies that permission to build battleships and submarines for Russia would be granted. Mr. Scott Ferris, the representative of the Soviet purchasing agency in the United States, Carp Export and Import Corporation of New York, had expressed his pleasure concerning the President's apparent pledge to Troyanovsky that every effort would be made to place contracts with American companies for war material. There is evidence that technical assistance contracts with firms producing aircraft in the United States were also being sought by Soviet representatives. All such efforts proved unsuccessful. Admiral Leahy and the Department of the Navy strongly opposed any large scale program of aid to a foreign government. Roosevelt would continue to push, however, for military assistance to Russia.[72]

IV

The Struggle
Commences

CHAPTER FOUR

THE STRUGGLE COMMENCES: APPEASMENT AND AGGRESSION

The Suggested Equipoise

The swords of war, so recently unsheathed and brandished, soon began to make their final incisions in a world order destined for destruction. The evisceration of the Versailles Peace was marked by the orchestrated themes of violence, revenge, and racial hatred as Germany, Japan, and Italy pursued their quest for dominance in Europe and Asia. The dismantling of the peace treaties signed in Paris after the first world conflagration proceeded with thundering swiftness. Germany's troops and mechanized armor moved into Austria without resistance in March, 1938, and in less than twenty-four hours the sovereignty of that nation merged imperceptibly into an Austro-German Union triumphantly proclaimed from Vienna. In the autumn months, Prime Minister Neville Chamberlain of Great Britain, French Premier Edouard Daladier, Reich President and Chancellor Adolf Hitler, and the Italian Duce Benito Mussolini signed the Munich accords sanctioning the initial truncation of Czechoslovakia. The failure of their endeavor to structure a settlement of lasting peace was evident to all within six months. In March, 1939, German, Hungarian, and Rumanian troops seized the last territorial remnants of Czechoslovakia. Three weeks later, Italy rushed to join the territorial spoilation and its troops began the invasion of Albania. Great Britain's belated guarantees to insure the inviolability of the Polish, Greek, and Rumanian borders failed to restrain Germany. The terrifying march to war culminated with the German invasion of Poland. French and British declarations of war finally confronted the German challenge, and the struggle was enjoined with irrevocable finality.

In the Far East, Japan methodically proceeded with the dismemberment of China. Indiscriminate bombings and executions awakened an observant audience to the brutal determination with which the Japanese military was completing the task of territorial absorption. Japan's ever widening hegemony was viewed with alarm by those powers which were determined to maintain their traditional spheres of influence in Asia. Great Britain, France, the United States, and the Netherlands anxiously watched the developing impending confrontation. Japan formally announced in November, 1938, that Manchuria and China were considered to be integral parts of the Japanese new order in East Asia. In the early months of the following year, Japan's army and navy began its initially hesitant move southward. The Spratly Islands and that of Hainan were occupied in February and March, 1939, and the fear of further territorial aggrandizement prompted an agonizing reappraisal of the consequences of the non-recognition doctrine. Perceptive analyzes of the future offered the certain prognostication of war.

Franklin Roosevelt was completely informed concerning the international events of these years. Germany's presupposed ambitions were delineated in hundreds of diplomatic despatches that were forwarded to the White House. A feeling of impending doom permeated the writing of the President's correspondents. In his speeches and letters there is abundant evidence that he shared the pessimistic appraisals of his representatives. The prospects of a German dominated Europe would eventually persuade the President that resistance to Hitler's ambitions was no longer a matter of choice, but sheer necessity.

This bleak outlook became more discouraging as the Soviet Union made known its desired diplomatic alignment during these years. Franklin Roosevelt had sincerely believed that Joseph Stalin would join the democratic coalition with France and Great Britain in opposition to Hitler's expansionist program. The German-Russian Non-Aggression documents initialed by Vyacheslav Molotov and Joachim Ribbentrop in August, 1939, made it apparent that this balance of power would not be immediately forthcoming. Russia's participation in the partitioning of Poland with Germany, and the subsequent invasion of Finland by the Red Army in the waning months of 1939, provided the President with a dramatic awakening to the meaning of Realpolitik. He was determined, however, to move cautiously in his dealings with Stalin. Assumptions that had been formulated during the years since recognition were not suddenly disposed by Franklin Roosevelt. He thought that the Soviet Union could still be enticed into the democratic coalition, and that it would one day take its place of shared leadership in the struggle for unconditional victory over fascism.

Great Britain and France presented to the President a shocking spectacle of military and moral weakness. Neville Chamberlain's belief that Germany could be appeased was not shared by Franklin Roosevelt. He became thoroughly disgusted with British pusillanimity during these years, and he feared a possible settlement with Germany that would leave that nation in control of continental Europe. The necessity of assuring Great Britain and France time to fully prepare for war persuaded the President to intervene at Munich, but only after it had become apparent to him that German air power could force a decisive victory. The final decision to challenge Germany after the invasion of Poland was strongly endorsed by the Chief Executive. Finally, the decisive engagement which he had always anticipated was to begin, and, given the alternatives available to all participants, there could be but one conclusion, total victory and total defeat.

The events of these years reinforced Franklin Roosevelt's sense of alarm and urgency. The President warned in his Annual Message to Congress in 1938 that stable civilization was threatened by nations abandoning the letter and spirit of treaties. Peace, he said, was most greatly jeopardized by those countries where democracy had been discarded or had never developed. He concluded that policies of aggression would have far reaching effects not only on their immediate neighbors, but also on the United States. The President observed a month later that at least one-fourth of the world's population was involved in a merciless devastating conflict in spite of the fact that a majority of mankind wished to live in peace. In Europe and the Far East, he told his audience, thousands of civilians were being driven from their homes and bombed from the air. Should the United States complacently assume that it could remain immune from aggression? Roosevelt did not think so. Military preparedness for coastal and hemispheric defense was deemed by the President to be necessary in the face of the fascist challenge.[1]

The words of the Chief Executive, which accurately describe his views of the threat posed by Germany, Italy, and Japan were followed by action. Military preparedness was but one means of defense. A secure military alliance would be more effective in throttling the ambitions of the dictators. Franklin Roosevelt earnestly attempted to lay the basis of such a military alliance with Great Britain and the Soviet Union. The President moved cautiously and secretly in this endeavor. Domestic criticism of any entanglement in European and Asian affairs was strong, and Congressmen were watchful for indications of collusion between the United States and foreign powers.

Public distrust was symbolized by a resolution sponsored by Louis Ludlow, a Democratic Congressman from Indiana, which would have provided for a national referendum for any declaration of war by the United States, except in the event of a direct invasion. The Ludlow Resolution was defeated in the House of Representatives by a very slim margin, and this vote dictated caution and reserve on behalf of the Administration's efforts to confront the fascist coalition. Franklin Roosevelt was pleased with its defeat. In a letter to his son James, he stated that in a modern war, with distance annihilated by advanced technology and weaponry, any delay in meeting a prospective challenge was dangerous. It would be far better, he reasoned, to meet the aggressor three or four thousand miles from the Pacific coast. Furthermore, as he acknowledged to William Bankhead, the Speaker of the House, such a war referendum would virtually cripple any President in his conduct of foreign affairs and would encourage other nations to believe that they could violate American rights with impunity. The intensity of his watchdog concern of the Congress did not immediately subside after the defeat of the Ludlow Resolution. In February, 1938, Senator Hiram Johnson of California asked the Administration in a very pointed manner whether or not there existed any alliance or proposed alliance between Great Britain and the United States, or if use of the navy with any other nation was contemplated either in a direct alliance or to patrol and police any particular area. Cordell Hull replied negatively to each section of this publicized inquiry. When questioned during a press conference if he, the President, would satisfy Senator Johnson's longing for more information of the Administration's foreign policy, Roosevelt replied, "I don't think so."[2]

Despite this distrustful inquisitiveness on the part of Congress and the American public, Franklin Roosevelt secretly set in motion plans which he hoped would result in the military coordination of the forces of Great Britain, the United States, and the Soviet Union in the event of the expected war, and in the isolation of the aggressors before the bar of world public opinion. The latter aim was suggested by Sumner Welles in his revived proposal for an international conference to promote world peace. In a memorandum to the President dated January 10, 1938, the Undersecretary of State urged that a meeting be held at which the European nations would jointly evolve a solution to the antagonisms threatening the European continent. This plan was rejected by British Prime Minister Neville Chamberlain after it was communicated to him by Franklin Roosevelt. Chamberlain feared that the President's proposal would hinder his efforts to reach agreement with Germany. Did the President really believe that Germany and Italy would have seriously participated in the proposed conference, or was he attempting to isolate the aggressors in anticipation of their rejection of international action to promote world peace? Roosevelt's attempts to reach agreement on the military coordination of the

American, British, and Russian armed forces in this same month of January, 1938, would seem to indicate that he was not sanguine about the prospects of success for the international conference. It would appear that he was making other plans in anticipation of its eventual failure.[3]

Franklin Roosevelt's proposals called for the cooperation of the American and British navies and the establishment of a military liaison with the Soviet Union. In late December, 1937, Captain Royal Ingersoll, Director of the War Plans Division, was sent to Great Britain to discuss with British Admiralty officials the coordination of the navies of Great Britain and the United States should they find themselves at war with Japan in the Pacific. Captain Ingersoll's mission was carried out at the direct request of Franklin Roosevelt. In a conversation with the President immediately before his departure for London, Ingersoll had received specific instructions on the objectives of his visit. Arrangements were to be made in regard to liaison officers, command relationships, communications, and code and cipher preparation. Ingersoll recalled later that everyone had realized that sooner or later the United States, the Netherlands, China, Great Britain and perhaps the Soviet Union, would be involved in a Pacific war. Arrangements had to be made to provide for a means of communicating with these nations in the united struggle against Japan. Although Captain Ingersoll did not say precisely that the Chief Executive shared this viewpoint, the conclusion that he did anticipate war with Japan, and that Ingersoll's mission was to prepare for that expected eventuality, would appear to be a logical deduction. Franklin Roosevelt must have stressed the need for secrecy for Admiral William Leahy, the Chief of Naval Operations, instructed an inquiring reporter from the *Christian Science Monitor* that there was to be no publicity regarding the employment of Captain Ingersoll. The Ingersoll mission concluded on January 29, 1938, with a personal report and discussion with the President on the current state of preparations for possible trouble in the future.[4]

Concurrent with these American-British discussions, proposals were also privately conveyed by Franklin Roosevelt to Ambassador Joseph Davies in January, 1938, for the purpose of exploring with Joseph Stalin the possibility of securing a liaison between the military and naval authorities of the United States and the Soviet Union. Ambassador Davies presented this suggestion to Soviet authorities at the request of the President. Soviet Foreign Minister Maxim Litvinov doubted that the liaison could be arranged secretly because of possible information leaks by the American participants in the plan. Stalin and Molotov expressed the same concern to Ambassador Davies. In a letter to Franklin Roosevelt, Davies said that while the Soviet dictator had been very chary about disclosing any military information, he had accepted the idea in principle and with every indication of friendliness. The Ambassador added that both Stalin and Molotov had expressed their approval of Colonel Philip R. Faymonville, an American Military Attaché in Moscow. Davies urged the President to retain Faymonville as a possible military liaison officer in the future should the Soviet authorities decide to fully accept Roosevelt's proposal. It is interesting to note that Colonel Faymonville did remain in Russia, perhaps because of the President's anticipation of the eventual military alliance. The Chief Executive may have shared the opinions expressed to him by his Ambassador in Moscow. Russia, wrote Davies, was devoted to international peace, and its army and government were much stronger than was generally recognized in certain European quarters . This prospective alliance partner had now received a very clear indication that Franklin Roosevelt would be most eager to accept the Soviet Union in any future coalition. Stalin probably assumed that he could depend on the support of the United States in any future struggle against the fascist powers. The impending alliance alignment was in its embryonic, yet formative, stage.[5]

Prelude to Fascist Revisionist Designs

The need to formulate more precise plans to meet the increasing belligerence of Germany, Japan, and Italy intensified considerably during this period. Germany remained the most serious concern of Franklin Roosevelt. The reports coming to him in the early months of 1938 were not optimistic concerning the future course of German foreign policy. Hugh Wilson had replaced William Dodd as the American Ambassador in Berlin, arousing hopes in some quarters that a less critical representative there might ease the diplomatic situation. William Bullitt believed that he and Wilson, working in unison, could bring about a Franco-German rapprochement thereby eliminating a major source of antagonism and probable dislocation. There occurred neither a lessening of tension, however, nor a perceptible change in Germany's expansionist ambitions.[6]

Prentice Gilbert, the American Chargé in Germany, offered an appraisal of the political and military aspects of Germany's foreign policy. In a memorandum forwarded to Franklin Roosevelt, Gilbert wrote that Germany was going after both colonial and continental claims. The incorporation of Austria and the Sudeten Germans into the Reich was one primary aim, said Gilbert. He noted too that the ideal of German racial unity was very deep in German consciousness, and that it was something much more fundamental than a mere

National Socialist doctrine. He warned that while Germany did not want war, its present leadership might go to unpredictable extremes in its internal and external affairs for there was confidence in Germany's inherent greatness and strength. He observed with alarm that the Yugoslav Foreign Minister had visited Berlin, and that this was an indication of that nation's receptivity to the furtherance of German influence in southern Europe. This trend of affairs, he added, could easily suggest eventual political developments of great importance. Gilbert's report may have heightened Roosevelt's fear, previously expressed during a cabinet meeting, that Romania and Yugoslavia were on the fascist path.[7]

There were other disconcerting observations concerning Germany which came to the President's attention. Arthur Murray wrote the Chief Executive on January 24, 1938 asserting that no agreements would be entered into by Berlin that would serve to check its expansionist aspirations. He predicted that a convulsion greater and more horrible than any that had yet occurred would be forthcoming. Vice-President John Garner cited a speech by Joseph Goebbels in which the propaganda chief was quoted as saying that Germany intended to pay no attention to treaties. The President thereupon suggested to Cordell Hull that he might wish to ask the German Ambassador if this was the official position of his country. Hitler's anti-Semitic policies continued to rankle the President. Gilbert had quoted the Führer's statement that he would proceed energetically against the Jewish inciters in Germany, and that as representatives of a Jewish Internationale they would be treated accordingly. Former Ambassador William Dodd wrote the Chief Executive on January 22, 1938, urging him to forbid Hugh Wilson from attending the Nuremberg Party rally where, he said, hundreds of thousands of German soldiers and Hitler youths were paraded about in order to scare Europe. Cordell Hull doubted the effectiveness of such abstention, and Ambassador Wilson did attend the ceremonies. Stephen Early informed Roosevelt in February, 1938, that Percy Winner, then in charge of the National Broadcasting Company's International Broadcast Service, had recently been fired from his job and that a group of South American fascist sympathizers were carrying on NBC's shortwave work. Early told the President that he had no reason to doubt Winner's word, and that such conduct on the part of NBC was almost unbelievable. Roosevelt suggested that some way must be found to counter German and Italian propaganda in South America. Herbert Pell offered perhaps the most succinct analysis for the President: "Looking at the international situation from here, I can only say that everything looks bad and the most hopeful are those who say it has looked bad for a long time."[8]

The most alarming reports concerning Germany's expansionist program were coming from Vienna, Austria. Prentice Gilbert had earlier warned from Berlin that those who believed Germany would embark on a radical course in foreign affairs were of the opinion that Austria might be the first nation to experience the German thrust. Evidence that this opinion was correct came to the White House from John Wiley, the American Chargé d'Affaires in Vienna. He wrote an extensive analysis of a meeting between the Austrian Chancellor Kurt von Schuschnigg and Adolf Hitler on February 12, 1938, at Berchtesgaden. Schuschnigg, reported Wiley, had described his visit with the Führer as the most horrible day of his life. The Austrian Chancellor depicted Hitler as a madman with a mission to unite 80 million Germans into a nation that would rule Europe. Austria, Hitler had told him, would be taken with greater ease than the Rhineland. The appointment of Arthur Seyss-Inquart, the leader of the National Socialist movement in Austria, as Minister of Interior, said Wiley, would not benefit the cause of Austrian independence. In the words of John Wiley, Austria would fall by force of arms. The only factor which awaited clarification was the time element.[9]

The time element was clarified on the night of March 11, 1938 as German troops marched into Austria. The Anschluss was complete and the Austro-German Union was proclaimed on March 13, 1938. Germany's action in Austria, wrote Hugh Wilson in a letter to Franklin Roosevelt, was another indication that its aims were guided largely by instinct rather than ratiocination. Wilson added that during a party given by Hermann Goering on the evening of March 11, 1938 there was apparent on every German face a mighty satisfaction and intense pride of power. The President was asked at a news conference if Austria still existed as a nation. He replied somewhat sardonically that legally, if there was such a thing as international law, there had as yet been no announcement from its Minister or otherwise that Austria had ceased to be an independent state. He also called the attention of reporters who complained that they were living under a dictator in the United States to a front page newspaper article entitled, "Newsmen Held Under Guns As Hitler Talks To Austria." Cordell Hull expressed the official position of the United States Government on March 19, 1938 saying that the Austrian incident was a matter of serious concern to his nation.[10]

Germany's success in Austria did not bring about any significant easing of the international crisis situation. It seemed to represent to many observers the real beginning of the restructuring of Europe. The continuing carnage in Spain was vividly described by Ambassador Claude Bowers in numerous letters to the President, and this information could only have served to heighten his already acute awareness of fascist aggression. He informed Roosevelt that the war in Spain was not a civil war at all, but a testing of the world's spirit by the fascist internationale. Germany and Italy, said Bowers, had converted Spain into a laboratory in which they were conducting experiments with their improved methods of destruction. He told the President that 1,000 kilo bombs had been dropped on Barcelona, in the very center of the city and on a Sunday, resulting in the slaughter of hundreds of women and children. Bowers' reports of German and Italian bombing were considered important enough by the Chief Executive to forward to the Secretaries of War and Navy. One such observation by Bowers was that the Republican forces were being defeated not by Franco, but by a deluge of German-Italian projectiles fired by German-Italian machines run by German-Italians. In May, the Ambassador warned Roosevelt that the success of fascism in Spain would give a tremendous impetus to fascism in South and Central America where Hitler and Mussolini were actively and arrogantly engaged in propagandizing against democracy. Bowers' opinion by August, 1938 was that the 100,000 Italians and Germans, and their planes, tanks and artillery were the key to Franco's probable success.[11]

In the European core area, there were no indications that Germany's expansionist ambitions had been satisfied. Samuel Fuller reported to the White House that Hitler was the one man for Germany now, and that the young Germans were most belligerent. One youth, said Fuller, typical of all, seemed to have Hitler and God all mixed up. Arthur Sweetzer, in an interview with the President on April 4, 1938 alarmingly reported that nothing in Central Europe could stop Hitler. Sweetzer believed that German opinion had been enormously exalted by its recent successes, and that the Führer could lead it wherever he desired. During the conversation, Roosevelt mentioned that he had just received a letter from a friend who had dined with six or eight of Schuschnigg's friends after the meeting at Berchtesgaden. The Austrian Chancellor, said the President, had apparently never dreamt of anything like it. Hitler had been unbelievable, said Roosevelt, for during his long tirades two names kept repeating themselves, Julius Caesar and Jesus Christ. Sweetzer observed that the Chief Executive seemed to think you could do very little with such a man. John Cudahy, writing from Warsaw, told the President, that all states, including Poland, east and south of Germany, were living in constant apprehension as to which might be the next victim of Hitler's expansionist program. Hugh Wilson, in a memorandum to Cordell Hull that was subsequently sent to Franklin Roosevelt, said that the Czech minister in Berlin was certain that Germany's foreign policy was based on the principle of the unity of the German race, wherever it may be found, under the direction of National Socialism.[12]

Signs that preparations were under way in Germany for another military move were clearly visible to diplomatic observers, and their reports were continuously forwarded to the President. The Ambassador in Berlin reported Foreign Minister Joachim von Ribbentrop's remark that Germany could not tolerate the mistreatment of 3,500,000 Germans in Czechoslovakia, and that the Reich was prepared for war. Ambassador Wilson wrote several weeks later that in army circles the eventual use of force against Czechoslovakia was viewed as inevitable. He apprised the President on July 11, 1938 of the enormous increase in the production of first line fighting planes in Germany. Six to seven thousand a year were being assembled, and as many as 17,000 yearly could be produced. This production in Germany, he continued, was of much greater importance to the world than was fully realized at home. John Wiley, writing from Vienna in July, 1938 cited reports of war preparation by German forces which were to be used in Czechoslovakia. He noted the opinion of one British passport control officer who believed that either war was imminent or the Germans were creating an atmosphere with a view to extracting far reaching concessions. Wiley reported four days later that preparations for offensive warfare were being rushed to completion. He observed that Austria was destined to be a springboard into the Balkans and that anti-Semitism emanating from Berlin would endeavor to play the same role as Pan Slavism which had been directed from St. Petersburg.[13]

There were some reports from informants that the Führer did not wish to use force against Czechoslovakia, and that he was reluctant to project Germany into a war. One of Hitler's closest associates had told Ambassador Hugh Wilson that Hitler would feel that his policy had been a failure if he had to shed German blood to accomplish it for he had been through war and knew its horrors. Wilson wrote on July 23, 1938 that Hitler seemed to be in a more friendly frame of mind, and that a breathing spell appeared to be evident. Major Truman Smith, the Military Attaché in Berlin, had reported earlier that he had seen no unusual troop movements in Silesia, Saxony, or Austria, and no evidence of troop concentrations, curtailments of leave, or calling up of reserves in border or interior areas.[14]

What were the President's expectations? Major Smith's memorandum mentioned that it was contrary to the strategic doctrine of the German Army to concentrate troops in frontier areas prior to an attack on a hostile country, and that such a method had been used neither in the Rhineland nor Austria. John Wiley's reports certainly indicated that preparation had begun for a military offensive. Ambassador Wilson observed from Berlin that mobilization would no longer be a prelude to offensive action by Germany. The army, he continued, was in a mobilized condition and troops could be sent on a march directly from their barracks for a given destination. He predicted that the Embassy would receive at most six or eight hours warning. Franklin Roosevelt did indeed expect a German advance in the near future. He sent a memorandum to Cordell Hull on August 31, 1938 which contained information from a person with intimate access to Mussolini. This individual had reported that Hitler had told Konrad Henlein, leader of the National Socialist movement in the Sudeten area of Czechoslovakia, in May, 1938 that Germany would complete its defense line in ten weeks, at which time that nation, Austria and Hungary would be ready to act against the Prague Government of Edouard Benes. Roosevelt noted for his Secretary of State that ten weeks from the end of May would be approximately the early part of September, 1938. It is clear that he expected action about that time.[15]

The alarming reports concerning Germany's prospective expansionist designs perhaps overshadowed the rather vague outlines of Italian foreign policy. Franklin Roosevelt's conviction, however, that Germany, Japan, and Italy were cooperating in achieving their aggressive ambitions does not seem to have been weakened by the equivocal reports coming from Rome. He informed Cordell Hull in January, 1938, that information had come to his attention concerning the shipment of Italian planes and aviators to Japan. Roosevelt told Hull bluntly that the time had come for Ambassador Phillips in Rome to officially ask the Italian Government categorically whether or not Italian airmen were being sent to Japan. William Phillips was unable to verify the veracity of the President's information. The reports of Italian operations in support of Japanese aggression in China were coming from Admiral Yarnell through William Leahy. Yarnell's phraseology probably left little doubt in Roosevelt's mind as to their authenticity. Yarnell wrote that the Italians were openly and avowedly in support of Japanese aggression in hopes of getting some droppings from the table and, he added, they were bootlicking the Japs at every turn. Substantive memoranda in earlier years had stressed the fact of Italian-Japanese collaboration. There is no evidence that the Chief Executive dismissed the above cited intelligence appraisals as false.[16]

The Axis unity of Germany and Italy does not seem to have been broken by events in the early months of 1938. The German absorption of Austria did not have a detrimental effect on the relations linking Rome and Berlin. In the first week of May, 1938 Adolf Hitler made a personal visit to Mussolini in Rome. Hugh Wilson summarized the German press coverage of this event as editorially stressing that Italy was ready to support with arms if necessary the joint policy of Italy and Germany. William Phillips reported that the visit had brought forth no new understandings, secrets, or commitments. He noted, however, that the talks had reaffirmed the solidarity of the Rome-Berlin Axis following the Anschluss, and had assured Italy of Hitler's guarantee of the inviolability of the Italian-German frontier. Roosevelt's Ambassador made the remark that there was no real public enthusiasm for Germany or the Germans during these moments of national rejoicing. American Counselor Edward Reed, however, stressed that government controlled Italian papers had emphasized the solidarity of the Rome-Berlin Axis as the dominant theme of editorial comment. Virginia Gaydo, the official press spokesman for the Italian Government, had written that if war should be perpetrated by the democracies, the combined strength of the Axis would be concentrated against them. Franklin Roosevelt evidently did not see any reason to disassociate the two nations from their collaborative efforts in behalf of fascism. In a letter to Phillips, the President remarked that ninety per cent of the American people were definitely anti-German and anti-Italian in sentiment, and he was not going to ask them to be neutral in thought. Claude Bowers' accounts of Italian-German action in Spain certainly influenced Roosevelt. Although Ambassador Phillips seemed to portray Italy as a less than eager participant in the Axis partnership, it would appear that the Chief Executive did not do so.[17]

The innumerable despatches which came to the White House concerning the international situation persuaded the President, whose detestation for fascism was already irrevocably firm, to begin what was to become an intensive campaign to awaken the American public to the dangers of isolation and to the threat posed by the Axis powers to the security of the United States. Cordell Hull's comments before the National Press Club in Washington on March 17, 1938 appeared to be the opening salvo in this campaign, and were vigorously endorsed by Roosevelt. The Secretary of State stressed the need for law, order, morality, and justice throughout the world. He told his audience that isolation was simply a fruitful source of insecurity. The Roosevelt Administration would safeguard America's legitimate rights in every part of the world, he pledged. Hull made it very clear that his government would not fail to arm when international lawlessness was on the rampage. He warned that to do less than that would lay open the country to unpredictable hazards.[18]

The President graphically illustrated during a press conference on April 20, 1938 what he considered as the unpredictable hazards in the present situation. Suppose there should occur a fascist revolution in Mexico, and suppose planes, officers, and guns were sent to Mexico, as had been done in Spain, said Roosevelt. Could we stand idly by and have this European menace right on our own borders, he asked? The President thought not, and an American counter action would be required, he added, whether the insurgents acted in Mexico or any-where else in the American hemisphere. The Monroe Doctrine, he admonished, applied to all of the Americas, and he was trying to keep an independent continent to the north and to the south. Perhaps to influence a skeptical audience, the Chief Executive related the story of a friend in China who had a brother three hundred miles southwest of Hankow, a pacifist who clung to the view that "We are so big, there is nobody that would dare to trouble us." Then the President added, in a rather allegorical manner, that this man's village in the Iowa of China had been completely wiped out and all residents had been killed when planes came over and dropped a bomb on the house where they were cooling off. Three hundred people in a nearby village were also killed and two minutes later the attackers were gone. They had wiped out one of the rural communities of the Iowa of China, he concluded, and no one had ever thought it would happen! In order to persuade the more incredulous reporters he informed them of German plans in 1918 to send an armed zeppelin to drop a cargo of bombs on New York City.[19]

These comments were intended to arouse a sleeping giant from its lethargic isolation. In an address at Queens University in Kingston, Ontario in August, 1938, he continued the theme of the threatened sanctuary. The Americas, said Roosevelt, were no longer a far away continent immune from controversies beyond the seas. He observed that all propaganda offices and general staffs were very much inter-ested in this hemisphere. He then directed his wrath squarely at the dictators, warning them that he could not prevent people from hold-ing an opinion in regard to wanton cruelty, undemocratic regimenta-tion, misery inflicted on helpless persons, or violations of accepted individual rights.[20]

Franklin Roosevelt was admitting that he personally had very strong feelings concerning the belligerent acts of the fascist powers. There is evident in the President's public statements a feeling of frustration con-cerning the fact that he could not do more to bring a halt to aggres-sion. Immediately after the Anschluss, a reporter asked him if there was any concrete step the United States could take to relieve the seri-ous situation in Europe. He answered that if there was such a plan, it would certainly not be announced at a press conference. In truth, there was no elaborate formula in the President's mind to counter German, Japanese, and Italian designs. The neutrality provisions that had been enacted by Congress were especially resented by him. The perplexing problems posed by their application were discussed by the Chief Executive on numerous occasions. He observed that had he applied the neutrality statutes to the Sino-Japanese conflict, they would have benefited Japan and hurt China, and that, he added, was not true neutrality. In Spain, however, he explained that he had not applied the neutrality provisions because Franco's forces, in complete control of the ocean, would have been able to get shipments of munitions from the United States. In Roosevelt's words,.he had been beating around the bush to keep the country neutral, which meant not helping one fellow more than the other.[21]

The President's anxiety during these years of uncontested aggression surfaced in a discussion with Arthur Sweetzer. Sweetzer had made some critical remarks about those nations which had given very little support to the League of Nations, and this prompted Franklin Roosevelt to vigorously defend his own efforts to aid the cause at Geneva. The Chief Executive said that he had joined everything over there that he could possibly join. "What more," he asked rhetorically, "would you have me do?" Then he admitted what was perhaps uppermost on his mind. The League had failed to halt the tide of war, and, in Roosevelt's opinion, it should in the future give up all political issues and keep to general non-controversial matters. He emphasized that all ideas of force or coercion must be abandoned. There is implied in these remarks a resigned pessimism concerning the present world situation. What was to be the future world order if there were no restraints to the ambitions of dictators? The President's vision was a dismal one. In June, 1938, after a visit from Ambassador Joseph Kennedy, a reporter asked the Chief Executive if Kennedy's report had made him feel cheerful or gloomy. He replied, "Made me feel just the way I have felt for the last two or three years." When asked if he was hopeful about the international situation, the President did not answer the question.[22]

The Prospective Coalition
Great Britain, France, and Russia on the Eve of Munich

A disquieting factor in the President's appraisal of the deteriorating international situation was the program of appeasement which the British were vigorously pursuing in their efforts to achieve a settlement with the fascist bloc nations. Prime Minister Neville Chamberlain's rejection of Roosevelt's proposed demarche in January, 1938 was followed by increasing evidence that Great Britain would silently acquiesce in a new European order dominated by Germany. Prentice Gilbert, reporting from Berlin on January 17, 1938, stated that Arthur Henderson, the British Ambassador to Germany, believed his Government must recognize Hitler's demands and accept German assurances as valid. If not, said Henderson, it would be better to abandon any idea of an understanding with Berlin. Chamberlain was intent upon following the path of least resistance. Herbert Pell informed the

President in February, 1938 that the fascist countries seemed to believe firmly that the British would never abandon their program of surrender. Pell observed that thus far the Axis nations had only been pecking at prestige, but they were convinced that the habit of surrender would continue when they begin to go directly after British interests. Anthony Eden's resignation this same month from the office of Secretary for Foreign Affairs in the Chamberlain Cabinet was another indication to Roosevelt that the Prime Minister's appeasement policies, much resented by Eden, would intensify. The President believed that Eden's departure was a prelude to further accommodation with the fascist powers. The Chief Executive foresaw two possibilities to Chamberlain's course of action. A deal by a Chief of Police with gangsters which results in no more holdups means that the Chief of Police will be called a great man. If the gangsters do not keep their word, however, the Chief of Police would go to jail. In Roosevelt's opinion, the British Prime Minister was taking very long chances, and was most likely breeding far more serious trouble in four or eight years.[23]

Franklin Roosevelt agreed with Ambassador Kennedy's impression that Hitler and Mussolini, having done so well for themselves by bluffing, were not going to stop bluffing until somebody very sharply calls their bluff. Arthur Murray told the President immediately after Germany's absorption of Austria that mistaken policies of the past had come home to roost and that the English people were ready to take up the sword against the German octopus. The despatches sent to the White House throughout 1938 indicated that Murray's judgment was not correct and that Chamberlain was earnestly seeking appeasement. It is doubtful that the logic provided the Chief Executive by the British economist, John Keynes, lessened Roosevelt's resentment of that nation's policies. Keynes had told him that the tragedy was that right minded countries had shown no indication of supporting one another. America won't support Britain, he continued, the British won't support France, and the French won't support Spain. When, asked Keynes, will we get together, and how much harm will be done by then?[24]

Roosevelt could have answered by pointing out the harm already done by Britain's pursuit of peace by appeasement. The President confided to Arthur Sweetzer that he had been having much difficulty with the British. He claimed to have personally sent a message to Stanley Baldwin at the time of the Italo-Ethiopian crisis urging the English and the French to stand solid against Mussolini. The only way to have stopped Italy, Roosevelt reflected, was resistance at the very start. Britain took no action, however, and the troops went on. Once again, recalled the Chief Executive, when the Rhineland was occupied, he had sent a message to the King of England through Vincent Astor Kent suggesting that a naval blockade of Germany would be effective in halting that nation's program of expansion. The answer he received from the King, said the President, was that it would have been an unneutral act. In a moment of reflection, Roosevelt asked Arthur Murray, "Why in the name of common sense can't the poor old world come together and cast their thoughts at least twelve months ahead? In the old days we used to try at least to think a generation ahead." [25]

The most vocal and impassioned criticism of Great Britain's foreign policy which came to the President's desk was contained in the letters of Claude Bowers. The British refusal to become involved in the Spanish Civil War was scathingly condemned by Roosevelt's Ambassador in Madrid. Bowers admitted that Chamberlain would be hailed as a hero if appeasement was successful, but, speaking for himself and the Chief Executive, he added that both hated compromise with principle. He praised the decision of Anthony Eden to break from what Bowers termed the fascistic policy of the British Prime Minister. The time had arrived, he said, when all democratic countries would have to stand up and be counted either for fascism or against it. In a letter to the President dated April 11, 1938, the Ambassador described Chamberlain's conduct as dishonorable, treacherous, anti-democratic, and deceptive. He had, said Bowers, consolidated his position only with Hitler and Mussolini, and in doing so he had plumbed the depths of hypocrisy and the garden variety of dishonesty. He concluded that he was having none of Mr. Chamberlain. Franklin Roosevelt seems to have agreed, but his criticism was tempered by an assumption not shared by Bowers. "I do wish," he wrote the Ambassador, "that our British friends would see the situation as it seems to be — but, as you know, they are doing everything to stall off controversy and possible war until at least 1941. It is amazing and sad to note that so many small nations have lost their confidence in England during the past two or three years." [26]

There were more temperate reports coming into the White House which tended to substantiate, in Roosevelt's opinion, the extremely captious remarks made by Bowers. The American Chargé in London, Herschel Johnson, observed that even the German Foreign Minister, Joachim von Ribbentrop, was convinced that the Englishman's bark was worse than his bite, and that neither Lord Halifax, the Foreign Secretary, nor the Prime Minister would stand in the way of German strength. Adolf Hitler, reported Johnson, thought that Halifax sympathized wtih Germany's aims in Austria, Memel, Czechoslovakia, and the colonial possessions. Ambassador Kennedy said that Chamberlain had likened Germany to a boa constrictor that had eaten a good meal and was trying to digest the meal before taking on anything else. The Prime Minister, therefore, saw no difficulties for the time being. Halifax, according to Kennedy, supported Hitler's right to expand in Eastern and Central Europe.[27]

Ambassador Hugh Wilson in Berlin wrote that French informants had told him that the cardinal policy of the British was the employment of every device to avoid a general war. In August, 1938, Herschel Johnson described the substance of a talk he had with Thomas Masaryk, the former President of Czechoslovakia. Masaryk, said Johnson, was certain that in order to keep out of war Britain would sacrifice Czechoslovakia in agreement with the four great powers. Eight days later the American Chargé in London added that Halifax was convinced that even the combined forces of France, Great Britain, and Russia could do nothing for Czechoslovakia reconstituted after a war fought on their behalf, reasoned Halifax. Joseph Kennedy quoted Chamberlain as saying that he would not sanction a war over Czechoslovakia unless he was absolutely forced into it. The Ambassador's opinion, however, was that even if Hitler should strike, the Prime Minister would use his influence to keep France and Britain out of the turmoil. In pensive meditation concerning these events, Franklin Roosevelt may have recalled the words of John Cudahy, his Ambassador in Warsaw, who had written that "those European nations seeking a face-saving formula for appeasement were becoming aware that it was no longer a question of saving face — for there was no face left to save — it was now merely a case of saving the rear end." [28]

William Bullitt writing from Paris was equally disparaging in his comments to Franklin Roosevelt on the topic of French foreign policy. Premier Camille Chautemps and his Foreign Minister Yvon Delbos were prepared to go ahead with their policy of reconciliation with Germany, said Bullitt. The German nation, he prophesized, would soon have a controlling position in Central and Eastern Europe, and France would accept the new arrangement in quiet acquiescence. Hitler is certain, wrote Bullitt, that he only need to be amiable and the French will accept his expansionist program. Ambassador Bullitt gave the President in May, 1938 a most critical appraisal of the condition of the French air force which would be vital in any encounter with Germany. When the French Minister for Air, Guy LeChambre, claimed that his nation would fight over Czechoslovakia, Bullitt asked sarcastically, "With what?" The American Ambassador did not believe that France could sustain the aerial bombardment which would surely come in any confrontation with Germany. William Bullitt dismissed France as a bulwark against fascist aggression. The present pursuit of appeasement with Germany might change in the future, but it seems doubtful that the President could have placed much faith in France's capacity to resist Hitler. The British lacked the will to challenge the Führer; France, the necessary requirements of war.[29]

The only encouraging information coming to the White House on the possible forces of resistance in the prospective encounter with Germany, Italy, and Japan emanated from Moscow in the observations of Joseph Davies. The President's strong desire to bring the Soviet Union into the democratic coalition must have been given added impetus by the expressed opinions of the American Ambassador. Davies, in a letter to Marvin McIntyre which was to be forwarded to Roosevelt, stressed that the Rome-Berlin-Tokyo Axis could only be halted by a London-Paris-Moscow union. The day would come, said the Ambassador, when the democracies of the world would be fortunate to have the power which Russia could supply in case the military fascists went "haywire." Davies' appraisal of the Soviet Union may have impressed the President. The Ambassador reported that Stalin, the Red Army, and the secret police or Gay-Pay-oo as he termed it, were all working overtime strengthening the nation against Hitler. The men in charge, he continued, were strong, able, and at least professed altruistic concepts of brotherhood in their justification of the terrible police state. Most important, he observed, was the fact that ideologically and politically it claimed to seek peace. If Ambassador Davies had any doubts about an alignment with Russia he dismissed them with the logic that, threatened by Hitler's fascism, Americans should hold hands with the Devil himself. The Devil appeared to many to be exceptionally active during these spring months as the purge trials and arrests continued with unremitting vengeance. Davies was certain, however, that they were justified. He believed that there had been a great deal of plotting on the part of many of the defendants to overthrow Stalin. Privately, he wrote, they apologized for these trials saying that they were only for the betterment of the people.[30]

In despatches brought to the Chief Executive's attention, analyses of Soviet foreign policy offered conclusions which appear to be in close agreement with the President's own opinions. Government officials in Moscow were described by Ambassador Davies as being greatly alarmed by British and French appeasement policies. Maxim Litvinov made numerous statements pledging that the Soviet Union would aid Czechoslovakia if France and Great Britain fulfilled their commitments. Editorial comment in the government controlled press was constantly analyzed for the President, and the theme of resistance to Germany was repeatedly emphasized. Editorials affirming that it was in the interest of all the powers to take counter measures against Hitler certainly were in accord with Roosevelt's views, as was the official diatribe in Moscow on the hesitance of Great Britain and France to meet the fascist challenge. The more accurate and perceptive insights of the American Chargé in Moscow, Alexander Kirk, were perhaps not appreciated by the Chief Executive. Kirk fully realized that although the Soviet Government was now concentrating its animosity against Nazi Germany in order to curtail the power of that state, it would welcome any measures to that end provided the costs would be borne by others.[31]

Franklin Roosevelt continued to press for a close American-Russian partnership. The President's desire to establish a military liaison with the Soviet Union was but one indication that he anticipated a meaningful partnership with Stalin. He specifically gave his support to plans calling for the construction of two battleships of approximately 35,000 tons and suggested that construction on two more battleships, each not to exceed 45,000 tons, should begin as soon as possible. Cordell Hull had informed Ambassador Troyanovsky that he was doing everything possible to facilitate the purchase of these ships. Charles Edison, the Assistant Secretary of the Navy, admitted that the only obstacle to the Chief Executive's requests, and one which he was never able to overcome, was that the major construction firms which could have produced the battleships had refused to take the risk of being man-handled by a Congressional investigation at a later date. They might be portrayed to the public as mercenary vultures who sold out the United States for dirty money.[32]

It is evident that President Roosevelt still considered the Soviet Union to be of major importance in the anticipated contest with Germany, Italy, and Japan. He was probably gratified by Maxim Litvinov's tribute to Joseph Davies during a dinner on June 7, 1937. The Russian Foreign Minister complimented Davies for doing his best to understand the Soviet Union, what was going on there, the motives behind such action, and the aims of the regime. Litvinov added that there was a great deal of latent, unexposed, unproclaimed, and unwritten mutual sympathy and respect between the peoples of the two countries. Ambassador Davies replied that the peoples of both countries were seeking to improve the lot of the common man and were trying to promote the well being of the greatest number. Davis persistent reiteration of the Russian leaders' admiration for Roosevelt in letters he wrote to the Chief Executive and to those with daily access to him, such as Marvin McIntyre and Steve Early, may have served to strengthen the President's resolve to construct a relationship of intimacy with the Soviet Union.[33]

Roosevelt and Munich
Appeasement or Tactical Compromise

The assumptions which Franklin Roosevelt had accepted concerning Germany's aggressive belligerence, Mussolini's strong attachment to the Führer, British appeasement, French weakness, and Russia's desire to halt fascism were strengthened during the Munich crisis. The President did not share the calm detachment which was evident in a memorandum sent to him by Assistant Secretary of State Adolph Berle on September 1, 1938. Berle predicted that Hitler would soon take all of Czechoslovakia in the course of his eastward march, but that he would never be able to hold together millions of Czechs, Ruthenians, Magyars, and Transylvanians. The Third Reich, like the old Habsburg Empire, thought Berle, would eventually collapse. He informed Roosevelt that emotion was obscuring the fact that were the actor anyone but Hitler, with his cruelty and anti-Semitic feeling, most would regard these events as the necessary and justifiable restructuring of the unsound work of Versailles. The President's subsequent actions would prove that he totally disagreed with all aspects of Berle's logic. The Munich denouement was but a temporary expedient. The democratic-fascist engagement, in Roosevelt's opinion, was certain to occur in the not too far distant future.[34]

Reports that Adolf Hitler was planning to seize the Sudetenland in Czechoslovakia were numerous throughout the summer months of 1938. During the first weeks of September, there was increasing evidence of Germany's intention to use force to achieve this aim, and Roosevelt was very cognizant of the Führer's serious determination to achieve his ambitions in Czechoslovakia. Ambassador Hugh Wilson, after having attended the Nuremberg festivities, remarked that he was more than ever impressed with Germany's solidarity and its determination to achieve results. He emphasized that this mighty power, completely obedient to one man, was a threat to peaceful European nations. The Ambassador's despatches often contained the warning that the Führer would move to crush any resistance. He wrote on September 13, 1938 that only prompt action somewhere could prevent the occurrence of that type and scope of disorder and bloodshed which might provoke Hitler into intervention. Wilson relayed information that Germany would indeed march on Czechoslovakia, and he noted a military attaché's report of reserves being gradually and secretly called to the colors. An air force of 400 bombers was said to be in readiness on airfields in Berlin. The situation appeared ominous as the President considered a response.[35]

Mussolini's resolve to support his Axis partner dispelled any doubts which Franklin Roosevelt might have had about Italy's membership in the fascist bloc. Ambassador William Phillips recounted in numerous despatches his observations and impressions of Italy's military preparedness to march on the side of Germany. The press spokesman for the Italian Government, Virginia Gaydo, had stressed the spiritual and political solidarity of the Axis union, and said that its armies should be considered a sure force for clarification and warning to other powers. Mussolini was quoted by the Ambassador as saying that Italy's stand against Czechoslovakia had already been taken, and that further pressure would be brought to bear on Benes' government. Franklin Roosevelt wrote Phillips on September 15, 1938, no doubt for Mussolini's consumption, and said that Americans were an emotional people who don't easily lose their heads, but would wade in with everything they have to give if the future of democratic government was threatened by a coalition of European dictators. Phillips could state with certainty a few days later that all measures of doubt regarding Italy's attitude toward the developing Czech crisis had been removed by Mussolini's statements, and it was now only a question as to what kind of military assistance would be given to Germany. He reported that the Italian dictator was fully prepared to wage war on England and France. Italy's determination would permit no hesitation, said the Duce. Finally, in a despatch dated September 27, 1938, and forwarded to the White House, an American Military Attaché cited instructions that had been sent to Italian units to make all secret preparations for a speedy mobilization.[36]

Why did Franklin Roosevelt decide to ask Mussolini to intercede on behalf of peace after having been given such discouraging information? Two factors might have played a role in his decision. One was a letter from Herbert Pell from Lisbon, stating his impression, gained while sojourning in Italy, that the Italian masses were thoroughly dissatisfied with the thought of the Germans on their border, and that the majority of Italians did not like the idea of the Rome-Berlin Axis. Pell recalled that as a boy he had seen the inscription "Death to the Germans" chalked on walls in Rome, and that he personally did not believe that this attitude had changed very much. There were others that he mentioned seeing on his recent trip to Italy which were not so encouraging such as "Believe-Obey-Fight," "Italy Fears No One," and "The Plough Opens the Land but the Sword Defends It." The most important criterion, however, which prompted the President to seek a compromise settlement was the appalling weakness of Great Britain and France.[37]

The information coming in the first weeks of September from Ambassador Joseph Kennedy in London, and the Charge Herschel Johnson, supported previous conclusions that the British were determined to appease Hitler, Neville Chamberlain and Foreign Secretary Halifax had given some intimation of stiffening in the bargaining with Germany, but no real resolve to do so was evident until the waning moments before the meeting at Munich. The Prime Minister noted as the crisis intensified that this really was not as much fun as shooting grouse, and herein seems to have revealed his ambivalence on whether or not to compromise with principle. The decision to seek peace and not a confrontation seemed firm by September 11, 1938 when Chamberlain rejected a plan to start destroyer fleet operations as a warning to Hitler that any provocative action would be firmly resisted. Kennedy could now affirm Chamberlain's resolution to move quickly with Hitler to see what could be done on a permanent basis for peace. Prior to the Prime Minister's departure to meet with the Führer on September 15, 1938, Ambassador Kennedy wrote that all efforts would be made to stall it off with Hitler, and to talk over any big plans for the peace of the world. In the President's opinion, as noted by Harold Ickes, Chamberlain appeared to be for peace at any price, and both England and France would soon wash the blood from their Judas Iscariot hands.[38]

The British Prime Minister and the Führer met at Berchesgaden on September 15, 1938. The result of the discussion was made clear to the President: the Sudetenland would go to Germany. Ambassador Wilson in Berlin relayed the request of British Ambassador Arthur Henderson that pressure should be firmly applied on Benes to force him to accede to German demands for dismemberment of Czechoslovakia. Joseph Kennedy reported that Hitler had threatened a world war if Britain and France resisted, and that Chamberlain had asked the Führer to hold off action until he could persuade his Cabinet to accept the new arrangements. Kennedy described the British as looking for a good excuse to stay out of any conflict. Hitler did promise not to move troops, and the Prime Minister expressed the opinion that while the Czechs might talk big, they would probably accede. Chamberlain also described the French as having come over with their tongues out looking for some way to save themselves from war. Kennedy commented with sardonic humor that the English were spending most of their time apologizing to Americans for the way they were acting. William Bullitt remarked to the President that the British and French were behaving like little boys doing dirty things behind the barn. Eleanor exclaimed to her husband, "The poor Zchecks! [sic] I don't some how like the role of England and France, do you?"[39]

Chamberlain, having discussed Hitler's requests with the British Cabinet, returned on September 22, 1938, for a second meeting with the Führer at Godesberg. Hitler, according to Kennedy's account of the discussions, wanted not only what everybody was willing to give him, but a great deal more. In the words of Arthur Cadogan, quoted by the Ambassador, there seemed to be no more sanity left in the man. Hugh Wilson in Berlin also feared that the German dictator would soon take matters into his own hands and precipitate events by launching an attack. Joseph Kennedy could confirm by September 26, 1938 that the situation appeared hopeless and gloomy and that finally the British and French were prepared to fight. "If war comes they know they are going to get hell," said Kennedy, "but they are now reconciled." [40]

The fear of Germany's military superiority over Great Britain and France convinced Franklin Roosevelt of the necessity for action. All incoming correspondence to the White House had been discouraging. Hugh Wilson had testified repeatedly on the strength and readiness of the German army and air force. William Phillips had no doubts about Mussolini's decision to enter the war as a full-fledged Axis partner. Joseph Kennedy was certain that Great Britain lacked the resolve and preparedness necessary to defeat Hitler. William Bullitt's letters contained predictions of immense catastrophic destruction in France should Germany decide on an air attack. It was apparent too that the Chief Executive took very seriously the Führer's statements concerning the willingness to precipitate a major conflict. He had urged on September 19, 1938 that plans be made ready to evacuate Americans from Europe if war should break out, and renewed his request for more ships for evacuation purposes one week later. Roosevelt expressed his concern to the Chief of Naval Operations, William Leahy, about the need to determine the location of all German warships on September 27, 1938. He fully expected the worst possible consequences. [41]

Despite his fear of strong public criticism and prejudicial press treatment of any meddling in the overseas turmoil, Franklin Roosevelt decided to intervene in the Czech crisis. In a message to the leaders of Czechoslovakia, Germany, Great Britain and France, dated September 26, 1938, he urged that a peaceful solution to the threat of war must be found through negotiation. Hitler's reply, containing an elaborate discussion of the injustices of the Versailles settlement and the oppression of the Sudeten Germans by the Benes Government, gave no evidence of a desire to compromise. The terrible fate of the Sudetens, said the Führer, no longer admitted of a further postponement of the solution to the problem. Roosevelt responded on September 27, 1938 with a renewed plea to the German leader to solve the dispute without resort to force, and on that same day he asked Benito Mussolini to intercede with the Führer on behalf of world peace. The resultant Munich Conference, attended by France,

Great Britain, Italy, and Germany did bring about a peaceful solution. The Sudetenland was ceded to Germany, and leaders of the four powers resolved to resort only to consultation to remove possible sources of difference.[42]

What had been the motives behind Franklin Roosevelt's actions during the Munich crisis, and what were his expectations concerning the post-Munich future? During a discussion with Josephus Daniels on January 16, 1939, the President acknowledged that if he had been in Chamberlain's place he would have felt constrained to have made terms to prevent war for which Germany was fully prepared. Roosevelt remarked to Daniels that he could not understand how Britain and France could have permitted themselves to get in such a comparatively weak position. The Chief Executive was convinced, he told Daniels, of the great superiority of the totalitarian countries, and was most concerned with a threatened German air raid attack on London before the Munich meeting. Roosevelt was certain of a German victory over the prospective British and French allies in September, 1938, and this was probably a major consideration in his decision to delay the inevitable encounter. Perhaps these thoughts were in the President's mind when he told a reporter on September 30, 1938, "It was, as we all know, a very definite crisis and though there are many things which are called crisis which are not, this one was." [43]

There is also evidence that Franklin Roosevelt was trying to rally public opinion aganist Germany in expectation of its rejection of requests to pursue a diplomatic solution. The phraseology of the President's second letter to Adolf Hitler clearly places the onus for irresponsible action on the Führer should he have decided to invade Czechoslovakia. It was not a question of error or injustices of the past, Roosevelt had said, but of the fate of the world and the mutilation and death of millions of citizens. The use of force, he warned Hitler, would be unnecessary and unjustifiable. Cordell Hull, Bullitt, Wilson, and Kennedy had repeatedly told the President that they had strong doubts that Germany would accede to requests for a diplomatic solution unless it received all of its territorial demands. The President may have been attempting to clarify the historical record for an ultimate judgment against Germany.[44]

President Roosevelt saw no lasting value in any agreement of appeasement with Germany. He had told Sir Ronald Lindsay, the British Ambassador in Washington, on September 20, 1938 that in all probability Hitler would soon overrun all of Czechoslovakia, and German expansion toward Denmark, the Polish Corridor, and Rumania would follow this success. The western powers, said the President, would shortly find themselves at war with Germany and Italy.

A war in which, thought Roosevelt, the British, French, and Russian forces would suffer terrific casualties and never get through. He then offered the ultimate solution, telling Ambassador Lindsay to keep secret all aspects of his proposal for if it leaked out he would surely be impeached and the suggestion would be hopelessly prejudiced. The Chief Executive renewed his call for a naval blockade of Germany with the participation of the United States. He also mentioned the value of bombing to attain the submission of Germany. Lindsay noted that the President, several times in the conversation showed himself quite alive to the possibility that his nation might become directly involved in the European war although he doubted that American troops could be sent to fight unless England was invaded by Germany. This interview presents interesting insights into Roosevelt's prognosis of the future, which remained completely unaffected by the Munich accords.[45]

Diplomatic despatches relayed to the White House, in addition to the numerous letters sent privately to the President, were unanimously in agreement with the view that Germany's drive for European hegemony had only been momentarily appeased. Anthony Biddle told Roosevelt that he was personally inclined to feel that Hitler's voracious appetite had been whetted by his recent gains, and that there would be no general European pacification. Lincoln MacVeagh warned the President that the shadow of Germany was creeping toward the Balkans, and that fear had become the order of the day everywhere. Claude Bowers continued his reporting of German and Italian murdering and mangling of women and children in peaceful villages by bombing from the air. John Cudahy described the Führer as intent on building not a ramshackle road like Napoleon once constructed, but one which would not tumble. He believed that an almost power drunk and super confident Germany intended to have no unsympathetic or undigested portions along the way toward its eastward goal. Hitler's program, wrote Josephus Daniels, envisaged control of all territory from Berlin to Baghdad. Joseph Davies was of the opinion that the Führer had crossed the Rubicon and could not stop. Germany was guided by a will for conquest, he observed, not a will for peace. Dictators ride bicycles, he concluded, and are unable to stand still. George Messersmith, Assistant Secretary of State, was certain that Germany would continue to expand and he claimed that even the Monroe Doctrine was as much an irritant to the present German Government as was the maintenance of the Czechoslovak state. Breckinridge Long's report to the President of observations he made while on tour of South America tended to support Messersmith's claims during these immediate post-Munich months. In Brazil, Long told Roosevelt, the whole German population was part of an organized propaganda network in that nation. In Argentina too, said Long, Italy and Germany were sending agents to organize their nationality groups for political activities against the Argentine Government. The President would probably agree with observers inside Germany who reported that Hitler would base his reliance first and foremost on Germany's armed might.[46]

In a speech delivered on October 26, 1938, Franklin Roosevelt made clear his personal interpretation of the real meaning of Munich. Peace by fear, he began, could have no higher or more enduring quality than peace by the sword. The recurrent sanctification of sheer force does not mean peace, he admonished. Americans must be prepared, he challenged, to meet with success any application of force against the United States. It is evident that the President fully shared the views of his diplomats. The critical point of encounter was fast approaching. He wrote Herbert Pell saying that his British friends must begin to fish or cut bait, and that the dictator threat from Europe was a good deal closer to the United States and the American continent than it was before.[47]

One other incident in this year would strengthen Franklin Roosevelt's hatred and fear of the National Socialist movement in Germany. In November, 1938, the German Government began what George Messersmith described as the wholesale arrest, plundering, pillaging, and terrorizing of innocent and helpless Jewish men and women throughout Germany. The program was undertaken as a reprisal for the assassination of a German diplomat in Paris by a young Jewish boy. Felix Frankfurter had kept the President informed of the Jewish persecutions in Germany during the summer months of 1938. The events of November, however, seemed far more horrifying in their compass. Roosevelt told reporters, concerning those Jews who were visiting in the United States, that from the point of view of humanity the government did not have the right to put them on ships and send them back to Germany's concentration camps. The formal statement of condemnation came on November 15, 1938. Ambassador Wilson was to return to Washington, he said, and, adding to the State Department draft of this announcement, he expressed his personal feelings: "I myself could scarcely believe that such things could occur in a twentieth century civilization."[48]

The seriousness of the international situation did not permit the Chief Executive to join others in their expressions of sarcastic cynicism at Munich. The President's perspective was perhaps best expressed by Joseph Kennedy who warned Roosevelt that Great Britain and France were very much on the defensive and were not strong enough to meet the offensive challenge of the totalitarian countries. The United States, according to Ambassador Kennedy, must either become the center of the world or she would watch the gradual disintegration of the old oceanic defences of democracy and become the last really independent democratic state. Roosevelt's seriousness about the present overseas crisis is evident in a memorandum he sent to Steve Early in which he expressed his anger concerning a Gridiron skit in which it was alleged that he, the President, had referred to another house party on the Banks of the Rhine after the collapse of the British Empire. The Chief Executive quoted an English friend as saying that this kind of talk coming from high Amercan sources hurt the British Empire at a very critical time in its history. What the British needed, thought Roosevelt, was time to strengthen their defenses. He informed Prime Minister Chamberlain, through Arthur Murray, that Great Britain would have all the industrial resources of the American nation behind it in the event of hostilities in the future. There were to be no more Munich surrenders.[49]

In The Shadows of War

The future was further darkened by events in China. Reports of the Japanese advance in that country were most disturbing to the President. In December, 1937, Japan had offered peace terms to China which included the demands that China abandon its anti-Japanese and anti-Manchukuo activities, cooperate with Japan against communism, and indemnify the Japanese Government for damage suffered during the hostilities. Roosevelt considered these demands to be utterly impossible to accept, and instructed Cordell Hull on January 4, 1938 to so inform the Chinese Ambassador. Two days later the President received from Admiral Leahy a copy of a letter written by Admiral Yarnell on the situation in China which could only have strengthened his resolve to support Chiang Kai-shek. Yarnell claimed that the Japanese were trying to destroy China's military forces and industrial establishments in order to take over all Chinese institutions. They were, he continued, systematically looting and burning China's mills and factories in occupied areas, and exhibiting a ruthless cruelty toward the Chinese people. What was Japan's ultimate ambition? Yarnell stated that Japanese intentions were to completely eliminate all British, French, and American influence from that area. He suggested that the United States should stick with the western powers in opposing Japanese designs. We could not afford to take the attitude that America was pulling British chestnuts out of the fire, said Yarnell, for England stands to pull out as many for us as we will for her.[50]

The destruction of American property in China by Japanese troops also rankled the President. He was certain that Japan's army was out of the control of its civilian government. He suggested to Cordell Hull that it seemed justifiable to hold Japan accountable in dollars for those malicious acts of destruction. He was most angered by reports of Japanese atrocities in China. They were so terrible in their details, he told members of the cabinet, that they could not be read out loud. The President did tell of soldiers carrying off Chinese women and raping them without limit. Several weeks after this cabinet session, Roosevelt received more information concerning such Japanese activities. William Leahy forwarded to the Chief Executive a letter from Captain Riley McConnell of the Asiatic Fleet. Captain McConnell described the murder, rape, and arson that went on in the wake of the Japanese army. He added that the current militaristic psychology of the Japanese people was not a temporary aberration but a revered tradition of the people, and that they would never be fit to live in the family of nations unless and until they were defeated so thoroughly that they would be unable to salvage a diplomatic victory. Included in this material which Leahy had given the President was a letter written, as the Chief of Naval Operations noted, by one of his most reliable officers stationed in China. The letter contained the statement that Japan was apparently a nation of drunkards, especially their military and naval personnel, and that even when sober they seemed so intoxicated with their victories that when drunk they became perfectly insane in their overbearing conduct. The President and the Secretary of State were also apprised of indiscriminate Japanese bombing of crowded Chinese cities, and on June 11, 1938 a formal statement condemning such action was issued by the Administration.[51]

The long term objectives of the Japanese drive into China became clearer to Franklin Roosevelt in the waning months of 1938. In a radio speech of November 3, 1938 the Japanese Prime Minister Prince Konoye announced that the Tokyo Government intended to establish a new order in Asia including China and Manchuria, and that all nations would have to adjust themselves to these new conditions prevailing in East Asia. Colonel Sato, Chief of the Information Bureau of the Japanese War Office, in a radio talk that was translated and sent to the President, proclaimed that Japan must aim at higher and bigger things, and in doing so must not budge an inch no matter what circumstances should arise. Every Japanese citizen, said Sato, except the sick and disabled, must take up arms and serve on the continent. Japan had not come 50 percent of the way, he concluded. Admiral Yarnell was most explicit and blunt about the Japanese design in another letter that came to the attention of the President. Yarnell claimed that the Minister of War was in actual control of Japan's foreign policy. The Japanese, said Yarnell, were presently engaged in the most gigantic land grabbing scheme in the world's history. China was to be reduced to the status of Manchuria. All American and European interests were to be eliminated from East Asia. Oil, iron ore, rubber and wool requirements would dictate Japan's absorption of the Philippines, Netherlands, Indies, and any other lands containing the necessary items. These were the specific goals of Japan, Yarnell claimed, and if achieved, her domination of the Far East would become an accomplished fact.[52]

These disturbing revelations assumed an even greater importance in the mind of the President when he was informed of the continued collaboration by members of the Berlin-Rome-Tokyo Axis. Joseph Grew reported that the Axis union was directed primarily against the democracies. He believed that Munich had impressed many nations with the preponderant strength of the fascist powers, and he noted that Japan seemed anxious to form a solid bloc with those nations whose will was uncontested at the appeasement conference, Germany and Italy. The authoritarian regimes, said Grew, had drawn closer together. This was not a favorable portent, in Roosevelt's opinion, of the future course of events.[53]

The information coming into the White House during the post-Munich months left no doubt in Franklin Roosevelt's mind that the eventual confrontation with the fascist bloc nations had simply been postponed. His appraisal of the critical international situation is revealed in the Annual Message to Congress on January 4, 1939. Yes, he acknowledged, a war had been avoided, but world peace had not been assured. All about us, said Roosevelt, were threats of aggression, both military and economic. In a phrase which indicated that the President anticipated the fascist program of territorial conquest to continue, he pledged all American aid short of war to the victims of aggression. In a request for additional appropriations for national defense which followed this speech, the Chief Executive warned that the United States could not be guaranteed a long period of time free from attack. The nation must be strong enough to ward off a sudden invasion. These words sound exceptionally grave, and they seem to reveal his personal interpretation of the succession of events in Europe and Asia and their consequences. The alarming tone of the speeches, and the inference that the United States was to play a more active role in world affairs, prompted a reporter to ask for a specific outline of the definite, hard, and fast foreign policy which the Administration was about to pursue. The President's response was politically tactful and concealing. No human being, he said, could define foreign policy except a columnist. Franklin Roosevelt would give the unmistakable impression in the days that were to come, however, of his resolve never to permit a fascist consolidation of power, no matter what means might be necessary to that end.[54]

The President was forced to become more reticent on this issue than he desired when an airplane crashed in California, killing an official of the French Air Ministry who was on board. The sale of planes to France was acknowledged on January 27, 1939 by the White House and this aroused the suspicions of those fearful of United States involvement overseas. Members of the Senate Military Affairs Committee were given an explanation of this transaction, and in the discussion Roosevelt was alleged to have instructed the Senators that, in his opinion, the frontier of America rested on the Rhine. During a press conference on February 3, 1939 he described the allegation as pure bunk, b-u-n-k, and reaffirmed his desire for no entangling alliances. He was unable to conceal his true convictions, as is proven by comments made to newsmen two weeks later. He again termed the accusation a deliberate lie, but asserted that the independence of Finland, Sweden, Norway, Denmark, Holland, Belgium, Portugal, Switzerland, Greece, Egypt, Turkey, and Persia served as protection for the democracies of the American hemisphere. He predicted that just as Austria had been absorbed, so too would Czechoslovakia, Hungary, Yugoslavia, Rumania, and Bulgaria. The frontier on the Rhine, in Roosevelt's opinion, seemed to be about to crumble.[55]

The President's attention during these early months of 1939 was directed toward Germany. The letters and memoranda coming before the Chief Executive had not been reassuring concerning the nation's future foreign policy. Prentice Gilbert, the Chargé in Berlin, reported that while the popular will of the Germans was against war, the Führer could embark on sudden and unforeseeable actions. He did not think that Hitler could be bluffed by a display of force out of any position that he might choose to take. Less than a week later, Gilbert warned of apprehension prevalent in certain states that some German military move to the west was imminent, although he personally doubted the validity of this information. Herschel Johnson, however, wrote from London that Edouard Benes was certain that war was inevitable and that Czechoslovakia was immediately threatened. The Germans, Benes had said, wanted to live down the 1918 military defeat; it was almost a crusade to them. He predicted that unless there was resistance to the dictators, France and Great Britain would go the way of Czechoslovakia. Chargé Johnson also told of reports among British diplomats that Germany was bound to move in February, 1938. An invasion of Holland, or an air attack on England was thought probable. One despatch from the British Foreign Office was quoted by Johnson. He wrote that Hitler's mental condition, his insensate rage against Great Britain, and his megolomania were consistent with the execution of a desperate coup against the western powers. A later cable from Prentice Gilbert predicted that Germany would try to form an autarchic bloc of all the states lying to the east and southeast down to and including Turkey over the next four years, and that economic association by these nations with Germany would be a prelude to a new political hegemony.[56]

The import of these predictive analyses was elaborated by Franklin Roosevelt. He told one correspondent that it was evident to him that the Germans were pushing their form of government all over the world. In a cabinet session held in January, 1939, he asserted that Germany's aim in controlling continental Europe was to dictate economic terms, and thereafter political terms, to the countries of South America which were dependent on these areas for sale of their exports. Hitler, he believed, could thereby strike a serious blow at the United States without even the thought of landing a soldier on our shores. The President told Harold Ickes on February 6, 1939 that he was concerned over prospects of a German attack on Holland and Switzerland in the near future. John Cudahy told Roosevelt that imminent action by the dictators didn't seem that probable because the Chief Executive's speeches had served notice on the dictators to stop, look, and listen. Ambassador Cudahy was wrong in his expectations. The remnants of Czechoslovakia were occupied by German troops on March 15, 1939, and the city of Memel was ceded to Germany by Lithuania on March 22, 1939. The President, recalled one cabinet member, seemed to be getting madder and madder.[57]

What did the latest German thrust portend? William Bullitt believed that henceforth in Europe diplomatic action would be almost impossible. Hitler, he said, had proven sevenfold that he had been an unscrupulous liar. Next year, he warned the President, you will wish you had an American army of two million men ready for action. Hitler, asserted Joseph Davies, definitely wanted war. Herbert Pell also thought that war seemed inevitable. The German machine, he informed Roosevelt, could not change its direction. Adolph Berle, the Assistant Secretary of State, recalled that no one had any illusions that the German Napoleonic machine would not extend itself almost indefinitely. Franklin Roosevelt shared this opinion. He considered the formal severance of diplomatic ties with Germany, but apparently backed down because of pressure from the State Department. An official condemnation of Germany's action in Czechoslovakia came on March 17, 1939, calling it an act of wanton lawlessness and arbitrary force. Roosevelt, in a letter to Edouard Benes, expressed his sympathies for the Czechoslovak people and the unfortunate circumstances in which for the time being they found themselves. The President's fears as to where events were leading were most sharply expressed during a press conference on March 31, 1939. The hope of last September, he began, that German policy was limited to bringing contiguous German people into the Reich has been dissipated by the events of the last few weeks. There appeared to be, said Roosevelt, no apparent limit to Germany's aims today. German domination, he exclaimed, could be expected to extend not only to the small nations of Europe, but to other continents. He shared the general fear that the German nation was attempting to attain world dominance.[58]

The ease with which Germany had accomplished its program of territorial expansion persuaded Mussolini to embark upon more aggressive policies. The despatches from Rome intimated that an armed initiative by Italy might be impending. William Phillips described the tone of anti-French polemics of Mussolini as being exceptionally violent. Some observers, said the Ambassador, were convinced that Mussolini was determined to get something for Italy from the present situation, perhaps French Tunisia. In a letter to the President on January 20, 1939, Phillips regretted to have to report that he had become less and less confident of the friendly assurances and words of the Italian Government, and that he was sure the Italians, who were presently spitting on the French in their pronouncements, were after something with the full support of their Axis partner, Germany.[59]

During the months of February and March, 1939, Ambassador Phillips expressed the opinion that although the Italian people were not anxious to become involved in a war, Mussolini might decide that something dramatic was necessary to strengthen his government. The mobilization of troops was being carried forth, said Phillips, to prepare for any eventuality. While there seemed to be some easing of the Italian-French antagonism in North Africa, the Ambassador observed that the Duce did not intend to remain a prisoner in the Mediterranean. Mussolini had also affirmed his unwavering support of Germany's aims in Central Europe, said Phillips, and had become belligerent and uncompromising after Hitler's uncontested success in Czechoslovakia.[60]

The Italian invasion of Albania on April 7, 1939 reaffirmed for the President the fact that Mussolini had cast his lot with the aggressors. The recent absorption of Czechoslovakia and this action by Italy compelled the Chief Executive to bluntly ask of the German and Italian leaders on April 14, 1939 if they were willing to pledge not to invade Finland, Estonia, Latvia, Lithuania, Sweden, Norway, Denmark, the Netherlands, Belgium, Great Britain, Ireland, France, Portugal, Spain, Switzerland, Liechtenstein, Luxemburg, Poland, Hungary, Rumania, Yugoslavia, Russia, Bulgaria, Greece, Turkey, Iraq, the Arabias, Syria, Palestine, Egypt, and Iran. Roosevelt fully realized, as William Bullitt had told him, that words no matter how wise would have small effect on Hitler and Mussolini. The President, according to Hull, wanted to place Hitler and Mussolini before the bar of world opinion to show to all that they were planners of the conquest of Europe. Roosevelt told Henry Morgenthau that once they had rejected this request sanctions would be imposed by the united forces of peace. In a speech on that same day, he directed a second question to the leaders of the two nations, phrased in a tone of accusatory sarcasm: "Do we really have to assume," he asked, "that nations can find no better methods of realizing their destinies than those which were used by the Huns and Vandals fifteen hundred years ago?" [61]

The most elaborate development of Franklin Roosevelt's views of the present crisis situation came during a press conference held on April 20, 1939. There were two nations, he charged, which had taken away the independence of three countries in the last four years. The Christian country of Ethiopia, whose Church was founded by St. Mark fourteen years before St. Peter went to Rome; Czechoslovakia, composed almost wholly of non-German people; and Albania — all have disappeared, said Roosevelt. Is it a pipe dream, he asked, to think that possibly these acts of aggression were but a prelude to an attempt to construct a world empire? Control of Europe by Germany, he reasoned, would mean that the fascist powers could dictate whatever they wished to the countries of South America which were dependent on their exports for an economic livelihood. Economic power would be translated into political power, followed by eventual military occupation of these nations of the American hemisphere, thought the President. Thereafter, he told members of the press, an air invasion of the United States was a very real possibility. He admitted that it all sounded irrational, fantastic, and like a pipe dream. Yet, he cautioned, who would have ever believed that in six years two nations could come so close to dominating Europe. It was all terribly hypothetical, he concluded, but it was time to consider it from the hypothetical point of view. [62]

The response of Adolf Hitler and Benito Mussolini to Roosevelt's message marked a further delineation of the coming war alliance. William Phillips described the Italian reaction as an outburst of rage and vituperation against the United States. The Führer's reply came on April 28, 1939. Hitler discussed in detail the injustices suffered by Germany because of the Versailles Treaty, and the legitimacy of his course of action, as dictated by Providence, to deliver his people from their frightful misery. Roosevelt's analysis of the effect of his challenge was that Hitler and Mussolini had closed the door in his face. The dictators' intentions were clear. Their military build-up foreshadowed offensive action. He charged that Germany's 1,800,000 men under arms and Italy's 1,200,000 troops were fully prepared for any initiative. He noted with alarm that German armed forces on the Dutch and Polish borders had been increased. [63]

The despatches and letters which were sent to Franklin Roosevelt during the critical summer months of 1939 contained incisive predictions of events which would soon transpire. Immediately after the absorption of Czechoslovakia, Chargé Raymond Geist in Berlin asserted that the Führer would pursue his program of expansion in Europe even though it would mean an eventual showdown with England. The resentment expressed by Germany against Great Britain's interference and haughtiness was best summarized by a National Socialist deputy in the Reichstag. Geist quoted Werner Daitz as saying that the British thought that God spoke English. America too, added Daitz, was acting like an immature child trying to instruct its mother! He also noted that the German press campaign against Poland resembled those which preceded the annexation of Austria, the Sudetenland, and the remnants of Czechoslovakia. The Chargé reported in April, 1939, that unusual military preparations were underway in Germany, and that there was developing an intensive war spirit directed toward Great Britain. Geist relayed information received from the Chief of the German General Staff that the Army would fully support whatever action might be necessary to secure Germany's aims and that it was entirely subordinate to the wishes of Hitler.[64]

In the months of May and June, 1939, the President received more precise analyses of Germany's probable intentions. John Wheeler-Bennett wrote to Roosevelt on May 3, 1939, telling him that former German Chancellor Heinrich Bruning had alerted him to the fact that Hitler had made up his mind to risk a general war for the sake of crushing Poland, and that his decision was unalterable. Nigel Law, an English acquaintance of the President, thought that the nations of Hungary, Yugoslavia, Bulgaria, Greece, and Rumania would all be tied to the German politico-economic steam roller. The President shared Law's pessimism, as did other diplomatic observers. Geist from Berlin warned ominously that Hitler was considering a sudden military movement against Poland. Alexander Kirk, recently appointed Chargé in Germany, agreed with this prediction but expected no action until September, 1939. He did admit, however, that the German Army was prepared to undertake an offensive against Poland at any moment. Alleged provocative acts by Poland were receiving heavy emphasis in the German press, said Kirk, and there was increasing danger of a major crisis through the development of incidents on either side. A note of caution and confusion was struck by Franklin Gunther in a letter to the President from Bucharest, Rumania. He told Roosevelt not to be certain of any definite move by Germany because Hitler was a neurotic whose brain, like Mussolini's, could not stand up to the strain of recent events. He believed that an unbalanced and disastrous decision should be expected.[65]

There was a general consensus, most succinctly phrased by Alexander Kirk, that the present situation could not endure many months longer. The Chargé's reports from Berlin throughout August, 1939 accurately described the hardening of Germany's resolve to liquidate the Polish problem. Demands for the return of Danzig to the Reich, said Kirk, had been affirmed categorically with emphasis and no thought of compromise. The Ambassadors to Germany from Poland and Great Britain, he reported, were of the opinion that Hitler had reached a point where he could not help himself even if he wished to solve the Polish-German dispute amicably. There were too many influences surrounding the Führer pressing for military action. The German people, said the Chargé, would march in blind obedience. Kirk wrote on August 21, 1939 that troop concentrations had been noted by foreign military observers in Germany, and that they were of such magnitude as to enable an offensive against Poland in three to five days. Poland, he predicted, was to be shattered. Franklin Roosevelt's fears of an imminent German offensive against Poland did not overshadow his much greater concern for what might follow such action. In a memorandum to Hull and Welles, he summarized what he personally termed as a very, very interesting report which had been sent to him by Harold Laski on August 8, 1939 from England. Laski, wrote Roosevelt, described Germany's basic aim as being the creation of a world empire of unassailable strength, hopefully to be accomplished without a world war. The despatches of these late days in August seemed to reveal that a world war would not stand in the way of the attempted achievement of this goal.[66]

The threat emanating from Germany, as conceived by Franklin Roosevelt, was augmented by incoming correspondence on the subject of Italian-German relations. The President had admonished the Italian Ambassador, Prince Colonna, on March 19, 1939 that Hitler intended to cast Italy aside once German ambitions had been fulfilled, and that Italy's real interests could be best served by cooperating with the western democracies. Reliable reports from Rome and Berlin indicated that Roosevelt's advice had not been heeded. In May, 1939 Virginia Gaydo boasted of the complete and unequivocal character of German and Italian unity. He pledged that the two nations would cooperate militarily in any struggle according to an organized plan. The two nations' air forces, armies, and navies, continued Gayda, would work in unison to secure a harmonious division of interests and spheres. There could be no peace, he said, until Italy and Germany have achieved sweeping worldwide territorial revisions in order to place them on a basis of economic parity with the wealthy powers. The signing of a German-Italian Military and Political Agreement on May 22, 1939 seemed to prove the substance of the above cited reports. Alexander Kirk quoted German editorials which described the created armored block of 150,000,000 men as being the decisive factor in European politics. Kirk acknowledged that some thought the arrangement with Italy might restrain the Führer from taking precipitous action. Others, he wrote, were certain that the alliance was complete, unconditional, and a preparatory action for war. Franklin Roosevelt, reading these despatches, agreed with the more pessimistic appraisals. He told William Phillips on June 7, 1939 that while he hoped Mussolini would be definitely against war, he was concerned about the size of the combined fascist armed forces. The President thought that both dictators shared the belief that their methods were succeeding. The alignment with Germany could not have been reassuring to the President.[67]

The perspective from the White House, darkened by prospects of armed action by members of the Axis alliance, was not appreciably improved by reports of a gradually stiffening will to resist manifested by the political leaders of Great Britain and France. Their weaknesses were so gravely presented to the President that the future must have appeared in very bleak outlines. Harold Laski, whose letters were forwarded to Roosevelt by Felix Frankfurter, had stated in January, 1939 that Prime Minister Neville Chamberlain's appeasement policies were losing ground. Initial reports coming out of London were more in line with the thinking of William Bullitt, however, who described the British as always willing to sacrifice the interests of other peoples. He predicted to Roosevelt that he, the President, would soon have to ask Chamberlain quietly not to behave like a S.O.B. Herbert Pell also believed that the Germans were convinced of their ability to bluff Britain on any issue, and ultimately to overwhelm, terrify, and starve both England and France. Ambassador Joseph Kennedy and Chargé Johnson were continually describing the British Prime Minister as hopeful of doing business with Hitler, certain that there would be no war, and eager to achieve a peaceful settlement with Germany. The President was moved to angrily write Roger Merriman that he hoped this attitude of the British that "We who are about to die, salute thee," would stop. Roosevelt sarcastically quoted Lord Lothian, British Ambassador to the United States, as saying that Hitler could be dealt with as a semi-reasonable human being. The President asserted that the British, who had for a thousand years been the guardians of Anglo-Saxon civilization, were now dropping the scepter, or the sword, or something like that from their palsied fingers. This defeatism, said the Chief Executive, made him mad clear through. He told Lothian that if that was the British attitude, then they weren't worth saving anyway. What the British need today, he concluded in the letter to Merriman, was a good stiff grog to induce some self-confidence. "In such an event they will have a lot more support from their American cousins — don't you think so?" asked the President.[68]

The month of March, 1939 brought a significant change in the direction of British foreign policy. The German acquisition of the remainder of Czechoslovakia prompted the toughening stance of Great Britain in negotiations with Germany. The British Foreign Secretary, Lord Halifax, was reportedly ready to break with Chamberlain over any continuance of the appeasement approach to Hitler. The Prime Minister himself, however, seemed to have swung to the war point of view. Ambassador Kennedy reported on March 24, 1939 that both Halifax and Chamberlain were ready to draw a line beyond which Germany must not transgress. The British, said the Ambassador, were no longer afraid to fight. A guarantee of Poland's boundaries in the event of a German attack was issued by the British Government on March 31, 1939, followed by a similar pledge to Greece and Rumania on April 13, 1939. In a note to Roosevelt, the British Government explained that Germany's recent action in Czechoslovakia marked the first departure from the Nazi racial theory and that there was little reason to suppose that it was not Germany's intention to extend its control over other countries in Europe. The situation was one of grave potential menace. In the words of William Bullitt, the British seemed to be awake at last.[69]

During the summer months of 1939 there was indisputable evidence that Great Britain fully intended to fight. Chamberlain was quoted as saying in April, 1939 that his own hopes that Hitler might hold back may have constituted wishful thinking. The Prime Minister was also very distrustful of Mussolini, according to Joseph Kennedy. Halifax told Roosevelt on April 5, 1939 that the British were determined to resist Germany. Ambassador Kennedy described the English press in May as uniformly agreeing that if Hitler goes to war over Danzig, a general conflagration would follow. It seemed that the British Prime Minister was fully prepared to accept the inevitable even though, reported Kennedy, he knew the attack would come just in time to spoil his vacation. The Ambassador noted at the end of June, 1939 that nation's fast crystallizing determination to resist every form of pressure for appeasement. The visit of King George VI and Queen Elizabeth to the United States during this month seemed to symbolize the closer relationship now being constructed between the two nations. The President was pleased with the change which had taken place in British foreign policy. He told William White that both the King and Queen had a real understanding of foreign affairs. It appeared to Roosevelt that, as Arthur Murray had said, the British Government was finally facing facts.[70]

Chamberlain's determination to challenge Germany's program of expansion did not waiver in the critical days before the invasion of Poland. No other policy except one of firmness towards Germany will be considered, wrote Ambassador Kennedy in July, 1939. Chamberlain, he said, would carry out his pledge to Poland. Herschel Johnson foresaw no overtures of appeasement by Britain. Johnson depicted the British public on August 9, 1939 as psychologically ready for war if one was to come in the days ahead.[71]

There was much disconcerting information pertaining to the international situation coming into the White House which made the belatedly heroic stiffening of Great Britain seem more an omen of difficult times than a prelude to the final halt of Germany's revisionist designs. William Bullitt's appraisal of the military weakness of France did not undergo any change. The analyses of the French Army and Air Force which had been sent to Roosevelt during the Munich crisis were applicable in 1939. In March, Bullitt bluntly warned that both Britain and France could go down to defeat unless aided by the United States in their rearmament programs. If we were to be drawn in, he concluded, as many men as possible would have to be sent to France. Ambassador Kennedy was equally pessimistic in his estimate of Britain's capacity to resist the Axis nations. He predicted that both the British and French would be forced to yield strategic positions that were vital to the security of the United States. Moreover, he cautioned Roosevelt, in the bitterness of their defeat, the manpower of Great Britain and France might be placed at the disposal of the authoritarian powers for action against America. Britain's collapse, which Kennedy fully expected, would mean a tremendous and decisive alteration in the balance of world forces at a grave disadvantage to the United States in the opinion of the Ambassador. These reports undoubtedly made the President especially anxious to help prospective allies in their preparations for war, but the situation was discouraging. The Senate Foreign Relations Committee in July, 1939 had deferred until the next Congressional session any action concerning the neutrality law despite the President's strong desire for revision of the mandatory embargo provisions of the statute. There could be no improvement in the decidedly weak condition in which the British and French found themselves. One other consequence of the lack of Congressional initiative in this area was also noted by the President. Hitler and Mussolini, he observed, had been given a definite stimulus to continue aggression.[72]

The most disquieting trend of events was to occur in the development of Soviet foreign policy in the crucial months before the war. Russia had always been considered by Franklin Roosevelt to be the bulwark of the future coalition against the Rome-Berlin-Tokyo Axis.

The role that Russia had played in international affairs had been greeted with approval by diplomats who were especially prolific in their correspondence with the President. Claude Bowers had applauded communist activities in Spain on behalf of the Republican forces. William Dodd was consistently looking to the Soviet Union as the most important member of any alliance partnership directed against the fascist powers. William Bullitt initially, and Joseph Davies continuously, had praised the democratic and peaceful intentions of the Soviet leadership, as well as the potential strength of Russia in any coming encounter. Recent events had not dispelled these previous assumptions.

The despatches that were forwarded to the White House during the Munich crisis reaffirmed the mistaken image of the Soviet Union as the staunch supporter of Czechoslovakia whose promise to aid that nation had been rendered meaningless by the appeasement approach of France and Great Britain. Criticism by Russian officials of Chamberlain and Daladier's conduct was not different than that given by American diplomats and the President. The vacillating policies of the two western nations received considerable emphasis in the Soviet press. Alexander Kirk, the Chargé in Moscow, sent translations of articles which were extremely critical of the negotiations with Germany by Great Britain and France. Accusations that Czechoslovakia was about to be betrayed; appeals for a halt to the aggressive ambitions of Germany; promises that Russia would carry out its international agreements; and exclamatory statements about the responsibility of the democracies for world peace were constantly given deliberate accentuation in Soviet newspapers.[73]

The incisive analyses offered by the Chargé were apparently never noticed by the President. Kirk reported on several occasions that self-interest and ideological motivation would dictate Russia's abstinence from the conflict which it in fact wished to provoke. There is no indication in Kirk's despatches that the Soviet Union was definitely planning to intervene on behalf of Czechoslovakia. He particularly emphasized the considerations which made such intervention appear highly unlikely. Kirk noted that geographic factors would make difficult the use of ground forces; that Stalin would be bound to act only if France fulfilled its treaty commitments; and that the Soviet leadership would not be prone to embark on any military venture that threatened the Russain defences.[74]

The editorial comment from Moscow on the Munich agreement was forwarded to the White House for the President. The opinions expressed herein seem to have been shared by Franklin Roosevelt. Statements such as those reaffirming that new demands of the aggressors would soon be advanced; that Munich was a capitulation, betrayal, and shameful act; that the fascist incendiaries of war had been given new impetus; and that France and Britain would pay for their cowardice were not strongly disputed by the Chief Executive. The Soviet Union remained for Roosevelt the most valued prospective ally.[75]

The intensifying crisis situation which was developing throughout 1939 reaffirmed the President's desire to bring the Soviet Union into a coalition with Great Britain and France. He was encouraged by such estimates as those of Anthony Biddle who wrote in April that Russia was effectively halting Japan in the Far East and would help ease the plight of Great Britain and France in the Mediterranean and Asia. Reports of Soviet aid to China were gratifying to Roosevelt. Colonel Joseph Fegan, a Marine Corps officer stationed in Shanghai told the President that Russian planes, pilots, gasoline, and small military arms were flowing into China. The Chief Executive expressed his pleasure to Fegan concerning the high number of casualties suffered by Japanese troops in their struggle with Soviet armed forces. The President's wife Eleanor asked that he read an article confirming that communists had come nearer to bringing equality and justice for the common working class in twenty years than the Tsar's Christianity had in centuries. The author of the article also noted that the Soviet Union had a more consistent peace record than any other nation. The consequences of such miscellaneous reports, as well as reflections on the fascist threat, encouraged continued attempts to entice the Stalin regime. Efforts by the Roosevelt Administration to aid the Russian shipbuilding program continued, but with no practical results. American manufacturers were not eager to undertake such a project, and some government officials feared that the press might discover this planned program of aid to Russia. The President undertook a more direct course of action, however, during the summer months of 1939 to promote the coalition which he thought was necessary to halt the fascist challenge: the union of Great Britain, France, and the Soviet Union.[76]

During the spring and summer months of 1939, British and French delegations proceeded to Moscow to discuss the terms upon which the Soviet Union would be willing to join an alliance against the fascist powers. Information received by the President indicated that the negotiations would be prolonged and difficult. Ambassador Joseph Kennedy's despatches in March, 1939 gave indication of the fact that Great Britain did not expect the Soviet Union to be of great potential value to the democratic alliance. Industrially, economically, and militarily, wrote Kennedy, the British felt that Russia was weak, and at most that it might send some ammunition to Poland in the event of trouble. In the months that followed, more disturbing reports seemed to foreshadow a most disquieting turn of events. Hitler and Stalin appeared ready to negotiate an alliance which would make war inevitable.[77]

Maxim Litvinov, considered to be a most vocal exponent of collective security arrangements against Germany and Japan, was replaced as Soviet Foreign Minister by Vyacheslav Molotov on May 3, 1939. Kennedy, reflecting on this event, said that the British were not sure whether Russian foreign policy would change with the resignation of Litvinov. Evidence that Litvinov's removal was a portent of closer Russian ties with Germany was soon noted by diplomats. The despatches of Consular Stuart Grummon, stationed at the American Embassy in Moscow, kept Franklin Roosevelt appraised of the negotiations. He reported on May 17, 1939 that the German Ambassador to Russia, Friedrich Schulenburg, had been called to Berlin for consultation with Ribbentrop. One week later, Grummon stated that the Soviet authorities were becoming very reluctant to sign any agreement with England and France because of their fears that the western nations might conclude a separate peace with Germany leaving the Soviet Union alone to fight a war in eastern Europe. Molotov's speech of May 31, 1939, in which he asserted that a German-Russian political arrangement was not out of the question, was viewed by Grummon as an admission that Stalin would not commit his nation to any anti-German coalition. In July, Consular Grummon relayed information given to him by members of the German Embassy in Moscow. They were now certain, he said, that a British-French-Russian pact would not be signed. He noted that Soviet diplomats had told their German colleagues that they were reluctant to join the western alliance. President Roosevelt decided at this critical moment to make a secret attempt to persuade Stalin to cast his lot with democratic allies.[78]

Franklin Roosevelt directed Under Secretary of State Sumner Welles on August 4, 1939 to urgently request of Ambassador Laurence Steinhardt in Moscow that he intercede with Soviet authorities on behalf of Great Britain and France with a special message from the Chief Executive. Welles' letter to Steinhardt went secretly through William Bullitt's Embassy in Paris. Bullitt was instructed to detail an officer for a special courier trip to Moscow, and was told to make no report on it other than the account for travel. The President's message contained the warning that an Axis victory would materially and immediately effect the position of both the United States and Russia, but especially that of the latter country. He expressed his belief that an agreement signed by British, French, and Soviet representatives would have a decidedly stabilizing effect in the interest of world peace, in the maintenance of which, of course, the United States, as well as the Soviet Union, had a fundamental interest. The President had become a most important fourth party in these critical negotiations at Moscow. Although the message did contain the qualification that the Chief Executive was making no suggestion, much less any official indication, of any desire on the part of the United States Government, there is implicitly suggested the avowed intention of the Roosevelt Administration to aid such a coalition and specifically the Soviet Union for the purpose of promoting world peace. Once again, however, the President was to receive a lesson in Realpolitik. Grummon reported on August 6, 1939 that Molotov and the German Ambassador Schulenburg had met with a view to normalizing relations between their countries. The results of this discussion seemed evident when Molotov replied to Roosevelt's proposal. He pointed out that general declarations were not the aim of the present negotiations with Great Britain and France, and that what must be forthcoming were specific obligations of mutual assistance in case of attack. The outcome of the negotiations, said Molotov, depends on others as well as the Soviet Union. The Soviet Union and Germany formally signed a Non-Aggression Pact one week later which would soon make possible the German and Russian invasions of Poland. Franklin Roosevelt succinctly commented to Arthur Murray that this event would make things infinitely more difficult for Great Britain and France, and added, "What a pure unadulterated devil Hitler is." [79]

The treaty commitments adopted by Germany and Russia coincided with a torrent of events which preceded the beginning of the European holocaust. Franklin Roosevelt anticipated war in early September, 1939. The diplomatic reports from Berlin, Rome, Moscow, and Paris throughout these summer months clearly revealed that the approaching climax could not be avoided. In the final days of August, 1939, President Roosevelt anxiously sought to make the historical record precise as to where the responsibility and onus for war was to reside. In messages to Adolf Hitler, King Victor Emmanuel of Italy, and President Ignacy Moscicki of Poland issued on August 24, 1939, the President urged that a peaceful solution to the present difficulties existing between Poland and Germany must be found. He admonished Hitler with the words that the United States Government opposed policies of military conquest and domination as well as the assumed right of any ruler to plunge countless millions of people into war. The Chief Executive again asked Italy to help avert the outbreak of war, and requested that Moscicki too search for a means to peace. The next day a second letter was sent to the Führer which served to precisely identify that nation which Roosevelt deemed responsible for the coming war. The President pointed out that Poland was not the country proffering claims and demanding concessions, and asked that the Government of the German Reich agree to the pacific means of settlement already accepted by the Government of Poland. Cordell Hull recalled that neither he nor Roosevelt expected these messages to have any effect on deterring Germany from aggression. In the words of the President, as recounted by Adolph Berle, this was an attempt to put the bee on Germany which nobody had done in 1914. The historical record had been graphically written by Franklin Roosevelt.[80]

The true slant of the Chief Executive's mind on the possibility of a negotiated settlement during these days of August is most clearly revealed in a discussion between the President and the British Ambassador, Lord Lothian. Reporting to Halifax on the substance of this interview on August 31, 1939, Lothian began by saying that there was nothing at all neutral about the President's attitude towards the conflict between the dictatorships and the democracies. Roosevelt, according to Lothian, had expressed the view that the most serious danger from the standpoint of American public opinion would be if it formed the conclusion that Hitler was entangling the British Government in negotiations leading to pressure on Poland by England and France to abandon vital interests. The Chief Executive was clearly warning his British colleague that American support would be lost if a second Munich betrayal took place. In trying to further stiffen the British in their resolve to oppose German demands, Roosevelt reasoned with Lothian that the British nation, if embroiled with Germany, would probably have no concurrent conflict with Japan. The President thought that the Russo-German agreement would lead to a fundamental realignment of Japanese foreign policy in the direction of coming to terms with China, Great Britain, and the United States. If not, said Roosevelt, the United States would apply pressure on Japan to halt its aggressiveness in the Far East by sending the American fleet to Hawaii and aircraft carriers and bombers to the Aleutian Islands. The President's logic was pointedly persuasive, and may have been purposefully presented at this crucial moment to make less likely a now highly unlikely second British and French capitulation to Adolf Hitler.[81]

Whatever doubts that Franklin Roosevelt might have entertained about the determination of Great Britain and France to confront the German challenge were removed in the first three days of September 1939. German troops invaded Poland on September 1, and two days later the British and French Governments formally declared war on Germany. Cordell Hull wrote vividly that during these tragic days Europe's lights had gone out. The President concurred and could possibly have added in the months ahead that the lights had dimmed considerably concerning the likelihood of a fascist defeat without the involvement of the United States in the overseas turmoil.[82]

The Prospective Future

Franklin Roosevelt's perspective of the events unfolding in the waning months of 1939 was a decidedly pessimistic one. The awesome preponderant military power of Germany, which had been clearly described in innumerable despatches, had become the essential force behind an activated drive for continental dominance on the part of this revisionist power. The President, based upon his own ideological convictions, his detestation of the National Socialist experiment in Germany, and his fear of the ultimate ambitions of Adolf Hitler, could not remain dispassionately objective concerning the new order emerging in Europe. There was also the very real concern that in the foreseeable future German ambitions and fascist revisionist demands would confront a weak and frail democratic alliance. This would insure the probable success of what appeared to Roosevelt to be an associative effort by Germany, Italy, and Japan to restructure the world balance of power. His primary objective during the two years of American abstinence from the European conflict will be to awaken an isolationist public to the precarious situation which would be created if Great Britain and France should be defeated by the combined forces of fascism. Did he foresee an American commitment to war as a necessary requirement in the task of preventing the dominance of the fascist bloc nations? Franklin Roosevelt's perspective would dictate this inescapable conclusion.

Politically astute, the Chief Executive did not exclaim in shrill alarm what he privately had accepted with much foreboding anxiety. He would endeavor to persuade his countrymen to accept the forthcoming commitment to war by patiently, yet forcefully, explaining to them the necessary requirements and dangers of the moment. In a fireside chat on September 3, 1939, the approach to be pursued by the President in this task may already be discerned. He began his remarks by saying that all people passionately desired detachment. He added, however, that every word coming through the air, every ship sailing the sea, and every battle being fought affected the American future. Roosevelt emphasized the need for defensive preparedness, and asserted that the immediate aim must be to keep war from coming to the Americas. The more revealing phrases uttered by the President were perhaps those stressing his belief that even a neutral should not be asked to close his mind or his consciousness. A neutral must take account of facts. Facts, assumptions, and ideological convictions, as accepted by Franklin Roosevelt, would necessitate the involvement of the United States in the ensuing struggle.[83]

The fact of German military superiority became clearly evident as Poland was smashed in less than three weeks. The President's criticism of the bombing of Polish towns and villages was a reflection of his personal disgust with this most recent act of aggression. The forces of the Soviet Union also invaded Poland two weeks later, and the two alliance partners soon signed a formal agreement providing for a ten year mutual assistance pact and the partition of Poland. Josephus Daniels had voiced praise for the Chief Executive's appeals on behalf of peace, but had warned that Hitler and the other dictators would not be deterred by words. They believe, said Daniels, that they have enough force to dominate the world and nothing can stop them. He could only express the hope in this letter to Roosevelt that Hitler's dreams of world domination, like those of Napoleon and the Kaiser, would be thwarted in the future. Adolph Berle, however, was more pessimistic in a memorandum that he wrote to the President. Berle predicted that the entire Danube Valley down to the Black Sea would fall automatically to Germany, and that the German-Russian domination from the Rhine to the Pacific would remain unchallenged. He thought that the Soviet Union and Japan would soon sign a non-aggression pact and divide China between them. Berle suggested that the wisest course of action would be for the United States to intensify efforts up to the limit to strengthen the countries of South America.[84]

Berle's pessimism was shared by other diplomatic observers. William Bullitt, writing from the American Embassy in Paris, brought no encouraging information to Franklin Roosevelt. He foresaw the possibility that Germany might quickly defeat both France and Great Britain by means of a full air force attack including gas and bacteria. The Ambassador was certain that Hitler's forces would one day have to be fought in the Americas. If Hitler should win, he emphasized in repeated letters, Germany would attack South America and then the United States. We are menaced by Hitler, he told Roosevelt, in a most terrible manner. In a despatch to the President on September 19, 1939, Bullitt included an account of a purported meeting of top National Socialist figures and the Führer which had taken place on March 8, 1939. The Ambassador noted that long range plans had been discussed for the conquest of Poland, Hungary, Rumania, France, England and the United States. Ambassador Joseph Kennedy in London echoed the dismal prognosis coming from Paris. He informed Roosevelt that he could find no military or naval expert who would give England a Chinaman's chance against Germany. The British would go down fighting, said Kennedy, but it would not do them the slightest bit of good. There was no one to lead them out of the valley of death. Joseph Davies, expecting a possible German invasion of Belgium, told Roosevelt that he could foresee only ineffective resistance there. Hitler held all the aces, Davies told Steve Early, and the outlook was not bright for the west. He wrote the President on

November 8, 1939 stressing that although Hitler was shrewd and cautious, he was totally unpredictable. Every contingency had to be guarded against. Lincoln MacVeagh offered a summation of the situation as it may have appeared to Franklin Roosevelt. In a letter to the Chief Executive he observed that "when one's whole sky is clouded, with storms on every horizon, there are no definite shadows, and all is more or less dark." [85]

What would be the foreign policy of those nations which had given their endorsement to Germany's program of territorial expansion? While there was uncertainty as to the precise actions which would be undertaken by Italy, the Soviet Union, and Japan, the President could not have been sanguine concerning probable developments in international affairs. William Phillips in Rome never came to firm conclusions about the future role of Mussolini. He informed Roosevelt on September 6, 1939 that Italy could and would remain neutral. He repeated his anticipation of continued neutrality by Italy in three subsequent letters during October. The Duce, said Phillips, was feeling his way inch by inch, and would avoid trouble with the Allies at all costs. Yet, as the year ended, the Ambassador returned to the ambivalent interpretive reporting which could not have been reassuring to the Chief Executive. Phillips told Roosevelt that although the Italian Government was clearly sympathetic to the allied cause, he was still of the opinion that Mussolini's leanings were towards Nazism. In brief, there could be no certainty about Italy's peaceful intentions. [86]

The abrupt departure of the Soviet Union from the President's proposed alliance structure after the signing of the Non-Aggression Treaty with Germany was followed by alarming instances of Russian abrasiveness in its relations with the United States, and blatant aggression in the invasion of Finland. Harold Laski wrote the President offering the opinion that Stalin had thrown away an opportunity to share in the moral leadership of the world, and that there could be no prospect of trust in his good faith for a long period to come. Roosevelt, as future events revealed, did not share Laski's judgment, but there did emerge in his public statements a momentary irritability with the actions of his perspective ally. The Chief Executive, in analyzing Russian actions, seemed reservedly angry, yet still hopeful that Stalin could be weaned into the anti-German coalition. Neither the President nor his Secretary of State desired to place the Soviet Union on the same belligerent footing as Germany for fear of thrusting that nation further into Hitler's arms. They shared the belief that Hitler had not abandoned his ambitions in Russia, and that mutual antagonism would break the alliance partnership. There is also no evidence to dispute the assumption that Franklin Roosevelt viewed the Russian alignment with Germany, and its invasion of Poland, as measures designed to protect the Soviet Union from immediate invasion. There is likewise nothing to indicate that the Chief Executive had ceased to accept the optimistic views of Joseph Davies concerning Russia. The recent metamorphosis of the Sovet Union from a vocal exponent of collective security to an acquiescent ally of Germany was certainly not a reflection of a diabolical design by Stalin, thought Davies. He commented in a letter to Steve Early that Britain and France had given Russia no choice but to join with Hitler. Whatever might have been the thoughts of Franklin Roosevelt, one thing is certain. He never considered the Soviet Union as a firm member of the fascist coalition.[87]

Irritants such as the internment by Russian authorities in Murmansk of the crew of an American steamer, the *City of Flint*, and the discourteous treatment accorded diplomats of the United States Embassy in Moscow rankled the President. Assistant Secretary of State George Messersmith was asked by Cordell Hull to draw up a list of incidents in which American diplomats had been harassed, insulted, and subjected to unusual investigative procedures. This compilation was forwarded to Franklin Roosevelt. The President's response to such outrages was unusually blunt. Every Soviet annoyance, he wrote, should be met by a similar annoyance against them. Rudeness by Stalin, Kalinin, and Molotov, wrote Roosevelt, must be met by an equivalent rudeness in Washington. The antagonistic attitude of Soviet officials was discomforting to the President, but his overwhelming objective would always be the defeat of Germany and fascism. The Roosevelt Administration's handling of the Russian invasion of Finland reveals that the Chief Executive did not wish to so damage relations between the two countries as to make impossible the formation of a future alliance against the fascist bloc nations.[88]

Rumors of an impending Russian attack on Finland were numerous. In October, 1939, Franklin Roosevelt was asked by the Crown Prince of Sweden, Gustav Adolf, to intercede in Finnish-Russian negotiations with the intent of exercising some restraint on Stalin. The President's message of October 11, 1939 expressed the hope that the Soviet Union would make no demands on Finland which would be inconsistent with the maintenance of peaceful relations between the two countries. The results of Roosevelt's intervention on behalf of Finland were inconsequential. The invasion by Russia commenced on November 30, 1939. Sumner Welles suggested that the time had come to sever relations with the Soviet Union. Cordell Hull was more cautious in formulating a response to this act of aggression, ever fearful of strengthening the German-Russian reapprochement.. Roosevelt agreed with his Secretary of State. He did condemn the invasion in diplomatically temperate, but not abrasive language, and addressed an appeal to both nations to halt the ruthless bombing of civilians. The

President publicly suggested that airplane manufacturers should not sell to nations engaged in such inhuman barbarism, and privately asked Secretary of the Treasury Henry Morgenthau to prevent the sale of aluminum to Russia. The restrained manner in which Franklin Roosevelt publicly and privately responded to this act of aggression, however, contrasts markedly with his repeated and vocal condemnation of Germany and its other allies. The Soviet Union was still viewed by the President as a prospective partner in the construction of a new world order and in the task of smashing fascism. It is evident that no action would be taken to undermine the possibility of such an eventuality. Nevertheless, Russia's aggression in Finland clouded the prospective future which had already been etched in very dark outlines.[89]

In the Far East, Japan's actions gave rise to increasing concern over the prospects of an eventual encounter with the western democracies, including the United States. Japanese troops occupied the island of Hainan during the month of February, 1939, and in March seized the Spratly Islands. The numerous warnings of a possible thrust by Japan southward toward French Indo-China and the Netherlands East Indies were given added emphasis by these aggressive moves. Ambassador Nelson Johnson wrote to the President stating that dictatorships like the one controlling Japan understood force and would yield only to superior power. The question, said Johnson, was whether the United States was ready to fight for the ideals necessary for peaceful existence. We must begin to show our teeth, he told Roosevelt, for one does not send a policeman armed with a truncheon to deal with a gangster armed with a machine gun. He concluded by advising the Chief Executive that this was not a question of saving British chestnuts for America's own chestnuts were involved. The Ambassador's viewpoint, from the President's perspective, was strengthened by continued reports coming to the White House of Japan's increasing resolve to firmly support the fascist allies in their struggle with the west.[90]

The despatches from Joseph Grew in Tokyo which were forwarded to Franklin Roosevelt were not reassuring in their content. There was evidence to support previous suspicions of firm collaboration by the fascist bloc nations of Germany, Japan, and Italy. Grew observed in February, 1939 that the Japanese Ambassadors in Berlin and Rome were pressing for a military alliance against the Soviet Union. The narrow application of the Anti-Comintern Pact by Japan, however, seems to have broadened during the following months. The Japanese Army, said Grew, had been very impressed by the irresistable power displayed by Germany in the Czech coup. He felt compelled on April 20, 1939 to warn Japanese authorities that if they were contemplating joining Germany and Italy in a war against Great Britain and France, then they must not discount the United States out of that war on the side of the western democracies. In May, 1939 Grew reported strong efforts by Germany and Italy to bring Japan into a definite fascist military alliance. He doubted that Japan would let others guide her destinies, but admitted that sinister influences were at work supporting the formation of such an alliance. The ever present possibility of Japan's firm commitment to an alliance with the fascist nations was not the President's sole reason for anxiety. There existed the possibility that a conflict with the United States had not been dismissed by Japan's army and navy leaders.[91]

Ambassador Grew personally told Roosevelt that a group of young Japanese officers were dictating policy to the higher command and to the government. These officers, Grew believed, had been responsible for the sinking of the Panay, and were anxious to create an incident that would involve the United States in war. The Ambassador also intimated in his conversation with the President that a program of sanctions against Japan might conceivably mean war. In particular, he predicted that the cutting of Japan's oil supplies would force her into the Dutch East Indies. The Chief Executive, recalled Grew, was not dismayed by these prospects, and had responded by saying that such a movement by the Japanese navy could be met by intercepting its fleet. This response by the President may have been given more serious reflection because later despatches from his Ambassador in Tokyo contained references to a possible agreement between Japan and the Soviet Union which would increase the chances of a drive southward. Japan, said Grew, would be in a better position to attack the East Indian possessions of the Netherlands, and might even be emboldened to go against the United States given an understanding with Russia. Eugene Dooman, Counselor in the American Embassy in Tokyo, reported in September, 1939 that Japanese newspapers were featuring sensational articles predicting a worsening of United States and Japanese relations, and that efforts were being made to develop public opinion against the American Government. A memorandum from the Office of Naval Intelligence affirmed that Japan's policy in China would continue to be directed toward the limitation of American political and economic influence there. William McAdoo cited the danger of the exposed condition at Pearl Harbor of the Navy's oil tanks which, he noted in a letter to Roosevelt, were wholly above ground and would be the first object of aerial attack if an enemy's planes got over the Island of Oahu. The President replied saying that he was thoroughly aware of the danger existing to the installation of the tanks at Pearl Harbor. Joseph Grew's most pessimistic appraisal of developments in the Far East came in December,

1939. Japan, he asserted, would not be defeated by any powers, or any military, social, economic, and financial circumstances. The new order in East Asia had come to stay, asserted the Ambassador, and to await the discrediting of Japan's army and military system was to await the millenium. He urged that moderation and forbearance, not intransigence, should guide America's relations with Japan. This last statement perhaps appeared as a non sequitur to Franklin Roosevelt for there is much to support the thesis that Japan's actions throughout 1939 demanded, in the President's opinion, a more determined stand of resistance. William Bullitt's suggestion that Japan, France, and England should ally against Germany was probably considered by the Chief Executive to be an utter impossibility. Japan's sentiments and policies had been fixedly identified by Franklin Roosevelt.[92]

President Roosevelt publicly and privately voiced his concern over the direction of Japan's foreign policies. He directed Cordell Hull to strongly protest the indiscriminate bombing conducted by Japan in China. In that same month, the Secretary of State, in agreement with Roosevelt, gave Ambassador Horinouchi formal notice of the intention of the United States to terminate its 1911 commercial treaty with Japan on January 26, 1940. The President, as related by Harold Ickes, was especially impressed by this rare instance of positive aggressive action by the usually overly cautious Secretary Hull. Roosevelt exclaimed, said Ickes, that he had felt like kissing Hull on both cheeks! In October, 1939 Joseph Grew delivered a marked warning to the American-Japanese Society in Tokyo. He expressed his personal fear that Japan's violation of treaties and its ruthless and indiscriminate bombing had aroused the antipathy of his fellow countrymen. Roosevelt praised his Ambassador for the speech, saying that it was done in the right way and at the right time. Japanese belligerence, now more pointedly directed toward the United States, continued to be a source of worry for the Chief Executive.[93]

These were the many considerations which occupied the President's mind as the nation faced the first full year of war. His most definite opinions seemed to revolve around the expectation that German aggression would continue unimpeded, and he feared the consequences of such a development. In conversations with Harold Ickes, Franklin Roosevelt revealed his ultimate concerns. He expected Adolf Hitler to unleash Germany's military might against the United States if the Führer's nation smashed France and Great Britain. He anticipated that this might be completed by June, 1940. The President also feared the possibility of dramatic technological achievements by Germany in war weaponry. Rumors of the existence of gas bombs capable of inestimable destruction were taken seriously by Roosevelt.

Memoranda written by the President reveal in these early months of the war his suspicions of possible hostile action by Germany in the American hemisphere. He told Acting Secretary of the Navy Charles Edison on October 9, 1939 that he had been disturbed by the failure to speed up, stay with, and identify patrols, surface ships and submarines. In this patrol business, he warned, time was of the essence and loss of contact with surface ships could not be tolerated. He instructed Sumner Welles on November 9, 1939 to keep close tabs on suspicious belligerent merchant ships in North Central and South American waters. Fear of Germany's intentions, combined with the possibility that Italy and Japan would enter the war against the democracies while the Soviet Union pursued a malevolent neutrality, left no room for comforting logic in the mind of the President. Roosevelt told William White on December 14, 1939 that the world situation was getting rather progressively worse as the weeks went by. He was not sure where the German-Russian arrangement would lead. An eventual confrontation was possible, thought Roosevelt, as was the conclusion of a definite alliance between the two nations to divide control of Europe, Asia, Persia, Africa, and various British, French, Dutch, and Belgian colonies. If the latter were true, he concluded, the existence of civilization was in peril.[94]

What would be the role of the United States in the coming struggle as envisaged by Franklin Roosevelt? He dismissed the notion entertained by many that America could serve as the intermediary for negotiation of a peace settlement. He was particularly angered by Ambassador Joseph Kennedy's persistent suggestion that an arrangement be worked out with the aggressors. Roosevelt told Henry Morgenthau that Joseph Kennedy always had been and always would be an appeaser. The President said that if Germany or Italy were to make a good peace offer tomorrow, Joseph would start working on the King and Queen, and from there on down, to get everybody to accept it. Kennedy, asserted Roosevelt bluntly, was just a pain in the neck. The Ambassador in London had earlier suggested that the President might wish to work out plans for world peace. The President had fired off an immediate response on the very same day that this unsolicited advice was received saying that the United States would not support any move for peace that would consolidate or make possible a survival of a regime of force and aggression. It would be incorrect to assume that Franklin Roosevelt sought to propose a peace settlement at this point in time, especially when German ascendance in Europe was an actual fact. He would never agree to any compromise settlement with the proponents of National Socialism and fascism. His plea for the cooperation of Pope Pius XII and other prominent religious leaders in a united effort to achieve peace was, as Roosevelt later admitted, didactic in its purpose. It was simply a plea that the moral forces of the world must strengthen their commitment to construct a world of decency and civility in the face of barbarism. This was not an appeasement proposal, but an appeal for the return to an ordered existence long since passed.[95]

Franklin Roosevelt did not accept the opinion of others who believed that the traditional American neutrality policy of non-alignment would spare the United States from war. He had officially proclaimed neutrality status on September 5, 1939, and had forbidden the export of arms and ammunition to all belligerents. In that same month, however, he went before Congress to urge a repeal of the non-discretionary embargo provisions of the neutrality law. This presentation to Congress was not a candid assessment by the President of the perils, as he saw them, in the present situation. Nowhere in this address is mentioned his very real fear of Germany's alleged ultimate ambitions. Nowhere does he reveal his concern for the weaknesses of Great Britain and France. Nowhere does he elaborate on the necessity of intervention in the ongoing struggle which he had accepted as a very real possibility. He could take some solace from passage of new neutrality legislation on November 4, 1939 which repealed the non-discretionary embargo and instituted a cash and carry policy beneficial to the French and British. The neutrality statutes, however, did not ease the anxiety of the President as he contemplated the prospective future. Harry Hopkins had written to Roosevelt offering the poetic rhyme of Joseph Warren who had foretold in 1775 of a free America in array against the forces of Europe and speaking in thunder to the nations of the world. Hopkins commented that it was certainly vigorous English. The President believed it was too vigorous for the moment. In his opinion there were too many who would have the United States enter the fray unprepared. Nevertheless, Franklin Roosevelt did not dismiss the real prospect of American intervention. Henry Morgenthau recounted that Roosevelt had told him that "if you have to decide along the lines that will not get us into war You [sic] decide, but if there is any decision which you think might get us into war, come and see me about it." Morgenthau added in his diary, "He left me with the distinct feeling that he might want to make decisions which might get us into war. I was terribly disappointed and evidently showed it. . . ."[96]

V

Approaching Encounter

CHAPTER FIVE

APPROACHING ENCOUNTER-
INEVITABLE CLIMAX

The Assertion of Fascist Dominance

The anticipated sequence of events during the years 1940 and 1941 served to strengthen Franklin Roosevelt's conviction that the entrance of the United States in the military conflict would be inevitably necessary if the fascist powers were to be halted in their drive for dominance in Europe and the Far East. In the brief span of several months, the precarious sovereignty of the weaker nations of Europe was extinguished by the decisively superior armed forces of Germany. Denmark, Norway, Belgium, Luxemburg, the Netherlands, and France were crushed in rapid succession. Italy, as the President had fully expected, officially entered the conflict in June, 1940 by declaring war on Great Britain and France, and began to press immediately for territorial acquisitions in Greece. Hungary, Rumania, and Slovakia, a skeletal remnant of the once independent nation of Edouard Benes, rushed to join the Axis coalition in what Roosevelt viewed as the spoilation of Europe. In the Far East, the aggressiveness of Japan added to the heightened sense of alarm shared by all the democratic powers. Japan appeared to be intent on establishing its imposed new order in China and Southeast Asia despite intensifying economic pressure by the United States. A ten year military and economic alliance signed by Germany, Japan, and Italy in September, 1940 reaffirmed Franklin Roosevelt's assumption that the free world was confronted by a concerted drive on the part of the revisionist powers to secure a global hegemony which would preclude any meaningful participation by the defeated nations in the restructured imbalance of power.

155

A pervasive pessimism marked the Chief Executive's appraisal of the future and his thoughts on the prospective role which the Axis leaders would accord to the United States after the consolidation of their victory. What might be America's future in the event of a very possible British defeat? Could there be any meaningful security for an impregnable fortress in imposed economic isolation? What did the reports of purported infiltration by German, Japanese, and Italian agents in the Latin American countries portend? These questions demanded crucial attention. In the months preceding Pearl Harbor, the fascist coalition had gained considerable momentum in its quest for continental supremacy. Bulgaria by willful acquiescence, and Greece and Yugoslavia by forceful subjugation became appendages to the expanding Third Reich. Great Britain, suffering heavy damage from air bombardment and sustaining intolerable losses on the seas, faced a most uncertain and crucial present. The Vichy Government in France, tolerated by Germany because of its weakness, seemed on the verge of adopting a course of firm collaboration with the Axis. The possibility that the French fleet might be added to the already dominant German navy was not dismissed by the President. What would be the outcome of the ensuing struggle if Japan, having moved its troops into Indo-China, proceeded to attack and secure British, French, and Dutch possessions in the Pacific? Would the Soviet Union be able to repel the German invasion of June, 1941 or a subsequent thrust by Japan? Russian resistance served to strengthen Roosevelt's determination to press for intervention in the near future. In his opinion, the Soviet Union was now a member of the coalition opposing fascism, and its manpower and resources would finally be available for use against Germany, Italy, and Japan. The most critical juncture of the war, thought the President, had been reached by December, 1941. The necessity of America's involvement in the struggle of finality was foreshadowed by the weakness of potential allies, the strength of potential aggressors, and the dim hope that the German-Russian confrontation would eventually turn the tide of battle. Japan's attack on Pearl Harbor and the declarations of war issued by the members of the fascist coalition against the United States forced the American commitment which Franklin Roosevelt realized would be inevitably necessary if the combined forces of Germany, Italy, and Japan were to be defeated.

The scenario of events in these two years was not entirely under the direction of Mussolini, the Führer, and Hirohito's military advisers. Franklin Roosevelt initiated efforts to aid Great Britain, Russia, and China that made inevitable an accumulation of incidents with Germany which may have eventually given the President a legislative mandate for war. The United States adopted a decidedly unneutral posture very early in the struggle. The exchange of American destroyers for British bases, the program of Lend-Lease, the occupation of Greenland and Iceland, the extension of ocean patrols, the convoying of ships to Iceland, the promulgation of the Atlantic Charter with its commitment to achieve the final destruction of Nazi tyranny, the order given to American ships to shoot on sight any German intruders, and the repeal of some of the most restrictive 1939 neutrality provisions were acts clearly aimed at impeding the German war effort. The sinking of America's *Robin Moor, Greer, Kearny,* and *Reuben James* by Germany, which did most to intensify public opinion against that nation, must be considered as an expected contingency of the policies pursued by the Roosevelt Administration. The winter months of 1941 were indeed critical ones, and there is no doubt that the President was seeking an incident, or a series of incidents, which would lead to embroilment in a war with Germany. He had for years accepted the assumption, now demonstrated, that German military power was far superior to that of any other nation. Adolf Hitler's firm retention of power and the continuation of Germany's program of expansion dictated the commitment to war which could no longer be postponed. The events of December, 1941 solved the dilemma of Franklin Roosevelt and secured the sought-after military commitment on the part of a united nation.

In his message to Congress on January 3, 1940, the President had set forth the considerations which would make impossible America's abstention from war. Months before the German blitzkrieg had begun, he candidly admitted that it would be disastrous for the United States to stand idly by as the rest of civilization was shattered. He pointedly condemned those who wishfully insisted, through innocence or ignorance, that Americans could live safely behind a high wall of isolation in a world ruled by force in the hands of a few. We must discern the future, said Roosevelt, and ask whether or not it would be possible to subsist as a mere appendage to vast and powerful military systems. He urged an abandonment of the ostrich-like attitude of burying one's head in the sand and avoiding realities. What was the alternative to the frail security of isolation? This question he did not attempt to answer, but the suggested response would seem to be implicit in the phraseology of his speech. The United States must soon become a participant of consequence in a struggle vitally related to its national security. When asked later if he thought it would be possible to stay out of the war, he answered cautiously by saying that "any statement holds until there is another one. That is the easiest way of putting it."[1]

Franklin Roosevelt, in the early months of 1940, contemplated no real alternative other than resistance to fascist aggression. A compromise peace with Germany had long since been removed as a subject of serious contemplation. A very misleading impression of Presidential intentions was given on February 9, 1940 when it was announced that Sumner Welles would visit Italy, France, Germany, and Great Britain in order to obtain information on conditions in Europe. Welles had initiated earlier peace initiatives, and a logical assumption seemed to be that this effort too was in reality a search for peace. The President, however, could not possibly have desired to sanction any negotiated settlement at this time. Cordell Hull said that Welles had literally pleaded with the Chief Executive for this opportunity. Harold Ickes noted that the Under Secretary had left without any specific instructions or any power to make or act on proposals. During a press conference, Roosevelt was pressed for an explanation of the mission. In his response, he offered no indication that any significant activity would be pursued by Sumner Welles other than that of reporting on the present European situation. He cautioned reporters not to exaggerate the importance of what was apparently an accession to persistent requests made personally by Welles to the President. "It is all in one sentence," said the Chief Executive, "and probably anything you add, any of you, columnists or anything else, to enlarge on this, you will be wrong."[2]

Franklin Roosevelt's appraisal of the Welles Mission was for him a foregone conclusion. The prospects for peace were nonexistent. Welles' reports, which were sent to the President, reinforced his assumptions concerning Axis ambitions. Roosevelt perhaps received very skeptically the view of his Under Secretary that there was a slight chance for the negotiation of a lasting peace. The Chief Executive could not have ignored Joachim von Ribbentrop's assertion that a victory over England was necessary for Germany's security, or Welles' description of the German Foreign Minister as a man saturated with hate for England, or the Führer's certitude about the overpowering might of Germany which would either ensure its triumph or bring the entire world down for better or for worse, or Deputy Rudolf Hess' absolute rejection of any negotiated settlement, or finally Welles' depiction of Benito Mussolini as a vindictive man, infatuated with force and power, obsessed with the idea of the reconstruction of the Roman Empire, and enormously impressed with German military strength. The President announced on March 29, 1940 that Sumner Welles had brought back no peace proposals from any source. Two weeks before this statement, he had made known his views about the nature of any prospective peace settlement. There could be no real or lasting peace, said Roosevelt, if it was to be based on oppression, starvation, cruelty, and human life dominated by armed camps. Welles' despatches had portrayed just such a picture of the status of affairs in Europe.[3]

Incoming despatches and memoranda arriving on the President's desk during the course of the Welles' sojourn in Europe contained alarming portents of expected future actions. John Cudahy, writing from Belgium, told of a large concentration of German troops on the Belgian border and predicted that Hitler would strike as soon as the weather became more favorable. He was sure that the Führer would have to risk all and bring off an offensive to maintain his great prestige. Cordell Hull had hurriedly called the Chief Executive in January, 1940 relaying information concerning a German attack on the Low Countries which could come in a matter of days. Roosevelt's antipathy toward Germany and his expectation of a further deterioration of the situation in Europe was increased too by descriptions of German occupation policies in Poland as being the most sadistically cruel in all history. Poles used for slave labor had been herded in droves into boxcars in subzero weather. Many had died of exposure, related the President during a cabinet session, their corpses being callously taken out of the boxcars and buried at the next stop. Jews had been treated in a similar manner. There is nothing to indicate that Roosevelt disagreed with the judgment of his close friend, Arthur Murray, who had defined Hitlerism as the denial of every Christian thought, sentiment, act, and ideal. Nazi Germany, wrote Murray, was behaving as the enemy of all mankind. This exponent of ruthless force, he added, had to be crushed if life was to be tolerable for peace-seeking, liberty-loving nations. No distinction should be made between the German Government and the German people, he told the President, for they had shown no perturbation over Hitler's aggressions and had willingly followed his leadership. Franklin Roosevelt's impressions of Germany's forceful expansion, based on numerous reports sent to him by diplomatic observers stationed throughout Europe, may not have been much different than those expressed by Arthur Murray. The violence and brutal suppression which followed in the wake of the German armies was noted by the President's most intimate correspondents. It would seem difficult for the Chief Executive to have remained dispassionately detached from the events which accompanied the horrifying onslaught of the German war machine.[4]

The predictions of an eventual blitzkrieg, as well as the assumption that there existed a solid unanimity in Germany for Hitler's war effort, were given added credibility on April 9, 1940 when German troops invaded Denmark and Norway. Franklin Roosevelt publicly denounced this act of aggression four days later. Civilization could only survive, he warned, when the rights of smaller nations to independence were respected by their more powerful neighbors. In a radio address on April 15, 1940 his comments were more pointed. There could be no illusions, he said, about the fact that dreams of universal empire were again rampant. Races claiming the right of mastery were trying to impose their way of life on other nations. Arthur Murray believed that the Germans had done the world a favor by their brazen invasion of the two countries for it had exposed Germany's treacherous tentacles and techniques of deceit to the world. Roosevelt could take no solace from these events in April, 1940. He informed Murray that the situation was extremely disturbing to him, and added that things ought to be speeded up a bit on the British side. "The only way to meet an almost perfect machine," said the President, "was to build an equally perfect machine."[5]

The President clearly anticipated another offensive move by Germany. John Cudahy expressed to him the opinion that this was just the beginning of a long war, that Hitler was now optimistic about his prospects of success, and that an air attack on England was to be expected soon. The Ambassador ominously predicted that the military phase of the war might be over before the end of 1940. Roosevelt replied saying that while he prayed to God the Germans would not move in the west, he would bear in mind that they were complete experts at hiding their moves, as was evident in the Scandinavian action. The veil of mystery covering Germany's aims was soon removed by the President's diplomatic correspondents. A report by an American Naval Attaché in London, which was sent to Roosevelt by the Navy Department, predicted a German invasion of Holland and Belgium if Italy should actively join the Axis coalition. William Bullitt's despatches to the President were most disconcerting. He noted the concentration of 15 German divisions close to the French, Belgian, and Dutch frontiers, and the menacing attitude of the Germans toward Sweden, the Netherlands, Belgium, Hungary, and Yugoslavia. Bullitt was convinced that Germany would launch new attacks in the future. Some observers, he told Roosevelt, believed that the neutrals of Central and Southern Europe would be so impressed by the superiority of the German army that they would fall in the maw of Germany and Italy without resistance.[6]

William Bullitt's analysis of the extensive scope of expected German aggression was partially verified when Germany's armies swept into Belgium, Luxemburg, and the Netherlands in the early days of May, 1940. The President told Ambassador Cudahy in Brussels that he hoped for resistance to the bitter end. He praised

Queen Wilhelmina of the Netherlands for the stand of Dutch armed forces against what he termed impossible odds, and expressed to King Leopold of Belgium his hope that German aggression would soon be halted. In truth, Franklin Roosevelt could not have been optimistic about the future. The forcefulness of the German onslaught had been vividly described to him by Crown Prince Olav, son of King Haakon of Norway. In the invasion of his nation, said Olav, the Germans subjected open cities and villages to severe bombing. The storm had struck with such ruthless force as could only be thought of in a nightmare. Olav was sure that the United States could not in the long run remain inactive in the struggle against those who believed in brutal aggression and serfdom for all except a handful of brutal men. Arthur Murray was again the most passionately descriptive of the President's correspondents. Hitler, the wild beast of Berchtesgaden, leader of the vilest gang of liars, perjurers, murderers and torturers that the planet had ever seen, said Murray, had launched his slaves and engines of war against innocent democratic peoples. A summer of brutality, agony, and ferocity was certain.[7]

The momentum gained by Germany's armed forces would soon carry them directly into the heart of France. William Bullitt's letters to the Chief Executive were exceptionally gloomy. The military situation for the French was appallingly bad. Germany had attacked in May, 1940, with colossal tanks and a totally overwhelming mass of bombardment planes. French Premier Paul Reynaud repeatedly stressed to the American Ambassador the need for war materials to counter the German superiority on air, land, and sea. The course of events by then, however, may have been predetermined. Bullitt informed the President on May 16, 1940 that Belgian resistance had collapsed, and that the German army was pouring all of its motorized and mechanized divisions into France. Unless God granted a miracle, he told Roosevelt, the French army would be utterly crushed. There would be no miracle for France, however. The Ambassador's correspondence throughout the months of May and June told only of surrender, reversals, and desperate heroism.[8]

Germany's achievements had markedly impressed its Axis partner Italy. Franklin Roosevelt had always feared the possibility that Mussolini would commit his nation and its armed forces to the war effort against the democracies, and he expected the Duce to embark on such a course of action during these propitious moments. In the early months of 1940, Counselor Alexander Kirk in Rome repeatedly emphasized in despatches that were forwarded to the President the likelihood of direct intervention by Italy to support the German offensive against France. Ambassador William Phillips, who had been cautiously optimistic about the prospects of continued Italian neutrality, now believed that it would always be necessary to reckon with Mussolini's pro-German attitude. Myron Taylor, appointed by Roosevelt as his special representative to Pope Pius XII, warned in April and May, 1940 that there was a real danger of Mussolini joining Hitler, and he urged the President to prevail on the Duce to remain nonbelligerent. Messages were sent by the Chief Executive to Mussolini on four occasions, and each one tactfully emphasized the possible consequences should Italy join the war on the side of Germany. Roosevelt personally attempted to persuade the Italian Ambassador, Don Ascanio Colonna, to press for Italy's neutrality.[9]

All such efforts proved to no avail. The jackal awaited only assurances of Germany's ultimate success. William Phillips' despatches throughout these crucial months made it clear to Franklin Roosevelt that he had failed in his attempts to keep Italy out of the war. The Ambassador was certain that the decision to join with Germany had been made by May 21, 1940, and he predicted some Italian act of aggression within four weeks. In a letter to Sumner Welles, which was sent to the President, he described Mussolini as bewitched by the accomplishments of Germany and ready to find a cheap victory for himself. Phillips bluntly told Roosevelt that the Duce's regime had gone mad territorially, and that Mussolini's Caesar complex was driving him to add to the Empire by hook or by crook without showing the slightest consideration for anyone in reaching this end. William Bullitt was certain that Italy would soon attack France. He told the President that Mussolini considered his requests for Italian neutrality to be indecent and immoral attempts to persuade him to break his pledged word to Adolf Hitler. The Ambassador sarcastically commented that to believe that the United States would be able to ever cooperate with Mussolini was as dangerous to the future of America as would be the belief that the Government could cooperate with Al Capone. Franklin Roosevelt could have had no doubts about the future course of Italian foreign policy. Mussolini's sympathies were clearly with Germany and its program of fascist expansion. The Duce's decision to join Hitler in the war against the democracies was expected by the Chief Executive.[10]

The most pessimistic appraisals of Italian foreign policy proved correct on June 10, 1940 when that nation formally declared war on Great Britain and a prostrate France. Bullitt impassionately wrote to Roosevelt saying that at this very hour another dictatorship had stabbed France in the back. The President, speaking at the University of Virginia that same day, echoed these sentiments. Italy, he said, had manifested its disregard for the rights and security of other nations by pursuing the gods of hate and force. The hand that held the dagger, he concluded, had struck it into the back of its neighbor.[11]

This discouraging turn of events was given added emphasis when German troops marched triumphantly into Paris on June 15, 1940. French Premier Paul Reynaud, having requested all American aid short of an expeditionary force, promised to fight in front of Paris, behind Paris, and in the provinces. The President, expecting a French defeat, responded cautiously in an inspirational manner. He pledged that French resistance efforts would be bolstered by ever-increasing quantities of materials and supplies. Realistically, he knew that a meaningful and successful commitment to halt fascist expansion would have to await a more propitious moment. It was evident to Roosevelt, however, that time was running out for the democracies. The tide of Axis victory might soon become irreversible.[12]

What might be the course of French foreign policy in the future? An armistice was signed with Germany on June 22, 1940 by representatives of a new French Government under the leadership of Marshal Henri Petain. A character sketch of Petain's administration, sent to the President by William Bullitt before his departure from France, was not encouraging. He described the French leaders as desirous of cutting loose from all that France had represented for the past two generations. Their physical and moral defeat had been absolute, wrote Bullitt. They seemed to have accepted the fate of becoming a favorite province of Nazi Germany, said the Ambassador. Petain's regime, governing from Vichy, France, appeared not only defeatist, but hostile toward Great Britain and the United States. Marshal Petain was certain that Germany would control all of France and thereafter crush Great Britain. Vice-Premier at Vichy, Admiral Jean Darlan, was outspokenly angry toward the British and seemed to regard with considerable pleasure the prospects of a British defeat. Bullitt had received promises that were intended to alleviate the Chief Executive's gravest concern. Petain and Darlan did pledge never to surrender the French fleet to Germany. Assurances from an assumed Axis collaborator were probably given scant credence by Franklin Roosevelt. The President did not dismiss the possibility that France might actually engage in war against Great Britain. The appearance of Vichy France made the plight of the democracies even more crucial.[13]

Germany's consolidation of power on the continent during the spring of 1940 would soon enable the Führer to direct major offensive operations against Great Britain. The future of America's hemispheric defense, in the opinion of Franklin Roosevelt, was dependent upon the continued independence and fighting capacity of the British

nation. Should Britain fall, he reasoned, the United States would be
forced to confront the Axis powers in a hopelessly weak position. The
accession of Winston Churchill to the office of Prime Minister on
May 10, 1940 was viewed by Roosevelt with sincere elation. The
defeatism of Neville Chamberlain had most often disgusted the President. It now appeared that England had a leader imbued with the
determination to crush the fascist powers at all costs. The former
First Lady of the Admiralty had kept the Chief Executive informed
of developments on the war front, and the two men seem to have
had a most understanding relationship prior to these crucial spring
months. He agreed with Arthur Murray's appraisal of the Prime Minister as a man representing the nation's unconquerable spirit and iron
resolve to destroy the Nazi Reich. Ambassador Joseph Kennedy, not
one to convey inspirational sentiments, was moved to write that
England would never give up as long as Churchill remained a power
in public life even if the country should be burnt to the ground. Kennedy's caustic pessimism could not be dismissed by Franklin Roosevelt
for Churchill himself was to graphically present in his letters to the
President the immediate gravity of a situation where imminent collapse of British resistance was a distinct possibility. Winston Churchill
began a series of blunt and impassioned requests for American
assistance five days after he had assumed his new office. He was not
optimistic concerning the prospects for the continued existence of the
democracies.[14]

He set forth his concerns of the moment in a letter to Roosevelt
on May 15, 1940. The small countries of Europe, he began, had been
smashed up like boxwood. He prophesied that a completely subju-
gated, Nazified Europe could be established with alarming swiftness,
and that the weight might be more than Britain could bear. Destroyers, aircraft, anti-aircraft equipment and ammunition would be
needed in abundant supplies, he told the President, and added that he
hoped America would give the stuff even if Britain could not afford to
pay for it. This letter, written before the French collapse, set a tone
of alarm and pessimism which pervaded Churchill's later correspondence with the Chief Executive. In a note dated June 20, 1940, the
Prime Minister warned that if his nation was left by the United States
to its fate no one could blame a later British Government for bargaining with Germany for the best terms possible. These terms, he said
pointedly, could best be secured by discussions concerning the British
fleet. This was a nightmarish vision, he admitted to the President, but
one that could take place in a nation where men in utter despair had
to accommodate themselves to the German will. Churchill repeated
these same dire admonitions to the Canadian Prime Minister Mackenzie King who, as intended, passed them on to Roosevelt. The

President, fearing a British collapse, contemplated a plan whereby that nation's fleet would be dispersed around the globe in order to avoid surrender to Germany. The future looked even more dismal after the German air forces began their attacks on Great Britain in July, 1940. In subsequent months, the intensity of the bombing reached awesome proportions. Destroyers stationed in the air-bombing area to prevent a seaborne invasion were particularly vulnerable to attack. Churchill repeatedly emphasized to the President the fact that continued loss of destroyers might be so serious as to break down the defense of the Atlantic food and trade routes. Hitler's full blow had not yet come, he told Roosevelt, and destroyers would be of precious help.[15]

Franklin Roosevelt was deeply concerned over the likelihood of a British defeat. Churchill had not been at all encouraging in his letters to the President, and his vivid presentations of contingent possibilities if England was left to fight alone were especially disturbing. In April, 1940 the Chief Executive told Henry Morgenthau that if things kept up the way they were going than the English would be licked. Roosevelt anticipated a demand by Germany that the British fleet be surrendered, and also reasoned that the English might capitulate before such a demand if the only alternative was a German occupation of their country. He told reporters in May, 1940 that the situation looked extremely serious. Germany was so infinitely strongly than England and France that, just on the doctrine of chance, he predicted, the Germans would win. During the summer months he began to seriously contemplate the ways and means of best aiding the British war effort.[16]

Winston Churchill's most pressing requests had been for destroyers. Public opinion in the United States was moving quickly toward a consensus in favor of giving more concrete help to the allies. William Allen White, head of the Committee to Defend America by Aiding the Allies, wrote to the President on June 10, 1940 saying that his correspondence was heaping up unanimously behind plans to aid the allies by anything other than war. He urged Roosevelt to catch up with public opinion if he expected to lead the American people. Frank Knox, soon to be appointed Secretary of Navy, told the Chief Executive in that same month that the Middle West, a bastion of isolationist sentiment, was overwhelmingly in support of aiding Great Britain. Steve Early could report by August 16, 1940 that the Gallup Poll taken that week found that 62 percent of the voters favored letting Britain have American destroyers. Assured of public support, worried about prospects of a British defeat, and eager to do something to impede the German advance, the President sought to conclude an agreement whereby destroyers could be transferred to

Britain. Henry Morgenthau, who believed it would be useless to expect England to fight on without destroyers, recalled that from the moment the transaction with Great Britain had been mentioned Roosevelt seemed to have made up his mind that this was something of the utmost importance. Formal agreements were signed on September 2, 1940, and fifty United States Navy destroyers were pledged to Great Britain in exchange for ninety-nine year leases to naval and air bases which were to be constructed in Newfoundland, Bermuda, the Bahamas, Jamaica, St. Lucia, Trinidad, and British Guiana. What Churchill called a decidedly unneutral act by the United States was justified by Roosevelt as an act of preparation for continental defense in the face of grave danger.[17]

The destroyers for bases deal did not immediately strengthen the deteriorating defenses of Great Britain. German air attacks were especially intensive in the fall of 1940, and Franklin Roosevelt's anxiety over the prospects of a British collapse continued to give him serious misgivings about that nation's ability to withstand the German attack. Cordell Hull gave a most pessimistic account of the plight of the English during a cabinet session just a few days after the agreement with Great Britain. Secretary Ickes believed that these were very anxious days for the British, and that it appeared as though the Germans were inflicting far greater damage than had been reported. Some, he added, even believed that the destroyers were sent too late to save the island's defense effort. Prime Minister Churchill tended to reinforce Hull's impression of England as a country on the verge of its greatest challenge in his letters to the President. He told Roosevelt in October, 1940 that the invasion danger had not passed. He described the Führer as having taken off his clothes and put on his bathing suit. The water would get colder in autumn, he wrote, so utmost vigilance was required at the moment. The British Prime Minister vaguely hinted too at the possibility of a declaration of war to be issued by Japan against Great Britain. Publicly and privately, Roosevelt seemed to be moving toward all-out aid to a beleaguered ally. He told Morgenthau on September 19, 1940 that the English could have everything they wanted and, as he later emphasized, the dollar sign should not be an obstacle to such aid. In homespun rhetoric, the President spoke of the need to lend a garden hose to a close neighbor to put out a fire. Certainly, he asked, one would not then quibble about the price to be levied for this transaction? We must get rid of that "silly, foolish, old dollar sign."[18]

Franklin Roosevelt's apparent fear of a collapse of British resistance was intensified by continued warnings of an expected Japanese drive to secure dominance in the Far East. The United States made known its disapproval of Japan's military and diplomatic policies on several occasions. The 1911 commercial treaty with Japan expired on January 26, 1940 with no subsequent renewal. Hull observed that henceforth trade with Japan would be on a twenty-four hour basis, and that commercial restrictions could always be imposed at wlll. Moral embargos had been applied to the export of aircraft and related materials, and on all items necessary for the production of high quality aviation gasoline. Exporters of vital war resources had to be licensed by the United States Government. An absolute prohibition on the exportation of aviation gasoline to Japan was another measure which some hoped would retard the Japanese advance southward. These imposed economic constraints may have appeared useful from the President's vantage point for a short time, but Japan's belligerent aggressiveness, he believed, would someday lead to war in the Far East. Francis Sayre, American Minister to the Philippines, had told Roosevelt that Japan was anxious to retire gracefully from China. He suggested that the Chief Executive might wish to extend his good offices to solve the Japanese-Chinese controversy. The time seemed propitious to Sayre, but not to the President. Sayre's letter of May 16, 1940 was one of the very few optimistic accounts of Pacific and Far Eastern developments.[19]

Intelligence memoranda contained numerous warnings of an imminent Japanese aggressive action. The President was informed in April, 1940 of a report by an American Naval Attaché in London that British officers had been expecting major developments in the Asiatic situation and that Japan might soon move toward the Dutch East Indies. The Chief Executive received information from the Office of Naval Intelligence in July, 1940 that the Japanese Foreign Minister, Hachiro Arita, had instructed Japan's diplomatic representatives to prepare for a southward offensive to seize the Malay Peninsula, Dutch East Indies, Australia, New Zealand, New Caledonia, and other British and French possessions. Reports of Japanese infiltration of Panama were sent to the White House in the autumn months. One other intriguing memorandum charged that the Japanese Ambassador, Kensuki Horinouchi, had been attempting to influence American public opinion by seeking favorable coverage for Japan from representatives of the Hearst and Scripps-Howard papers.[20]

Diplomatic despatches discussing expected Japanese policies were equally disquieting. Francis Sayre's previous optimism concerning the prospects of a peaceful settlement with Japan had been replaced by urgent warnings to the President that fifth column activities by the Japanese in the Philippines were of such scope that the Army and Navy intelligence units there needed additional funds to handle the demands for more extensive surveillance. He thought that the chances were fifty-fifty on the possibility of a Japanese attack on Indo-China,

Hong Kong, or the Dutch East Indies. Ambassador Grew relayed a statement from Foreign Minister Arita in June, 1940 in which he expressed Japan's resentment concerning the stationing of the American fleet in Hawaii and Pearl Harbor because it implied suspicion of Japanese intentions with regard to the South Seas and Netherlands East Indies. The significance of Arita's pointed criticism of the American naval presence at Pearl Harbor might have been apparent to Franklin Roosevelt several months later. Admiral James Richardson, Commander of the Pacific Fleet, met with the President on October 8, 1940. Admiral Richardson attempted to impress upon the Chief Executive that the fleet in Hawaii was undermanned, unprepared for war, and therefore disadvantageously disposed for preparing for or initiating war operations. The Admiral believed that the presence of the ships served no useful purpose. Roosevelt, recalled the Admiral, replied that on the basis of his information the Pacific fleet was exercising a restraining influence on Japan, at least for the moment. However, the President added, the United States would enter a war against Japan sometime in the future for someday they would make a mistake. The fleet did remain at Pearl Harbor, but it is doubtful that it had the much desired effect of impeding Japanese expansionist aims.[21]

A new government under Premier Fumimaro Konoye came to power in Tokyo in July, 1940. Hull recalled that Konoye was Premier when Japan intensified its drive into China in July, 1937. Konoye's Foreign Minister, Yosuke Matsuoka, was as crooked as a basket of fishhooks according to the Secretary of State. The direction which Konoye's administration would take in foreign affairs became known on September 27, 1940 when Germany, Italy, and Japan signed a Three Power Pact in which they pledged to stand by and cooperate with each other in their efforts to control Greater East Asia and Europe. Article Three of the pact was what most concerned American statesmen. Political, economic, and military assistance was promised by all three signatories if one was attacked by a power presently not involved in the European war or the Sino-Japanese conflict. This was a pointed reference to the United States. The signing of this pact significantly intensified the already hostile relations between the United States and Japan. Ambassador Grew, in a despatch dated October 6, 1940, and sent to the White House, observed that he could not and did not underrate the future possibility of intensified difficulties between the two countries. He felt compelled on November 26, 1940 to send a translation of a statement by Retired Admiral Ryozo Nakamura. The Admiral emphasized that it would be impossible to construct an East Asia co-prosperity sphere or settle the China incident without ("repeat without" was added by Grew) war with the United States. Nakamura concluded by challenging Japan to enter the fight against America in the most daring spirit. Matsuoka, said Ambassador Grew one month later, had asserted that Japan must soon take some action to give concrete assistance to its allies in the war effort. The Office of Naval Intelligence also provided the President with a report, gained from unimpeachable sources, that Japan, Germany, and Italy were fully collaborating with each other. The Chief of Naval Operations warned of the possibility of war at any moment, and urgently proposed that a conference be held with British, Dutch, and Canadian officials to discuss the perilous situation.[22]

Franklin Roosevelt could have been under no misapprehensions about the inevitability of an eventual encounter with Japan. What was necessary, as he had told Henry Morgenthau, was not to push Japan too much as such pressure might compel her to seize the Dutch East Indies. There seemed to be one contingency, however, which would force the President to intervene against Japan. Francis Sayre had written the Chief Executive on November 13, 1940 urging him to avoid being sucked into a war with the Japanese. Roosevelt's reply gives a most accurate account of his thoughts on what might compel the United States to commit its military forces in the Far East and European controversy. He told Sayre that of course he did not wish to be drawn into any war anywhere. There was, however, said the President, a very close connection between Far Eastern developments and those in eastern Europe and the Mediterranean. There was going on, he emphasized, a world conflict in which there were aligned on one side Japan, Germany, and Italy, and on the other side China, Great Britain, and the United States. There could be no doubt where America stood, he affirmed. Then he elaborated on his most agonizing concern. If Japan should seize the Netherlands East Indies, or the Malay Peninsula, he reasoned, would not the chances of Germany defeating Great Britain be increased? The President seems to have accepted the necessity of war in the Far East once British forces came under attack from Japan, especially given the German dominance on the Atlantic front.[23]

Joseph Grew offered a summary analysis of Japanese foreign policy on December 14, 1940 which was very much in agreement with Franklin Roosevelt's personal opinions on this subject. The Ambassador in Tokyo was convinced that a head on showdown with Japan would have to come someday. He depicted the Japanese nation as an open and unashamed predator. No Japanese leader or group of leaders could reverse the expansionist program and hope to survive, said Grew, and he predicted the ascendancy of a more extremist government in the future. The President voiced his decided agreement with these conclusions. He disagreed, however, with his Ambassador's suggestion that the logic of postponing any conflict with Japan was, as an end in itself, a wise policy. Roosevelt advanced the same line of reasoning as contained in his letter to Frank Sayre. He appears to have reaffirmed his decision to enter what he termed a single world conflict if a British defeat, which would be an even greater possibility if Japan entered the fray, seemed imminent. A commitment to war, while neither formal nor binding, was accepted personnally by the Chief Executive given the contingent circumstance of a prospective British collapse. The appraisals of Japanese foreign policy through-out this year indicated that the approaching storm was not far distant.[24]

Franklin Roosevelt, The Axis Threat, and America's Security

Franklin Roosevelt's perspective concerning the aims of the fascist powers was not limited to Europe and the Far East. Reports that agents of the Axis nations were active in several Latin American coun-tries became more numerous throughout the year. The President had always assumed that Germany's aggression would one day reach the Western Hemisphere unless it could be halted far from American shores. The extent to which he related overseas developments to the security of the United States is revealed by his statement to Adolph Berle that one of the consequences of Hitler's invasion of Holland would be the leasing of Dutch islands in the Caribbean by Germany. He may have interpreted this as a prelude to a German invasion. He directed the Chief of Naval Operations, Admiral Stark, in April, 1940 to prepare plans to either occupy the Island of Fernando Noronha off the coast of Brazil with sufficient forces to repel an attack, or to make ready an air force which could destroy the airfield there so that it could not be used by land planes or amphibians. These plans were to become operative if any European nation attempted to seize the island. The continuance of German military victories on the Euro-pean continent prompted the President to engage in very interesting speculation. He envisaged the bombing of Washington, D.C., and sternly directed the Secretary of War to solve the logistics of rail and highway transportation if any marked disruption of the means of communication should occur. The validity of Roosevelt's assump-tion that an attack on the United States by Germany was a distinct possibility was shared by some intelligence and diplomatic represen-tatives who forwarded to the White House their observations on fascist penetration of the American hemisphere.[25]

Claude Bowers, Ambassador to Chile, informed the President in May, 1940 that although he did not think there was any real danger of an immediate fascist coup, there was always that possibility. He believed that if the Nazis were so stupid as to attempt to inject themselves by force into the American scene, it would be in Chile that they would strike. In a report entitled "Purported German Nazi Plans in Chile" which was enclosed in this letter to Roosevelt, Bowers noted that the German population in that country was primarily militantly Nazi. He thought that it would not be entirely fantastic to consider the likelihood of an attempted overthrow of the Chilean Government by German agents. He concluded that there was a greater danger of a Nazi attempt in Chile than in any other country because of the German population and its aggressive attitude in the present war. The President replied on May 24, 1940 and voiced his conviction that, in the event of continued German victories in Europe, German agents in many of the Latin American countries would undertake immediate activities with a view to overthrowing existing governments. He urged Bowers to send to him by telegram all information of a disquieting character. Disquieting information from Bowers did come the very next day. Chile's nitrate and copper, said Bowers, would attract Germany. Brazil too, he told Roosevelt, was a most fertile field for Nazi agents. Rumors had been circulating, added the Ambassador, which told of as many as 30,000 Germans drilling for war purposes in Brazil. He admitted that the numbers might be a bit extreme, but that one could never tell. In this same month, Edwin Wilson, American Minister to Uruguay, reported an increase in Nazi activities in that nation with serious possibilities for the future. The President was disturbed by Wilson's memorandum, and directed Sumner Welles to get word to the Uruguayan Government to do something about such activities for any press leakage of them might harm Pan American solidarity. The most direct warning to come to the White House in May, 1940 came not from diplomats in Latin America, however, but from William Bullitt. Hitler's attack on America, he told Roosevelt, was an absolute certainty.[26]

Bowers' letters may have been responsible for the increased attention which the President gave to reports of internal subversion at this time. He requested Sumner Welles to investigate J. Edgar Hoover's charge that the German Consul in New York City was making inquiries of persons of German origin in reference to their radio activities in the United States. When Adolph Berle informed Roosevelt of the operations of a registered German foreign agent who directed the German Library of Information at 17 Battery Place, New York City, the President suggested that someone should look into the matter. He was most upset with the speeches of Charles Lindbergh concerning Germany's military superiority, and confided to Henry Morgenthau that if he, Roosevelt, should die today, he wanted the world to know that he was absolutely convinced that Lindbergh was a Nazi. The President ordered Sumner Welles to supply him with a list of Americans who had been awarded decorations by the German Government since 1933. He was not prepared to tolerate other Lindberghs. His suspicions about espionage activities even led him to suggest to Pierre-pont Moffat that Grand Manon, an island in the Bay of Fundy, would make a good internment camp with its high cliffs and icy waters.[27]

Fears of internal subversion did not seem to be of primary concern to the Chief Executive. The continued reports of German political actions in Latin America, however, attracted his close scrutiny. Bowers' letters were the most explicit on this subject, and the most alarming in tone and content. The Germans in Chile, he could report on June 1, 1940, were numerous and thoroughly organized for a coup d'etat. The President seemed as engaged in the subject as his Ambassador for he told Bowers to be on the lookout and to keep the closest watch of developments. This was zealously done by the Ambassador. He told the Chief Executive on June 7, 1940 that Gestapo agents from Germany were in Chile. The whole German movement, he wrote, was directed from Berlin. A certain German-Chilean by the name of Dr. Fuchs had purportedly said to Bowers that the Germans already had 7,000 trained men ready for action in Chile, with 20,000 others armed and ready to help. Nine Nazi officers were on their way over to direct operations. He informed the President on June 19, 1940 that there were approximately thirty German officers in Chile, and that their armies were in possession of light machine guns smuggled in from Germany. What was going on, Bowers reminisced, was an exact repetition of the methods adopted in Spain. Ambassador Norman Armour in Argentina sent a despatch to Cordell Hull which was made available to Roosevelt. Armour quoted an informant of the Argentine Naval Air Service as saying that if Italy joined sides with Germany three million fascists in Argentina would be thrown into the Nazi camp. This would bring the forces of the totalitarians in the country to almost one-third of the population. The Latin fear of Anglo-Saxon domination had done much to darken the Argentine image of America, said the officer. Sumner Welles described Armour's message as of very real significance. The President probably concurred. Josephus Daniels in Mexico also wrote to Roosevelt asserting that there were Nazis and communists there who would like to make trouble, but that the Embassy was vigilant to get their number with the active aid of the Mexican Government.[28]

The arrival of these letters and memoranda coincided with that of an emotionally charged message from Alexander Kirk, Consul in Berlin. He warned that the United States was the only power in the world which could effectively oppose Hitler in the future and that the Führer knew it. Kirk was personally convinced that there would be no place for the United States in the new order envisaged by the

German dictator. Hitler, he wrote, would attempt to eliminate America as a great power as soon as possible, not by force, but by gradual economic and financial strangulation. He concluded ominously that the defeat of the Allies in the present battles meant ultimately the defeat of the United States. Reports of Germany's continued penetration of Latin America appeared to Roosevelt as confirmation of Kirk's dismal prognosis.[29]

Information concerning purported German political activity in Latin America continued to reach the Chief Executive during the remaining months of 1940. A memorandum from the Office of the Chief of Naval Operations on July 10, 1940 concluded with the warning that there was a possibility of fifth column activities in all the Latin American countries. Argentina, Brazil, Chile, Uruguay, Ecuador, and Costa Rica were considered to have the most numerous organized espionage groups, and urgent action was suggested in the latter two nations to halt fascist influence. There was also contained in this intelligence report a cautionary prediction that the Axis powers would attempt to control the Panama Canal and invade Brazil, Argentina, and Uruguay. An assistant to the President, Tom Corcoran, forwarded a letter to Roosevelt which he had received from a United Press Correspondent in Brazil. The author, Jim Miller, had written that America's presence was needed in South America or the countries there would go Nazi. The President considered the information important enough to send to Sumner Welles to read and return. Cornelius Vanderbilt, after a trip through Mexico and the Central and South American countries, told the Chief Executive that Hitler planned to invade the United States immediately. In Columbia, Costa Rica, and Mexico, Vanderbilt reported having seen advanced preparations for the Nazi invasion including private Nazi airports, Nazi bombers, and German civilians training natives. There could be no quibbling, he said, America must get ready to withstand this immediately planned onslaught. Roosevelt apparently did not dismiss such information for in September, 1940 he requested that Sumner Welles should obtain naval rights from Mexico in places like Magdelena Bay, Salina Cruz, and the northeast corner of Yucatan. He seems to have been considering in this directive the occupation of key areas from which to resist a German invasion or subversive activities in close proximity to American shores. A letter from Samuel Fuller to Franklin Roosevelt contained a capsule expression of the latter's views at the close of this year. Fuller had written forcefully that the United States must defeat its enemy, the Germans, or chaos would result in the nations of the Western Hemisphere. In Fuller's view, Britain was but a temporary protection. The Germans, he continued, were terribly ruthless, and would strike at the United States when such was good strategy. He advised the President, however, that they could be beaten for their characteristic weaknesses were brutality to all under them, national conceit, and an inability to accept reversals manfully. Roosevelt replied, "There is something so wholehearted and frank about your letter of November eleventh that I want you to know that I received it with deep gratitude and appreciation. After all, we are in agreement on essential things."[30]

What were Franklin Roosevelt's personal views concerning the nature of the fascist threat to the United States? Official proclamations issued by the President during 1940 indicate that in his estimation there was the possibility that America might become directly involved in the war. He requested ever increasing funds for national defense. He sought authority to call out the National Guard in July, 1940 because of the increasing seriousness of the international situation. A Permanent Joint Board of Defense was formed on August 18, 1940 after conversations between Franklin Roosevelt and the Prime Minister of Canada, Mackenzie King. Selective Service registration was announced by the White House one month later. These essentially war preparedness measures reveal at the very least that the Chief Executive had not dismissed from most serious consideration America's participation in the overseas struggle. The question that remains to be answered more fully is why Franklin Roosevelt believed the United States to be threatened by the fascist powers.[31]

The evidence presented to the President concerning fascist penetration of Latin America does not seem to have been of sufficient depth to warrant the definite assumption that any one of the Axis nations was preparing an immediate invasion of the United States. Roosevelt had innumerable sources of information and reason dictates that if there had truly been a concerted effort by Germany or Japan at this moment to achieve political control in strategically contiguous territories, such activities would have been reported to him in far greater detail and from a much larger number of observers than was in fact the case. What were the assumptions on which Franklin Roosevelt based his conviction that the United States would one day come under direct attack? In numerous public addresses and press conferences the President emphasized several major themes in his analysis of the fascist threat. Roosevelt's thoughts on this subject stem not only from the events of 1940, but from impressions gained over a seven year period. Diplomatic correspondence, intelligence cables, letters from overseas, and the President's applied intuition were the bases of the confirmed opinion that the United States would probably face invasion in the future.

The personality of Adolf Hitler, as interpreted by Franklin Roosevelt, was at the very core of the President's personal assumptive convictions. During a press conference on April 18, 1940, Roosevelt offered the following psychological appraisal of the Führer. What would you do, he asked, if your name happened to be Hitler? Victorious Hitler's, he answered, would want to extend their power. It would be only natural for them to do so. Napoleon and Alexander did not think in terms of world domination at first. The thing tended to grow, he said. If the Führer was to achieve control over Europe, he continued, why should he wish to leave an entire continent, North, Central, and South America alone? World domination would be an enticing objective to the mass Hitler mind, asserted Roosevelt. The theme of the compulsive conqueror was reiterated on May 30, 1940 before an audience of newsmen. Hitler would say to himself, assumed the President, "I have taken two-thirds of the world and I am all armed and ready to go, why shouldn't I go the whole hog and control, in a military way, the last third of the world, the American?" Victors and conquerors always say they only want so much more, exclaimed Roosevelt, and when they get that they request the whole known world. Speaking to an American Youth Congress on June 5, 1940, the Chief Executive asked his listeners to imagine themselves as victorious Hitlers. Would you go back and paint pictures as some say the Führer will do, he asked them? He may do it, mused Roosevelt, or he might do as other successful conquerors have done and strive for world domination. He concluded, "I am not saying that is a probability, because it would be silly. I am saying it is a possibility, which is correct, and therefore, if it is a possibility, which it is, we have got to say to ourselves, 'We have got to prepare against it'."[32]

The second assumptive conviction accepted by Franklin Roosevelt was that Germany's planned conquest of the United States would come by invasion and bombing from strategic contiguous territories which would gradually fall under its control either by military occupation or economic blackmail. Bombers could reach America's shores in two hours and fifty minutes from Venezuela, seven hours from the Cape Verde Islands, and fourteen hours from the home base of a European unnamed country. His geography lessons were numerous and explicit. He urged listeners on many occasions to look at a map and check the proximity of Greenland, Alaska, Canada, Costa Rica, Columbia, Mexico, Venezuela, Brazil, Bermuda, and the West Indies. Then too if Great Britain were to be defeated even the ocean barrier would be disastrously weakened, thought the President. He replied to those who had accepted Hitler's pledge that he had no intention of invading America by saying simply that it brought back memories and recollections. Why should we accept assurances that we are immune, he asked? Such assurances had been previously given, he noted, to numerous other nations. Americans, Roosevelt emphasized, must begin to think about the potentialities of the war in relation to the United States, and that, he thought, would be a "damn good thing" to do. It is evident that he had been doing much thinking about this subject.[33]

Economic blackmail of the Latin American nations by a victorious Germany, in Franklin Roosevelt's opinion, might also enable that country to prepare for an eventual attack on the United States. Argentina, he speculated, would be told by the Germania Corporation that it could not sell its cattle, mutton, or sheep anywhere except through the Germania Corporation. Similar coerced arrangements would be made with other smaller countries. Political domination would then follow closely on the heels of economic subjection. Roosevelt believed that an actual invasion of America might not be necessary once economic dominance had been attained by Germany. He described imposed economic isolation as the "helpless nightmare of a people without freedom — the nightmare of a people lodged in prison, handcuffed, hungry, and fed through the bars from day to day by the contemptuous, unpitying masters of other continents."[34]

The intensity with which Franklin Roosevelt expressed these views was due to his firm conviction concerning their validity, and to a strong detestation of National Socialist Germany, its ideology, and its government. The German dictatorship, he asserted, represented the threat of a new enslavement in which men could not speak, could not listen, and could not think. The grave danger posed by National Socialism to democratic institutions, said Roosevelt, was evident in the German experience. The cult of Nazism, he charged, had abolished free elections and free choice in Germany. He assumed that it could happen elsewhere. The domination of the world by what he termed the Nazi forces and their fascist lieutenants was for him an abhorrent vision.[35]

The assertive tone of steadfast conviction concerning the fascist threat, which permeated Franklin Roosevelt's press conferences and speeches, was momentarily discarded in the 1940 election campaign. In accepting an unprecedented third term nomination on July 19, 1940, he had said that it was his simple, plain, and inescapable duty to arouse his countrymen to the danger of the new forces let loose in the world. This he had done in earnest before July, sporadically in the months immediately thereafter, and not at all during the autumn campaign. Roosevelt's decision to accept the party's nomination was clearly related to the international situation. He desired to participate wholeheartedly in the struggle against fascism. Henry Morgenthau noted in his diary that the President had said on January 24, 1940 that he definitely knew what he wanted to do with regard to the third term issue. He assumed that Roosevelt would accept the nomination. Numerous friends had urged him to accept a third term because of the threat of war. Herbert Pell, an acquaintance of the President from boyhood days, reflects in a letter to Roosevelt the thoughts of many other of the Chief Executive's correspondents. The desire for convenience, pleasure, and needed rest must be sacrificed, wrote Pell, to the needs of the world and the country. Louis Wehle, another longtime associate, instructed Roosevelt that war in Europe compelled him to forsake retirement and accept another four years in office. Francis Sayre confided to the President that he was the one man best able to lead the nation through the crucial months ahead. Franklin Roosevelt probably needed little prodding. He knew the confrontation which had long been expected was soon to come, and he especially would never have relinquished leadership in the struggle against fascism.[36]

The appointment of two Republicans to public office, Frank Knox as Secretary of the Navy and Henry Stimson as Secretary of War on June 19, 1940 seemed to indicate that the President was about to embark on a campaign to gain bipartisan support for the war effort. Political realism silenced Franklin Roosevelt. His campaign speeches were not at all candid if compared in their content to earlier addresses by the President. Emphasis was given to the pledge that the United States would not become involved in a war except in case of attack. This last proviso was discarded during a speech in Boston on October 30, 1940 when he said again, and again, and again that American boys would not be sent into any foreign wars. In delivering his remarks, he also mentioned his delight in welcoming home Joseph Kennedy. Neither statement was truthful. One month later, Roosevelt bluntly declared that the United States would not go to war. The President, in truth, knew that involvement in war would be a necessity.[37]

The election victory over the Republican opponent Wendell Willkie in November, 1940 enabled Franklin Roosevelt to resume his campaign to prepare Americans for acceptance of participation in the coming struggle. In a fireside chat on December 29, 1940 he reiterated the themes which had previously provided the substance of his speeches. The Axis powers, he declared, were determined to unite in ultimate action against the United States if America should interfere with their program of world domination. What possibilities did he foresee in the future? If Britain should fall, he warned, the Axis countries would control Europe, Asia, Africa, Australia, and the high seas. The Americas, said the President, would then be living at the point of a gun loaded with explosive economic and military bullets. Occupation of any South American country by the Nazis would enable them to attack the United States. What course of action, given these contingencies, did the President prescribe? There could be no appeasement, for one could not tame a tiger into a kitten by stroking it. There could be no negotiated peace with a gang of outlaws in control of Austria, Czechoslovakia, Poland, Norway, Belgium, the Netherlands, Denmark and France. There could be no civilized life with the constant threat of extermination, shooting, chains, and concentration camps. The United States, he said, must become the great arsenal of democracy. The question which the President did not answer was whether or not an arsenal would be sufficient to halt fascism. Roosevelt knew the answer, and he hoped that events in Europe and the Far East would awaken public opinion to the necessity of war involvement which he anticipated with certainty.[38]

Moments for Decision

Franklin Roosevelt approached the new year with grave concern. Germany's military dominance in Europe was an established fact, and the Führer's ambitions, as perceived by the President, had not been fully realized. The attack on Great Britain had not succeeded, but English losses were continuing to be extremely heavy. Vichy France seemed anxious to join with Germany on a basis of full collaboration. Reports of Axis penetration of Latin America were read in earnest seriousness by the Chief Executive, and served to confirm his intuitive hunch that Hitler did not intend to limit German expansion to the European continent. Italy appeared to be firmly within the fascist coalition, as a subservient and willing partner. Japan, having officially joined the Tripartite Pact, was intensifying its military activities in the Far East. The momentum of victorious conquest was clearly on the side of the Axis powers. The events of this year, 1941, were to convince the President of the need to intervene militarily against the victorious belligerents. He had always known that this moment of intervention would have to come if Germany, Italy, and Japan were to be prevented from achieving world dominance. The time for decision was rapidly becoming propitious and necessary.

Germany remained the primary focus of the President's attention. His immediate fear was that an invasion of England would be the next major thrust planned by Hitler. During a cabinet session on February 2, 1940, Cordell Hull predicted an attack on Great Britain within sixty to ninety days. Reports that 250,000 German parachute troops, dressed in English uniforms and fluent in the English language, had been assembled for this purpose were revealed during this meeting. It was also learned that Germany had produced great quantities of arsenic gas for use in the campaign. The expected invasion, however, did not materialize in the subsequent months.

Roosevelt could not have interpreted this postponement as a sign of weakness on the part of Germany. He believed that the Führer had decided to first achieve total mastery of Europe. An invasion of England could come later.[39]

Franklin Roosevelt's expectation of continued aggression by Germany was based on numerous sources. John Franklin Carter, a former journalist, Foreign Service officer, and State Department official, sent several reports to the President which discussed the capabilities of Germany to conduct its offensive operations. Carter's opinion, based on secret contacts with knowledge of domestic conditions in Germany, was that the German nation was prepared for a long war. Supplies of raw materials, he wrote, were far from desperate, food was perfectly adequate, morale was good, the army enjoyed extreme popularity, and public opinion appeared to express an assured confidence about winning the war. Carter described Germany's aims as the unification of Europe along Nazi lines. He added that Americans were privately hated by German authorities because of their desire to block the war program. Popular sentiment, said Carter, seemed to hold that it was now or never for Germany to become a great nation. He was not entirely pessimistic in his correspondence with Roosevelt for he noted that there existed a general belief that the Germans lacked guts, loved to win but were craven losers, and could not take it. Carter's restrained optimism could not have comforted the Chief Executive for thus far Germany had proven its invincibility, and from all indications intended to maintain its triumphant conquests.[40]

The Balkans appeared to be the next objective of the German advance. Colonel William Donovan had been sent on an overseas fact-finding mission by Roosevelt in August, 1940. He reported on February 26, 1941 that the United States should take action at once to create a Balkan bloc which would serve as a barrier toward any German drive to the southeast. Action must be taken immediately, warned Donovan, or it would be too late. Donovan's views distressed the President, but Hull's reply to Roosevelt's request that something be done along the lines of Donovan's advice, was even more discouraging. The Secretary of State tersely observed that the message had come too late, and that anyhow nothing could have been done. Where events in the Balkans were leading was foretold by Lincoln MacVeagh in Athens. Leg-over, leg-over, the dog went to Dover, and country by country the Germans had come to Greece and Turkey, he told the President. In this same month, Bulgaria and Yugoslavia joined the Axis coalition. Roosevelt had hoped for Yugoslav resistance, and a coup d'etat on March 27, 1941 did succeed in ousting those favoring acceptance of Germany's demands. The victory of the anti-fascist forces led by King Peter and Premier Dushan Simovich was shortlived. Reports that the Germans would soon retaliate were widespread, and on April 6, 1941 German troops began the invasion of Yugoslavia and Greece.[41]

In less than three weeks the two nations became mere appendages to a burgeoning German dominion. Herbert Pell, Ambassador to Hungary, grimly surveyed the present European situation for the President after these most recent conquests by the German army. Pell predicted that Hitler would organize all of Europe into a group of helot semi-independent states which would consume the products of an industrial Germany and provide it with raw materials and food. The Ambassador reported that he could see no justification for a cheerful outlook. The great strength, excellent equipment, good spirit, and magnificent work of the German military organization seemed absolutely unbeatable, said Pell. He confided to Roosevelt that there was no point at which the German army could be effectively attacked, and that its exhaustion would take a very long time and would result in the destruction of civilization. Pell's analysis of the trend of events in Europe was reaffirmed by Franklin Gunther, United States Minister to Rumania. In a letter to Roosevelt, Gunther wrote that one had to see first hand, month by month, the long German columns to realize the tremendous military strength of the Germans, their efficiency, discipline and organization. Rumania's Chief of State, General Jon Antonescu, said Gunther, was of the opinion that the German army would never be beaten on land. Minister Gunther suggested that the best way to finish off this impregnable Germany was to engage in merciless retaliatory bombings of the large population centers of Germany. He thought that fifteen successive nights of bombing Berlin and the German people would demand peace or rebel against their leaders. Vienna, said Gunther, where three million Germans had arrived seeking shelter, would be an excellent target. The Minister's prescription for the defeat of Germany must have revealed to Roosevelt the extreme strength of the invincible German forces. Gunther's message reporting that Antonescu had gone over to the Germans lock, stock, and barrel concluded this depressing outlook depicted by diplomats during the spring months.[42]

German activities in the Western Hemisphere continued to engage the President's interest. Roosevelt's Administrative Assistant, Lowell Mellett, had sent to the White House on January 8, 1941 excerpts from a letter of a close friend who, said Mellett, had exceptional connections in South America. The informant predicted that if Britain did fall, Brazil, Argentina, and Chile would all "go Hitler" within two weeks. The armies of these countries, said the unnamed source, were ready to go over to the German side in a minute. The President seemed impressed by these allegations for he wrote to Cordell Hull asking for a conference to discuss them. Roosevelt also received a confidential memorandum on the internal conditions and international relations of various Latin American republics. Columbia was described as a real danger spot with one of the most efficient Nazi organizations in Latin America. Ecuador was another key country for German Nazi agents. In Peru, German, Italian and Japanese agents were cooperating in a common front on behalf of Nazism. Chile, it was alleged, had the best organized Nazi movement, and in Brazil over two million Germans were working hard. Claude Bowers in Chile was initially quite confident that the Chilean government could handle any subversive initiatives. He reported, however, that there was an increasing collaborative effort on the part of the German, Italian, and Japanese Embassies to work in close cooperation in commercial and propaganda activities. Josephus Daniels was more sanguine in his letters about German infiltration in Mexico. Nazi propaganda efforts, wrote Daniels, were in evidence, but were carried on underground with little effect. John Franklin Carter was not so optimistic about propaganda activities in Argentina. He informed the President that five major Argentine newspapers were subsidized with German funds.[43]

Franklin Roosevelt expressed his concern over German activities in the Western Hemisphere on several occasions. He instructed Sumner Welles to look into the possibility that a German air base might be constructed in Haiti. He ordered the Secretary of War, Henry Stimson, to investigate reports that twenty-five German officers were expected in the French West Indian possessions. One of the intelligence services, he told Stimson, should inspect Martinique, Guadeloupe, French Guiana, and other smaller French islands. This was coming pretty close to home, concluded the President. He ordered Stimson and Secretary of the Navy Frank Knox to prepare contingency plans to militarily hold Scoresby Sound should Germany try to establish a base in northeast Greenland. Roosevelt told Henry Morgenthau in May, 1941 that American troops would have to take the Azores and Cape Verde islands if Germany pushed into Portugal or Spain. The Chief Executive did not ignore defense matters closer to American shores. He directed the Secretary of the Navy to begin patrols on the Hudson Bay during the summer months to prevent some German raider, submarine or otherwise, from entering the bay and destroying shipping, docking, mining, and smelting facilities. The President seems to have taken seriously a report by Ambassador Bowers in Chile that German Nazis had been sent from Berlin to Washington with orders to assassinate him. A memorandum containing excerpts from Bowers' letter was sent by Roosevelt to Colonel Edward Starling of the Secret Service on June 25, 1941.[44]

In addition to Germany's actions, the posture of the other fascist powers continued to give Franklin Roosevelt cause for concern. Italy seemed to be firmly encamped in the Axis alliance. Ambassador William Phillips initially informed the President that there had been a general condemnation of the war and open criticism of Mussolini. Public sentiment against the Duce, however, seemed to change in the months thereafter. The Ambassador could report in February, 1941 that the daily war bulletins issued by the government in Rome were extolling the glorious achievements of the Italian army, navy, and air forces. Italians appeared anxious to associate themselves with Germany's triumphant march. The feeling of certainty in Italy regarding an Axis victory had given added impetus to Mussolini's desire to pass under German domination. Phillips still entertained the vague hope that the Italian people would eventually overthrow their leaders and cast their lot with the Allies. He suggested to Roosevelt that perhaps a distinction should be made between the Italian Government and the Italian masses in diplomatic relations with the United States. The President responded quickly and negatively. Roosevelt saw little possibility that the Italians were willing to do more than passively accept the ignominious position which their alliance with Germany had forced upon them. He was convinced, as he had always been convinced, that Germany and Italy were working closely together. In support of this view, the Chief Executive had received two reports asserting that Italy under Mussolini's direction would not hesitate to commit its armed forces in a situation of direct hostilities with America.[45]

The third member of the Axis triumvirate assumed a momentarily equivocal posture in its relations with the United States. It is doubtful, however, that Franklin Roosevelt seriously considered the possibility that Japan was earnest and sincere in its quest for a peaceful understanding with its Far Eastern neighbors and America. The brief moments of optimism were generated in February, 1941 by Bishop James Walsh and Father Drought, Catholic priests who had just returned from Japan with what they believed were meaningful proposals for peace. Cordell Hull immediately informed Roosevelt that any suggestions for peace from Japan were valid only insofar as the United States was willing to stand aside while Japan proceeded by force to subjugate neighboring areas and strengthen its partnership with Germany in establishing a new world order. He saw little or no likelihood that Japan would accept any agreement in good faith other than that which would assure its dominance in the Far East. Intimations that Japan was considering an adjustment of its differences with the United States did persist, however. Admiral Kichisaburo Nomura, the recently appointed Japanese Ambassador to Washington, held several conversations with the President and his Secretary of State in which it appeared as though the liberal elements in Tokyo were desirous of a peaceful accommodation. Memoranda to the President from Joseph Davies and Admiral Pratt on their conversations with Nomura also contained information that tended to support the credibility of Nomura's offer of serious negotiations. The appearance in May, 1941 of Colonel Hideo Iwakuro representing the Japanese Army and Tadao Wikawa of the Cooperative Bank of Japan, served to strengthen the impression that Japan wished to achieve a cordial understanding with the United States. Japanese and American peace proposals were exchanged throughout the months of May and June, but no significant progress was made in these discussions. Franklin Roosevelt, meanwhile, had other sources of information which reaffirmed his personal conviction that any accord with Japan, other than that premised on the elimination of all western influence from the Far East, was an impossible prospect.[46]

Ambassador Joseph Grew sent to the State Department on January 27, 1941 what was in retrospect a most significant document. He reported that a Japanese official had told of plans for a surprise mass attack on Pearl Harbor, and that while the project seemed fantastic, there were so many sources speaking of such an operation that he was prompted to pass on the information. Grew's cable was sent to the President for his perusal. The next day another despatch from Grew, also forwarded to the White House, cited press reports of radio addresses delivered in Tokyo to the Japanese in North America in which was affirmed Japan's willingness to go into a war with the United States, a war for which Japan was fully prepared. The commentator asked Japanese everywhere to serve their country in various positions. Admiral Stark, Chief of Naval Operations, sent his appraisal of Japanese intentions to Roosevelt on February 5, 1941. He offered a most pessimistic portrayal of the future. Stark wrote that the Japanese peace negotiations were to be pursued only for the sake of obtaining legal rights to Indo-China and Thailand as a prelude to an invasion of Malaya and British North Borneo. Stark believed that Japan desired to move against the British, the Dutch, and the United States in succession, and that it wanted to avoid at all costs a war with the three powers simultaneously. Roosevelt appears to have reached the conclusion that the negotiations were a delaying tactic for reasons set forth in Stark's memorandum. He told Sumner Welles that the instructions of Foreign Minister Matsuoka to Nomura seemed to have been the product of a deeply disturbed mind incapable of thinking quietly or logically. Roosevelt also took a cynical view of

Matsuoka's visits to Berlin and Rome in the month of February, 1941 for he asked either Welles or Hull to express a slight raising of the eyebrows in surprise because of the Foreign Minister's failure to visit Washington on his way home.[47]

In the weeks that followed the beginning of the Nomura-Hull conversations, the despatches of Grew which were forwarded to Franklin Roosevelt were confusing in their content. Despite some evidence which pointed toward a drive by Japan to reconcile differences with the United States, these cables continued to warn of military and naval pressure by Japanese officers for precipitate action in the Pacific region. The President was probably not pleased over the report from Grew on March 25, 1941 that Osaka street signs carried pictures of Churchill, Roosevelt, and Chiang Kai-shek being struck by a hammer with the caption "Strike the enemies of the imperial nation." In April, 1941 Francis Sayre described the situation in the Philippines as one of considerable uneasiness because of concern over a possible Japanese invasion. John Carter relayed information to the President concerning extensive Japanese fifth column activities in the Philippines. The island outpost of Hawaii, however, was described as the strongest fortress in the world by Army Chief of Staff, General George Marshall, so at least Roosevelt could assume the defenses were secure. The signing of a neutrality treaty by the Soviet Union and Japan on April 13, 1941 must have heightened the concern of those who feared a Japanese drive southward. Hull, trying not to antagonize the Soviet Union, declared the pact to be simply descriptive of a situation which had existed for some time past. Grew had previously reported that the Japanese Foreign Office was aware of the intentions of Russia which were to promote a Japanese-American war. It is obvious, as will be shown, that Franklin Roosevelt did not view Soviet foreign policy in such a tactical manner. He agreed with Adolph Berle, however, who interpreted the agreement to mean that Japan was now free to blast southward and head for Singapore. In summary, Roosevelt's opinions concerning the fascist threat in the Far East had not changed. Japan remained intent upon pursuing a course of aggression in concert with Germany. He may have accepted as true Matsuoka's comment, cited in a despatch from Grew on May 19, 1941, that a war between Germany and the United States would mean a Japanese-American war too. The prospects of an encounter in the Pacific seemed very real from the perspective of the President.[48]

The threat of continued fascist aggression was but one of the considerations in the mind of Franklin Roosevelt as he speculated on the necessity of American intervention in the war. The weaknesses of a previous ally, now Vichy France, and Great Britain were also compelling factors in assessing the inevitability of a war commitment by the United States. Marshal Petain's government presented a most discouraging image in these critical months of 1941. William Leahy had been named Ambassador to Vichy in December, 1940 and his letters to the President were most alarming. Petain and his cabinet, said Leahy, were so certain of a German victory that they would accept almost any compromise with Berlin. In Leahy's view, the French desired an early peace at almost any price. He acknowledged that France was beaten down and thoroughly sick of war, that there were one and a half million war prisoner hostages, and that any way out of the situation would appeal to most of the inhabitants. Vichy officials, wrote Leahy, were too timid to resist German demands and, added the Ambassador, whatever the Germans might request would be granted. Petain was quoted as saying that the French had no arms, no organization, and very little fighting spirit. He was worried too about German retaliation on French prisoner hostages should they offer any resistance. The attitudes of Vice-Premier Admiral Darlan especially irritated the President who feared ever increasing collaboration with Germany. The status of the French fleet was probably uppermost in the minds of American diplomatic observers. Darlan met with Adolf Hitler in May, 1941 and later signed an agreement with Germany which assured that nation of the use of Syria, Bizerte in Tunisia, Dakar in West Africa, French ships to convoy German goods across the Mediterranean, and supplies of French trucks and guns. Roosevelt issued a statement saying that it would be inconceivable for France to engage in collaboration with Germany for the utter destruction of liberty, freedom and popular institutions. In truth, he could not have been that certain. The substance of Leahy's messages and the French-German accord offered no assurances that France would not someday commit its naval forces, in concert with Germany, to an invasion of England. Vichy France was an uncertainty of major concern.[49]

Great Britain's capability to sustain its war effort, especially if left to fight alone, was very much in question. Franklin Roosevelt no doubt wished that the Ship of State would sail on strong and great, but most observers were becoming very skeptical about the capacity of the British to resist the military might of Germany. Reports reaching the President were decidedly pessimistic. Admiral Stark described for Roosevelt the difficulties that the English were facing in these early months of 1941. Britain's supply of munitions, he wrote, was constantly imperiled. The nation's minimum food supply might be reached in a very few months. Its air defense could not sustain a constant wearing attrition in the shape of sporadic bombardments which were diminishing industrial capacity and straining morale. If invaded in the near future, which the Admiral thought likely, the British would receive a heavy blow from large reserves of German air power. Stark also observed that British forces would probably be defeated in the Far East if Japan should move against them. The American Consul in London, James Wilkinson, characterized the amazing resiliency of the English people in the face of German bombardment as a grimness born almost of despair. Hershel Johnson, the Chargé in Great Britain, reported that the number of weapons available to Great Britain in 1941, while sufficient to enable her to resist, would not enable her to conquer. Roosevelt thought that Johnson's appraisal was important enough to forward to John Winant, the recently chosen Ambassador to London. Winant saw for himself the pitiable plight of a courageous people under seige. In response to Roosevelt's requests for a description of the effects of the bombing, the Ambassador described the result of one 4,000 pound German bomb: 400 people killed and 400 houses destroyed. Reports such as these were the causal factors behind the Chief Executive's decision to give increased aid to the British. The dire assessments of diplomatic observers portrayed a beleaguered ally whose future existence seemed to be in grave doubt.[50]

Harry Hopkins was sent to Great Britain in January, 1941 as the personal emissary of the President. His letters to Roosevelt urged that immediate aid be sent to the English. Hopkins was visibly impressed by Winston Churchill's fighting determination to resist Germany. His depiction of Churchill offered to the President a few moments of inspiration, but Hopkins' emphatic insistence that the English desperately needed American help was of more meaningful import at the moment. He reported that British officials expected a German invasion in the early spring, and that now was the time to act promptly and boldly to get supplies to England. Decisive action could mean the difference between defeat and victory, he concluded. Roosevelt pondered such alternatives throughout these anxious moments. Averell Harriman, who was sent to Great Britain in May, 1941 to discuss Lend-Lease requirements, also shared Hopkins' views about the dependence of England on the United States for a successful final outcome of the war.[51]

Winston Churchill's correspondence with the President reveals a courageous doggedness to struggle on against heavy odds and the possible prospects of defeat. Germany, wrote the Prime Minister, was persevering in its preparations for invading England, and Hitler's forces for this mission were quite large. Japan might strike in the Pacific, he added, and the weight of the Japanese navy there would be beyond the scope of Britain's naval resources. A Japanese attack, he said, would result in the awful enfeeblement of the British war effort. This enfeeblement feared by Churchill was visible by May, 1941. The situation in North Africa, Greece, and the Middle East was not at all encouraging. The British Prime Minister warned Roosevelt not to underrate the gravity of the consequences which might follow from a Middle Eastern collapse. He pointed out that if all Europe, Asia, and Africa became a part of the Axis system, a war maintained by the British Isles, the United States, Canada, and Australia against such a mighty agglomeration would be a hard, long, and bleak proposition. The Chief Executive, pondering the necessity of American intervention, agreed with Churchill's opinion.[52]

A most important consideration for Franklin Roosevelt in his decision to press forward resolutely for a war commitment in the struggle against fascism was the position of the Soviet Union. He had attempted, unsuccessfully, to persuade Stalin to cast Russia's lot with that of the democracies. He had hoped for military cooperation from that nation and had attempted to lay the basis for the eventual military coordination of American and Russian armed forces. The Soviet Union's non-aggression pact with Germany, the invasion of Poland and Finland, the occupation of Estonia, Latvia, and Lithuania marked by mass deportation of so called dissidents, the espionage activities carried on by Russia in the United States, and the neutrality treaty with Japan seemed to have had very little effect on Roosevelt's strategy of tactfully conducting diplomacy with the Soviet Union in the hope that Stalin would some day enter the struggle against fascism. The President's aim was the defeat of Germany, and Russia's participation in this task was deemed an essential necessity. In 1941, by default, Stalin entered the democratic alliance upon request, and he was heartily and overzealously welcomed by Franklin Roosevelt.

Cordell Hull wrote that minor irritations from Russia rankled the President after the signing of the non-aggression pact with Germany. Ambassador Laurence Steinhardt in Moscow had complained about hastily imposed restrictions on the Embassy staff. Roosevelt suggested reciprocal action in Washington, saying to Hull that what was sauce for the goose might well be sauce for the Russian Ambassador, Constantine Oumansky. Speaking before the American Youth Congress on February 10, 1940, he offered an unusually harsh criticism of the Soviet Union's aggression against its infinitesimally small neighbor Finland. The President later praised the Finns for their heroic resistance and condemned the indiscriminate bombing by Russia. Thereafter, however, he seems to have pursued a policy described most accurately by his Secretary of State. Good relations were to be maintained, the Soviet Union was never to be given the slightest impression that the United States was either a present or potential enemy, and the door to friendship was always to be wide open.[53]

The Chief Executive did know of Russian espionage activities. He was informed by Adolph Berle that French police had sure evidence that Mrs. Marguerite Spiridovitch, a friend of his mother, Sara Roosevelt, was an active agent for the Soviet Union. He also received from Sumner Welles a report from Steinhardt which described the efforts of the Soviet Government to enlist as agents in the United States persons immigrating to America from territory under Soviet control. Permits to deport, said Steinhardt, were contingent upon one's willingness to engage in espionage operations. The President could not have been ignorant of Tyler Kent's spy apparatus in London, and the delivery of letters sent between Roosevelt and Churchill to Russian accomplices. The President, however, was not going to permit what he termed minor irritations to interfere in the important task of defeating the fascist powers.[54]

Franklin Roosevelt anticipated an eventual German-Russian clash. He might have been encouraged by despatches from Embassy officials in Moscow in which Stalin was portrayed as a wily strategist waiting for the opportune moment to strike Germany. Chargé Walter Thurston reported that the Soviet dictator did not feel in a position to risk a conflict with Germany's army at the present time and preferred the possibility of a future war with that nation at the very real risk of a military defeat at the present time. Laurence Steinhardt quoted the British Ambassador Sir Stafford Cripps as saying that Stalin had decided to await the outcome of the British-German struggle before engaging the armies of the Soviet Union in a war with Hitler. Stalin, said Cripps, was waiting for the serious impairment of German military power before making any commitment. Roosevelt apparently interpreted Stalin's alignment with Germany as tenuous and without substance for he told Henry Morgenthau on October 3, 1940 that he did not believe that the Russians had come to any real agreement with Germany but were still sitting mugwump on the fence.[55]

Most observers agreed that the alignment with Germany was under a severe strain. Steinhardt's despatch of October 2, 1940 contained information from reliable observers stating that the Germans were concentrating large forces in the Scandinavian countries in areas which might serve as eventual bases of operation against the Soviet Union. Leland Morris, Chargé in Germany, reported in November, 1940 that the Foreign Ministers of Germany and Russia, Joachim von Ribbentrop and Vyacheslav Molotov, had not been able to reach an agreement over Soviet requests for the Dardanelles and Finland during their conversations in Berlin. The extent of the German-Russian antagonism became known in January, 1941 when Sam Woods, the United States Commercial Attaché in Berlin, informed Cordell Hull that Germany would invade the Soviet Union. Preparations for the German attack were to be completed by the spring of 1941. The Secretary of State, having assured himself that Woods' reports were credible, brought the matter to the President's attention. Roosevelt immediately directed that a despatch be sent to Soviet officials warning of the impending German invasion. The phraseology of this message was most unusual and probably created in the minds of Stalin and his associates certain significant impressions. Hull said that his Government did not feel that it would be to the common interest of the countries which had thus far succeeded in maintaining political and economic independence in the face of German aggression for it to remain silent while in possession of such important information. The unique manner in which Russia had faced German aggression before this moment was not explained. The Soviet Union, ironically, was portrayed as a fascist opponent instead of a collaborator in a joint program of territorial acquisition. American naivete was perhaps noted by Stalin and Molotov.[56]

Rumors of an imminent invasion became more numerous in the months preceding June, 1941. Leland Morris in Germany and Ambassador Steinhardt in Moscow sent several despatches citing reports of an expected clash between the two nations. Cordell Hull, evidently expecting a break in Russian-German relations, cabled Steinhardt and set forth the principles which were to guide relations between the United States and the Soviet Union. No approaches were to be made to Russia. Any approaches which the Soviet Government might make were to be treated with reserve until such time as the Soviet Government could demonstrate that it was not engaging in maneuvers to obtain unilateral concessions and advantages for itself. A strict quid pro quo was to be exacted for anything given to the Soviet Union. No sacrifices in principle were to be made in order to improve relations. It was to be stressed that any improvement would help the Soviet Union more than the United States. Finally, day to day relations were to be based on the principle of reciprocity. The signatures on this despatch were those of Cordell Hull and Stanley Hornbeck. The immediate abandonment of the guidelines cited above must be credited to a decision by Franklin Roosevelt. In the days after German armies invaded Russia on June 22, 1941, it was the President who most strongly demanded that every request of the Soviet Government be fulfilled as hurriedly as possible. The prospects for the defeat of the Axis coalition appeared more probable, in Roosevelt's estimation, because of Russia's manpower and resources.[57]

Pressing Toward the War Commitment

William Bullitt had written Franklin Roosevelt on May 21, 1941 urging him to embark on a program of bold leadership in the task of preparing Americans for their participation in the coming struggle against the fascist powers. The time, said Bullitt, was 11:59. The people must be told the facts and the requirements of the situation. Initially, Roosevelt seems to have been reluctant to engage in the bellicose oratory of a partisan interventionist. The President momentarily preferred, as he told Henry Morgenthau, to wait for the Germans to force the United States into war by an incident which he expected at any time. Morgenthau was sure that the Chief Executive wanted to be pushed into the battle rather than lead his fellow countrymen into the European turmoil. Roosevelt's appraisal of events transpiring in the first half of this crucial year 1941, however, compelled him to put forth an even more forceful presentation of the dangers to American security than he had done in the past. He seems to have accepted the advice given to him by Felix Frankfurter. One reaches minds, wrote Frankfurter on May 24, 1941, by repetition and concreteness. The people must understand, he continued, that this struggle was their struggle because fascism was an immediate menace to everything that Americans cherish in the country's institutions. They must not be deceived by the notion that Uncle Sam was simply Lady Bountiful engaged upon an altruistic enterprise in aiding Great Britain. All men must know, he told Roosevelt, that it is their own skins and souls at stake. Tell them, he prodded the President, that the nature of the threat and our readiness to resist it have already been decided. If such is our policy, said Frankfurter, then we must not withhold execution of it by waiting on what is called an incident. A powerful and self-reliant nation will not determine its policy by the accident of an incident. What the people want, he concluded, is a "let's go." They want to know why, where, and how.[58]

Germany's military dominance of Europe, the collaborationist temperament of the officials of Vichy France, the precarious condition of Great Britain, the President's assumptions concerning Hitler's aims in the Western Hemisphere, and the uncertainties surrounding Russian resistance were the determinants in the decision to seek the involvement of necessity. Roosevelt had explained to Jan Ciechanowski, the Ambassador of Poland's government in exile, that he was endeavoring to make citizens world conscious and to lift them out of a home townish foreign policy. They must realize, said the President, that this was a war for fascist territorial expansion, a war in defense of fundamental democratic principles, and a war of irreconcilable ideologies and aims. The advice given by Felix Frankfurter was intended to be used in the radio address proclaiming an unlimited national emergency. Roosevelt's attempt to awaken Americans to the facts as he had portrayed them to Ciechanowski intensified with this speech on May 27, 1941.[59]

His introductory remarks were ominous and blunt. The Nazis were engaged in a world war for world domination. The advance of Hitler-ism had to be forcibly checked or else the Western Hemisphere would soon be within range of Germany's weapons of destruction, said the President. Some people, he charged, mistakenly believe that we are not attacked until bombs drop in Chicago, New York, San Francisco, or New Orleans. Czechoslovakia began with Austria, he continued, Norway began with Denmark, and Greece began with Albania and Bulgaria. Roosevelt thought it would be suicide to wait until Germany was in America's front yard. The Bunker Hill of tomorrow might be several thousand miles from Boston.[60]

It is evident from this speech that Franklin Roosevelt yearned to confront the German challenge before a direct attack by that nation on the United States. In numerous public addresses he conveyed a crisis mood of war expectation. He instructed a gathering of magazine and newspaper editors to give to the reading public an accurate pre-sentation of the terrible seriousness of the Axis threat. He told his listeners that America had to quit all this silly business of "business as usual." The nation must be made to realize that if the fascist powers win, the United States would be put in a vice, a strait jacket, from which it would not recover for one hundred years. The media, Roosevelt demanded, must be frank with the public. Aid to Britain was not of itself a wise slogan for more might be demanded of Amer-icans who must arm themselves for the future. The seriousness of the situation, he suggested, should be played up all the time. He often elaborated on this theme of war preparation. We've got to buckle down to the determination to fight the war through, said Roosevelt, by hard, tough fighting in which somebody will get hurt. Against naked force, he reasoned, the only possible defense was naked force. The defenders against aggression must match destruction with more destruction, said the President, and slaughter with greater slaughter. The United States, he emphasized, could not escape its collective responsibility for the kind of life that would emerge from the present ordeal. Roosevelt seems to have been asking the nation to prepare for a long arduous trial which would call for a commitment beyond the arsenal contribution.[61]

In attempting to prepare national sentiment to accept the respon-sibility of direct involvement in hostilities, Franklin Roosevelt would give extensive treatment to the nature of the German menace. Why should Americans fight in battles far from presently secure shores? The President assumed that they would have no other choice. The theme of the compulsive conqueror was reiterated in speeches this year. Do business with Hitler, he would ask? Live at peace with Hitler? The only peace with the Führer, he warned, would be one of complete surrender. What the German dictator desired, Roosevelt would say, was world domination. Germany, he thought, would literally parcel out the world, hoisting the swastika over vast territories and populations. What would life be like in this new world order? The vast majority, said the President, would live in tyrannical enslavement. These men and their hypnotized followers, he charged, sought the regimentation of all human beings. In the place of the Bible, Roosevelt would tell his listeners, the Nazis would offer Mein Kampf; in place of the cross, the Swastika; and in place of love and mercy, blood and iron. All those who resisted, he concluded, would be mowed down by the firing squads of the Gestapo. The vivid expressiveness of these phrases seemed designed to promote fear and anger. Such responses would be necessary to secure the war commitment.[62]

Where, when, and how was the United States going to come to terms with the fascist threat? Franklin Roosevelt believed that the moment for military engagement would come when America and the Western Hemisphere were threatened. He seemed to believe that this moment had already arrived. The President's thoughts concerning the perimeters within which the United States Navy was to conduct its patrol operations reflect his appraisal of the Germana menace and reveal his strategy for encounter. In February, 1941, Roosevelt defined the Atlantic zone of security as halfway between the most westerly part of the western continent, North, Central, and South America, which was the "sticky out" point of Brazil, and the same relative point on the other side, which was, he said, the "sticky out" point of Africa. In the Pacific, asserted Roosevelt, the perimeter within which American patrols would operate was set by the international date line. Two months later, however, he seemed to indicate that there were no limits to the patrol activities. Ships were directed to patrol as far on the waters of the seven seas as might be necessary for the defense of the American hemisphere. He compared these activities to those of wagon train scouts of old. They did not wait until the Indians were two miles within striking distance. No one could draw a line around the Western Hemisphere, he declared, which would guarantee the security of the Americas. He offered the example of an old lady who, having just crossed the Arctic Circle, observed that she had not been able to see it. So it is with any line of demarcation, said the President. In rendering aid to Great Britain's Atlantic defense efforts by reporting the location of Axis raiders, it was inevitable that American patrol vessels would eventually come under fire from German ships. This must have been evident to Franklin Roosevelt. He had intentionally placed no geographical limits on these defense operations. The accident of an incident must have been an expected contingency in the mind of the President, and perhaps an awaited contingency too.[63]

The first encounter came on May 21, 1941 when the merchant ship *Robin Moor* was sunk by a German submarine. Roosevelt declared that this brutal act revealed that Germany intended to pursue a policy of intimidation, terror, and cruelty in its effort to drive American commerce from the oceans and seize control of the high seas. The United States destroyer *Greer* was sunk on September 4, 1941, and the President used this incident to once again generate anger, fear, and a desire for revenge in the mind of the American public. The Nazi design, he charged, was to abolish freedom of the seas and to acquire absolute control of the oceans surrounding the Western Hemisphere. The next step, asserted Roosevelt, would be to use the German bridgeheads in Uruguay, Argentina, Bolivia, and Columbia for a concerted attack on American possessions. A permanent world system based on force, terror, and murder would then be created under German auspices. In pressing toward the war commitment, the President declared that the time had come to say that the Axis shall go no further. If you see a rattlesnake poised to strike, you do not wait until he has struck before you crush him. In Roosevelt's opinion, the time had come for prevention of attack. American ships were ordered in September, 1941 to shoot on sight any German or Italian vessel entering waters within the American defense perimeter, a zone which the President had previously hinted was nonexistent. The sinking of the *USS Kearney* on October 17, 1941 and the loss of the *Reuben James* two weeks later served to further dramatize the Chief Executive's earlier warnings.[64]

In truth, Franklin Roosevelt realized that Hitler's strategy was to avoid any encounter with American destroyers or merchant ships. William Phillips had told him on August 30, 1941 that neither the Germans nor the Italians were going to do anything which might bring the United States into the war. The Ambassador reported that Hitler had issued orders to his submarine commanders not to sink any American ship and that any who did so would suffer capital punishment. The President seemed to be deliberately trying to make it impossible for the Führer to carry out his strategy of avoidance. He probably hoped that the public reaction to these incidents would one day sustain a declaration of war against Germany. The occupation of Greenland, Iceland, Trinidad, and British Guiana by American troops during the spring and summer months of this year may also have been intended for both defensive and tactical purposes. In the case of Iceland, Roosevelt directed the Secretaries of War and Navy to order the occupation forces to attack Axis planes flying over that territory for reconnaisance purposes. His expectation of an incident was based on the clear realization that the likelihood of such an occurrence was a distinct possibility.[65]

The seriousness with which Franklin Roosevelt anticipated the military involvement of the United States in war is also evident in America's relations with Great Britain during this year. American and British military officials met in Washington from January to March, 1941 to prepare plans for the coordination of the two nations' armed forces should the United States be compelled to resort to war. No specific commitments were to be made except as to technical methods of cooperation. The resultant ABC-1 and ABC-2 Plans called for further consultation between the military representatives of both sides to allocate the principal areas of responsibility, and to determine the major lines of military strategy to be pursued, the strength of the forces which each side might be able to commit, and command arrangements. It was agreed that the Atlantic and European area was to be considered the decisive theater, with Germany cited as the primary target for offensive action by British and American forces. The President, who fully approved the purpose of these staff discussions, did not ignore the possibility that the United States might soon find itself at war with Germany. Preparation of war plans had begun in earnest seriousness.[66]

Material and financial aid to Great Britain also increased substantially during these critical months. The Chief Executive signed into law the Lend-Lease Act on March 11, 1941 and requested $7 billion to finance this program of aid to the Allies. Averell Harriman was appointed to expedite shipments to England. This law seemed to make binding what Harry Hopkins referred to as the common-law marriage of the sister democracies. Scientific information was now exchanged, military intelligence was pooled, security operations were coordinated, American military and civilian specialists were sent to England, damaged British warships were repaired in American shipyards, and plans for military collaboration had begun. Hopkins made a second trip to London in July to arrange for a future meeting between Roosevelt and Churchill and to discuss other pertinent matters relating to British-American cooperation. He remarked that there were then in London all manner of missions, and that the American Embassy was bursting at the seams with representatives from the United States. It remained for the Prime Minister and the President to personally sanction what was in reality a partnership in the war effort against Germany.[67]

The meeting of Franklin Roosevelt and Winston Churchill in Argentia Harbor off the coast of Newfoundland must have signified to the Axis powers that Great Britain and the United States had finally sealed their collaborative commitments to halt the advances of

Germany, Italy, and Japan. The attendance at this conference of the chief military advisers of the President and Prime Minister gave sure indication to interested observers that war preparations were being discussed at the highest levels of both governments. The enunciation of the principles of the Atlantic Charter on August 14, 1941 marked the two nations complete rejection of fascist revisionist designs. Roosevelt and Churchill pledged to seek no aggrandizement, territorial or other; to refrain from making any territorial changes which were not in accord with the freely expressed wishes of the people; to respect the right of all peoples to choose the form of government under which they would live; to assure access to all nations on equal terms to trade and raw materials; to bring about full economic collaboration; to establish a secure peace; to obtain freedom of the seas; and to insure the abandonment of the use of force by all nations. A most important phrase which was contained in the sixth principle of the Charter was the call for the final destruction of the Nazi tyranny. These words could have left no doubt as to where Franklin Roosevelt and the United States stood in present hostilities. Given the information in the hands of the President, the commitment to destroy the Nazi tyranny must be considered as a commitment to engage the Axis powers with America's military forces. In no other way were Germany and Italy going to be defeated in a decisive manner. True, as Hopkins notes, the Atlantic Charter was never inscribed on parchment, signed, sealed, and taped. In Roosevelt's words, however, the conversations had clarified many things and, he added, they had discussed operations. A most important operation, and one revealed by Harry Hopkins to Joseph Davies, which was discussed by Roosevelt and Churchill was a second front to aid the Soviet Union. It seems impossible to believe that the British were contemplating such military aid to Russia with a view to engaging only their own armed forces. They were already under severe strain in the struggle against Germany. A second front could have only been created as a joint American and British effort. It is clear from Hopkins' candid admission to Davies that America's involvement in the war was considered by Roosevelt to be only a matter of a very short time.[68]

Franklin Roosevelt's efforts to construct a firm American-British alliance in anticipation of the intervention of the United States in the war effort against fascism were concurrent with his attempts to strengthen the Soviet Union in its endeavor to resist the German invasion. The President had said on June 24, 1941 that the United States would give all the aid it could to the Soviet Union. The zealousness with which the President undertook the task of all out aid to Russia seems to reveal more than a desire to save the Red Armies from a crushing defeat by Germany. The Soviet Union was to become a member of the emerging triumvirate against the Axis coalition. Foreseeing America's entrance into the war, Roosevelt wanted to secure Stalin's wholehearted participation in the eradication of fascism and in the construction of a new world order.

Initially, he may have had serious doubts about the capacity of Russia to sustain resistance under the German onslaught. Secretary Stimson thought its defenses might collapse in one to three months time. Secretary Knox predicted that it would take six weeks to two months for Hitler to clean up in Russia. John Franklin Carter reported to the President that a knowledgeable observer believed Moscow would be taken in three weeks although Russian resistance might continue beyond this time span which had been allotted by Germany for the conquest of European Russia. Serge Obolensky, a former Russian officer and acquaintance of Roosevelt, expressed little hope that the Red Army could hold back the invasion for more than a month or so after which the Germans would set up a puppet Russian government. Obolensky's comments were not entirely pessimistic, however, for he believed that Russia's 200,000 man Far Eastern army would continue the battle against German intruders and that its generals might even agree to form a Siberian democratic government. The Chief Executive remained optimistic concerning this issue despite the opinions of many that Russia would collapse. He expressed his particular interest in Obolensky's estimate of the Far Eastern army's ability to ultimately defeat Germany's forces in Russia. The President told William Leahy that the Russian diversion might mean the liberation of Europe from Nazi domination, and that the United States really did not need to worry about Russian domination in the future. Reports reaching the Chief Executive in the months to come would further strengthen his belief that Germany's defeat was becoming a very real possibility. Yet it was during these months that Roosevelt, disregarding the advice of State Department officials to warily approach a former Axis collaborator, stressed most earnestly the necessity for meeting all Russia's requests. The future unity of the war coalition of the United States, Great Britain, and the Soviet Union in the final destruction of the fascist nations was perhaps the primary aim of Franklin Roosevelt in this endeavor.[69]

The armies of the Soviet Union, while suffering heavy losses, did manage to impede the German advance to a far greater extent than most observers had thought possible. British intelligence sources reported to the President on July 19, 1941 that the situation in Russia was completely under control, that the General Staff of the Soviet Union and the Commander of the Air Force appeared to be full of confidence, and that large counter attacks might be launched in the near future. The next day Roosevelt met personally with the Soviet Ambassador Oumansky and promised to supply urgently the requests of the Soviet Union. The enactment of Lend-Lease permitted the President to aid any country whose defense was deemed vital to the defense of the United States, and with this authority the aid program began hurriedly in July, 1941. The announcement of Russia's inclusion in Lend-Lease arrangements was not made until November 7, 1941 primarily because of Roosevelt's fear that public opinion would be violently opposed to it. The administration of the aid program was conveniently placed in the Division of Defense Aid Reports of the Office of Emergency Management. Hopkins noted that the title suggested a dusty, fusty, bookkeeping agency which would be an inconvenient target for criticism. It was not until October 28, 1941 that the Office of Lend-Lease Administration was established under the direction of Edward Stettinius. In the intervening months, the President, acting through Harry Hopkins, had committed the United States to fulfilling the demands of Stalin and his representatives. William Knudsen, Director General of the Office of Production Management, Major General James Burns, Executive Officer of the Division of Defense Aid Reports, and the Secretaries of War and Navy were ordered by the Chief Executive in July, 1941 to give prompt and effective assistance to the Soviet Union. The coalition necessary to achieve success in the struggle against fascism was to be secured at all costs.[70]

Harry Hopkins was sent to Moscow in July, 1941 as the personal envoy of the President to Joseph Stalin. Hopkins had suggested the visit in a letter to Roosevelt dated July 25, 1941 for it was his opinion that the Russian dictator had to know in an unmistakable way that the United States meant business on a long term supply job. The Chief Executive saw another purpose in the Hopkins' mission and that was to lay the basis of cordiality, friendship, and trust between himself and Stalin. Roosevelt asked Stalin to treat his representative with the identical confidence which would be accorded to himself, the President. In his first conference at the Kremlin, Hopkins told Stalin of the need to defeat Hitler, the enemy of mankind. The Soviet leader responded with words intended for Franklin Roosevelt. The Germans, he asserted, could never be trusted and were an anti-social force in the present world. He was certain that these views on Germany coincided with those of the President. Detailed discussions then followed concerning the aid program. Hopkins rose to leave, and reiterated to Stalin the President's determination to do everything to assist the Soviet Union in its valiant struggle against the German invaders. Stalin might have interpreted this last statement to mean that Roosevelt would be willing to declare war on Germany for this request was

made to Hopkins the very next day. American troops would be welcomed on any part of the Russian front, said Stalin. Roosevelt never
answered this appeal with an outright rejection. The President's impressions of the Soviet dictator must have been favorable ones. Hopkins was treated most cordially and courteously. Stalin's expressed
determination to crush Nazism, despite its belated assertion, coincided
with the Chief Executive's most desired objective. The leader whom
Hopkins described as modest, informal, forthright, and democratic
was, thought Roosevelt, a necessary allied associate in the war
coalition.[71]

Hopkins' optimistic reports about the status of Russian resistance
to the German invasion coincided with those of other diplomatic
observers. Hull sent to Roosevelt the observations of Laurence Steinhardt, Ambassador in Moscow, who had reported that the German
advance toward Leningrad and the capital city was making little
progress and would soon encounter determined and perhaps effective
resistance. Two days later, the Secretary of State reported the dis-
covery of a second Soviet defense line of more than one hundred fresh
divisions. A despatch from Leland Morris in Berlin on that same
day described the Germans increasing uneasiness about the difficulties
in Russia. Morris believed that public unrest in Germany might reach
serious dimensions if the Soviet defense continued. John Carter, sending information he had obtained from a private source, said that the
Nazi forces would be defeated in Russia within twelve months. Heavy
rains would soon make Russia an impossible quagmire, he told Roosevelt, and the bogged down Nazi panzer divisions would then be subjected to guerilla attacks by fanatical Russians who would fire their
guns until they were killed. An observer in the Soviet Union expressed
his feeling of elation concerning the Russian war effort. In a letter
sent to the President, he said that it was literally unthinkable that
the Germans could conquer in this vast, immeasurably powerful
united, and heads-up country. The President told Henry Morgenthau
that he expected the German drive to come to a halt soon because of
the use of inferior lubricating oil. Franklin Roosevelt had received
information asserting that the German advance into Russia would not
be immediately successful and that the invading armies were meeting
very determined resistance. The view that all out aid to Russia was
due to that nation's possible imminent collapse would appear to be
weakened by the despatches previously cited. It was at this moment,
however, that the Chief Executive, ignoring the advice of State Department officials, chose to embark on a course of unquestioning
fulfillment of Stalin's every demand.[72]

Franklin Roosevelt pressed for action in his program of aid to
Russia in the midst of the increasingly optimistic reports on the capa-

bility of the Soviet Union to halt the German armies. He told Wayne Coy, the Liaison Officer for Emergency Management, that if he, Roosevelt, were a Russian he would feel that he had been given the run-around in the United States. He directed Coy to act as a burr under the saddle and to get things moving. Step on it, ordered the President. Roosevelt told Stimson and Knox that it was of paramount importance to deliver all reasonable munitions help to Russia. The Chief Executive confided to his cabinet officers that he was sick and tired of hearing that the Soviet Union was going to get this or going to get that. What he wanted to hear from now on was that it was underway. Why was Franklin Roosevelt so eager to meet the demands of Stalin? Why was the principle of reciprocity, as suggested by the State Department, so readily abandoned in the program of aid to Russia? The threat of an easy German victory over the Soviet Union had disappeared in the autumn months. Perhaps the letter sent by Churchill and Roosevelt to Stalin on August 15, 1941 may provide an answer to the above questions. In this note, the President and Prime Minister requested a meeting in Moscow to consult on the requirements of the Russian war effort. The most significant phrase would seem to be that stating that the three powers must direct their attention to a more long term policy for there was still a long and hard path to be traversed before the final victory. What was this more long term policy if it was not the political and military alignment of Britain, America, and the Soviet Union in the war against fascism? [73]

Franklin Roosevelt's readiness to aid the Soviet Union was evident too in the assignment of Averell Harriman as Chairman of a Special War Supply Mission which visited Russia in September and October, 1941. Harriman presented a note from the President in which Stalin was assured that ways would be found to provide the material and supplies necessary to fight Hitler. Harriman pointedly pledged, in his first meeting with the Russian dictator, that the fullest possible assistance would be given to the Soviet Union until the ultimate victory was secured. The United States had a vital and lasting interest in the outcome of the struggle, said Harriman. The subsequent discussions were most cordial, and on one occasion Stalin even proposed a toast to American industry and the assistance that it was providing to Russia. The needs of the Soviet Union were listed in detail and sent to the President for his immediate action. This Moscow Conference must have assured Stalin of the President's zealous eagerness to meet his demands. The Soviet leader wrote to him on October 3, 1941 expressing his certainty that the Chief Execuive would do everything necessary to insure the carrying out of the decisions of the Moscow Conference as speedily and as completely as possible. Roosevelt replied saying that all military equipment and munitions had been approved for shipment and that he had ordered the delivery of raw materials to be expedited. The Chief Executive also told Stalin that the Soviet Union would be charged no interest for its indebtedness. Payment for American supplies was not to commence until five years after the war's conclusion. Roosevelt directed Lend-Lease officials and government agencies to promptly fulfill the requests which his Special Envoy had received from Stalin.[74]

There is other evidence that Franklin Roosevelt sought a long term relationship with the Soviet Union in the war effort. He was careful to cultivate the understanding of Pope Pius XII concerning aid to an avowedly atheistic regime. Myron Taylor was given the task of convincing the Pope of the following assumptions as set forth by Roosevelt: Russia's attack on churches from 1918 on was based on the primary objective of removing the Orthodox Church from politics; Russian churches were open for worship and attended by a very large percentage of the population; and Russia was in no sense the aggressor nation. The President reiterated these same thoughts in a personal letter to the Pope on September 3, 1941. Pope Pius, who was far more knowledgeable about the state of religious persecution in Russia, cordially replied to Roosevelt but made no references to the President's assumptions concerning religion in the Soviet Union. It is difficult to disagree with the advice of Father Leopold Braun, Chaplain to American Catholics in Moscow. In a letter forwarded to the President by Myron Taylor, Father Braun suggested that now was the time to beat the iron while it was hot and soft on the need for religious freedom and an end to religious persecution in Russia. Franklin Roosevelt did ask Harriman to urge Stalin to ease restrictions on religious worship.[75]

The increasing danger of hostilities with Japan was a major consideration in the President's determination to strengthen military and diplomatic relations with those nations opposing Germany. Ambassador Joseph Grew retrospectively commented that the Roosevelt Administration had reached the conclusion that Japan was incorrigible and should, in the fullness of time, be dealt with in summary fashion. This point of view was shared by Franklin Roosevelt. Negotiations with Japanese diplomats Ambassadors Nomura and, after November 7, 1941, Saburo Kurusu, would continue in the critical months before Pearl Harbor, but the prospects for peaceful accommodation were, in Roosevelt's opinion, exceedingly dim. Japanese aggression in the Far East had been of constant concern to the President since 1933. Nothing except a complete withdrawal of Japan's forces from China and southeast Asia would have modified Roosevelt's assumptions about the inevitability of war between the United States and Japan. He hoped that the day of reckoning could be postponed through tactful, but firm, diplomatic maneuvering.[76]

The President's expectation of war with Germany, and hence his desire to avoid a confrontation with Japan, is evident in letters he wrote to Harold Ickes concerning the possibility of an oil embargo. The Secretary of Interior had suggested that oil exports to Japan should be curtailed to restrain its war effort. The President thought otherwise. He told Ickes that the present requirement was to keep peace in the Pacific primarily because of the need to control the Atlantic supply routes. He also noted that there just was not enough navy to go around. Roosevelt expressed a similar view to Henry Morgenthau, saying that a stoppage of all oil shipments to Japan would drive that nation down to the Dutch East Indies and would mean war in the Pacific. The Chief Executive made an interesting proposal to Nomura in this same month. During a discussion on July 24, 1941, Roosevelt proposed the neutralization of Indo-China if Japan would withdraw its forces from that area. He did not anticipate a favorable response to this neutralization scheme, and he did not receive one. Japanese troops were to remain in French Indo-China until the China Incident was settled. Once again, however, as in the decision not to embargo oil, the President had attempted to prolong negotiations and maintain peace in the Pacific. He may have been motivated, as Ambassador Grew has observed, by a desire to place the United States in an unassailable position from the point of view of history.[77]

The President could not have been optimistic concerning the neutralization proposal. Japan's occupation of Indo-China had already begun weeks before he had advanced the suggestion to Nomura. The decoding of intercepted diplomatic messages to and from Japan, termed Operation MAGIC, made available to Roosevelt the real intentions and dimensions of the Japanese drive southward. The thrust into Indo-China, as revealed by the intercepts, would not be halted. The President knew that the reasons for occupying the area were to prepare for an advance on the Netherlands East Indies with the eventual aim being to crush all Anglo-American military power. The Chief Executive was asked about the Japanese danger during a press conference. He replied that he did not know what today's move would be, or tomorrow's, or the next day. If there was something specific that we could count on happening, he added, then we could talk about it. In truth, he knew that the momentum of Japanese military policy was carrying it quickly toward war in the Pacific. Japan's action in Indo-China, he told Josephus Daniels, had created new problems with far reaching implications. The issuance of an Executive Order on July 26, 1941 freezing all Japanese assets in the United

States, and thereby bringing trade with that nation under firm government control, was perhaps an indication that while the President wished to engage in continued negotiations with Japan, he would not be an unwitting accomplice to Japan's program of imperialist aggression. He agreed with Francis Sayre's opinion that the threat of further advances on Singapore, Thailand, the Netherlands East Indies, and the Philippines was now very real.[78]

Franklin Roosevelt was still, however, unwilling to confront Japanese aggression with stronger measures that would lead to war. Prime Minister Churchill had pressed the President for a definite war commitment if Japan should attack any third power, most particularly Great Britain, and for a pledge to undertake any and all steps of whatsoever character against Japan if that nation's conquests continued in southeast Asia. Roosevelt had told Churchill during the discussions at the Atlantic Conference that every effort must still be made to prevent the outbreak of war with Japan. A statement was given by the President to Nomura on August 17, 1941 which tactfully avoided the blunt language suggested by the British Prime Minister. The primary enemy was Germany. A Pacific encounter would gravely weaken the Atlantic war effort.[79]

In the months of August and September, 1941, Premier Fumimaro Konoye formally requested a meeting with Franklin Roosevelt to discuss all important problems between Japan and America covering the entire Pacific area, and to explore the possibility of saving the situation. Vice-President Henry Wallace wrote a letter to the President the day after Konoye had made this proposal. Wallace suggested to Roosevelt that he take an exceedingly firm stand with Japan. An appeasing or partially appeasing stand, said the Vice-President, was certain to bring bad results with regard to Japan and the situation in Europe. A strong stand, however, would impress the Axis and would strengthen the psychology of the American people. Wallace strongly advised the President to go to the absolute limit in firmness in dealing with Japan. Any sign of weakness, concession, or appeasement would be misunderstood by Japan and the Axis, and would cost America many millions of hours of man labor and much suffering. Wallace's advice could not have come at a more critical moment in American-Japanese relations. The President had initially favored a meeting with Konoye. Ambassador Grew had urgently suggested that prayerful consideration be given to Konoye's offer. The Vice-President's thoughts may have brought to mind the Munich betrayal and more importantly its aftermath. Roosevelt, although anxious to avoid a confrontation with Japan as he watched closely war developments with Germany, was not willing to risk the charge of pusillanimous appeasement should Japan choose to continue its mission of conquest.

He may have wondered privately why Konoye could not have achieved an accommodation with the United States without a summit spectacle. If the position of the Prime Minister was as precarious as Ambassador Grew indicated, and given the belligerent sentiment in Japanese military circles, what could be the chances of implementing any agreements which might come from a meeting with Konoye? Roosevelt apparently did not believe that a settlement of the Far Eastern controversy could be achieved in a dramatic and ceremonial encounter between the two leaders. He never issued a flat rejection of Konoye's offer, but did insist that broad agreements first be reached concerning respect for territorial integrity and the sovereignty of all nations, the principle of non-interference, equality of commercial opportunity, and the non-disturbance of the status quo in the Pacific excepting change through pacific means. He told Ambassador Nomura that the fundamental and essential questions had to be answered first. Roosevelt's approach to the Konoye proposal was perhaps not a momentary decision, but one reached after deliberating over the course of Japanese aggression during the last ten years. Could the tide of militarist imperialism be halted so suddenly? The President did not think so.[80]

The resignation of Konoye on October 17, 1941 and his replacement by Premier General Hideki Tojo, former Minister of War, was a portent of disconcerting significance. An area very directly threatened by the continued intensity of Japanese offensive activities was China, and Chiang Kai-shek plaintively appealed for American aid in the struggle against Japan. The tone of the Generalissimo's letter was foreboding. A real collapse of resistance might be possible, he told Roosevelt. Japan, he asserted, intended to defeat its opponents in the Far East one by one. He asked for American air support to meet the Japanese invasion. The President refused to commit the United States to a course of action which might mean war with Japan. The primary theater of war still remained in Europe and the Atlantic.[81]

There occurred a sudden deterioration in American-Japanese relations in the month of November, 1941. Ambassador Grew, in a despatch that was sent to Roosevelt, warned on November 3, 1941 that it would be a grave mistake not to think seriously of Japan's willingness to enter a war with the United States. The Japanese, he wrote, whose sanity was not measured by western logic, have the capacity to rush headlong into a suicidal conflict. They would exploit all available tactical advantages including initiative and surprise, he added later, and admitted that the Embassy in Tokyo should not be relied upon to give adequate warning of attack. Mounting evidence that a sudden aggressive move by Japan might be forthcoming did not persuade the President to abandon his strategy of delay and caution in meeting the Japanese threat. Admiral Stark and General Marshall had advised Roosevelt to seek time to build up the defensive forces in the Far East, and to remain committed to the primary objective of defeating Germany. The President continued his pursuit of what Hopkins called a policy of stalling and holding off in negotiations with Japan. The attempt to avoid a confrontation was becoming increasingly more difficult.[82]

FDR fully realized that the crisis was reaching its inevitable climax. A proposed *modus vivendi,* which called for Japan's withdrawal from southern Indo-China and an end to the freeze placed on Japanese assets, was abandoned at a time when, as Roosevelt told Morgenthau, the situation with Japan was coming to a head and prospects were not too good for a favorable settlement. Winston Churchill and Chiang Kai-shek were decidedly opposed to any compromise arrangement. Marshall and Stark, however, again suggested that the most essential consideration was to gain time. In the midst of conflicting advice, the President chose not to offer the *modus vivendi.* In a letter to Francis Sayre dated November 26, 1941, Roosevelt expressed his conviction that Japan contemplated the extension of its control by aggression into the whole of the Pacific area. He advised that Japanese aggression might soon cause an outbreak of hostilities between the United States and Japan.[83]

Franklin Roosevelt was certain of imminent action by Japan. There were several possible targets of Japanese aggression thought the President. The Philippines, East Indies, Burma, Malaya, and Thailand were in the path of the Japanese advance. MAGIC intercepts in the first week of December, 1941 left no doubt that Japan contemplated a war action which would involve the United States. Roosevelt confided to Henry Morgenthau on December 1, 1941 that he could not guarantee anything and that it was all in the laps of the gods. He added that it was likely to be worse in the next week. He was sure the Japanese were simply stalling until they were ready. Nomura and Kurusu, said the President, were running around like a lot of wet hens when asked to explain the Japanese build-up in Indo-China. The President admitted that he was talking with the British about where and when the United States and Great Britain should strike and, said the Chief Executive, that he was still awaiting a clarifying response on this issue. Roosevelt had decided by this time to issue a war warning to Japan, in conjunction with an identical note by Great Britain, should Japan move its troops southward. In a letter to Emperor Hirohito on December 6, 1941, he warned of tragic possibilities in the Pacific area if the Japanese advance continued. In the evening hours of that same day Roosevelt read through thirteen points of a fourteen point memorandum which was soon to be delivered by Nomura and Kurusu. The Tokyo regime herein denounced the United States for opposing Japanese efforts to create its New Order in East Asia. The phraseology of the notes also made unmistakably clear Japan's intentions to eliminate the American and British presence in the Pacific and to achieve military dominance of the Far East. FDR, reflecting on the content of the thirteen points, said tersely "This means war." [84]

The debacle at Pearl Harbor brought a united and angry nation into the war against the fascist powers. Franklin Roosevelt was apparently certain that Japan's declaration of war against the United States would bring Germany and Italy into the conflict. In considering on December 7, 1941 whether or not to include the fascist allies in the declaration of war against Japan, Roosevelt expressed the view that Japan's decision to declare war on the United States would automatically bring in its Axis partners. America did declare war solely on Japan on December 8, 1941. The Chief Executive's prescience proved to be terrifyingly correct, as indeed it had been throughout the years preceding the war holocaust. Germany and Italy, as had been expected by the President, declared a state of war with the United States three days later. America responded with a similar statement within twenty-four hours. The inevitable encounter had come at last.[85]

Conclusion

CHAPTER 6

CONCLUSION

FDR's Personal Perspective on the Inevitability of War

Franklin D. Roosevelt had foreseen with certainty the inevitability of the American war commitment. He was personally convinced that the enormous strength and determined resolve exhibited by the revisionist powers of Germany, Japan, and Italy would insure their ultimate victory in Europe and the Far East if the United States chose to remain out of the global conflict. He was certain that the consequences of fascist predominance would be disastrous for the future security of America and the countries of the Western Hemisphere. The decision to intervene was not a matter of choice from the perspective of the President. It was a requirement of urgent necessity. There was never a moment in which Franklin Roosevelt considered the possibilities of a permanent accommodation with the victorious Axis coalition. He never believed that a compromise peace would be possible with the proponents of fascism. There was only one course of action which could potentially turn the tide of battle in favor of those nations which opposed the Axis triumvirate. The formal entrance of the United States into the global conflict was the necessary determinant.

The decision to enjoin the ideological, military, and economic struggle with the authoritarian regimes of Germany, Japan, and Italy, however, was not simply a product of necessity borne of imminent danger. Franklin Roosevelt had always been eager to halt the fascist advance. He was implacably opposed to fascist ideology and its espousal of the doctrines of racial supremacy and subjugation through forceful conquest. There existed a deep personal hatred and detestation of those regimes and their leaders who had accepted the notion that military might conferred legitimacy on a nation's mission to

209

achieve its territorial ambitions. The consideration of possible actions to crush the members of the Axis coalition began years before the crucial events and developments preceding Pearl Harbor. The abhorrence of fascism and all that it represented called forth from the President a yearning commitment to silence those voices trumpeting the bellicose oratory of martial fanaticism and the gospel of vengeful racial hatred. The requirements of national security dictated a commitment to war. The fear of an inevitable confrontation with a dominant fascist coalition and a personal loathing repugnance toward the prophets of the new order determined the response of engagement.

Germany was the war fulcrum which determined Franklin Roosevelt's response to events in Europe. During the first world war, Franklin, as Assistant Secretary of the Navy, displayed an innate enmity toward Germany. He was most anxious to enter the war against Kaiser Wilhelm and was always suspicious of German intentions toward the United States. Neither sabotage nor a daring submarine attack on America's shores were dismissed as distinct possibilities. The European Inspection Trip taken by the Assistant Secretary in 1918 also impressed upon him the horrors of war, and he made a point of noting in detail what he described as the Hun atrocities. The church destroyed in Cierges, the bombed hospital in Doullens, and the account of young French girls removed enceinte from the Germans were the bases of lasting impressions.

The accession to power of Adolf Hitler compelled Franklin Roosevelt to focus his attention once more on Germany. The Führer seemed to possess those qualities which the President found to be particularly repugnant. Hitler was seen as insensitive, overbearing, gross, and aggressively German. Detestation and dread were the feelings engendered in Roosevelt by the appearance of the German dictator. Under his leadership, preparations for the revision of the Versailles Treaty began in earnest. Diplomatic despatches were never reassuring on the probable course of German foreign policy. The correspondents of the President were certain in their assumption that Germany was soon to become a marching nation and a forceful exponent of ferocious anti-semitism and fanatical racism. Germany's withdrawal from the Geneva Disarmament Conference and the League of Nations convinced Franklin Roosevelt of that country's will for war. He would often expound on German war preparations and that nation's mission to conquer and control the world, and he did so before the territorial spoilation of Europe had become a reality. He anticipated the coming storm, and awaited an offensive thrust by Germany.

Franklin Roosevelt watched with alarm as the German nation prepared to secure a position of absolute equality with former victors. The

Saar plebiscite, he was told, was simply a big drink of Schnaps for Germany, and attempts to recover lost areas of racial affinity seemed certain to follow this initial elective union. The imposed limits on the size of Germany's armed forces were unilaterally disposed in March, 1935 with the introduction of universal conscription and the creation of an air force and 500,000 man army. Whither Germany asked most observers, including Franklin Roosevelt. A nation of 67,000,000 people, described by diplomats, intelligence officers, and private sources of the President as a day to day menace to the peace of all nations, was rapidly achieving an armed capability to meet all eventualities.

Germany's occupation of the Rhineland on March 7, 1936 was described by the President as a thoroughly disgusting spectacle of aggressive militarism. The impunity with which Hitler had violated the sanctity of the Versailles Treaty clauses, thought Roosevelt, would lead to further transgressions by Germany. He was certain that the momentum gained by unimpeded territorial revisions would carry the Führer on to further ambitious schemes. Austria entered the German Reich in March, 1938. The President was thoroughly informed concerning this impending action. The descriptions of Hitler's tirades during an interview with the Austrian Chancellor Kurt von Schuschnigg, and the alleged comparisons made by the Führer of himself to Julius Caesar and Jesus Christ, led most observers to expect a continuance of German expansion. Confirmation of their predictive analyses was received in the short space of several months. War preparations for an advance on Czechoslovakia were reportedly in their final stages when the Munich Accords permitted the peaceful truncation of that nation as the Sudetenland entered the German hegemony. Franklin Roosevelt was certain that the fascist drive for continental dominance would continue, and his informed assumption was soon proven correct. The remains of Czechoslovakia were absorbed in March, 1939, and plans for the advance on Poland were prepared immediately thereafter. In September, 1939, Poland too fell before the blitzkrieg fury. The German war machine appeared to be invincible from the perspective of the President.

Germany's European Axis associate, Italy, served to augment the fascist menace in the opinion of Franklin Roosevelt. His critical assumptions concerning Italian foreign policy were sharpened by the failure of Benito Mussolini to maintain an initial impression of cordiality, friendship, and sincere warmth in his approach to the United States. Roosevelt had been informed that the Duce could be counted upon to lead the drive for disarmament and would even join France in opposition to Germany should that nation continue its aggressive revisionist designs. The fascist movement itself, he had been told, had produced efficiency, respectability, prosperity, and individual dignity. These misconceptions were dispelled with the invasion of Ethiopia. The President agreed with the description of this attack as deliberate, determined, obdurate, ruthless, and vicious. The blinded, burnt, and pitted bodies of children, victims of Italian bombings in Ethiopia, were horrifying reminders of the consequences of the Duce's unleashed martial spirit. The brutal manner in which this act of lawlessness was carried out by Mussolini's armies convinced the President that Italy was, and would always remain, a nation committed to the aims of conquest, subjugation, and fascist dominance. He never doubted the fact that Italy was, in its ideology and ultimate ambition, a firm partner in the fascist coalition. The Duce had faithfully supported Adolf Hitler's determined stand at Munich, and had accepted the possibility of participation in a war against Britain and France. The invasion of Albania in April, 1939 seemed to follow logically the path already set forth by Germany. Diplomats and other representatives of the President would offer some equivocal analyses of Mussolini's intentions, but they were rejected by Roosevelt. Italy's momentary neutrality in September, 1939 was not expected to last for long. Axis unity would soon demand a significant military contribution by Mussolini, and the President expected him to willingly fulfill his pledges to the Führer.

In the Far East, the third member of the Axis triumvirate was preparing for a final effort to oust all British, French, Dutch and American influence from Asia and the Pacfic. Franklin Roosevelt assumed that Japan had imperialistic designs which would not permit accommodation or a negotiated settlement of outstanding differences. He had received, as Assistant Secretary of the Navy, innumerable memoranda giving details of the Japanese program of conquest. Reports of plans to absorb all of China, of the probable invasion of the Philippine and Hawaiian Islands, and of Japanese espionage activities in the United States, Canada, and Mexico were disconcerting and, most important, were often reiterated in the years before the final engagement between America and Japan. The participation of Japan in the Washington Conference and the London Naval Conference for the limitation of naval armaments brought only a momentary revision in Roosevelt's assumptions concerning the aggressive belligerence of a nation in search of empire. The invasion of Manchuria and the withdrawal of Japan from the League of Nations dispelled hopes for a peaceful future in the Far East. The President became increasingly certain that a one hundred year plan for the expansion of Japan, as revealed to him by a Japanese friend at Harvard in 1902, was the real aim of what he called the Junker crowd in Tokyo. China, Korea,

Manchuria, Mongolia, Australia, New Zealand, and all the islands of the Pacific were to be absorbed by a nation intent, thought Roosevelt, on achieving the subjugation of all the yellow races.

The correspondents of Franklin Roosevelt were united in their belief that war would be the primary instrument of national policy for Japan. This nation, he was told, was not a small or weak country. Its size, if Manchukuo was included, was even greater than that of France, Germany, Spain, Switzerland, Belgium, the Netherlands and Denmark combined, and its total population of about 120,000,000 was equal to that of the United States. Observers predicted that a people so nationalistic, war-loving, aggressive and unscrupulous would attempt to achieve the conquest of Asia in the manner of the Mongol hordes and Genghis Khan. Japan's mission in Asia was ultimately to eliminate all vestiges of western inffuence. The invasion of China was believed to be the real beginning of Japan's attempt to realize its imperial ambitions in the Far East, and Franklin Roosevelt was convinced of the fact that this was just an initial thrust which would ultimately bring war between the Japanese militarists and the United States. The violent and brutal occupation policies which marked Japan's advance into China further intensified the President's concern for the fascist challenge in Asia. Reports of Japanese espionage activities in the Bering Sea, the Philippines, and Panama heightened Roosevelt's suspicions of Japanese intentions. He had directed the Chief of Naval Operations in 1936 to definitely identify all Japanese residents in Hawaii who were observed greeting ships from Japan, or who appeared to have connections wtih Japanese officers. Their names were to be placed on a special list of those who would be the first to be interned in concentration camps in the event of war. Franklin Roosevelt clearly anticipated an eventual confrontation. The sinking of the *Panay,* the continued dismemberment of China, the indiscriminate bombing of crowded Chinese cities, and the announcement of plans to create a Greater East Asia Co-Prosperity Sphere served to confirm what was a conviction in the mind of the President: Japan was embarked on the greatest land grabbing scheme in its history. He fully realized that there could be no compromise, no conciliation, no appeasement, no neutralization scheme, and no avoidance of a final engagement. It was simply, from the President's perspective, a matter of time.

The fascist threat was not visualized as a segmented and compartmentalized challenge on three separate geographic fronts. Germany's thrust for continental dominance, Italy's advance in the Mediterranean, and Japan's consolidation of power in the Far East were viewed by Franklin Roosevelt as manifestations of a concerted and orchestrated attack on the western nations, their democratic institutions, and the values esteemed and prized by the community of civilized man. The civil war in Spain was believed to be the beginning of an international fascist conspiracy against democracy. German and Italian troops, war supplies, tanks, planes, and bombs were tested in the human laboratory of the Spanish Civil War. The President was certain that the Spanish conflict was but a prelude to other undeclared wars against the democracies in Europe. The Anti-Comintern Pact signed by Germany and Japan, and the Three Power Pact formed by Italy's adherence to what Roosevelt now saw as the Fascist Internationale, strengthened the assumption, firmly accepted by the Chief Executive, that the Rome-Berlin-Tokyo Axis was solidly united and ready to engage in an all out war for world dominance. Reports of the exchange of military and naval officials between and among the fascist bloc nations confirmed what the President had always suspected: the eventual encounter would be global in its scope and final in its resolution.

Franklin Roosevelt searched in vain for a response to the fascist challenge. He was constrained by isolationist sentiment, neutrality restrictions, and the appeasement solutions offered by other nations. Despite these impediments, however, the President formulated and suggested proposals which were designed to throttle the Axis dictatorships before the presumed final encounter. His acceptance of defensive preparedness had given way during the first world war to a belief in the necessity of intervention. This same transition came much more suddenly as events pushed men and nations rapidly toward war. He chastized those responsible for the great inertia which he described as the failure to recognize the grave and precarious position of the United States as a nation if it were to assume an isolated monastic seclusion from world affairs. America, he always believed, was the keystone of the arch of world peace. Its active participation in the community of nations was required if outlaw nations were to be prevented from running amuck, murdering, maiming, and despoiling their weaker neighbors. These thoughts he had enunciated with emphasis and conviction during the election campaign in 1920, and they became essential components of his approach to world affairs after the 1932 election victory. He had warned that another Napoleon, another Caesar, or another Alexander the Great would one day stridently march in search of glorious conquest if nations failed to unite in a solid front against aggressors. He had once said that the power of the United States carried with it a great responsibility. America, he had emphasized, must play the part of a man, and lead the fight for the collective union of peace loving nations. This he earnestly wished to do, and despite both domestic and foreign impediments, attempted to do with circumspection and tactful restraint.

He had predicted in 1920 that a future war would of necessity involve the United States. If you wish to send men overseas again, he lectured audiences, simply remain in the insecure confines of the Western Hemisphere and avoid all disturbing developments elsewhere. Franklin Roosevelt was convinced that democracy could never survive in isolation; America was not an impregnable fortress. He always knew that the failure to create a united front against Germany, Italy, and Japan would one day call for definite ships and definite men on a definite day.

He encouraged the delegates attending the Geneva Disarmament Conference to enter into a solemn and firm pact of non-aggression, and pledged that the United States would be willing to consult with other nations in case of a threat to world peace and would refrain from any action tending to defeat a collective effort to restore peace. The collapse of the Geneva Conference, the growing distrust among British, French, and American statesmen, the requirements of congressional support for needed depression legislation and later foreign policy initiatives, and traditional isolationist criticism of any involvement in European affairs persuaded the President to hurriedly abandon his proposed endorsement of some form of collective security arrangement for maintaining peace and taking action against aggressor nations. He personally, however, never abandoned the desire to initiate collective punitive measures against the fascist nations.

He discussed a plan with close associates during the months of 1935 calling for the naval blockade of Germany by England, France, Italy, Belgium, Holland, Poland, Czechoslovakia, Austria, and Russia. Economic strangulation would be the antidote to Adolf Hitler's armament program. In this same year, he also seriously considered the possibility of a naval blockade of Japan by the United States, France, and Great Britain. During the Italo-Ethiopian war, Roosevelt pushed for strong action against Mussolini and used neutrality legislation and moral embargoes to lead the League of Nations in a determined effort to constrain Italy. He personally suggested to the British Prime Minister Stanley Baldwin that England and France must stand rigid against the Duce. Roosevelt refused to sanction Italy's brazen act of aggression, and official diplomatic recognition of the Italian conquest was not proffered by the President. Germany's advance into the Rhineland prompted the Chief Executive to send a message to the King of England proposing a naval blockade to halt the German program of expansion. He desired to aid the Republic of Spain in its struggle with the fascist supported armies of Franco but was prevented from doing so by neutrality legislation, the muddled domestic reaction to embroilment in this civil war, and especially the non-intervention policies pursued by Great Britain and

France. Any effective initiative was in this instance an impossibility.

The famous Chicago Quarantine Address was not simply a verbal inducement to consider a response to aggression, nor was it solely intended to enlighten public opinion to the dangers lurking overseas. In the President's mind, the word quarantine meant economic blockade. He fully realized that the necessary support for this endeavor was absent among the leaders of the western nations, but he still eagerly anticipated the opportunity for implementing such a program of strangulation against Germany, Italy, and Japan. His plans to convert oil burning merchant ships so that they could remain at sea for an extended period, could carry eight or ten planes for flight over a wide area, could ward off small air attacks, and sink less powerful merchant ships were intended to prepare the United States for participation in what Roosevelt considered as the ultimate solution to aggression at this moment in time. He was not willing, however, as was evident at the Brussels Conference, to be pushed into the forefront of any campaign of sanctions against the aggressors by nations whose actions in meeting the fascist threat he had characterized thus far as pusillanimous and self-seeking. All nations would have to unanimously endorse the imposition of economic strictures against members of the Axis coalition before the President would assume leadership of any concerted drive to halt the advance of fascism.

His reluctance to appear as the messiah was based on his belief that Great Britain and France would not be willing to join wholeheartedly in the struggle against Germany, Italy, and Japan. The collapse of the London Economic Conference had ushered in years of mutual mistrust among those nations which would bear the brunt of Axis aggression. British and French appeasement policies often disgusted the President. He threatened to approach Canada, Australia, New Zealand, and South Africa in an effort to inform the dominions that their future security was tied to that of America if England did not abandon its policies of accommodation with Japan. He was compelled to suggest in 1935 that no advances be made to the British Government because of its tendency to exhibit a national selfishness which made mutual helpfulness very difficult to accomplish. Great Britain's apparent eagerness to appease Adolf Hitler, as evident in the Anglo-German Naval Agreement, its reluctance and that of France to constrain Mussolini as seen in the Hoare-Laval proposals, and its willingness to consider peace with Japan were disheartening to the President. The non-interventionist policy of the western democracies during the Spanish Civil War was viewed by Roosevelt as an expected sequel to years of cowardly retreat. Franklin Roosevelt publicly admitted that he ardently desired an offensive-defensive alliance to implement an Anglo-Saxon *Pax Romana*. He was very disappointed by the actions of potential allies in their responses to the fascist threat. Neville Chamberlain's rejection of a proposed meeting with the President in 1937 appeared as the final confirmation of his belief that the British sought not to resist but to appease the proponents of fascism. His estimation of the French was even more critical for not only did they engage in pursuit of appeasement, but their weaknesses, as conveyed to Roosevelt, were appalling. Confusion, discord, and chaotic strife characterized the domestic scene in France. Corruption, dishonesty, bribery, scandal and intrigue were the norm in French politics. Its military capacity was never judged to be of any practical worth if compared to that of its fascist neighbors. The approaching encounter with the armies of the Rome-Berlin-Tokyo Axis appeared as a most distressing thought in the mind of Franklin Roosevelt.

The world situation on the eve of the European conflict was not encouraging from the perspective of the President. The overwhelming preponderance of Axis power and the assumed weaknesses of the western democracies called forth a most depressing vision of the future. There were some who thought seriously of a compromise peace with the fascist nations based on their conviction that defeat was inevitable in any contest with so powerful a coalition. Franklin Roosevelt never shared nor entertained this assumption. The decision to postpone the encounter which he knew had to come eventually rested on the hope that with sufficient time remedies could be found for the appalling deficiencies in the military preparedness of the British, French, and American armies. The President's intervention in the Munich crisis was posited solely on the assumption that in September, 1938, Great Britain and France would have been defeated in a devastating attack by German and Italian land and air forces. Roosevelt never believed that the Munich Accords would provide a lasting peace in Europe. He had always rejected appeasement as a possible solution to the fascist challenge. He only wished to delay the inevitable engagement for a more propitious moment. The future, however, looked no brighter after this momentary respite. Perhaps he believed that needed support for the cause of the western allies could be found in the few months remaining before the invasion of Poland.

The nation which had always occupied paramount importance in the mind of Franklin Roosevelt as he contemplated the approaching war was the Soviet Union. The cardinal principle of the President's foreign policy was to establish close, personal, and cordial relations with Joseph Stalin. The strength of Russia, economically and militarily, would be essential if Germany, Japan and Italy were to be defeated in the inevitable encounter. The establishment of diplomatic relations with the Soviet Union was directly related to the emerging constellation of great powers. The final defeat of fascism in Europe and the Far East, thought Roosevelt, would be possible only with the cooperation of Russia.

The President ignored what he considered as minor irritants in the search for detente. The debt controversy was described as simply a flyspeck on the wall. Comintern propaganda activities were not to be criticized by order of the Chief Executive. FDR never clearly grasped the scope of the purge trials or the intensity of the terror under Stalin's tyrannical regime. The misinformation often sent by his representative in Russia, Joseph Davies, did nothing to further clarify the President's perspective. Ambassador Davies was certain that the terror was inspired primarily for reasons of national security. Spies and saboteurs, the American Ambassador in Moscow had noted, had to be ferreted out of government circles in preparation for a war with Germany and Japan. The nuances of Soviet foreign policy, as perceived by experienced diplomats, were not understood by Franklin Roosevelt. He always assumed the veracity of Russian proposals for collective resistance against the aggressors. The Division of Eastern European Affairs in the State Department, whose analyses had often been incisively critical of Russia, was abolished and its staff merged with the Division of Western European Affairs under the direction of a man with no specialized training in the study of the Soviet Union. Nothing would be permitted to interfere with Franklin Roosevelt's determination to enlist Russia's might in the war against fascism.

The selection of Joseph Davies as Ambassador to the Soviet Union in 1937 reflects Roosevelt's determination to entice Stalin into a firm alignment with the United States. Preparations were made for the President's proposal to establish a military and naval liaison with representatives of the Soviet armed forces. Inducements such as the construction of battleships and submarines for the Russian navy, and the granting of technical assistance contracts to Soviet representatives for aircraft production in the United States had the Chief Executive's personal endorsement and only the fear of future congressional investigations and press publicity prevented the accomplishment of these programs of aid. The liaison proposal was made in June, 1938, and a seemingly eager opponent of the Axis coalition rejected the Roosevelt proposition. Stalin now knew, however, of the President's eagerness to gain Russia's support in the coming struggle. He could be assured of America's aid in the ultimate showdown with Germany. One more attempt was made to persuade the Soviet dictator to cast his lot with the allies. In the summer months of 1939, Roosevelt secretly sent a message to Russian leaders urging them to sign an agreement with Great Britain and France. Implicitly, the President was proposing to aid such a coalition, and specifically the Soviet Union, for the purpose of defeating the Axis triumvirate. Stalin's rejection of this unsolicited advice from the Chief Executive did not dampen Roosevelt's enthusiasm for political and military entente with the Soviet Union, but the signing of the German-Russian Non-Aggression Pact in August, 1939 eliminated for the moment the sole remaining hope for successful resistance to the fascist war machine.

The anticipated sequence of events during the initial two years of the war made the American war commitment an urgent necessity. The assertion of fascist dominance was achieved without any meaningful opposition. Germany's war machine swept across Europe in a terrifying display of awesome military preponderance. Denmark, Norway, Belgium, Luxemburg, the Netherlands, France, Yugoslavia, and Greece fell victim to the invincible German armies. Bulgaria, Rumania, and Hungary, anxious to share the spoils of war, eagerly joined the Axis powers in the forceful reconstruction of Europe. Italy, awaiting the successful outcome of the German advance, rushed to participate in the truncation of its prostrate neighbor, France. Franklin Roosevelt had never doubted Mussolini's allegiance to the fascist cause. The jackal's propitious decision to cast its fate with the victor of the moment had come as no surprise to the President. The combined forces of the continental Axis sovereigns prepared to dispatch with the sole belligerent opponent to the construction of the new order. Great Britain stood alone, precariously poised to receive the fascist onslaught. The continued existence of the western democracies, from the perspective of the Chief Executive, appeared to be in grave danger of extinction.

Franklin Roosevelt had always assumed that Adolf Hitler envisaged the eventual subjugation and control of the nations of the Western Hemisphere, and most particularly the United States. The President did receive from several sources alarming information concerning fascist penetration of the Latin American countries. Chile reportedly possessed the most militantly Nazi German population. The likelihood of an attempted overthrow of the Chilean Government by German agents was, in the opinion of the American Ambassador in that country, a real possibility. Argentina too was described as ready to join the fascist cause if the Axis powers continued their triumphant march in Europe. There were additional reports of fifth column activities in Brazil, Uruguay, Ecuador, Costa Rica, Panama, and Mexico. An acquaintance of the President, having recently returned from a trip through Mexico and the Central and South American countries, alleged that advanced preparations for the Nazi invasion were already in evidence. Airports, aircraft, and German advisers were purportedly scattered throughout Columbia, Costa Rica, and Mexico. Fascist propaganda efforts were said to be the most intense in Brazil, Argentina, and Chile. The President, convinced of the probability of a German invasion, took most seriously these warnings of fascist infiltration throughout Latin America.

His interpretation of the alleged instances of active preparation of fascist agents for a concerted attempt to achieve control of the nations of the Western Hemisphere was based on several assumptive convictions. The personality of Adolf Hitler would drive the Führer to seek world domination, he assumed. The theme of the compulsive conqueror was often emphasized in Roosevelt's speeches. He was convinced too that Germany's planned conquest of the United States would come by invasion and bombing from strategic contiguous territories. He would repeatedly instruct his listeners as to the proximity of adjacent areas where the possibilities for launching expected attacks were always present. Economic blackmail of the Latin American nations by a victorious Germany, in Roosevelt's opinion, might also enable that country to prepare for the eventual subjugation of the United States. The Führer's methods might vary, but his objective, as alleged by Roosevelt, was ultimately the destruction of the impregnable fortress of America.

The seriousness with which the President assayed the fascist menace is evident in his response to reports of espionage and subversion. The Federal Bureau of Investigation was directed to investigate activities of registered German agents. A list of American citizens who had been awarded decorations by Germany was requested by the White House. Charles Lindbergh was referred to by the Chief Executive as a Nazi. Grand Manon, an island in the Bay of Fundy, was suggested by Roosevelt as a good internment camp for subversives. The President urged the acquisition of naval rights in Magdelena Bay, Salina Cruz, and Yucatan to prevent any German offensive action from emanating from adjacent territories. An inquiry was ordered into reports that a German air base might be constructed in Haiti. The Chief Executive instructed the Secretary of War to inspect Martinique, Guadeloupe, French Guiana, and other smaller French islands to see if German officers were present in these areas. Plans to occupy the Azores, Cape Verde Islands, and the Island of Fernando de Noronha were prepared for implementation. Navy patrols were also undertaken on the Hudson Bay in search of possible German raiders. Reports that German agents had been sent from Berlin to Washington to assassinate the President were forwarded to the Secret Service. The fascist threat to the American hemisphere was taken most seriously by Franklin Roosevelt.

A crucial consideration in the opinion of the President as he attempted to judge the urgency of securing the war commitment was the probable course of action which would be pursued by Vichy France. Diplomatic despatches were not optimistic concerning the anticipated foreign policy of Marshal Petain's regime. France's physical and moral defeat seemed absolute; defeatism pervaded the highest offices of the Vichy Government. The possibility that the French fleet might be given to Germany was a most pressing fear in the mind of the President. The hostility of the leaders of Vichy France toward Great Britain and the United States might stimulate the already prevalent desire for full collaboration with Germany in the conquest of Britain. The appearance of Vichy France made even more critical the plight of the democracies as appraised by the Chief Executive.

The weakening of Great Britain's defenses, as conveyed to Franklin Roosevelt, was of crucial importance in persuading the President to press for the war commitment. The nation's unconquerable spirit and its iron resolve to continue the struggle against what appeared to some as overwhelming odds was an inspiration to those anxious for the defeat of Germany, but the probability that this desired objective would be attained grew more distant with the passage of time. The nightmarish vision of a compromise peace with Germany, secured by the surrender of the English fleet by a defeated British government was pointedly brought to the attention of the President. Dire admonitions that a British collapse was imminent became numerous as the air bombardment of English towns intensified, and the sinkings of British ships multiplied alarmingly. The dispatch of destroyers to America's beleaguered ally did not seem to stem the increasing enfeeblement of Britain's war effort. Lend-Lease aid to England was hurriedly rushed to prevent a precipitate collapse of resistance. In the estimation of the President, the war commitment could not be delayed much longer.

The necessity of American military intervention was dictated too by the probability that Japan was about to join Germany and Italy in their program of conquest. The anticipated southward offensive by Japan was reportedly in the final stages of preparation. Roosevelt was certain that Japan would soon give concrete assistance to its fascist allies by attacking the British forces stationed throughout the Pacific and the Far East, and the President had serious doubts about the capacity of Great Britain to sustain a two front war. Negotiations between American and Japanese representatives in Washington were making no progress. MAGIC intercepts revealed that throughout the diplomatic discussions Japan's military preparations for the occupation of French Indo-China and Thailand, in anticipation of an eventual drive against Malaya, British North Borneo, the Dutch East Indies, and the Pacific possessions of the United States were being hurriedly rushed to completion. Franklin Roosevelt sought to delay the inevitable encounter with Japan by engaging in conversations, which he had always assumed would be futile, with the emissaries from Tokyo. Economic sanctions against Japan were applied gradually in the hope of impeding that nation's war preparations without forcing a sudden move southward to obtain vital raw materials. The freezing of Japanese assets in the United States, and the refusal of the President to meet with Prime Minister Konoye until definite and firm agreements had been reached concerning Japan's aggression in the Far East, were reflections of the Chief Executive's conviction that the moment of impending attack had arrived, and that the avoidance of engagement was no longer a possible option. There would be momentary thoughts of seeking a possible accommodation with Japan, but important considerations would persuade the President to abandon this last minute proposal. What concerned Franklin Roosevelt the most during the early autumn months before Pearl Harbor was the likelihood of a British defeat if Japan entered the war. This possibility compelled the President to clarify for the American public the issues at stake in the inevitable future conflict.

A most important consideration for Franklin Roosevelt in his decision to press forward in the task of preparing the nation for the struggle against fascism was the position of the Soviet Union. Incoming despatches predicted with certainty that a break in Russian-German relations would soon occur, and that preparations for invasion had already been completed by Adolf Hitler and his military advisers. The President had attempted, unsuccessfully, to persuade Stalin on numerous occasions to cast his lot with that of the democracies. Roosevelt had assiduously pursued the search for entente with Russia from the moment of recognition. He probably realized that a war commitment to defeat the fascist powers would be incapable of complete success without the use of the huge manpower reserves of the Soviet Union. He had earnestly hoped for military cooperation from that nation, and throughout his terms of office, had attempted to lay the basis for the eventual military coordination of American and Russian armed forces against the members of the Axis coalition. The Soviet Union's non-aggression pact with Germany, its invasion of Poland and Finland, its seizure of Estonia, Latvia, and Lithuania, and the mass deportation of peoples in these areas, as well as Russia's efforts to carry on extensive espionage activities in the United States did not substantially alter Roosevelt's foreign policy design. The President's aim was the unconditional surrender of the fascist powers, and Russia's participation in this task was deemed to be an essential necessity. The coalition to defeat Germany, Italy, and Japan came into existence, in the mind of the

Chief Executive, in June, 1941 with Germany's invasion of Russia. Russia's manpower and resources would make possible and probable the complete defeat of the authoritarian regimes.

Franklin Roosevelt anxiously emphasized the theme of war preparedness. In innumerable speeches he attempted to persuade his countrymen to confront the German challenge before a direct attack by that nation on the United States. A crisis mood of war expectation pervaded his public addresses. The arsenal contribution to Great Britain would no longer be sufficient, thought the President. Americans, he would stress, would have to be ready to engage in hard tough fighting in which somebody was going to get hurt. The Chief Executive combined this presentation of future realities, as he foresaw them, with the reiteration of his personal assumptive convictions concerning the personality of Adolf Hitler, the Führer's desire for world domination, and the prospective German invasion or economic strangulation of the United States. The vivid and emotional expressiveness which characterized Franklin Roosevelt's presentation of these selected subject themes was intended to promote both fear and anger in his listeners, and such responses would be necessary in the forthcoming struggle against fascism.

The Chief Executive's actions reveal that he was preparing for the moment in the immediate future when America's military intervention would become a reality. The patrol activities conducted by the United States Navy seemed to have been extended for both defensive and tactical purposes. Publicly, Roosevelt had declared that there should be no limits placed on the perimeters within which patrol vessels were to conduct their operations. Privately, he had received information that the Führer had embarked on a strategy of avoidance and had ordered his submarine commanders, under penalty of death, not to engage any American ships. The President had confided to a close associate that he wished to be dragged into the war through the accident of an incident. He had earlier expressed to this same individual his desire to make decisions that would push the United States into the global conflict. The extension of patrol operations, while ordered for reasons of security and convoy protection, would appear to have been one of those decisions which would make possible the accident of an incident. The President would thereby be able to defeat the avoidance strategy of Hitler, and secure the public support that would be necessary for the needed congressional declaration of war. Certainly, FDR did not anticipate nor calculate the actual sinking of American ships. The loss of the *Robin Moor, Greer, USS Kearney,* and *Reuben James,* however, provided opportunities for the President to expound forcefully on the immediate threat of the fascist menace. In related developments, American forces proceeded to occupy Greenland, Iceland, Trinidad, and British Guiana for perhaps both defensive and tactical purposes. Roosevelt had ordered occupation troops to fire on Axis planes flying over Iceland for reconnaissance purposes. His expectation of an incident was based on the realization that the likelihood of such an occurrence was a distinct possibility.

Preparations to insure the effectiveness of the inevitably approaching war encounter were also undertaken in earnest. American and British military officials met in Washington to draw up plans for the coordination of the two nations' armed forces in the coming encounter. Military and civilian specialists were subsequently dispatched to England to continue the elaboration of war plans necessary for the collaborative struggle against Germany. Politically, too, the common-law marriage of the sister democracies in their effort to crush fascism was confirmed by the meeting of Franklin Roosevelt and Winston Churchill in Argentia Harbor. The principles of the Atlantic Charter marked the complete rejection of fascist revisionist designs by the United States and Great Britain. The pledge to obtain the final destruction of the Nazi tyranny could have meant nothing else to the President, given his perspective of the preponderant power of Germany, other than a commitment to engage the Axis powers with America's military forces for in no other way were Germany and Italy going to be defeated in a decisive manner. There is evidence too that the possibility of establishing a second front to aid the Soviet Union was also discussed during these conversations. British armed forces, already under severe strain in the struggle against Germany, would not have provided sufficient manpower to conduct such an operation alone. A second front could only have been created as a joint American and British effort. Politically and militarily, America's involvement in war was in the final stages of preparation.

Franklin Roosevelt's zealousness in the task of providing aid to Russia also reveals his determination to secure the armed forces of the Soviet Union in order to make effective the approaching war commitment. Numerous despatches which were forwarded to the President indicated that the German advance against Russia would not be immediately successful. The eagerness with which the Chief Executive sought to assure Stalin that his every request would be fulfilled could not have emanated solely from Roosevelt's fear of a precipitate collapse of Russian resistance. He knew that the prospects for a German victory over the Red Armies were growing dimmer and dimmer with each passing day. Why then did he ignore the advice of State Department officials who had earlier insisted that all approaches to the Soviet Union be made on the strict basis of reciprocity? A former Axis collaborator, they had cautioned, had to be treated warily. The President, however, was determined not only to sustain the Russian resistance, but to insure that Joseph Stalin and the military forces of the Soviet Union would wholeheartedly join Great Britain and the United States in the struggle against fascism. The effectiveness of the forces against fascism, which in Roosevelt's opinion had to be sufficient to achieve the unconditional surrender of the Axis triumvirate, would be determined by Russia's participation in the coalition. Stalin fully realized the intensity of Roosevelt's desire to gain the support of the Russian armies, for he bluntly asked for a declaration of war by the United States against Germany. The President never directly rejected this request from the Soviet dictator. He expected America's military intervention in the near future. It would appear as though Franklin Roosevelt was seeking an ally for a long and arduous struggle against the fascist nations. He even attempted to persuade the papacy to publicly sanction Russia's membership in the community of morally righteous powers. The long anticipated confrontation with Germany, Italy, and Japan was about to begin and the prospects for success in the coming struggle appeared to be much brighter with the assured participation of the resources and manpower of the Soviet Union.

The inevitable encounter would originate in the Far East. Franklin Roosevelt was convinced that the Japanese course of expansion through aggression in the Pacific was irrevocable. He had witnessed the belligerence of Japan's war machine for years and was consistently and accurately informed of its ultimate ambitions. The President fully realized that the authorities in Tokyo would accept nothing less than abject surrender and were engaging in negotiations solely for the purpose of furthering their war preparations prior to a final thrust against the Far East possessions of America, Great Britain, France, and the Netherlands. Japan's attack on Pearl Harbor marked the beginning of the engagement which FDR had foreseen with certainty. Germany, Italy, and Japan stood united in their war declarations against the United States and its allies. The Chief Executive had predicted with prescient foresight that the Axis triumvirate would act in unison in their concerted effort to create a world hegemony based on violence, naked force, the law of the sword, brutal oppression, and the doctrine of racial supremacy. Franklin Roosevelt's vision of the terrifying apocalypse had proven tragically correct. The inevitable encounter had come at last. The struggle against fascism was enjoined with irrevocable finality.

ENDNOTES

CHAPTER ONE

1. Josephus Daniels, *The Wilson Era*, 2 vols.(Chapel Hill: University of North Carolina Press, 1944-1946), 1:127; and FDR Speech, April 10, 1913, no. 20, FDR Papers, President's Personal File, Speech File, Franklin D. Roosevelt Library, Hyde Park, New York (hereinafter cited as PPF and FDRL).

2. Basil Rauch, ed., *The Roosevelt Reader* (New York: Rinehart and Co., 1957), pp. 18-20.

3. U.S. Congress, House, *Hearings Before the Committee on Naval Affairs on Estimates Submitted by the Secretary of the Navy*, 63rd Cong., 2nd Sess., 1915, p. 979; and ibid., 3 vols., 64th Cong., 1st Sess., 1916, 3: 3444-497, 3528, 3531, 3535.

4. FDR, "On Your Own Heads," *Scribner's Magazine,* January-June 1917, pp. 413-16; and idem, "What the Navy Can Do For Your Boy," *The Ladies Home Journal,* June 1917, pp. 25, 88.

5. Daniels, *Wilson Era,* 2: 258; and FDR to Winston Churchill, April 18, 1917, FDR Papers, Papers as Assistant Secretary of the Navy, 1913-1920, FDRL.

6. Daniels, *Wilson Era,* 2: 258; Elliot Roosevelt, ed., *FDR His Personal Letters,* 4 vols. (New York: Duell, Sloan and Pearce, 1947), 2: 233, 238-39, 243, 339; and Eleanor Roosevelt, *The Autobiography of Eleanor Roosevelt* (London: Hutchinson and Co., 1937), p. 75. See also Alfred Rollins, Jr., *Roosevelt and Howe* (New York: Alfred A. Knopf, 1962), p. 239.

7. Roosevelt, ed., *FDR Personal Letters,* 2: 240, 246, 249, 267. Eleanor wrote to her husband on August 7, 1914, saying that "the only possible quick solution to me seems the banding together of France, Russia and England" in Joseph Lash, *Eleanor and Franklin* (New York: W.W. Norton, 1971), p. 202.

8. Roosevelt, ed., *FDR Personal Letters,* 2: 270, 283; his mother Sara was against "dealings with the German criminals," see Lash, *Eleanor and Franklin,* p. 204; on Wilson's remarks see Samuel Rosenman, ed., *The Public Papers and Addresses of Franklin D. Roosevelt,* 13 vols. (New York: Random House, 1938-1950), 8: 117 (hereinafter cited as *Public Papers*).

9. FDR Speech, May 9, 1917, no. 68, FDR Papers, PPF, Speech File, FDRL.

10. FDR, Memorandum to Josephus Daniels, October 29, 1917, Box 15, Josephus Daniels Papers, Library of Congress, Washington, D.C. See also FDR letter to Daniels, February 21, 1921, ibid.; Daniels, *Wilson Era,* 2: 83-84; and Roosevelt, ed., *FDR Personal Letters,* 2: 364-67.

11. Roosevelt, ed., *FDR Personal Letters,* 2: 351. On the possibility of sabotage see FDR Memorandum to the Office of Naval Intelligence, June 22, 1917, FDR Papers, Assistant Secretary of the Navy, FDRL.

12. FDR, Diary Entry, July 30, 1918, European Inspection Trip, FDR Papers, Assistant Secretary of the Navy, FDRL; see also, Roosevelt, ed., *FDR Personal Letters,* 2: 391.

13. FDR, Diary Entry, August 4, 1918, European Inspection Trip, FDR Papers, Assistant Secretary of the Navy, FDRL.

14. FDR, Diary Entry, August 5, 1918, European Inspection Trip, FDR Papers, Assistant Secretary of the Navy, FDRL. Letters to Sara on the subject of German atrocities are in Roosevelt, ed., *FDR Personal Letters,* 2: 451, 462.

15. Alfred Mahan to FDR, August 18, 1914, FDR Papers, Assistant Secretary of the Navy, FDRL.

16. Theodore Roosevelt to FDR, May 10, 1913; Bradley Fiske to FDR, May 13, 1913; and A. Bielaski, Memorandum to the Secretary of the Navy, May 20, 1913, FDR Papers, Assistant Secretary of the Navy, FDRL.

17. Office of Naval Intelligence, Unsigned Memorandum to the Secretary of the Navy, June 9, 1916, FDR Papers, Assistant Secretary of the Navy, FDRL.

18. Office of Naval Intelligence, Unsigned Memorandum to the Assistant Secretary of the Navy, December 20, 1919; Director, Office of Naval Intelligence, Report to the Assistant Secretary of the Navy, January 13, 1920; and Office of Naval Intelligence, Unsigned Memorandum to the Assistant Secretary of the Navy, March 22, 1920, FDR Papers, Assistant Secretary of the Navy, FDRL.

19. Unsigned Memorandum, no. 35, "What America's Policy Should be in China," January 21, 1920, FDR Papers, Assistant Secretary of the Navy, FDRL.

20. Eleanor Roosevelt to Lorena Hickok, undated letter, cited in Lash, *Eleanor and Franklin,* p. 556.

21. Eleanor Roosevelt, *Autobiography,* p. 88; James Roosevelt and Sidney Shalett, *Affectionately FDR* (New York: Harcourt, Brace and Co., 1959), pp. 61, 79; Daniels, *Wilson Era,* 2: 270, 273; and Grace Tully, *FDR My Boss* (New York: Charles Scribner's Sons, 1949), p. 59. The Wilson-FDR meeting is in Roosevelt, ed., *FDR Personal Letters,* 2: 477, 496-497; and James Cox, *Journey Through My Years* (New York: Simon and Schuster, 1946), pp. 241-45.

22. FDR Speech, July 18, 1919, no. 98, FDR Papers, PPF, Speech File, FDRL. The acceptance speech is in Roosevelt, ed., *FDR Personal Letters,* 2: 500-03.

23. FDR Speech, August 23, 1920, no. 149, FDR Papers, PPF, Speech File, FDRL.

24. FDR Speeches, August 12, 1920, no. 134; August 14, 1920, no. 158; August 21, 1920, nos. 147, 151; September 18, 1920, no. 172; and September 28, 1920, no. 180, FDR Papers, PPF, Speech File, FDRL.

25. FDR Speeches, August 14, 1920, no. 138; August 20, 1920, no.

144; September 22, 1920, no. 176; October 20, 1920, no. 219; October 23, 1920, no. 224, FDR Papers, PPF, Speech File, FDRL.

26. Rosenman, ed., *Public Papers*, 10: 152.

27. Roosevelt, ed., *FDR Personal Letters*, 2: 213.

28. FDR to William A. White, July 28, 1921, and White to FDR, August 17, 1921, Box 58, William A. White Papers, Library of Congress, Washington, D.C.

29. FDR to Violet Loroy, January 11, 1922, Woodrow Wilson Foundation Correspondence Folder, FDR Papers, Papers Pertaining to Family, Business and Personal Affairs; and FDR to A. C. Coolidge, May 9, 1924; FDR to Isadore Dockweiler, September 3, 1925; FDR to W. Earl Hopper, December 19, 1927, Walter Hines Page Memorial Correspondence Folder, FDR Papers, Family, Business, and Personal Affairs FDRL.

30. FDR to George Marvin, January 29, 1924, American Peace Award Correspondence Folder, FDR Papers, Family, Business and Personal Affairs, FDRL.

31. The Peace Plan may be found in Eleanor Roosevelt, *This I Remember* (New York: Harper and Bros., 1949), pp. 353-66; see also, Drafts and Notes File, 1901-1933, FDR Papers, Family, Business and Personal Affairs, FDRL.

32. Donald S. Carmichael, ed., *FDR Columnist* (Chicago: Pellegrini and Cudahy, 1947), pp. 63-65.

33. FDR to Norman Davis, March 30, 1928; Davis to FDR, April 12, 1928 and April 17, 1928, Box 51, Norman Davis Papers, Library of Congress, Washington, D.C.

34. FDR, "Our Foreign Policy: A Democratic View," *Foreign Affairs* 6 (July 1928): 573-86; and see Roosevelt, ed., *FDR Personal Letters*, 3: 141-42, 213.

35. The article, dated September 20, 1928, is in Carmichael, ed., *FDR Columnist*, pp. 132-36.

36. Roosevelt, ed., *FDR Personal Letters*, 3: 106-07, 147, 163, 195. The draft of the article on Japan, "The Japs-A Habit of Mind," is in FDR Papers, Family, Business and Personal Affairs, FDRL. See also Carmichael, ed., *FDR Columnist*, pp. 57-60.

37. Francis Sayre to FDR, October 13, 1932, and November 30, 1932; FDR to Sayre, November 19, 1932, Box 7, Francis Sayre Papers, Library of Congress, Washington, D.C.; and Arthur Sweetzer to FDR, July 29, 1932, Box 34, Arthur Sweetzer Papers, Library of Congress, Washington, D.C.

38. *New York Times*, February 3, 1932, p. 4.

39. Norman Davis to Frank Polk, February 17, 1932, Box 47, Davis Papers, and Louis Wehle, *Hidden Threads of History, Wilson through Roosevelt* (New York: MacMillan Co., 1953), p. 110.

40. Norman Davis to FDR, November 18, 1932; FDR to Davis, November 28, 1932, Box 51, Davis Papers; and Felix Frankfurter to FDR, November 12, 1932, and FDR to Frankfurter, November 17, 1932, Box 97, Felix Frankfurter Papers, Library of Congress, Washington, D.C.

CHAPTER TWO

1. Rosenman, ed., *Public Papers FDR,* 2: 14, 3: 11-12, 4: 410-12.

2. Ibid., 5: 9-12.

3. Key Pittman to FDR, February 19, 1933, Box 81, Key Pitman Papers, Library of Congress, Washington, D.C.

4. Norman Davis to FDR, January 10, 1933, Box 51, Davis Papers; Orville Bullitt, ed., *For the President, Personal and Secret* (Boston: Houghton Mifflin Co., 1972), pp. 21, 27, 30; Louis Wehle to FDR, August 13, 1932, Box 39, Louis Wehle Papers, FDRL, Hyde Park, New York; and Wehle, *Hidden Threads of History,* pp. 117-18, 123.

5. Ramsay MacDonald to FDR, February 10, 1933, and FDR to MacDonald, undated and not sent, FDR Papers, President's Secretary's File, Diplomatic Correspondence, Great Britain, FDRL (hereinafter cited as PSF, DC); see also, Edgar Nixon, ed., *Franklin D. Roosevelt and Foreign Affairs,* 3 vols. (Cambridge: Belknap Press of Harvard University Press, 1969), 1: 11, 14, 16; FDR to Arthur Murray, April 14, 1933, ibid., p. 54; and Press Conferences, Nos. 14, 14B, April 26, 1933, *Complete Presidential Press Conferences of Franklin D. Roosevelt,* 25 vols. (New York: Da Capo Press, 1972), 1: 163, 180-84.

6. Paul Claudel to Paul Boncour, January 11, 1933, and February 21, 1933, cited in Ministere Des Affaires Etrangeres, *Documents Diplomatiques Francais, 1932-1939,* 6 vols,. 1st Series (Paris: Imprimerie Nationale, 1966-), 2: 414-17, 670-71; Press Conference No. 15, April 26, 1933, in *Complete Press Conferences,* 1: 186-87. See also U.S., Department of State, *FRUS, 1933,* 5 vols. (Washington, D.C.: Government Printing Office, 1949-1950), 1: 623.

7. U.S., Department of State, *FRUS, 1933,* 1: 492, 623, 670-71; FDR to MacDonald, May 22, 1933, in Roosevelt, ed., *FDR Personal Letters,* 3: 347-48; Robert Bingham to FDR, June 16, 1933, in Nixon, ed., *FDR Foreign Affairs,* 1: 243; see also Rosenman, ed., *Public Papers FDR,* 2: 264-66.

8. Robert Bingham to Cordell Hull, September 19, 1933, U.S., Department of State, *FRUS, 1933,* 1: 749; Herbert Feis, *1933: Characters in Crisis* (New York: Little, Brown and Co., 1966), p. 236; and Cordell Hull, *The Memoirs of Cordell Hull,* 2 vols. (New York: MacMillan Co., 1948), 1: 268-69.

9. William Bullitt to FDR, dated only December, 1932, in Bullitt, ed., *For the President,* p. 23.

10. Rexford Tugwell, *In Search of Roosevelt* (Cambridge: Harvard University Press, 1972), pp. 251, 253-54; and idem, *The Democratic Roosevelt* (Garden City, New York: Doubleday and Co., 1957), p. 439.

11. John Cudahy to FDR, December 27, 1933, FDR Papers, President's Personal File, No. 1193, FDRL (hereinafter cited as PPF).

12. William Dodd to Cordell Hull June 10, 1933, Box 34, Cordell Hull Papers, Library of Congress, Washington, D.C.

13. William Dodd to FDR, July 30, 1933, August 12, 1933, October 13, 1933, October 28, 1933, Box 42, William Dodd Papers, Library of Congress, Washington, D.C.

14. William Dodd to FDR, November 27, 1933, Box 42, Dodd Papers, Library of Congress; see also Dodd to FDR, December 23, 1933, FDR Papers, PSF, DC, Germany, FDRL. Rudolf Hess, Hitler's secretary, was described as "greatly disturbed", see John Coar to FDR, September 9, 1933, PPF, No. 3716, FDRL.

15. George Earle to FDR, November 27, 1933, FDR Papers, PSF, DC,

Austria, FDRL; Memorandum on the Austrian situation by Louis Einstein, undated, ibid.

16. Samuel Fuller to FDR, May 11, 1933, FDR Papers, PPF, No. 2616, FDRL; and FDR to Hull, May 27, 1933, Nixon, ed., *FDR Foreign Affairs*, 1: 172-74.

17. Ibid.

18. Press Conference No. 6, March 24, 1933, *Complete Press Conferences*, 1: 77; William Phillips to Louis Howe, March 31, 1933, FDR Papers, Papers as President, Official File, No. 20, FDRL; I. C. Blackwood to FDR, March 31, 1933, and FDR to Blackwood, April 12, 1933, PPF, No. 256, FDRL; and Irving Lehman to FDR, May 10, 1933, May 24, 1933, FDR to Lehman, May 18, 1933, FDR Papers, PPF, No. 436, FDRL.

19. Felix Frankfurter, Memorandum on German Refugees, April 16, 1933, and Frankfurter to Hull, May 23, 1933, Box 137, Frankfurter Papers, Library of Congres; Frankfurter to FDR, October 17, 1933, Box 97, Frankfurter Papers. See FDR's comments to Schacht on Jewish issue, U.S., Department of State *DGFP*, Series C, 5 vols. (Washington: Government Printing Office, 1957-'66), 1: 392-93; and Dodd to FDR, July 30, 1933, August 12, 1933, Box 42, Dodd Papers, Library of Congress.

20. Press Conference No. 4, March 17, 1933, *Complete Press Conferences*, 1: 50. FDR on disarmament see Nancy Hooker, ed., *The Moffat Papers* (Cambridge: Harvard University Press, 1956), p. 92; and U.S., Department of State, *DGFP*, Series C, 1: 173-75.

21. MacDonald Plan is in *FRUS, 1933*, 1: 43-54, 2: 476-93; Press Conference No. 19, May 10, 1933, *Complete Press Conferences*, 1: 231-48.

22. Norman Davis to FDR, April 23, 1933, Box 51, Davis Papers, Library of Congress; Felix Frankfurter to FDR, May 9, 1933, Box 97, Frankfurter Papers, Library of Congress; and Press Conference No. 20, May 12, 1933, *Complete Press Conferences*, 1: 257.

23. Rosenman, ed., *Public Papers FDR*, 2: 185-88; see also Press Conference No. 21, May 16, 1933, *Complete Press Conferences*, 1: 267, and *FRUS 1933* 1: 144-45,

24. Rosenman, ed., *Public Papers FDR*, 2: 187-88; Press Conferences Nos. 21 and 22, May 16, 1933, May 19, 1933, *Complete Press Conferences*, 1: 266-67, 282; FDR to Cordell Hull, May 6, 1933, FDR Papers, OF, No. 198, FDRL. Hitler's speech is in Norman Baynes, ed., *The Speeches of Adolf Hitler*, 2 vols (London: Oxford University Press, 1942), 2: 1053.

25. Hull, *Memoirs*, 1: 228; Davis' speech is in U.S., Department of State, *Peace and War, United States Foreign Policy, 1931-1941* (Washington: Government Printing Office, 1943), pp. 188-89.

26. Press Conference No. 47, August 25, 1933, *Complete Press Conferences*, 2: 221-22; Owen Johnson to FDR, May 12, 1933, and FDR to Johnson, June 24, 1933, FDR Papers, PPF, No. 611, FDRL; FDR to MacDonald, August 30, 1933, Davis Papers, Box 51, Library of Congress and *FRUS, 1933*, 1: 210.

27. FDR to Norman Davis, August 30, 1933, Box 51, Davis Papers, Library of Congress, and see *FRUS, 1933*, 1: 209. FDR to William Dodd, September 13, 1933, Box 42, Dodd Papers, Library of Congress.

FDR, Hull, Davis telephone conversation in Box 22, Davis Papers, Library of Congress, and *FRUS 1933*, 1: 247.

28. Arthur Sweetzer to FDR, January 15, 1934, and FDR to Sweetzer, February 6, 1934, Sweetzer Papers, Library of Congress.

29. William Dodd to FDR, August 15, 1934, and FDR to Dodd, August 25, 1934, Box 45, Dodd Papers, Library of Congress; R. W. Moore to FDR, November 20, 1934, and Dodd to Moore, November 5, 1934, FDR Papers, PSF, DC, Germany, FDRL.

30. J. MacMurray to FDR, March 27, 1934, FDR Papers, OF, No. 909, FDRL; Robert Bingham to FDR, May 8, 1934, FDR Papers, PSF, DC, Great Britain, FDRL; Lincoln MacVeagh to FDR, August 6, 1934, FDR Papers, PSF, DC, Greece, FDRL; John Montgomery to FDR; July 13, 1934 and FDR to Montgomery, August 29, 1934, FDR Papers, OF, No. 507, FDRL; and William Phillips to FDR, June 5, 1934, enclosing Messersmith Memorandum of June 4, 1934, FDR Papers, PSF, DC, Germany FDRL.

31 Felix Frankfurter to FDR, May 7, 1934, Box 97, Frankfurter Papers, Library of Congress; Leonard Elmhirst to Miss Le Hand, October 4, 1934, FDR Papers PPF, No. 4320, FDRL; and Marvin McIntyre to Herbert Pell, May 30, 1934, and Pell to FDR, November 6, 1934, Box 12, Herbert Pell Papers, FDRL, Hyde Park, New York.

32. Press Conference No. 142, September 7, 1934, *Complete Press Conferences*, 3: 58-61; and E. Roosevelt, *This I Remember*, p. 84.

33. Baynes, ed., *Hitler's Speeches*, 2: 1195-96; Breckinridge Long to FDR, February 8, 1935, FDR Papers, PSF, DC, Italy, FDRL; and Press Conference No. 192, March 20, 1935, *Complete Press Conferences*, 5: 168.

34. FDR to William Dodd, December 2, 1935, FDR Papers, PSF, DC, Germany, FDRL, and Roosevelt, ed., *FDR Personal Letters*, 3: 530-31.

35. William Dodd to FDR, May 9, 1935 and July 29, 1935, Box 47, Dodd Papers, Library of Congress.

36. Robert Bingham to FDR, March 26, 1935, FDR Papers, PSF, DC, Great Britain FDRL; Edward House to FDR, April 20, 1935, FDR Papers, PPF, No. 222, FDRL; Lincoln MacVeagh to FDR, May 4, 1935, FDR Papers, PSF, DC, Greece, FDRL; John Cudahy to FDR, October 11, 1935, FDR Papers, PSF, DC, Poland, FDRL; John J. Pershing to Marvin McIntyre, September 6, 1935, FDR Papers, PPF, No. 1179, FDRL; C. H. Sherrill, Memorandum, August 24, 1935, FDR Papers, PSF, DC, Germany, FDRL; and Samuel Fuller to FDR, October 11, 1935, FDR Papers PPF, No. 2616, FDRL. The Fuller memorandum was sent to Hull, October 28, 1935, Box 38, Hull Papers, Library of Congress.

37. Henry Kannee to FDR, April 30, 1935, FDR Papers, OF, No .198, FDRL; Henry Morgenthau, Jr., Diary Entry, March 18, 1935, Book 4, p. 112, Henry Morgenthau Papers, FDRL. FDR had earlier suggested a boycott of German goods, see William Phillips Memorandum, May 25, 1934, *FRUS, 1934*, 5 vols. (Washington: Government Printing Office, 1949-'51), 1: 70, and Norman Davis' account of a discussion with the President in Box 21, State Department Memoranda Folder, March-June, 1933, Davis Papers, Library of Congress.

38. FDR to Edward House, April 10, 1935, FDR Papers, PPF, No. 222, FDRL.

39. FDR to William Bullitt, April 21, 1935, cited in O. Bullitt, ed., *For the President*, p. 113.

40. Henry Stimson and McGeorge Bundy, *On Active Service in Peace and War* (New York: Harper and Bros., 1947), pp. 235-36, 292-93, 297; Tugwell, *In Search of Roosevelt*, pp. 249-51; Raymond Moley, *After Seven Years* (New York: Harper and Bros., 1939), pp. 94-95; Louis Wehle to FDR, December 1, 1932 and January 17, 1933, Box 39, Wehle Papers, FDRL; and see Stimson-FDR conversation on January 13, 1933, in *FRUS, 1933*, 3: 53.

41. Washington treaties are in *FRUS, 1922*, 2 vols. (Washington: Government Printing Office, 1938), 1: 33-37, 247-66, 276-82. Kellogg-Briand Pact is in *FRUS, 1928*, 3 vols. (Washington: Government Printing Office, 1942-'43), 1: 153-57. London accords of 1930 are in *FRUS, 1930*, 3 vols. (Washington: Government Printing Office, 1945), 1: 107-25.

42. Tugwell, *In Search of Roosevelt*, pp. 249-51; James Farley, *Jim Farley's Story: The Roosevelt Years* (New York: Whittlesey House, 1948), p. 39.

43. Norman Davis to FDR, January 10, 1933, Box 51, Davis Papers, Library of Congress.

44. Stanley Hornbeck, Memorandum to William Phillips, April 3, 1933, and Phillips to FDR, April 3, 1933, FDR Papers, PSF, DC, Japan, FDRL; and Hornbeck, Memorandum to William Phillips, May 9, 1933 and Phillips to FDR, May 9, 1933, FDR Papers, PSF, DC, China, FDRL.

45. Otohiko Matsukata to FDR, February 20, 1934, FDR Papers, PSF, DC, Japan, FDRL; and Stanley Hornbeck to Cordell Hull, February 26, 1934, FDR Papers, PSF, DC, Japan, FDRL.

46. Stanley Hornbeck, Memorandum to Cordell Hull, April 5, 1934, and brought to the President's attention, see William Phillips to Louis Howe, April 20, 1934, FDR Papers, PSF, DC, Japan, FDRL.

47. Cordell Hull to FDR, May 29, 1933, enclosing Hornbeck note of May 27, 1933, and Joseph Grew letter to Hull, May 11, 1933, FDR Papers, PSF, DC, Japan, FDRL. Report of military attaché, R. S. Bratton, May 8, 1933, No. 6777, was attached to Grew letter, FDR Papers, PSF, DC, Japan, FDRL.

48. William Phillips to FDR, January 15, 1934, and Joseph Grew to Cordell Hull, No. 608, December 12, 1933, FDR Papers, PSF, DC, Japan, FDRL.

49. Cordell Hull to FDR, January 22, 1935, enclosing Joseph Grew to Hull, No. 1102, December 27, 1934, FDR Papers, PSF, DC, Japan, FDRL. See also *FRUS, 1935*, 4 vols. (Washington: Government Printing Office, 1952-'53), 3: 822-28, 842-43, 843-52. (These despatches from Grew are in FDR Papers, PSF, DC, Japan, FDRL.)

50. Lin Sen to FDR, May 19, 1933, FDR Papers, OF, No. 404, FDRL; Breckinridge Long to FDR, July 17, 1933, FDR Papers, PSF, DC, Italy, FDRL; Arthur Sweetzer to FDR, January 15, 1934, FDR Papers, PPF, No. 506, FDRL; Henry Roosevelt to FDR, March 2, 1934, FDR Papers, PSF, Subject File, London Naval Conference, FDRL; Grenville Emmet to FDR, August 17, 1934, FDR Papers, PPF, No. 372, FDRL; and Arthur Holcombe to FDR, February 6, 1935, FDR Papers, PPF, No. 2325, FDRL.

51. Hull, *Memoirs*, 1: 279. The Amau statement is in *FRUS, Japan, 1931-1941*, 2 vols. (Washington: Government Printing Office, 1943), 1: 31-41, 224-25.

52. FDR to Edward House, April 5, 1933, in Roosevelt, ed., *FDR Personal Letters*, 3: 343; FDR to Malcolm Peabody, August 19, 1933 FDR Papers, PPF, No. 732, and Hirohito to FDR, May 20, 1933, FDR Papers,

OF, No. 404, FDRL. See also Stimson and Bundy, *On Active Service,* pp. 301-02.

53. Hull, *Memoirs,* 1: 281-85. Hull's memoranda of the conversations with Saito are in FDR Papers, PSF, DC, Japan, FDRL; and see FDR to Hull, May 10, 1934, Box 36, Hull Papers, Library of Congress.

54. Press Conference No. 148, October 5, 1934, *Complete Press Conferences,* 4: 108; and Norman Davis, Memorandum of Hull, Davis, FDR conversation, April 28, 1934, Box 21, Davis Papers, Library of Congress.

55. FDR to Norman Davis, October 5, 1934 and November 9, 1934, FDR Papers, PSF, Subject File, London Naval Conference, FDRL; Davis to FDR, October 31, 1934 and November 6, 1934, Box 51, Davis Papers, Library of Congress; and Press Conference No. 167, December 21, 1934, *Complete Press Conferences,* 4: 294-95.

56. Norman Davis to FDR, December 20, 1935, FDR Papers, PSF, Subject File, London Naval Conference, FDRL; Hull, *Memoirs,* 1: 449; *FRUS, Japan, 1931-1941,* 1: 297; and Press Conference No. 267, January 17, 1936, *Complete Press Conferences,* 7: 79.

57. Henry Morgenthau, Jr., Diary Entry, March 18, 1935, Book 4, p. 112, Henry Morgenthau Papers, FDRL; Ray Newton, E. Johnson, and G. Clark to FDR, April 18, 1935, FDR Papers, OF, No. 66, FDRL; S. Hornbeck, Memorandum No. 1012, January 3, 1935, and Joseph Grew to Cordell Hull, Memorandum No. 1156, February 6, 1935, FDR Papers, PSF, DC, Japan, FDRL.

58. Benito Mussolini to FDR, April 24, 1933, FDR Papers, PSF, DC, Italy, FDRL.

59. Breckinridge Long to FDR, June 1, 1933, and FDR to Long, June 15, 1933, Box 105, Breckinridge Long Papers, Library of Congress, Washington, D.C.

60. Breckinridge Long to FDR, June 1, 1933, and June 9, 1933, Box 105, Long Papers, Library of Congress.

61. Breckinridge Long to FDR, July 17, 1933, and December 15, 1933, and FDR to Long, September 11, 1933, Box 105, Long Papers, Library of Congress.

62. Breckinridge Long to FDR, September 14, 1933, Box 105, Long Papers; Long to FDR, February 3, 1935, February 8, 1935, April 19, 1935, May 10, 1935, Box 114, Long Papers, Library of Congress.

63. Breckinridge Long to FDR, June 27, 1933, Box 105, Long Papers, Library of Congress.

64. Breckinridge Long to FDR, February 15, 1935, Box 114, Long Papers, Library of Congress; and Hull to FDR, August 19, 1935, Alexander Kirk to Hull, August 19, 1935, and FDR to Hull, August 20, 1935, FDR Papers, PSF, DC, Italy, FDRL.

65. Breckinridge Long to FDR, September 6, 1935, and October 30, 1935, Box 114, Long Papers, Library of Congress. Louis Howe wrote to FDR on October 18, 1935, stating that "Long has been hypnotized by Mussolini. Is sending five or six cables a day little short of absolute Italian propaganda" see FDR Papers, OF, No. 200, FDRL.

CHAPTER THREE

1. Press Conference No. 246, November 6, 1935, *Complete Press Conferences,* 6: 249-50.

2. Dave Morris to FDR, December 26, 1935, FDR Papers, PSF, DC, Belgium, FDRL; FDR to Long, March 9, 1935, and September 19, 1935, Box 114, Long Papers, Library of Congress; FDR to Dodd, August 14, 1935, Roosevelt, ed., *FDR Personal Letters,* 3: 501; FDR to Josiah Bailey, August 29, 1935, FDR Papers, PPF, No. 2518, FDRL.

3. FDR to Ray Baker, March 20, 1935 and FDR to Dodd, January 6, 1936, Roosevelt, ed., *FDR Personal Letters,* 3: 467, 543.

4. Robert Bingham to FDR, May 22, 1933, FDR Papers, OF, No. 491, FDRL; idem, March 8, 1934, and April 23, 1934, FDR Papers, PSF, Subject File, London Naval Conference, FDRL.

5. Hull to FDR enclosing Phillips Memorandum, April 26, 1934, and Bingham to FDR, May 8, 1934, FDR Papers, PSF, Subject File, London Naval Conference, FDRL.

6. FDR to Nicholas Butler, September 26, 1934, FDR Papers, PPF, No. 445, FDRL; Davis to FDR, October 31, 1934, Box 51, Davis Papers, Library of Congress; FDR to Davis, November 9, 1934, and Davis to FDR, November 27, 1934, FDR Papers, PSF, Subject File, London Naval Conference, FDRL; and FDR to Stimson, December 8, 1934, Roosevelt, ed., *FDR Personal Letters,* 3: 440.

7. Bingham to FDR, June 28, 1935 and FDR to Bingham, July 11, 1935, FDR Papers, PSF, DC, Great Britain, FDRL; Dodd to FDR, July 29, 1935, FDR Papers, PSF, DC, Germany, FDRL; Davis to FDR, February 18, 1936, FDR Papers, PSF, Subject File, London Naval Conference, FDRL; and Henry Morgenthau, Diary Entry, July 10, 1935, Book 8, p. 50, Morgenthau Papers, FDRL.

8. Press Conference No. 25, May 31, 1935, *Complete Press Conferences,* 1: 322; Long to FDR, February, 7, 1934, FDR Papers, PSF, DC, Italy, FDRL; Straus to FDR, February 27, 1934, and January 2, 1936, FDR Papers, PSF, DC, France, FDRL; FDR to Straus, February 13, 1936 and June 8, 1936, Roosevelt, ed., *FDR Personal Letters,* 3: 555, 593-94.

9. Beatrice Berle and Travis Jacobs, eds., *Navigating the Rapids, 1918-1971* (New York: Harcourt, Brace, Jovanovich, Inc., 1973), pp. 45-49; Frances Perkins, *The Roosevelt I Knew* (New York: Viking Press, 1946), pp. 86-87. He told Perkins, "I don't understand the Russians. I just don't know what makes them tick. I wish I could study them. Frances, see if you can find out what makes them tick" ibid.; see also Tugwell, *Democratic Roosevelt,* p. 346. Charles Bohlen's criticism of FDR's views on Russia are in his *Witness to History, 1929-1969* (New York: Norton and Co., 1973), p. 141. Raymond Robins, a vocal exponent of Russian recognition, thought Roosevelt's views toward the Bolshevik revolution were too favorable, see Robins to FDR, October 28, 1933, FDR Papers, OF, No. 200, FDRL.

10. Hull, *Memoirs,* 1: 297, 304, 306, 378; Sumner Welles, *Where Are We Heading?* (New York: Harper and Bros., 1946), p. 375; William Phillips, *Ventures in Diplomacy* (Portland, Maine: Anthoensen Press, 1952), p. 156; Wehle, *Hidden Threads,* pp. 114-15; Tugwell, *Democratic Roosevelt,* pp. 438-39; Bohlen, *The Transformation of American Foreign Policy* (New York: W. W. Norton, 1969), pp. 16-17; and FDR, *On Our Way* (New York: John Day Co., 1934), p. 131.

11. Press Conference No. 12, April 14, 1933, No. 23, May 24, 1933, No. 39, August 4, 1933, and No. 40, August 5, 1933, *Complete Press Conferences,* 1: 143-44, 301, 2: 102-03, 133, 142; Phillips to Marvin McIntyre, April 28, 1933, FDR Papers, PSF, DC, Russia, FDRL; Hull,

Memoirs, 1: 293-94; Bullitt to FDR, July 8, 1933, FDR Papers, PSF, Subject File, London Economic Conference, FDRL.

12. Kalinin-Roosevelt correspondence is in *FRUS, 1933,* 2: 794-95; see also Harold Ickes, *The Secret Diary of Harold Ickes,* 3 vols. (New York: Duell, Sloan and Pearce, 1950), 1: 114; John Blum, *From the Morgenthau Diaries,* 3 vols. (Boston: Houghton Mifflin Co., 1959-'67), 1: 55-57; Frankfurter to FDR, October 29, 1933, Box 97, Frankfurter Papers, Library of Congress; and Daniels to FDR, October 21, 1933, Box 16, Daniels Papers, Library of Congress.

13. Litvinov-Roosevelt notes in *FRUS, 1933,* 2: 805-10; on debt issue see ibid., p. 804; on views of Kelley, Hull, and Bullitt see ibid., pp. 783-87 and U.S. Department of State, *FRUS, The Soviet Union, 1933-1939* (Washington: GPO, 1952), pp. 10-12, 16-17.

14. Press Conference No. 70, November 17, 1933, *Complete Press Conferences,* 2: 461-62; FDR speech of November 18, 1933 is in Rosenman, ed., *Public Papers FDR,* 2: 492-93; FDR to Litvinov, November 23, 1933, in *FRUS, 1933,* 2: 820. Litvinov's comments are in *FRUS, 1934,* 1: 189-90. For a retrospective critical view see W. Averell Harriman, *America and Russia in a Changing World* (New York: Doubleday, 1971), p. 11.

15. Bullitt to FDR, January 1, 1934, and FDR to Bullitt, January 7, 1934, FDR Papers, PSF, DC, Russia, FDRL.

16. Hornbeck Memorandum, "Russo-Japanese Conflict, Problem: What Should Be the Attitude and Course of Action of the United States," January 31, 1934, FDR Papers, PSF, DC, Japan, FDRL.

17. Bullitt to Hull, No. 188, October 2, 1934, "Personal Observations on Conditions in the Soviet Union," FDR Papers, PSF, DC, Russia, FDRL.

18. Bullitt to FDR, January 1, 1934, April 13, 1934, September 8, 1934, April 8, 1935, and Bullitt to Hull, No. 604, April 22, 1934, FDR Papers, PSF, DC, Russia, FDRL.

19. Bullitt to FDR, April 13, 1934, FDR to Bullitt, May 9, 1934, and Hull to Bullitt, No. 11, March 17, 1934, FDR Papers, PSF, DC, Russia, FDRL; R. W. Moore to Bullitt April 24, 1934, May 8, 1934, June 4, 1934, Box 3, R. W. Moore Papers, FDRL. FDR requested that Russia be exempt from the Johnson Bill which prohibited loans to governments which had not paid instalments on debts owed to the United States, see Nixon, ed., *FDR Foreign Affairs,* 1: 616.

20. Bullitt to FDR, May 1, 1935, FDR to Bullitt, June 3, 1935, Bullitt to Hull, No. 552, April 26, 1935 and forwarded to FDR, May 16, 1935, FDR Papers, PSF, DC, Russia, FDRL.

21. Bullitt to FDR, July 15, 1935, FDR Papers, PSF, DC, Russia, FDRL; Bullitt to Moore, July 15, 1935 and Moore to Miss Le Hand, August 1, 1935, and Moore to Bullitt, September 3, 1935, Box 3, Moore Papers, FDRL; *FRUS, The Soviet Union, 1933-1939,* pp. 222, 248-51, 254, 258-59; and Press Conference No. 225, July 3, 1935, *Complete Press Conferences,* 6: 65-66. Two veteran diplomats approved of Bullitt's stiffening attitudes toward Russia, see George Kennan, *Memoirs, 1925-1950* (Boston: Little, Brown and Co., 1967), p. 80 and Bohlen, *Witness to History,* p. 34.

22. Bullitt to Moore, September 8, 1934, Moore to FDR, October 23, 1934, Box 4, Moore Papers, FDRL; Bullitt to FDR, April 7, 1935, April

8, 1935, August 3, 1935, FDR Papers, PSF, DC, Russia, FDRL; Dodd to FDR, December 15, 1935, FDR Papers, PSF, DC, Germany, FDRL. Dodd urged Moore to emphasize to FDR the necessity of a united American, British, and Russian front, see Dodd to Moore, January 18, 1934, Box 5, Moore Papers, FDRL.

23. Rosenman, ed., *Public Papers FDR*, 4: 40-41; FDR to Joseph Robinson, January 30, 1935, FDR Papers, OF, No. 202, FDRL; FDR to Stimson, February 6, 1935, FDR Papers, PPF, No. 20, FDRL; Press Conference No. 177, January 23, 1935, *Complete Press Conferences*, 5: 67-68.

24. Rosenman, ed., *Public Papers FDR*, 4: 345-47; FDR to House, September 17, 1935, Roosevelt, ed., *FDR Personal Letters*, 3: 506; Dodd to FDR, December 2, 1935, FDR Papers, PSF, DC, Germany, FDRL. The 1935 Neutrality Law is in U.S., Department of State, *Peace and War, United States Foreign Policy 1931-1941* (Washington: GPO, 1943), pp. 266-70.

25. Rosenman, ed., *Public Papers FDR*, 4:315, 412-18, 440; Press Conference No. 238, September 13, 1935, *Complete Press Conferences*, 6: 160-61; and *FRUS, 1935*, 1: 794.

26. FDR to Hull, October 10, 1935, Nixon, ed., *FDR Foreign Affairs*, 3: 18; Ickes, *Secret Diary*, 1: 462; Hull, *Memoirs*, 1: 432-33; Press Conference No. 244, October 30, 1935, *Complete Press Conferences*, 6: 228; Henry Morgenthau, Diary Entry, October 31, 1935, Book 10, p. 196, Morgenthau Papers, FDRL.

27. Hull, *Memoirs*, 1: 436-40; FDR to Hull, November 27, 1935, Box 38, Hull Papers, Library of Congress. Hull's account of the conversations with Rosso are in FDR Papers, PSF, DC, Italy, FDRL.

28. Phillips to FDR, August 6, 1935, and August 9, 1935, FDR Papers, PSF, DC, Italy, FDRL. The Ethiopian mobilization order is in ibid.; Henry Morgenthau, Diary Entry, November 12, 1935, Book 11, p. 372, Morgenthau Papers, FDRL; Hubbard Wynant to FDR, December 12, 1935, FDR Papers, PSF, DC, Ethiopia, FDRL; FDR to Robert Skinner, December 19, 1935, FDR Papers, OF, No. 502, FDRL.

29. Cornelius Engert to FDR, January 10, 1936, FDR Papers, PSF, DC, Ethiopia, FDRL; Rosenman, ed., *Public Papers FDR*, 5: 89-91, 92-94. The 1936 Neutrality Law is in U.S., Department of State, *Peace and War*, pp. 313-14.

30. Press Conference No. 292, May 5, 1936, *Complete Press Conferences*, 7: 233; Hull, *Memoirs*, 1: 471; Long to FDR, June 15, 1936 and June 23, 1936, Box 117, Long Papers, Library of Congress; MacVeagh to FDR, June 13, 1936, FDR Papers, PSF, DC, Greece, FDRL.

31. Norman Davis to FDR, February 18, 1936, Box 37, Davis Papers, Library of Congress; FDR to Long, February 22, 1936, Box 117, Long Papers, Library of Congress.

32. FDR to Anthony Biddle, March 12, 1936, FDR Papers, PSF, DC, Norway, FDRL; FDR to Dodd, March 16, 1936, FDR Papers, PSF, DC, Germany, FDRL; Long told FDR that this was the most dangerous time since 1918, see Long to FDR, March 13, 1936, Box 117, Long Papers, Library of Congress.

33. FDR to Bullitt, March 16, 1936, Bullitt, ed., *For the President*, p. 150; Cudahy to FDR, March 20, 1936, FDR Papers, PSF, DC, Poland, FDRL; and Dodd to FDR, April 1, 1936, Box 49, Dodd Papers, Library of Congress.

34. Bowers to FDR, August 26, 1936, and September 9, 1936, with enclosure of September 7, 1936 of Bowers to Hull, FDR Papers, PSF, DC, Spain, FDRL.

35. Bowers to FDR, August 26, 1936, September 9, 1936, September 16, 1936, December 16, 1936, and Bowers to Hull, September 23, 1936, and October 30, 1936, FDR Papers, PSF, DC, Spain, FDRL.

36. Dodd to FDR, October 19, 1936, FDR Papers, PSF, DC, Germany, FDRL.

37. Dodd to FDR, May 9, 1935 and October 31, 1935, FDR Papers, PSF, DC, Germany, FDRL; and Hull, *Memoirs,* 1: 489.

38. Rosenman, ed., *Public Papers FDR,* 5: 285-92; Josephus Daniels told FDR that his presence at Buenos Aires would insure epoch-making declarations, see Daniels to FDR, November 2, 1936, Box 16, Daniels Papers, Library of Congress.

39. Bowers to FDR, February 16, 1937, March 31, 1937, July 21, 1937, August 11, 1937, October 11, 1937, and Bowers to Hull, May 18, 1937, FDR Papers, PSF, DC, Spain, FDRL.

40. Roosevelt, *This I Remember,* pp. 161-62; Hull, *Memoirs,* 1: 511-15; Rosenman, ed., *Public Papers FDR,* 6: 185-93; Ickes, *Secret Diary,* 2: 569; *FRUS, 1936,* 2: 471. The 1937 Neutrality Act is in U.S., Department of State, *Peace and War,* pp. 355-65.

41. Davis to Hornbeck, Memorandum of a conversation with FDR, March 23, 1937, Box 27, Davis Papers, Library of Congress. Neutralization proposal is discussed in R. W. Moore to Hull, November 19, 1936, Box 40, Hull Papers, Library of Congress, and FDR to Hull, March 1, 1937, Roosevelt, ed., *FDR Personal Letters,* 3: 662-64; FDR to the Chief of Naval Operations, August 10, 1936, FDR Papers, PSF, Departmental Correspondence, War, FDRL; and unsigned memorandum, "The Military Coup in Tokyo," February 26, 1936, FDR Papers, PSF, DC, Japan, FDRL.

42. Hull, *Memoirs,* 1: 535.

43. Grew to Hull, 793.94/9732, No. 321, August 27, 1937, FDR Papers, PSF, Confidential File, Japan, FDRL (hereinafter cited as CF); Leahy to FDR, October 11, 1937, forwarding a report of Major Bales, FDR Papers, PSF, Departmental Correspondence, Navy, FDRL; Leahy to FDR, November 30, 1937 forwarding Admiral H. Yarnell to Leahy, November 7, 1937, FDR Papers, PSF, Departmental Correspondence, Navy, FDRL; and Grew to Hull, 793.94/10946, No. 510, November 2, 1937, enclosing a report of Military Attaché Major Cresswell, FDR Papers, PSF, CF, Japan, FDRL.

44. FDR to Leahy, Memorandum, "Japanese Vessels in the Bering Sea," August 22, 1937, FDR Papers, PSF, Departmental Correspondence, Navy, FDRL; Charles Barnett undated memorandum "Japanese Penetration of the Philippine Islands" and Harry Woodring to FDR July 2, 1937, FDR Papers, PSF, DC, Japan, FDRL. FDR called the Japanese the Prussians of the East, see R. McIntyre, *White House Physician* (New York: G. P. Putnam, 1946), p. 109.

45. Press Conference No. 392, August 17, 1937, *Complete Press Conferences,* 10: 166-67; and Rosenman, ed., *Public Papers FDR,* 6: 354.

46. Henry Morgenthau, Diary Entry, January 4, 1937, Book 51, p. 17, Morgenthau Papers, FDRL; FDR to Dodd, August 5, 1936, and Dodd to FDR, September 21, 1936 and October 19, 1936, Box 49, Dodd Papers,

Library of Congress; Joseph Davies, Diary Entry, August 28, 1936, and Davies to FDR, January 22, 1937, Box 3, Joseph Davies Papers, Library of Congress, Washington, D.C.; FDR to Dodd, January 9, 1937, Roosevelt, ed., *FDR Personal Letters,* 3: 649; Dodd to FDR, April 13, 1937, Box 51, Dodd Papers, Library of Congress.

47. Ludwig to FDR, August 15, 1936, FDR Papers, PPF, No. 3884, FDRL; Dodd to FDR, September 21, 1936, Box 49, Dodd Papers, LC; Fuller to Miss Le Hand, October 22, 1936, FDR Papers, PPF, No. 2616; Bullitt to FDR, November 24, 1936, FDR Papers, PSF, DC, France, FDRL; Law to FDR, November 26, 1936, FDR Papers, PPF, No. 6032, FDRL.

48. Bullitt to FDR, January 10, 1937, and April 12, 1937, and FDR to Bullitt, April 21, 1937, FDR Papers, PSF, DC, France, FDRL; FDR to Phillips, February 6, 1937, Roosevelt, ed., *FDR Personal Letters,* 3: 656; Dodd to Hull, 762.63/368, No. 156, July 12, 1937, FDR Papers, PSF, CF, Austria, FDRL; Davis to FDR, undated, and Dodd to FDR, May 24, 1937, FDR Papers, PSF, DC, Germany, FDRL; and Pell to FDR, September 11, 1937, Box 12, Pell Papers, FDRL.

49. MacVeagh to FDR, February 17, 1937, FDR Papers, PSF, DC, Greece, FDRL; Phillips to FDR, April 27, 1937, and FDR to Phillips, May 17, 1937, Phillips, *Ventures in Diplomacy.* pp. 204-05; Kirk to Hull, 762.65/302, No. 205, May 6, 1937, and Phillips to Hull, 762.65/318, No. 258, June 2, 1937, and idem, 762.65/322, No. 415, June 11, 1937, FDR Papers, PSF, CF, Italy, FDRL.

50. Rosenman, ed., *Public Papers FDR,* 6: 406-11.

51. Hull, *Memoirs,* 1: 544-45; Hooker, ed., *Moffat Papers.* pp. 153-54; Berle and Jacobs, eds., *Navigating the Rapids,* p. 140; and Press Conference No. 400, October 6, 1937, *Complete Press Conferences,* 10: 248-52.

52. Leahy to FDR, November 8, 1937, enclosing Yarnell to Leahy, October 18, 1937, FDR Papers, PSF, Departmental Correspondence, Navy, FDRL; Ickes, *Secret Diary,* 2: 274; Welles, *Seven Decisions,* p. 8; Phillips, *Ventures in Diplomacy,* p. 207; Leahy believed the President's policy of quarantine would "almost certainly bring about a war with Japan" see Leahy, Diary Entry, Diary 3, Box 1, William Leahy Papers, Library of Congress, Washington, D.C.

53. Grace Tully, *FDR My Boss* (New York: Charles Scribner's Sons, 1949), pp. 231-32; Welles, *Seven Decisions,* p. 13; Samuel Rosenman, *Working with Roosevelt* (New York: Harper and Bros., 1952), p. 10; Ickes, *Secret Diary,* 2: 213; Hull, *Memoirs,* 1: 545; Hooker, ed., *Moffat Diary,* p. 156.

54. Dodd to FDR, March 3, 1936 and April 1, 1936, FDR Papers, PSF, DC, Germany, FDRL; MacVeagh to FDR, April 30, 1936, and FDR to MacVeagh, May 1, 1936, FDR Papers, PSF, DC, Greece, FDRL; Frankfurter to FDR, July 11, 1936, Box 98, Frankfurter Papers, LC; Bullitt to FDR, February 22, 1936, FDR Papers, PSF, DC, Russia, FDRL; Straus to FDR, May 13, 1936, FDR Papers, PPF, No. 283, FDRL. FDR believed that if England had shut the Suez Canal, Italy would have been halted, see Ickes, *Secret Diary,* 2: 84.

55. Bowers to FDR, December 16, 1936, February 16, 1937, March 31, 1937, FDR Papers, PSF, DC, Spain, FDRL; FDR to Hull, June 29, 1937, Box 41, Hull Papers, LC. FDR probably agreed with Bernard

Baruch's suggestion of an English-American alliance, but British appeasement policies must certainly have dampened FDR's effort to achieve such,
see Baruch to FDR, November 18, 1936, Box 40, Hull Papers, LC.

56. Dodd to Moore, August 31, 1936, FDR Papers, PSF, DC, Germany, FDRL; Moore to FDR, September 15, 1936, Box 17, Moore
Papers, FDRL; Bingham to FDR, September 4, 1936, November 13,
1936, January 5, 1937, FDR Papers, PSF, DC, Great Britain, FDRL.
FDR thought that Bingham's last letter was important enough to forward
to Hull for his persual, see Box 40, Hull Papers, LC.

57. Press Conference No. 360A, April 15, 1937, *Complete Press Conferences,* 9: 301-02; Davis to Chamberlain, June 10, 1937, Chamberlain
to Davis, July 8, 1937, and FDR to Chamberlain, July 28, 1937, Box 8,
Davis Papers, LC.

58. Press Conference No. 381, July 13, 1937, and No. 400, October
6, 1937, *Complete Press Conferences,* 9: 42-43, 10: 249-52; Bingham to
Hull, June 16, 1937, and FDR's comments on Bingham's despatch, memorandum to Hull, July 7, 1937, Box 41, Hull Papers, LC.

59. Bullitt to FDR, October 24, 1936, November 8, 1936, November
24, 1936, December 7, 1936, January 10, 1937, April 12, 1937, and
May 10, 1937, FDR Papers, PSF, DC, France, FDRL.

60. Memorandum of Roosevelt-Davis conversation is in *FRUS, 1937,*
4: 85; see also Hull to Davis, October 8, 1937, ibid., p. 84; Berle and
Jacobs, eds., *Navigating the Rapids,* pp. 141, 147; FDR's comments on
the Brussels Conference are in *FRUS, Japan, 1931-1941,* 1: 401; Davis'
speech at Brussels is in ibid., pp. 405-07; and see Hooker, ed., *Moffat
Papers,* pp. 157-58, 183.

61. Hooker, ed., *Moffat Papers,* pp. 161, 166, 174; Bohlen, *Witness to
History,* p. 42; Davis to FDR and Hull, No. 19, November 6, 1937, and
No. 22, November 7, 1937, *FRUS, 1937,* 4: 157-59, 162-63. In the interview with Jules Henry, FDR had said that if Japan attacked Hong Kong
or Indo-China or the Dutch East Indies, this would mean an attack on the
Philippines and we would all act together. However, to view this as a
commitment to France is to take it totally out of context. FDR, angered
over French temerity toward Japan, was not about to unilaterally secure
any French territory. Discussion of this interview is in Ministere des
Affaires, *Etrangeres Documents Diplomatiques Francais, 1932-1939,* 2nd
Series, 7 vols. (Paris: Imprimerie Nationale, 1964-1972), 7: 355-56;
FRUS, 1937, 3: 666-67, 4: 173; and Press Conference No. 412, November 26, 1937, *Complete Press Conferences,* 10: 374.

62. Ickes, *Secret Diary,* 2: 275-76; Grew to Hull, 762.94/214, No.
2660, November 13, 1937, *FRUS, Japan, 1931-1941,* 1: 160; Phillips to
Hull, 762.94/215, No. 654, November 17, 1937, and 762.94/176, No.
468, November 7, 1937, FDR Papers, PSF, CF, Italy, FDRL; and FDR
to Biddle, November 10, 1937, FDR Papers, PSF, DC, Poland, FDRL.

63. Hull, *Memoirs,* 1: 559-62; Ickes, *Secret Diary,* 2: 275; FDR to
Hull, December 13, 1937, FDR Papers, PSF, DC, Japan, FDRL; Leahy,
Diary Entry, December 14, 1937, Box 1, Diary 3, Leahy Papers, LC. The
account of the *Panay* attack sent to FDR is in *FRUS, Japan, 1931-1941,*
1: 535-37, and FDR Papers, PSF, DC, China, FDRL. Roosevelt probably
agreed with the views expressed to him by Henry Stimson. Stimson characterized the Far East crisis as extremely serious for the United States.
He condemned Japan, and urged the President to alleviate the disparity

under which China was fighting. FDR replied that while Stimson's considerations were ever present in his mind, he had not as yet found a solution to the problem. Herbert Feis wrote to Stimson, "I can hardly doubt but what the President must agree with the whole train of your presentation," see Stimson to FDR, November 16, 1937, FDR to Stimson, November 24, 1937, FDR Papers, PPF, No. 20, FDRL; and Feis to Stimson, November 22, 1937, Box 26, Herbert Feis Papers, LC, Washington, D.C.

64. Bullitt to Hull, Memorandum, "Policy of the United States with Respect to the Soviet Union and Communism," No. 1537, April 20, 1936, FDR Papers, PSF, DC, Russia, FDRL.

65. Henderson to Hull, No. 1850, September 1, 1936, FDR Papers, PSF, DC, Russia, FDRL. Eleanor Roosevelt described Vyshinsky as one of Russia's great legal minds, a skilled debater, and a man with the ability to use the weapons of wit and ridicule, see *The Autobiography of Eleanor Roosevelt* (London: Hutchinson and Co., 1937), p. 240; see also Perkins, *The Roosevelt I Knew*, pp. 156-57.

66. Kennan, *Memoirs*, pp. 82-83; Bohlen, *Witness to History*, pp. 45, 52; and Bullitt to Moore, June 15, 1937, Box 3, Moore Papers, FDRL.

67. Davies to FDR, January 25, 1937, Box 3, Davies Papers, LC; Davies to FDR, March 5, 1937, Davies to Early, March 9, 1937, Davies to McIntyre, March 15, 1937, Box 4, Davies Papers, LC; and Mrs. Marjorie Davies to Eleanor Roosevelt, March 3, 1937, FDR Papers, PSF, DC, Russia, FDRL.

68. Davies to Early, February 8, 1937, and Davies to FDR, February 17, 1937, Box 3, Davies Papers, LC.

69. Davies to FDR, February 4, 1937, Davies to McIntyre, January 25, 1937, Box 3, and Davies to FDR, July 10, 1937, and Davies to McIntyre, July 10, 1937, Box 5, Davies Papers, LC. Davies, recalled Bohlen, asked Alfred Chollerton of the *Daily Telegraph* what he thought of the trials. Chollerton replied, "Mr. Ambassador, I believe everything but the facts" see Bohlen, *Witness to History*, p. 52.

70. Kennan, *Memoirs*, pp. 84-85; Bohlen, *Witness to History*, pp. 39-41; Bullitt to Hull, July 19, 1937, and Hull to Bullitt, August 3, 1937, Box 41, Hull Papers, LC. A possible related development in this action may be found in a letter of Arthur Bliss Lane to R. W. Moore from Riga, which was forwarded to FDR. Lane criticized his Russian section for lack of an open mind on Russia. He said that too many saw Russia as a separate entity, rather than in terms of Russia's relationship to Europe and the rest of the world. He stressed that he desired a section not fundamentally anti-Soviet in its attitude. The specialists were like students preparing a doctor's thesis, he wrote, they were unfitted to deal with broad issues. He suggested that they be sent to Latin America. Lane's letter was enclosed in R. W. Moore to FDR, September 23, 1936, Box 17, Moore Papers, FDRL.

71. FDR complained of the biased reporting against the communists' role in Spain as expressed in the Hearst papers; see FDR to Bowers, September 16, 1936, and Bowers to FDR, December 16, 1936 and March 31, 1937, FDR Papers, PSF, DC, Spain, FDRL. See also Bowers to Hull, September 23, 1936, forwarded to FDR by Hull, October 10, 1936, stating that the communists were under rigid discipline and supporting the constituted authorities, Box 39, Hull Papers, LC. On Litvinov, see Davies

to Hull, 740.00/114, No. 31, February 5, 1937, and 740.00/193, No. 164, July 10, 1937, FDR Papers, PSF, CF, Russia, FDRL. On the Japanese-Soviet situation, see Davies to Hull, 761.94/958, No. 152, March 26, 1937, FDR Papers, PSF, CF, Russia, FDRL, and Grew to Hull, 761.94/969, No. 2445, May 29, 1937, FDR Papers, PSF, CF, Japan, FDRL. Morgenthau, Diary Entry, December 17, 1936, Book 48, pp. 261-62.

72. Ickes, *Secret Diary,* 1: 494, 2: 111; Blum, ed., *Morgenthau Diaries,* 1: 224; Leahy, Diary Entry, January 2, 1937, Diary 3, Box 1, Leahy Papers, LC; see also Leahy's notes of a meeting with Troyanovsky, December 9, 1937, ibid.; and *FRUS, the Soviet Union, 1933-1939,* pp. 467-68, 475-90. For Hull's activities see ibid., pp. 463-64, 485. On possible aircraft purchases see ibid., pp. 466-67, 474, and William Standley and A. Ageton, *Admiral Ambassador to Russia* (Chicago: Henry Regnery, 1955), pp. 40-41.

CHAPTER FOUR

1. Rosenman, ed., *Public Papers FDR,* 7: 1-2, 69-71.

2. FDR to James Roosevelt, January 20, 1938, Roosevelt, ed., *FDR Personal Letters,* 4: 750-51; Hull, *Memoirs,* 1: 563-64, 573-74; FDR to William Bankhead, Janaury 6, 1938, Rosenman, ed., *Public Papers, FDR,* 7: 37; Press Conference No. 433, February 11, 1938, *Complete Press Conferences,* 11: 146. FDR wrote to William A. White the following words, "Get back to your writing as soon as you can, for we all need to jog people into speeding up their evolutionary processes of thinking," see FDR to White, January 17, 1938, Series C, Box 290, White Papers, LC.

3. *FRUS, 1938,* 1: 115-17; Neville Chamberlain to FDR, January 14, 1938, and FDR to Chamberlain, January 17, 1938, ibid., pp. 118-22 and in PSF, DC, Great Britain, FDRL.

4. U.S. Congress, *Hearings before the Joint Committee on the Investigation of the Pearl Harbor Attack,* 79th Cong., 2nd Sess., 1946, 39 vols. (Washington, GPO, 1946), 9: 4272-278; and William Leahy, Diary Entry, January 25, 1938 and January 29, 1938, Diary 4, Box 2, Leahy Papers, LC.

5. Joseph Davies, "Supplementary and Final Report on Discussion had with Messers. Stalin and Molotov prior to Departure from Soviet Union," January 17, 1939; Davies to FDR, January 18, 1939; and Davies to Welles, January 17, 1939, Box 9, Davies Papers, LC. Davies stated that he talked with Molotov and Stalin about this proposal on June 5, 1938, see Davies to Hull, January 17, 1939, 800.5W89USSR/247 Diplomatic Division, Record Group 59, National Archives, Washington, D.C.

6. Bullitt to FDR, December 7, 1937, and January 10, 1938, FDR Papers, PSF, DC, France, FDRL.

7. Prentice Gilbert to Hull, January 3, 1938, 762.00/152, No. 3804, FDR Papers, PSF, Confidential File, Germany, FDRL; idem, January 19, 1938, 760C.62/350, No. 19, ibid.; and Ickes, *Secret Diary,* 2: 286. Future references to the Confidential File will be abbreviated CF.

8. Murray to FDR, January 24, 1938, FDR Papers, PSF, DC, Arthur Murray, FDRL; FDR to Murray, February 10, 1938, Roosevelt, ed., *FDR Personal Letters,* 4: 757; Gilbert to Hull, February 25, 1938, 762.00/175,

No. 79, FDR Papers, PSF, CF, Germany, FDRL; Ickes, *Secret Diary*, 2: 291; Dodd to FDR, January 22, 1938, FDR Papers, PSF, DC, Germany, FDRL; Hull to FDR, January 25, 1938, and FDR to Hugh Wilson, June 10, 1938, FDR Papers, PSF, DC, Germany, FDRL; Stephen Early, Memorandum to FDR, February 3, 1938, Box 23, Early Papers, FDRL; and Herbert Pell to FDR, February 25, 1938, Box 12, Pell Papers, FDRL. See too Ickes, *Secret Diary*, 2: 317.

9. Gilbert to Hull, February 11, 1938, 762.00/160, No. 49, FDR Papers, PSF, CF, Germany, FDRL; Wiley to Hull, February 15, 1938, 762.63/428, No. 20; idem, February 16, 1938, 762.63/440, No. 25; idem, February 19, 1938, 762.63/461, No. 31; idem, February 19, 1938; 762.63/484, No. 129; idem, February 16, 1938, 762.63/432, No. 59; idem, February 26, 1938, 762.63/473, No. 83, FDR Papers, PSF, CF, Austria, FDRL.

10. Wilson to FDR, March 12, 1938, FDR Papers, PSF, DC, Germany, FDRL; Press Conference No. 442, March 15, 1938, *Complete Press Conferences*, 11: 224-25; Hull, *Memoirs*, 1: 575; FDR's desire for a strong condemnation of Germany is in Berle and Jacobs, eds., *Navigating the Rapids*, pp. 169-69.

11. Bowers to FDR, February 20, 1938, FDR Papers, PSF, DC, Spain; Bowers to FDR, February 22, 1938, and FDR to Secretaries of War and Navy, February 28, 1938, FDR Papers, PSF, Departmental Correspondence, Navy; Bowers to FDR, May 7, 1938 and August 18, 1938, FDR Papers, PSF, DC, Spain, FDRL.

12. Fuller to FDR, March 21, 1938, FDR Papers, PPF, No. 2616, FDRL; Arthur Sweetzer, memorandum of April 4, 1938, of interview with FDR, Box 34, Sweetzer Papers, LC; Cudahy to FDR, April 10, 1938, FDR Papers, PSF, DC, Poland, FDRL; and Wilson to Hull, April 28, 1938, 760F.62/224, No. 205, FDR Papers, PSF, CF, Germany, FDRL.

13. Wilson to Hull, May 24, 1938, 760F.62/333, No. 266; idem, June 4, 1938, 760F.62/392, No. 292, FDR Papers, PSF, CF, Germany, FDRL; Wilson to FDR, July 11, 1938, FDR Papers, PSF, DC, Germany, FDRL; Wiley to Hull, July 22, 1938, 760F.62/503, No. 271; idem, 760F.62/577, No. 345, July 26, 1938; idem, August 18, 1938, 760F.62/671, No. 378; idem, August 24, 1938, 760F.62/672, No. 397, FDR Papers, PSF, CF, Austria, FDRL.

14. Wilson to Hull, June 4, 1938, 760F.62/392, No. 292; idem, June 29, 1938, 760F.62/455, No. 334; and idem, July 23, 1938, 760F.62/504, No. 357, FDR Papers, PSF, CF, Germany, FDRL. Major Truman Smith, Military Attaché, Memorandum, June1 5, 1938, 760F.62/461, No. 183, FDR Papers, PSF, CF, Germany, FDRL.

15. Wilson to FDR, August 31, 1938, FDR Papers, PSF, DC, Germany, FDRL; FDR to Hull, Memorandum, August 31, 1938, Box 42, Hull Papers, LC, and FDR Papers, PSF, DC, Italy, FDRL.

16. FDR, Memorandum to Hull, January 29, 1939, Roosevelt, ed., *FDR Personal Letters*, 4: 754; Yarnell to Leahy, December 22, 1937 and Leahy to FDR, January 6, 1938, FDR Papers, PSF, DC, China, FDRL.

17. Wilson to Hull, May 7, 1938, 762.65/429, No. 229, FDR Papers, PSF, CF, Germany, FDRL; Phillips to Hull, May 11, 1938, 762.65/439, No. 106, FDR Papers, PSF, CF, Italy, FDRL; Phillips to FDR, May 5, 1938 and May 13, 1938, FDR Papers, PSF, DC, Italy, FDRL; Reed to Hull, May 20, 1938, 762.65/457, No. 917, FDR Papers, PSF, CF, Italy,

FDRL; FDR to Phillips, September 15, 1938, FDR Papers, PSF, DC, Italy, FDRL.

18. Hull, *Memoirs,* 1: 576-77, and Box 42, Hull Papers, LC.

19. Press Conference No. 452A, April 20, 1938, *Complete Press Conferences,* 11: 330-34.

20. Rosenman, ed., *Public Papers FDR,* 7: 492-93.

21. Press Conferences Nos. 443, March 18, 1938, 452A, April 20, 1938, 452B, April 21, 1938, *Complete Press Conferences,* 11: 237, 326-28, 365-68.

22. Arthur Sweetzer, Memorandum of interview with FDR, April 4, 1938, Box 34, Sweetzer Papers, LC; and Press Conference No. 468, June 21, 1938, *Complete Press Conferences,* 11: 478-81.

23. Gilbert to Hull, January 17, 1938, 741.62/221, No. 16, FDR Papers, PSF, CF, Germany, FDRL; Pell to FDR, February 25, 1938, Box 12, Pell Papers, FDRL; Ickes, *Secret Diary,* 2: 333; Hull, *Memoirs,* 1: 581; FDR to Cudahy, March 9, 1938, Roosevelt, ed., *FDR Personal Letters,* 4: 766; and FDR to Cudahy, April 16, 1938, ibid., p. 776.

24. Kennedy to FDR, March 11, 1938, FDR Papers, PSF, DC, Great Britain, FDRL; Murray to FDR, March 26, 1938, FDR Papers, PSF, DC, Arthur Murray, FDRL; Keynes to FDR, March 25, 1938, FDR Papers, PSF, DC, Great Britain, FDRL.

25. Arthur Sweetzer, Memorandum of interview with FDR, Box 34, Sweetzer Papers, LC; FDR to Murray, May 13, 1938, FDR Papers, PSF, DC, Arthur Murray, FDRL.

26. Claude Bowers to FDR, March 7, 1938, February 20, 1938, and April 11, 1938; FDR to Bowers, August 31, 1938, FDR Papers, PSF, DC, Spain, FDRL.

27. Johnson to Hull, March 22, 1938, 741.62/258, No. 69 and March 22, 1938, 741.62/257, No. 71, FDR Papers, PSF, CF, Great Britain, FDRL; Kennedy to Hull, April 11, 1938, 741.65/530, No. 296, and May 16, 1938, 760F.62/264, No. 411, FDR Papers, PSF, CF, Great Britain, FDRL.

28. Wilson to Hull, May 6, 1938, 760F.62/238, No. 226, FDR Papers, PSF, CF, Germany, FDRL; Johnson to Hull, August 16, 1938, 760F.62/571, No. 779, and August 24, 1938, 760F.62/597, No. 815, FDR Papers, PSF, CF, Great Britain, FDRL; Kennedy to Hull, August 30, 1938, 760F.62/628, No. 838, FDR Papers, PSF, CF, Great Britain, FDRL (Kennedy's despatch emphasized by Adolph Berle, Memorandum to FDR, August 31, 1938, FDR Papers, PSF, Departmental Correspondence, State Department, FDRL); Cudahy to FDR, June 19, 1938, FDR Papers, PSF, DC, Poland, FDRL.

29. Bullitt to FDR, January 20, 1938, FDR Papers, PSF, DC, France, FDRL; and idem, May 12, 1938, May 20, 1938, and June 13, 1938, ibid.

30. Davies to McIntyre, April 4, 1938, Box 7, Davies Papers, LC; and Davies to Early April 4, 1938, ibid.

31. Davies to Hull, May 22, 1938, 760F.62/287, No. 123; Kirk to Hull, August 29, 1938, 760F.62/614, No. 271; idem, August 31, 1938, 760F.62/631, No. 273; idem, August 31 ,1938, 760F.62/632, No. 274, FDR Papers, PSF, CF, Russia, FDRL. Concerning the Japanese threat, Davies wrote that Russia was shipping enormous quantities of military supplies to China to be used against Japan, see Davies to FDR, March 3, 1938, Box 7, Davies Papers, LC. FDR praised communist forces in China, see Ickes, *Secret Diary,* 2: 327-28.

32. Leahy, Diary Entry, April 8, 1939, Diary 4, Box 2, Leahy Papers, LC; Hull, Memorandum, March 26, 1938, Box 61, Hull Papers, LC; and Charles Edison, Memorandum to the President, February 23, 1938, FDR Papers, PSF, Departmental Correspondence, Navy, FDRL.

33. Joseph Davies, Memorandum, June 7, 1938, FDR Papers, PSF, DC, Russia, FDRL. Davies wrote "Personally, I do not think that the world is in any real danger from communism, for many years to come. Communism won't work. It hasn't worked here. This government is not communism. It is a socialism.", see Davies to Steve Early, April 4, 1938, Box 7, Davies Papers, LC. FDR discussed his approach to communism at a news conference saying that he was labeled a communist back in 1911-1912 when he was trying to get passage of the 54 House Law for women and children in industry. He said, "We were that kind of communists and we bragged about it. We admitted it.", see Press Conference No. 479, August 26, 1938, *Complete Press Conferences*, 12: 54-58.

34. Berle, Memorandum to FDR, September 1, 1938, FDR Papers, PSF, Departmental Correspondence, State Dept., FDRL.

35. Wilson to Hull, September 8, 1938, 760F.62/701, No. 425, FDR Papers, PSF, CF, Germany, FDRL; for reports of expected German military action see idem, September 13, 1938, 760F.62/785, No. 436; idem, September 25, 1938, 760F.62/1090, No. 493; idem, September 26, 1938, 760F.62/1089, No. 492, and 760F.62/1106, No. 495, FDR Papers, PSF, CF, Germany, FDRL.

36. Phillips to Hull, September 13, 1938, 760F.62/786, No. 240; idem, September 13, 1938, 760F.62/789, No. 241, FDR Papers, PSF, CF, Italy, FDRL; Phillips to FDR, September 29, 1938, and FDR to Phillips, September 15, 1938, FDR Papers, PSS, DC, Italy, FDRL; Phillips to Hull, September 18, 1938, 760F.62/877, No. 252; idem, September 19, 1938, 760F.62/910, No. 254; idem, September 24, 1938, 760F.62/1070, No. 258; idem, September 26, 1938, 760F.62/1120, No. 261; idem, September 27, 1938, 760F.62/1177, No. 263, FDR Papers, PSF, CF, Italy, FDRL. Phillips reported to the Chief Executive that Mussolini's recital about going to war with Germany against France and Great Britain had "left me literally gasping for air", see Phillips to FDR, September 29, 1938, FDR Papers, PSF, DC, Italy, FDRL.

37. Pell to FDR, September 26, 1938, Box 12, Pell Papers, FDRL. Ambassador Wilson also reported that Mussolini wanted to avoid a European struggle, see Wilson to Hull, September 19, 1938, 760F.62/911, No. 462, FDR Papers, PSF, CF, Germany, FDRL.

38. Kennedy to Hull, September 10, 1938, 760F.62/723, No. 893; idem, September 11, 1938, 760F.62/732, No. 987; idem, September 11, 1938, 760F.62/733, No. 899; idem, September 13, 1938, 760F.62/767, No. 910; idem, September 14, 1938, 760F.62/797, No. 923, FDR Papers, PSF, CF, Great Britain, FDRL; and Ickes, *Secret Diary*, 2: 468.

39. Wilson to Hull, September 18, 1938, 760F.62/897, No. 456, FDR Papers, PSF, CF, Germany, FDRL; Kennedy to Hull, September 17, 1938, 760F.62/866, No. 950; idem, September 17, 1938, 760F.62/871, No. 953; idem, September 17, 1938, 760F.62/891, No. 960; idem, September 19, 1938, 760F.62/914, No. 970; idem, September 21, 1938, 760F.62/973, No. 983, FDR Papers, PSF, CF, Great Britain, FDRL; Bullitt to FDR, September 20, 1938, FDR Papers, PSF, DC, France,

FDRL; and Eleanor to FDR, September 21, 1938, cited in Lash, *Eleanor and Franklin,* p. 573.

40. Kennedy to Hull, September 24, 1938, 760F.62/1055, No. 1011, FDR Papers, PSF, CF, Great Britain, FDRL; Wilson to Hull, September 25, 1938, 760F.62/1090, No. 493, FDR Papers, PSF, CF, Germany, FDRL; Kennedy to Hull, September 26, 1938, 760F.62/1102, No. 1030; idem, September 26, 1938, 760F.62/1127, No. 1035, FDR Papers, PSF, CF, Great Britain, FDRL.

41. Bullitt to FDR, May 12, 1938, May 20, 1938, June 13, 1938, and September 28, 1938, FDR Papers, PSF, DC, France, FDRL; and Leahy, Diary Entry, September 17, 1938, September 19, 1938, September 26, 1938, September 27, 1938, Diary 4, Box 2, Leahy Papers, LC.

42. In the President's concern and anger about press criticism of his possible response to the Czech situation see Press Conference No. 484, September 9, 1938, *Complete Press Conferences,* 12: 83-84. The microfilm copy of this press conference contains these words of FDR. When asked if he was leading a Stop Hitler movement, he replied "And do not put words into people's mouths that they have not said. Make that very, very clear. The Press of this country is behaving rather badly on this whole foreign policy situation." When pressed he exclaimed, "It means no news for you, any of you today, and do not try to guess and do not try to interpret when I say there is no news. And now, that is all there is." Conversations with Bullitt and Kennedy on the proposed message of the President are on September 26-27, 1938, 760F.62/11117, 1/10-8/10, and September 27, 1938, 760F.62/11117A, FDR Papers, PSF, CF, Germany, FDRL. Message is in Rosenman, ed., *Public Papers FDR,* 7: 531-32; Hitler's reply, ibid., pp. 532-35; FDR's second message in ibid., pp. 535-37; and FDR to Phillips for Mussolini in U.S., Department of State, *Peace and War,* p. 427.

43. Daniels, Record of conversation with FDR, January 16, 1939, Box 7, Daniels Papers, LC; and Press Conference No. 487, September 30, 1938, *Complete Press Conferences,* 12: 117.

44. Hull, *Memoirs,* 1: 591-95.

45. E. Woodward and R. Butler, eds., *Documents on British Foreign Policy, 1919-1939* Third Series, 9 vols. (London: His Majesty's Stationery Office, 1946-'65), 7: 627-29. The naval blockade is discussed further in Ickes, *Secret Diary,* 2: 469.

46. Biddle to FDR, October 6, 1938, FDR Papers, PSF, DC, Germany, FDRL; MacVeagh to FDR, November 22, 1938, FDR Papers, PSF, DC, Greece, FDRL; Bowers to FDR, November 17, 1938, FDR Papers, PSF, DC, Poland, FDRL; Daniels to FDR, October 3, 1938, Box 16, Daniels Papers, LC; Davies to Early, October 7, 1938, Box 9, Davies Papers, LC; Hull to FDR, October 1, 1938, *FRUS, 1938* 1: 704-06; Long to FDR, November 18, 1938, FDR Papers, PSF, DC, South America and Central America, FDRL; and Donald Heath to Hull, November 12, 1938, 762.00/215, No. 429, PSF, CF, Germany, FDRL. FDR's fear of German penetration of South America is mentioned in Ickes, *Secret Diary,* 2: 484, and Press Conference No. 500, November 15, 1938, *Complete Press Conferences,* 12: 230.

47. Rosenman, ed., *Public Papers, FDR,* 7:564-65; and FDR to Pell, November 12, 1938, Roosevelt, ed., *FDR Personal Letters,* 4: 826.

48. Frankfurter to FDR, April 12, 1938, April 27, 1938, June 18,

1938, and July 5, 1938, Box 98, Frankfurter Papers, LC; Press Conference No. 501, November 18, 1938, *Complete Press Conferences,* 12: 239; Messersmith to Hull, November 14, 1938, *FRUS, 1938,* 2: 396-97; Hull, *Memoirs,* 1: 599.

49. Kennedy to FDR, December 19, 1938, FDR Papers, PSF, DC, Great Britain, FDRL; FDR, Memorandum to Steven Early, December 20, 1938, Box 23, Early Papers, FDRL; and Murray to FDR, December 15, 1938, FDR Papers, PSF, DC, Arthur Murray, FDRL.

50. FDR, Memorandum to Hull, January 4, 1938, Roosevelt, ed., *FDR Personal Letters,* 4: 741-42; Leahy to FDR, January 6, 1938, enclosing letter of Admiral Yarnell to Leahy, December 22, 1937, FDR Papers, PSF, DC, China, FDRL.

51. FDR to Hull, January 21, 1938, January 28, 1938, Roosevelt, ed., *FDR Personal Letters,* 4: 752-53; Ickes, *Secret Diary,* 2: 302; Leahy to FDR, February 19, 1938, enclosing Capt. Riley McConnell to Leahy, January 27, 1938 and an unsigned letter on conditions in China, FDR Papers, PSF, DC, China, FDRL; and Hull, Memoirs, 1: 569.

52. Konoye's statement is in *FRUS, Japan, 1931-1941,* 1: 480; Sato's speech of November 1, 1938 is in FDR Papers, PSF, DC, Japan, FDRL; and Leahy to FDR, December 15, 1938, enclosing Yarnell to Leahy, November 25, 1938, FDR Papers, PSF, DC, Japan, FDRL.

53. Grew to Hull, December 2, 1938, 762.94/264, No. 3502, PSF, CF, Japan, FDRL.

54. Rosenman, ed., *Public Papers FDR,* 8: 1-12, 70-71; and Press Conference No. 520, January 24, 1939, *Complete Press Conferences,* 13: 85-86.

55. Press Conferences Nos. 523 and 525, February 3, 1939 and February 17, 1939, *Complete Press Conferences,* 13: 112-18, 140-42.

56. Gilbert to Hull, January 25, 1939, 762.00/239, No. 550, idem, January 31, 1939, 762.00/231, No. 79, FDR Papers, PSF, CF, Germany, FDRL; Johnson to Hull, January 30, 1939, 760F.62/1919, No. 1967; idem, January 24, 1939, 740.00/548, No. 94, FDR Papers, PSF, CF, Great Britain, FDRL; Gilbert to Hull, February 4, 1939, 762.00/240, No. 90, FDR Papers, PSF, CF, Germany, FDRL.

57. FDR to Hugh Gaffney, January 20, 1939, FDR Papers, PPF, No. 5824, FDRL; Cudahy to FDR, March 4, 1939, and FDR to Cudahy, March 4, 1939, FDR Papers, PS, DC, Poland, FDRL. FDR's views on German expansion in Ickes, *Secret Diary,* 2: 597.

58. Bullitt to FDR, March 18, 1939, FDR Papers, PSF, DC, France, FDRL; Davies to Hull and FDR, March 22, 1939, No. 32, FDR Papers, PSF, DC, Belgium, FDRL; Berle and Jacobs, eds., *Navigating the Rapids,* pp. 199, 201; FDR to MacVeagh, March 24, 1939, FDR Papers, PSF, DC, Greece, FDRL; FDR to Benes, March 27, 1939, FDR Papers, PSF, DC, Czechoslovakia, FDRL; Hooker, ed., *Moffat Papers,* p. 232; Rosenman, ed., *Public Papers FDR,* 8: 166; and Press Conference No. 534, March 31, 1939, *Complete Press Conferences,* 13: 237-38.

59. Phillips to Hull, January 17, 1939, 741.65/697, No. 19; idem, January 24, 1939, 751.65/506, No. 21, FDR Papers, PSF, CF, Italy, FDRL; Phillips to FDR, January 20, 1939, FDR Papers, PSF, DC, Italy, FDRL; FDR, angry over criticism of him by the Italian press told Phillips, "Isn't it curious that while the veneer in Italy is so highly polished, it peels off at the first opportunity.", see FDR to Phillips, February 4, 1939,

FDR Papers, PSF, DC, Italy, FDRL. FDR was told that Germany would support Italy's Mediterranean claims, see Welles to FDR, January 3, 1939, enclosing Edwin Wilson to Welles, December 21, 1938, FDR Papers, PSF, DC, Germany, FDRL.

60. Phillips to FDR, March 17, 1939, FDR Papers, PSF, DC, Italy, FDRL; Phillips to Hull, February 21, 1939, 751.65/549, No. 59; March 6, 1939, 751.65/573, No. 74; idem, March 17, 1939, 751.65/594; No. 94; idem, March 30, 1939, 751.65/622, No. 109; idem, March 22, 1939, 765.00/125, No. 97; idem, March 26, 1939, 765.00/130, No. 102, FDR Papers, PSF, CF, Italy, FDRL.

61. Rosenman, ed., *Public Papers FDR,* 8: 203; Bullitt to FDR, April 10, 1939, No. 693, FDR Papers, PSF, DC, France, FDRL; Hull, *Memoirs,* 1: 620; Morgenthau, Diary Entry, April 14, 1939, Book 1, Presidential Diaries, FDRL; Hooker, ed., *Moffat Papers,* p. 239; Berle and Jacobs, eds., *Navigating the Rapids,* p. 213; Ickes, *Secret Diary,* 2: 619-20. FDR told Leonard Elmhirst that his message was intended to make world opinion clear to Hitler and Mussolini, June 15, 1939, FDR Papers, PPF, No. 4320, FDRL.

62. Press Conferences Nos. 539 and 540A, April 15, 1939 and April 20, 1939, *Complete Press Conferences,* 13: 273-78, 302-24.

63. Phillips to FDR, April 20, 1939, FDR Papers, PSF, DC, Italy, FDRL; and Press Conference No. 557A, June 23, 1939, *Complete Press Conferences,* 13: 461-63.

64. Geist to Hull, March 29, 1939, 741.62/343, No. 213; idem, March 29, 1939, 760C.62/476, No. 212; idem, April 6, 1939, 740.00/742, No. 237; idem, April 13, 1939, 740.00/794, No. 247; and idem, April 24, 1939, 740.00/1362, No. 724, FDR Papers, PSF, CF, Germany, FDRL.

65. Wheeler-Bennett to FDR, May 3, 1939, FDR Papers, PSF, DC, Germany, FDRL; Law to FDR, May 24, 1939, and FDR to Law, June 6, 1939, FDR Papers, PPF, No. 6032, FDRL; Geist to Hull, May 3, 1939, 760C.62/546, No. 310; Kirk to Hull, May 12, 1939, 760C.62/574, No. 350; idem, May 13, 1939, 740.00/1457, Nos. 355 and 356; idem, May 26, 1939, 760C.62/619, No. 417, FDR Papers, PSF, CF, Germany, FDRL; and Gunther to FDR, June 19, 1939, found in Box 44, Hull Papers, LC.

66. Kirk to Hull, July 21, 1939, 760C.62/724, No. 682; idem, August 12, 1939, 760C.62/806, No. 789; idem, August 16, 1939, 760C.62/834, No. 809; idem, August 19, 1939, 760C.62/875, No. 833; idem, August 21, 1939, 760C.62/896, No. 849; and idem, August 18, 1939, Memorandum — Germany Public Opinion Regarding the Current International Situation, 760C.62/1151, No. 1324, FDR Papers, PSF, CF, Germany, FDRL; and FDR, Memorandum to Hull and Welles, August 25, 1939, enclosing Laski to FDR, August 8, 1939, FDR Papers, PSF, DC, Germany, FDRL.

67. FDR, Memorandum for Colonna interview, April 3, 1939, Roosevelt, ed., *FDR Personal Letters,* 4: 875-76; Phillips to Hull, May 22, 1939, 762.65/605, No. 202; idem, June 1, 1939, 762.65/620, No. 212; idem, June 2, 1939, 740.00/1717, No. 1455, FDR Papers, PSF, CF, Italy, FDRL; Kirk to Hull, May 18, 1939, 762.65/595, No. 386; idem, May 25, 1939, 762.65/616, No. 416; idem, June 5, 1939, 762.65/634. No. 938, FDR Papers, PSF, CF, Germany, FDRL; FDR to Phillips, June 7, 1939, Roosevelt, ed., FDR Personal Letters, 4: 891. Kirk relayed informa-

tion that Italy would join Germany in a war against Britain and France, see Kirk to Hull, August 18, 1939, 760.62/862, No. 827, FDR Papers, PSF, CF, Germany, FDRL. FDR told Berle that a German and Italian victory could not be excluded from consideration, see Berle and Jacobs, eds., *Navigating the Rapids,* p. xxv.

68. Laski to FDR, January 5, 1939, Box 98, Frankfurter Papers, LC; Bullitt to FDR, January 1, 1939, Bullitt, ed., *For the President,* p. 307; Pell wrote that there seemed to be no limit to British patience, see Pell to FDR, March 14, 1939, Box 12, Pell Papers, FDRL; on Chamberlain and appeasement see Kennedy to Hull, February 17, 1939, 740.00/588, No. 246; idem, February 20, 1939, 740.00/589, No. 255; idem, February 27, 1939, 740.00/598, No. 275; Johnson to Hull, March 10, 1939, 740.00/615, No. 321, FDR Papers, PSF, CF, Great Britain, FDRL; and FDR to Merriman, February 15, 1939, FDR Papers, PSF, DC, Great Britain, FDRL.

69. Kennedy to Hull, March 18, 1939, 740.00/630, No. 360; idem, March 20, 1939, 740.00/638, No. 370; idem, March 24, 1939, 740.00/681, No. 399; idem, March 27, 1939, 740.00/690, No. 403; idem, March 30, 1939, 740.00/710, No. 420, FDR Papers, PSF, CF, Great Britain, FDRL; and Bullitt to FDR, March 23, 1939, Bullitt, ed., *For the President,* p. 332.

70. Kennedy to Hull, April 4, 1939, 740.00/736, No. 440, FDR Papers, PSF, CF, Great Britain, FDRL; Halifax to FDR, April 5, 1939, FDR Papers, PSF, DC, Great Britain, FDRL; Kennedy to Hull, April 14, 1939, 741.65/729, No. 478; idem, May 6, 1939, 760C.62/567, No. 630; idem, June 9, 1939, 740.00/1684, No. 807, June 9, 1939; idem, June 30, 1939, 740.00/1839, No. 918; Johnson to Hull, June 13, 1939, 741.62/368, No. 2487 FDR Papers, PSF, CF, Great Britain, FDRL; FDR to White, June 15, 1939, Series C, Box 32, White Papers, LC; and Murray to FDR, June 21, 1939, FDR Papers, PSF, DC, Arthur Murray, FDRL.

71. Kennedy to Hull, July 1, 1939, 760C.62/670, No. 931; idem, July 10, 1939, 760C.62/698, No. 966; Johnson to Hull, August 8, 1939, 760C.62/770, No. 1139; and idem, August 9, 1939, 740.00/2035, No. 1146, FDR Papers, PSF, CF, Great Britain, FDRL.

72. Bullitt to FDR, March 23, 1939, Bullitt, ed., *For the President,* pp. 332-34; Kennedy to FDR, March 3, 1939, FDR Papers, PSF, DC, Great Britain, FDRL; Hull, *Memoirs,* 1: 653; Rosenman, ed., *Public Papers FDR,* 8: 381-88; and FDR to Caroline O'Day, July 1, 1939, Roosevelt, ed., *FDR Personal Letters,* 4: 900-01.

73. Criticism of France and Great Britain before Munich is in Davies to Hull, May 22, 1938, 760F.62/287, No. 123; Kirk to Hull, August 31, 1938, 760F.62/632, No. 274; idem, September 14, 1938, 760F.62/796, No. 291; idem, September 16, 1938, 760F.62/853, No. 296; idem, September 17, 1938, 760F.62/872, No. 297; and idem, September 21, 1938, 760F.62/1100, No. 310, FDR Papers, PSF, CF, Soviet Union, FDRL.

74. Kirk believed that the Soviet Union would not act to help Czechoslovakia, see Kirk to Hull, August 29, 1938, 760F.62/614, No. 271; idem, September 11, 1938, 760F.62/726, No. 284; idem, September 12, 1938, 760F.62/740, No. 287; idem, September 16, 1938, 760F.62/853, No. 296; and idem, September 21, 1938, 760F.62/978, No. 301, FDR Papers, PSF, CF, Soviet Union, FDRL.

75. Kirk to Hull, September 30, 1938, 760F.62/1344, No. 327; idem,

October 4, 1938, 760F.62/1464, No, 337; idem, October 6, 1938, 760F.62/1499, No. 344; idem, October 11, 1938, 760F.62/1595, No. 352 idem, October 29, 1938, 760F.62/1778, No. 373; and idem, October 31, 1938, 760F.62/1780, No. 374, FDR Papers, PSF, CF, Soviet Union, FDRL.

76. Biddle to FDR, April 18, 1939, FDR Papers, PSF, DC, Poland, FDRL; Fegan to FDR, June 3, 1939, and FDR to Fegan, June 29, 1939, FDR Papers, PSF, Departmental Correspondence, War Department, FDRL; Eleanor to FDR, April, 1939, enclosing an article by Jerome Davis, "Why not be fair to the Soviet Union" from *Protestant Digest*, FDR Papers, PSF, DC, Russia, FDRL; on fear of leakage to the press see Robert Carney to Daniel Callaghan, July 7, 1939, FDR Papers, PSF, Departmental Correspondence, FDRL; and on battleship construction aid to Russia see *FRUS, Russia, 1933-1939*, pp. 882-85, 892.

77. Kennedy to Hull, March 24, 1939, 740.00/681, No. 399, FDR Papers, PSF, CF, Great Britain, FDRL; and Bullitt to FDR, March 18, 1939, Bullitt, ed., *For the President*, p. 365.

78. Kennedy to Hull, May 8, 1939, 740.00/1381, No. 640, FDR Papers, PSF, CF, Great Britain, FDRL; Grummon to Hull, May 17, 1939, 761.62/511, No. 251; idem, May 24, 1939, 741.61/639, No. 263; idem, June 2, 1939, 741.61/662, No. 285; idem, July 19, 1939, 741.61/779.

79. Welles to Steinhardt, August 4, 1939, 741.61/824A, Diplomatic No. 393, FDR Papers, PSF, CF, Soviet Union, FDRL.
Division, Decimal File, Record Group 59, General Records of the Department of State, National Archives, Washington, D.C.; Welles to Bullitt, August 4, 1939, 741.61/826 ibid.; Steinhardt to Welles, August 16, 1939, 741.61/828 1/2, ibid.; Welles to FDR, August 29, 1939, with the comment "I think you will find this very interesting", ibid.; Grummon to Hull, July 19, 1939, 741.61/779, No. 393, FDR Papers, PSF, CF, Soviet Union, FDRL; and FDR to Murray, August 24, 1939, FDR Papers, PSF, DC, Arthur Murray, FDRL.

80. Berle offers the date September 10, 1939 as FDR's estimation on the outbreak of war, see Berle and Jacobs, eds., *Navigating the Rapids*, p. 235; on the purpose of FDR's messages see ibid., p. 244 and Hooker, ed., *Moffat Papers*, p. 253. The messages are in Rosenman, ed., *Public Papers FDR*, 8: 444-50; and Hull, *Memoirs*, 1: 662-63.

81. Lothian to Halifax, August 31, 1939, in Woodward and Butler, eds., *Documents on British Foreign Policy*, 3rd Series, 7: 428-29. Hopkins told FDR that another Munich "would be fatal to the democracies", see Hopkins to FDR, August 31, 1939, Box 96, Harry Hopkins Papers, FDRL.

82. For FDR's perspective of events in the days before the war see Kennedy to Hull, August 27, 1939, 760C.62/1059, No. 1278; idem, August 29, 1939, 760C.62/1135, No. 1299; idem, August 29, 1939, 760C.62/1138, No. 1300; and Johnson to Hull, August 30, 1939, 760C.62/1297, No. 3285, FDR Papers, PSF, CF, Great Britain, FDRL. Only in one despatch is it strongly suggested that Chamberlain might appease Hitler, and this one day before FDR's interview with Lothian, see Kennedy to Hull, August 30, 1939, 760C.62/1208, No. 1325, FDR Papers, PSF, CF, Great Britain, FDRL. For the view from Germany see Kirk to Hull, August 31, 1939, 760C.62/1210, No. 964, FDR Papers, PSF, CF, Germany, FDRL. FDR thought the United States might be-

come seriously embroiled in the war, see Leahy, Diary Entry, August 30, 1939, Diary 5, Box 2, Leahy Papers, LC; and during a cabinet meeting FDR noted that all was ready "in the event of our going to war" see Morgenthau, Diary Entry, September 1, 1939, Book 2, Presidential Diaries, FDRL. Publicly, FDR pledged to stay out of the conflict, see Press Conference No. 575, September 1, 1939, *Complete Press Conferences,* 14: 132.

83. Rosenman, ed., *Public Papers FDR,* 8: 462-64; and see FDR's neutrality views in FDR to Robert Wood, October 12, 1939, Roosevelt, ed., *FDR Personal Letters,* 4: 938-84. Rosenman, ed., *Public Papers, FDR,* 8: 511; Daniels to FDR, September 4, 1939, FDR Papers, PSF, DC, Mexico, FDRL; and Berle to FDR, September 18, 1939, FDR Papers, PSF, Departmental Correspondence, State Department, FDRL.

84. Rosenman, ed., *Public Papers FDR,* 8: 511; Daniels to FDR, September 4, 1939, FDR Papers, PSF, DC, Mexico, FDRL; and Berle to FDR, September 18, 1939, FDR Papers, PSF, Departmental Correspondence, State Department, FDRL.

85. Bullitt to FDR, September 8, 1939, September 13, 1939, September 16, 1939, September 19, 1939, Bullitt, ed., *For the President,* pp. 320-21, 368-69, 372, 374; Kennedy to FDR, September 30, 1939, FDR Papers, PSF, DC, Great Britain, FDRL; Davies to FDR, September 23, 1939 and Davies to Early, September 25, 1939, Box 10, Davies Papers, LC; see also Davies to FDR, October 7, 1939, FDR Papers, PSF, DC, Belgium, FDRL, and idem, November 8, 1939, Box 10, Davies Papers, LC; and MacVeagh to FDR, December 3, 1939, FDR Papers, PSF, DC, Greece, FDRL.

86. Phillips to FDR, September 6, 1939, FDR Papers, PSF, DC, Italy, FDRL; Phillips to Hull, October 3, 1939, and to FDR, October 23, 1939, FDR Papers, PSF, DC, Italy, FDRL; and see Phillips to Hull, December 18, 1939, 765.00/165, No. 562, FDR Papers, PSF, CF, Italy, FDRL; Phillips to FDR, October 18, 1939, Phillips, *Ventures in Diplomacy,* pp. 243-44; and idem, December 24, 1939, FDR Papers, PSF, DC, Italy, FDRL.

87. Laski to FDR, September 5, 1939, FDR Papers, PSF, DC, Great Britain, FDRL; Hull, *Memoirs,* 1: 685; Davies to Early, September 11, 1939, Box 10, Davies Papers, LC. The threat of "the Russian steam roller . . . from the Baltic to the Rumanian border" was cited by MacVeagh in a letter to FDR, October 13, 1939, FDR Papers, PSF, DC, Greece, FDRL. FDR made no reference to this comment in his reply, see FDR to MacVeagh, December 1, 1939, ibid.

88. City of Flint issue is in *FRUS, The Soviet Union, 1933-1939,* pp. 988, 990, 1007; Messersmith to Hull, December 16, 1939, ibid., p. 865; see also Steinhardt's complaints, ibid., pp. 864-65, 916; Hull, *Memoirs,* 1: 708-09; FDR, Memorandum to Hull and Welles, December 22, 1939, Roosevelt, ed., *FDR Personal Letters,* 4: 974-75; and Ickes, *Secret Diary,* 3: 50.

89. Hooker, ed., *Moffat Papers,* pp. 270-71; Rosenman, ed., *Public Papers FDR,* 8: 538-39. The original draft of this message by FDR is harsher, warning against violations of the independence, integrity, and vital interests of Finland; see draft copy, October 11, 1939, Box 17, R. W. Moore Papers, FDRL; Hull, *Memoirs,* 1: 702-03, 709; Rosenman, ed., *Public Papers FDR,* 8: 587-89; Morgenthau, Diary Entry, December 4, 1939, Book 226, Morgenthau Diaries, p. 264, FDRL; see also Hjalmar

Procope, Finnish Ambassador in Washington, to FDR, December 1, 1939, describing the Finnish alternative "voluntarily to submit to all the horrors of communist terror or to risk to be attacked," FDR Papers, PSF, DC, Finland, FDRL. FDR wrote to Francis Sayre, December 13, 1939, saying "No human being can tell what the Russians are going to do next", Box 7, Sayre Papers, LC.

90. Hull, *Memoirs*, 1: 628-29; Johnson to FDR, February 27, 1939, FDR Papers, PSF, DC, China, FDRL.

91. Grew to Hull, February 27, 1939, 762.94/301, No. 3709; idem, March 31, 1939, 762.94/310, No. 161; idem, April 20, 1939, 762.94/321, No. 188; idem, May 5, 1939, 762.94/340, No. 215; idem, May 8, 1939, 762.94/373, No. 3879; and idem, August 8, 1939, 762.94/402, No. 394, FDR Papers, PSF, CF, Japan, FDRL.

92. Ickes, *Secret Diary*, 2: 653; Joseph Grew, *Turbulent Era: A Diplomatic Record of Forty Years, 1904-1945*, 2 vols. (Cambridge: Riverside Press, 1952), 2: 1212; Grew to Hull, November 27, 1939, 761.94/1162, No. 626; idem, November 27, 1939, 761.94/1163, No. 631; idem, December 1, 1939, 711.94/1396, No. 4359; Dooman to Hull, September 19, 1939, 711.94/1296, No. 484; idem, September 22, 1939, 711.94/1299, No. 489, FDR Papers, PSF, CF, Japan, FDRL; W. S. Anderson, Memorandum for the Chief of Naval Operations, November 17, 1939, FDR Papers, PSF, Departmental Correspondence, Navy, FDRL; McAdoo to FDR, September 19, 1939, FDR Papers, PPF, No. 308, FDRL; and Bullitt to FDR, August 28, 1939, FDR Papers, PSF, DC, China, FDRL.

93. FDR to Hull, July 7, 1939, Box 44, Hull Papers, LC; Hull, *Memoirs*, 1: 636-37; Ickes, *Secret Diary*, 2: 692; FDR said that the abrogation of the 1911 treaty was "the constructive thing to do at this time" see FDR to Admiral Richard Byrd, August 2, 1939, FDR Papers, PPF, No. 201, FDRL; and FDR to Grew, October 23, 1939, Roosevelt, ed., *FDR Personal Letters*, 4:945 (Grew's speech is in FDR Papers, PSF, DC, Japan, FDRL).

94. Ickes, *Secret Diary*, 2: 720, 3: 9, 37, 85; FDR to Edison, October 9, 1939, FDR Papers, PSF, Departmental Correspondence, Navy, FDRL; FDR to Welles, November 9, 1939, FDR Papers, PSF, Departmental Correspondence, State Department, FDRL; FDR to White, December 14, 1939, Series C, Box 320, White Papers, LC; and see Berle and Jacobs, eds., *Navigating the Rapids*, p. 258.

95. Morgenthau, Diary Entry, October 3, 1939, Book 2, Presidential Diaries, FDRL; Kennedy to Hull, September 11, 1939, and FDR to Kennedy, September 11, 1939, FDR Papers, PSF, Safe File, Joseph Kennedy, FDRL. Ickes recounts FDR's sarcastic humor when told that Kennedy might receive an invitation to join the Chamberlain Cabinet, see Ickes, *Secret Diary*, 2: 712. FDR rejected William Rhodes Davis' attempts to arrange a German-American peace, see Hooker, ed., *Moffat Papers*, pp. 272-75, and Berle and Jacobs, eds., *Navigating the Rapids*, pp. 265-66. FDR rejected similar efforts by Adam von Trott to secure peace. He ordered J. Edgar Hoover and the FBI to investigate von Trott and have his room gone through, see Morgenthau, Diary Entry, October 9, 1939, Book 2, Presidential Diaries, FDRL; Rosenman, ed., *Public Papers, FDR*, 8: 606-09; Hull, *Memoirs*, 1: 715, and Press Conference No. 614, January 12, 1940, *Complete Press Conferences*, 15: 68-69.

96. Rosenman, ed., *Public Papers FDR*, 8: 464-78, 512-25. 559-61;

Neutrality Law of November 4, 1939, is in *Peace and War*, pp. 494-506; Hopkins to FDR, December 16, 1939, Box 96, Hopkins Papers, FDRL; FDR to Hopkins, December 18, 1939, Roosevelt, ed. *FDR Personal Letters*, 4: 969-70; and Morgenthau, Diary Entry, December 9, 1939, Book 2, Presidential Diaries, FDRL.

CHAPTER FIVE

1. Rosenman, ed., *Public Papers FDR*, 9: 2-4; Press Conference No. 620, February 2, 1940, *Complete Press Conferences*, 15: 115.
2. Hull, *Memoirs*, 1: 737-38; Ickes, *Secret Diary*, 3: 138; Press Conference No. 622, Feb. 9, 1940, *Complete Press Conferences*, 15: 140-43.
3. *FRUS, 1940*, 1: 39, 41, 49, 51, 63, 73, 77, 88, 113-14, 116-17; see also FDR to Marriner Eccles, March 4, 1940, Roosevelt, ed., *FDR Personal Letters*, 4: 1004; and Roseman, ed., *Public Papers, FDR*, 9: 103. Robert Murphy described Welles' trip as solely for domestic politics, see Murphy, *Diplomat Among Warriors* (New York: Doubleday and Co., 1964), p. 38.
4. Cudahy to FDR, January 19, 1940, February 2, 1940, FDR Papers, PSF, DC, Belgium, FDRL; Hull to FDR, January 14, 1940, FDR Papers, PSF, DC, Belgium, FDRL; FDR expected a German invasion of Belgium, see Berle and Jacobs, eds., *Navigating the Rapids*, p. 284; Ickes, *Secret Diary*, 3: 115; and Murray to FDR, February 8, 1940 and April 5, 1940, FDR Papers, PSF, DC, Arthur Murray, FDRL.
5. Rosenman, ed., Public Papers FDR, 9: 157, 161; Murray to FDR, April 25, 1940 and FDR to Murray, April 30, 1940, FDR Papers, PSF, DC, Arthur Murray, FDRL.
6. Cudahy to FDR, April 15, 1940 and FDR to Cudahy, April 17, 1940, FDR Papers, PSF, DC, Belgium, FDRL; D. J. Callaghan to FDR, April 17, 1940, FDR Papers, PSF, Departmental Correspondence, Navy Department, FDRL; and Bullitt to FDR, April 18, 1940, April 28, 1940, Bullitt, ed., *For the President*, p. 409.
7. FDR to Cudahy, May 8, 1940, FDR Papers, PSF, DC, Belgium, FDRL; FDR to Queen Wilhelmina, May 18, 1940, Roosevelt, ed., *FDR Personal Letters*, 4: 1027; FDR to Leopold III, May 11, 1940, Rosenman, ed., *Public Papers, FDR*, 9: 189; Prince Olav to FDR, May 10, 1940 and Florence Harriman to FDR, April 30, 1940, FDR Papers, PSF, DC, Norway, FDRL; and Murray to FDR, May 12, 1940, FDR Papers, PSF, DC, Arthur Murray, FDRL.
8. Bullitt to FDR, May 14, 15, 16, 26, 30, 1940 and June 4, 1940, Bullitt, ed., *For the President*, pp. 415, 419, 425, 427, 430, 440, 449.
9. Kirk to Hull, March 9, 1940, 762.65/809, No. 603; idem, March 18, 1940, 762.65/820, No. 685, FDR Papers, PSF, CF, Italy, FDRL; Phillips to FDR, February 9, 1940, Phillips, *Ventures in Diplomacy*, p. 261; idem, April 1, 1940, FDR Papers, PSF, DC, Italy, FDRL, and see Phillips to Hull, 740.0011EW1939/2433, No. 285, April 23, 1940 and idem, 740.0011EW1939/2920, No. 341, May 14, 1940, FDR Papers, PSF, CF, Italy, FDRL; Taylor to FDR, April 19, 20, 1940 and May 11, 1940, *FRUS, 1940*, 2: 686-88, 702; FDR's messages to Mussolini, ibid., pp. 691-92, 704-05, 710-11, 713-14; Mussolini's responses, ibid., pp. 698, 706; Colonna-FDR interview, ibid., pp. 695-98.

10. Phillips to Hull, May 21, 23, 29, 1940, June 7, 1940, 740.0011EW-1939/2855, Nos. 392, 402, 429, 480, FDR Papers, PSF, CF, Italy, FDRL; Phillips to Welles, May 31, 1940, FDR Papers, PSF, DC, Italy, FDRL; Phillips to FDR, May 31, 1940, Phillips, *Ventures in Diplomacy*, p. 276; Bullitt to FDR, May 29, 1940, and May 31, 1940, FDR Papers, PSF, Safe File, FDRL; and Ickes, *Secret Diary*, 3: 203.

11. Bullitt to FDR, June 10, 1940, FDR Papers, PSF, Safe File, FDRL; Rosenman, ed., *Public Papers, FDR*, 9: 260-63, 265-67; Hull, *Memoirs*, 1: 787; Ickes, *Secret Diary*, 3: 210.

12. Reynaud to FDR, June 10, 1940 and FDR to Reynaud, June 15, 1940, Rosenman, ed., *Public Papers FDR*, 9: 265-66.

13. Bullitt to FDR, July 1, 1940, Bullitt, ed., *For the President*, p. 481; French-German Armistice in *Documents on German Foreign Policy*, Series D, 9: 671; FDR's concern for French fleet in Hull to Bullitt, May 26, 1940, Bullitt, ed., *For the President*, p. 431 and FDR to Leahy, November 16, 1940, Roosevelt, ed., *FDR Personal Letters*, 4: 1080-81; see also Churchill's fears on the surrender of the French fleet, Churchill to FDR, June 14, 1940, September 23, 1940, Winston Churchill, *Their Finest Hour* (Boston: Houghton Mifflin, 1949), pp. 188, 487-88; and see FDR to Churchill, June 14, 1940, Francis Loewenheim, Harold Langley, Manfred Jonas, eds., *Roosevelt and Churchill, Their Secret Wartime Correspondence*, (New York: Saturday Review Press, E. P. Dutton, 1975), p. 103.

14. FDR to Churchill, February 1, 1940, Roosevelt, ed., *FDR Personal Letters*, 4: 995; Kennedy to FDR, May 15, 1940, FDR Papers, PSF, Safe File, FDRL; Kennedy earlier wrote that the US would have nothing to work with given the condition of Britain and France, see idem, June 12, 1940, FDR Papers, PSF, Safe File, FDRL, Claude Bowers wrote "The cause of liberty and democracy won a major victory when the insufferable ass, pro-fascist at heart, Chamberlain, was pried loose from appeasement and Churchill was put in", see Bowers to FDR, May 14, 1940, FDR Papers, PSF, DC, Chile, FDRL.

15. Churchill to FDR, May 15, 1940, June 20, 1940, and Churchill to King, June 5, 1940, June 24, 1940, Churchill, *Their Finest Hour*, pp. 24-25, 56-57, 145-46, 227; Hooker, ed., *Moffat Papers*, pp. 310-11, 319-20; and Churchill to FDR, July 31, 1940, August 15, 1940, August 22, 1940, Churchill, *Their Finest Hour*, pp. 406, 410-12.

16. Morgenthau, Diary Entry, April 29, 1940, Book 2, Morgenthau Presidential Diaries, FDRL; Ickes, Secret Diary, 3: 187-88. Bullitt predicted the establishment of a fascist government in England under Oswald Mosely, see Bullitt to FDR, May 16, 1940, Bullitt, ed., *For the President*, p. 427. FDR didn't fear German retaliation while considering aid to England. He thought if they wanted war then a cause would be found, see FDR to Senator David Walsh, August 22, 1940, Roosevelt, ed., *FDR Personal Letters*, 4: 1056-57.

17. White to FDR, June 10, 1940, Series C, Box 347, White Papers, LC; Knox to FDR, June 7, 1940, FDR Papers, PPF No. 4083, FDRL; Early to FDR, August 16, 1940, Box 24, Early Papers, FDRL; see FDR memorandum on the cabinet meeting of August 2, 1940 in Roosevelt, ed., *FDR Personal Letters*, 4: 1050-51; Morgenthau to Grace Tully June 18, 1940, August 14, 1940, Book 3, Morgenthau Presidential Diaries, FDRL; Rosenman, ed., *Public Papers FDR*, 9: 392-407; and Churchill, *Their Finest Hour*, p. 404.

18. Ickes, *Secret Diary*, 3: 314, 394; Churchill to FDR, October 4, 1940, *Their Finest Hour*, pp. 497-98; see also Kennedy's description of difficult plight of the English, Kennedy to FDR and Hull, September 27, 1940, *FRUS, 1940*, 3: 48-49; Morgenthau, Diary Entry, September 19, 1940, December 17, 1940, Morgenthau Presidential Diaries, FDRL; Press Conference No. 702, December 17, 1940, *Complete Press Conferences*, 16: 354-55. On aiding England William A. White wrote "And don't pull your punches on appeasers. Shoot the works." See White to FDR, December 28, 1940, Series C. Box 347, White Papers, LC.

19. Hull, *Memoirs*, 1: 729; *FRUS Japan 1931-1941*, 2: 189, 203-04, 211-18; Sayre to FDR, May 16, 1940, Box 7, Sayre Papers, LC; and FDR to Sayre, June 4, 1940, ibid. See also FDR's anger over Japanese bombing in China, FDR to Hull, June 13, 1940, Roosevelt, ed., *FDR Personal Letters*, 4: 1040.

20. D. J. Callaghan to FDR, April 17, 1940, FDR Papers, PSF, Departmental Correspondence, Navy, FDRL; idem, July 16, 1940, enclosing report by W. S. Anderson of the Office of Naval Intelligence, "Japanese Policy of Empire Expansion," FDR Papers, PSF, Departmental Correspondence, Navy, FDRL. Japanese penetration of Panama is discussed in W. S. Anderson to Admiral Harold Stark, Chief of Naval Operations, December 11, 1940, FDR Papers, PSF, Departmental Correspondence, Navy, FDRL; and on press contacts see idem, October 11, 1940, FDR Papers, PSF, Departmental Correspondence, Navy, FDRL.

21. Sayre to FDR, July 2, 1940, Box 7, Sayre Papers, LC; Grew to Hull, June 10, 1940, 711.94/1525, No. 431, FDR Papers, PSF, CF, Japan; and see *Pearl Harbor Hearings*, 1: 265-66.

22. The Pact is in *FRUS Japan 1931-1941*, 2: 165-66; Grew to Hull, October 6, 1940, 711.94/1740, No. 950; idem, November 26, 1940, 711.94/1842, No. 1204; idem, December 10, 1940, 741.94/460, No. 1314, FDR Papers, PSF, CF, Japan, FDRL. Grew had earlier reported that the Germans had overplayed their hand with the Japanese and had caused some resentment because of this, see Grew to Hull, August 21, 1940, 762.94/469, No. 725, FDR Papers, PSF, CF, Japan, FDRL. See also Anderson to Stark, November 6, 1940 and Stark to Knox, November 12, 1940, FDR Papers, PSF, Departmental Correspondence, Navy, FDRL.

23. Morgenthau, Diary Entry, August 17, 1940, Book 3, Morgenthau Presidential Diaries, FDRL; Ickes, *Secret Diary*, 3: 314; FDR to Sayre, December 31, 1940, Box 7, Sayre Papers, LC; Grew to FDR, December 14, 1940, FDR Papers, PSF, CF, State Department, FDRL; and Roosevelt to Grew, January 21, 1941, *Pearl Harbor Hearings*, 2: 623-33.

24. Grew to FDR, December 14, 1940, FDR Papers, PSF, CF, State Department, FDRL; FDR to Grew, January 21, 1941, *Pearl Harbor Hearings*, 2: 632-33. FDR's position seems to have changed considerably from that which he held in the spring months. He told Morgenthau in June, 1940 that he would like to join with Japan in a treaty to keep peace in the Pacific. See Morgenthau, Diary Entry, June 3, 1940, Book 3, Morgenthau Presidential Diaries, FDRL.

25. Berle and Jacobs, eds., *Navigating the Rapids*, pp. 284, 293, 299-301; FDR to Stark, April 30, 1940, FDR Papers, PSF, Departmental Correspondence, Navy, FDRL; and FDR to Woodring, March 11, 1940, Roosevelt, ed., *FDR Personal Letters*, 4: 1007.

26. Bowers to FDR, May 14, 1940 enclosing Bowers to Hull, May 14, 1940; idem, May 25, 1940 and Bowers to Welles, May 25, 1940, and FDR to Bowers, May 24, 1940, FDR Papers, PSF, DC, Chile, FDRL; Wilson to Hull, May 15, 1940, and FDR to Welles, May 20, 1940, *FRUS 1940*, 5: 1147; and Bullitt to FDR, May 30, 1940, Bullitt, ed., *For the President*, p. 441.

27. FDR to Welles, May 20, 1940; Berle, Memorandum to FDR, May 31, 1940; FDR to Berle, May 28, 1940 and Welles to FDR, June 8, 1940, FDR Papers, PSF, CF, State Department, FDRL; Morgenthau, Diary Entry, May 20, 1940, Book 3, Morgenthau Presidential Diaries, FDRL; and see Hooker, ed., *Moffat Papers,* p. 325.

28. Bowers to FDR, June 1, 7, 1940 and FDR to Bowers, undated, FDR Papers, PSF, DC, Chile, FDRL; see also Bowers to FDR, June 12, 1940 warning of submarines in Brazilian and Argentine waters, and idem, June 19, 1940, ibid.; Armour to Hull, June 6, 1940 and Welles to FDR, June 14, 1940, FDR Papers, PSF, DC, Argentina, FDRL; and Daniels to FDR, June 28, 1940, FDR Papers, PSF, DC, Mexico, FDRL.

29. Kirk to Miss Le Hand, June 19, 1940, FDR Papers, PSF, DC, Germany, FDRL. See Berle's comments with Kirk, June 11, 1940 in Berle and Jacobs, eds., *Navigating the Rapids,* p .322; and Kirk to FDR, September 1, 1940, FDR Papers, PSF, DC, Germany, FDRL.

30. Callaghan, Memorandum to the Chief of Naval Operations, July 10, 1940, FDR Papers, PSF, Departmental Correspondence, Navy, FDRL; Bickel to Corcoran enclosing Jim Miller to Bickel, undated, and FDR to Welles, July 16, 1940, FDR Papers, PSF, Departmental Correspondence, State Department, FDRL; Vanderbilt to Miss Le Hand, August 27, 1940, FDR Papers, PPF, No. 104, FDRL; FDR to Welles, September 28, 1940, FDR Papers, PSF, Departmental Correspondence, Navy, FDRL; Fuller to FDR, November 11, 1940 and FDR to Fuller, November 15, 1940, FDR Papers, PPF No. 2616, FDRL. See also Bowers to FDR, October 26, 1940 enclosing Bowers to Frank Oliver, undated. Bowers writes that fascist propaganda "fairly reeks with the most fantastic fabrications aimed at us, and with the most indecent denunciations of Roosevelt", FDR Papers, PSF, DC, Chile, FDRL.

31. Rosenman, ed., *Public Papers FDR,* 9: 94-95, 198-205 ,250-53, 313-14, 357-59, 428-31; and *FRUS 1940,* 3: 146.

32. Press Conferences Nos. 636A, 647A, 649A, April 18, 1940, May 30, 1940, June 5, 1940, *Complete Press Conferences,* 15: 281-82, 414-15, 501-02.

33. Press Conferences Nos. 635, 636A, 645A, 652A, April 12, 18, 1940, May 23, 1940, June 14, 1940, *Complete Press Conferences,* 15: 251, 272,-78, 361, 570; and Rosenman, ed., *Public Papers FDR,* 9: 199-200, 466. He hoped that the extension of the combat area in April, 1940 would persuade people to think about the proximity of war. He stated, "it is a damn good thing for Americans to think about the subject and not take everything for granted", see Press Conference No. 643, April 9, 1940, *Complete Press Conferences,* 15: 241-42; and Rosenman, ed., *Public Papers, FDR,* 9: 127.

34. Press Conference No. 636A, April 18, 1940, *Complete Press Conferences,* 15: 282; and Rosenman, ed., *Public Papers FDR,* 9: 261-62.

35. Press Conferences Nos. 647, 658, May 30, 1940, July 5, 1940,

Complete Press Conferences, 15: 413, 16: 18-19; and Rosenman, ed., *Public Papers FDR*, 9: 288-89, 439.

36. Rosenman, ed., *Public Papers FDR*, 9: 302; Morgenthau, Diary Entry, January 24, 1940, "The inference I got from this was that Roosevelt is anxious to keep on and keep his mouth shut", Book 2, Morgenthau Presidential Diaries, FDRL and see Diary Entry, June 28, 1940, Book 3, ibid.; Pell to FDR, June 11, 1940, Box 12, Pell Papers, FDRL; Sayre to FDR, March 4, 1940, Box 7, Sayre Papers, LC; Wehle to FDR, June 15, 1940, Box 39, Wehle Papers, FDRL; and see Samuel Rosenman, *Working with Roosevelt* (New York: Harper and Bros., 1952), p. 193.

37. Rosenman, ed., *Public Papers FDR*, 9: 488, 495, 517-20, 543, 546; Rosenman, *Working with Roosevelt*, p. 242; and Robert Sherwood, *Roosevelt and Hopkins, An Intimate History* (New York: Harper and Bros., 1948), p. 191.

38. Rosenman, ed., *Public Papers FDR*, 9: 633-44.

39. FDR to Hull, January 30, 1941, Roosevelt, ed., *FDR Personal Letters*, 4: 1115; Ickes, *Secret Diary*, 3: 422-23. Grew wrote that a member of the German Embassy in Tokyo had predicted a German victory this year, Grew to Hull, March 27, 1941, 762.94/490, No. 474, FDR Papers, PSF, CF, Japan, FDRL.

40. John Carter to FDR, March 6, 1941, March 31, 1941, FDR Papers, PSF, Subject File, John Franklin Carter, FDRL.

41. Press Conference No. 669, August 10, 1940, *Complete Press Conferences*, 16: 111-12; Donovan to Hull and FDR, February 26, 1941, and Hull to FDR, March 3, 1941, Box 48, Hull Papers, LC.

42. Pell to FDR, May 16, 1940, Box 12, Pell Papers, FDRL; Gunther to FDR, June 18, 1941, June 19, 1941, FDR Papers, PSF, DC, Rumania, FDRL. See also Gunther to Hull for FDR, January 30, 1941, FRUS 1941, 2: 860; and Ickes, *Secret Diary*, 3: 480-81.

43. Lowell Mellett to FDR, January 8, 1941, Box 5, Group 60, Lowell Mellett Papers, FDRL, Hyde Park, New York; FDR to Hull, January 9, 1941, FDR Papers, PSF, DC, South America/Central America, FDRL; "Confidential Memorandum on Internal Conditions and International Relations of Various Latin American Republics," no source given, January 7, 1941, FDR Papers, PSF, DC, South America/Central America, FDRL; Bowers to FDR, March 7, 14, 1941, April 10, 1941, May 14, 1941, FDR Papers, PSF, DC, Chile, FDRL; Daniels to FDR, March 18, 1941, June 3, 1941, FDR Papers, PSF, DC, Mexico, FDRL. FDR complimented Daniels for following subversive activities, see FDR to Daniels, June 17, 1941, Box 17, Daniels Papers, LC; and John Carter to FDR, April 15, 1941, Memorandum on Nazi Newspapers in Buenos Aires, FDR Papers PSF, Subject File, John F. Carter, FDRL.

44. FDR to Welles, January 21, 1941, FDR Papers, PSF, Departmental Correspondence, State Department, FDRL; FDR to Stimson, April 26, 1941, FDR Papers, PSF, Departmental Correspondence, War, FDRL; FDR to Sitmson and Knox, April 30, 1941, FDR Papers, PSF, DC, Greenland, FDRL; Morgenthau, Diary Entry, May 22, 1941, Book 4, Morgenthau Presidential Diaries, FDRL; White House Memorandum to Colonel Starling, June 25, 1941, FDR Papers, PPF, No. 85, FDRL. FDR also worried about the concentration of plants along the Atlantic seaboard, Cleveland, and Detroit, see Ickes, *Secret Diary*, 3: 521-22.

45. Phillips to FDR, January 21, 1941, February 17, 24, 1941, March

4, 1941, May 17, 1941, and FDR to Phillips, May 24, 1941, June 11, 1941, FDR Papers, PSF, DC, Italy, FDRL; see also Phillips, *Ventures in Diplomacy*, pp. 295-97, 308, 310, 313. Italy's willingness to engage in war with the United States is in Phillips to Hull, April 28, 1941, 711.65/148, FDR Papers, PSF, CF, Italy, FDRL; and Morris to Hull, March 27, 1941, 762.94/488, No. 1144, FDR Papers, PSF, CF, Germany, FDRL.

46. Hull, *Memoirs*, 2: 984; Hull, Memorandum to FDR, February 5, 1941, *Pearl Harbor Hearings*, 20: 4289-91; Memoranda of conversations, Hull and Nomura, March-April, 1941, FDR Papers, PSF, DC, Japan, FDRL and *FRUS Japan 1931-1941*, 2: 387, 389, 396, 402, 406; see Berle's account of FDR's "sobbing routine" with Nomura, another indication that the President did not accept the alleged Japanese sincerity in the negotiations, Berle and Jacobs, eds., *Navigating the Rapids*, p. 359; D. J. Callaghan, Memorandum for the President, enclosing W. V. Pratt, Interview with Nomura, March 11, 1941, *Pearl Harbor Hearings*, 20: 4296-98; Davies to Early, March 13, 1941, ibid., pp. 4301-03; American and Japanese proposals for peace are in *FRUS Japan 1931-1941*, 2: 420, 432, 439, 446, 486. Grew was initially optimistic, Grew to Hull, January 22, 1941, 711.94/1925, No. 102, FDR Papers, PSF, CF, Japan, FDRL.

47. Grew to Hull, January 22, 1941, 711.94/1935, No. 125; idem, January 28, 1941, 711.94/1937, No. 131, FDR Papers, PSF, CF, Japan, FDRL; Stark, Memorandum for the President, "Analysis of the Situation in Indo-China", February 5, 1941, *Pearl Harbor Hearings*, 16: 2152; FDR to Welles, February 19, 20, 1941, FDR Papers, PSF, Departmental Correspondence, State Department, FDRL.

48. FDR was kept informed of the changing status of the peace negotiations by Joseph Grew. The Ambassador's appraisals of the Japanese peace proposals are in March-April despatches, FDR Papers, PSF, CF, Japan, FDRL; Sayre to FDR, April 23, 1941, Box 7, Sayre Papers, LC; Carter to FDR, May 14, 1941, Memorandum on Japanese Fifth Columns in the Philippines, FDR Papers, PSF, Subject File, John F. Carter, FDRL; Hull on Japanese-Russian neutrality pact, *FRUS Japan 1931-1941*, 2: 186; Grew to Hull, February 27, 1941, 761.94/1283, No. 321, FDR Papers, PSF, CF, Japan, FDRL; Berle and Jacobs, eds., *Navigating the Rapids*, p. 368; Matsuoka's comment is in Grew to Hull, May 19, 1941, 711.94/2099, No. 707, FDR Papers, PSF, CF, Japan, FDRL.

49. Leahy to FDR, January 25, 1941, February 24, 1941, March 19, 1941, April 18, 1941, April 21, 1941, FDR to Leahy, undated, arrived May 23, 1941, Diary, 6 Box 3, Leahy Papers, LC; Hull, *Memoirs*, 2: 962-63, 958; and *FRUS 1941*, 2: 171.

50. FDR to Churchill, January 19, 1941, Roosevelt, ed., *FDR Personal Letters*, 4: 1109; Stark to FDR, January 22, 1941, *Pearl Harbor Hearings*, 20: 4275-80; Herschel Johnson to Hull, enclosing James Wilkinson, "Bomb Damage in English Cities," January 8, 1941, FDR Papers, PSF, DC, Great Britain, FDRL; FDR to Winant, February 8, 1941, enclosing Johnson, February 7, 1941, No. 470, FDR Papers, PSF, DC, Great Britain, FDRL; and Winant to FDR and Hull, April 3, 1941, No. 1309, FDR Papers, PSF, Subject File, John Winant, FDRL.

51. Press Conference No. 706, January 3, 1941, *Complete Press Conferences*, 17: 2-6; Sherwood, *Roosevelt and Hopkins*, pp. 239, 243, 257-58, 259-60; and Averell Harriman to FDR, May 7, 1941, FDR Papers, DC, Harriman File, FDRL.

52. Churchill to FDR, January 28, 1941, February 15, 1941, May 4,

1941, Winston Churchill, *The Grand Alliance* (Boston: Houghton Mifflin, 1951), pp. 25-26, 178-79, 235-36.

53. Hull, *Memoirs,* 1: 709; FDR, Memorandum to Hull, January 10, 1940, Roosevelt, ed., *FDR Personal Letters,* 4: 987; FRUS, 1940, 3: 244-45; Rosenman, *Public Papers FDR,* 9: 93, 100-01. The President urged curtailment of gas line shipments and scrap iron deliveries to Russia, see FDR to Hull, January 27, 1940, FDR Papers, PSF, Departmental Correspondence, State Department, FDRL.

54. Berle to FDR, April 19, 1940, FDR Papers, PPF No. 8, Sara Roosevelt, FDRL; Welles to FDR, November 22, 1940, FRUS 1940, 3: 236; Hull, *Memoirs,* 1: 701, 743, 810, 2: 993 for a discussion of America's Russia policy; and on the Tyler Kent affair see Breckinridge Long diary in Fred Israel, ed., *The War Diary of Breckinridge Long* (Lincoln: University of Nebraska Press, 1966), pp. 97-101, 111-13.

55. Thurston to Hull, August 27, 1940, 741.61/898, No. 1078; Steinhardt to Hull, September 22, 1940, 741.61/899, No. 1202, FDR Papers, PSF, CF, Russia, FDRL; and Henry Morgenthau, Diary Entry, October 3, 1940, Morgenthau Presidential Diaries, FDRL.

56. Steinhardt to Hull, October 2, 1940, 740.0011EW1939/5837, No. 1267, FDR Papers, PSF, CF, Russia, FDRL; Morris to Hull, November 12, 1940, 761.62/789, No. 4671, FDR Papers, PSF, CF, Germany, FDRL; Hull, *Memoirs,* 2: 967-69; and Hull to Steinhardt, February 28, 1941, 740.0011EW1939/8656, Diplomatic Division, Record Group 59, National Archives, Washington, D.C.

57. FDR was kept informed of the Russian-German antagonism throughout the months of April-May, 1941, see FDR Papers, PSF, CF, Russia, FDRL and FDR Papers, PSF, CF, Germany, FDRL. On the guidelines for the approach to be taken by the United States toward the Soviet Union see Hull to Steinhardt, June 13, 1941, 740.0011EW1939/11970, Diplomatic Division, Record Group 59, National Archives, Washington, D.C.; William Bullitt, *The Great Globe Itself* (New York: Charles Scribners Sons, 1946), p. 21; and see FDR to Fulton Oursler, June 25, 1941, FDR Papers, PPF No. 2993, where Roosevelt states that the primary aim of aiding the Soviet Union is to prevent world domination by Hitler.

58. Bullitt to FDR, May 21, 1941, Bullitt, ed., *For the President,* p. 520; Henry Morgenthau, Diary Entry, May 17, 1941, Book 4, Morgenthau Presidential Diaries, FDRL; and Frankfurter to FDR, May 24, 1941, Box 98, Frankfurter Papers, LC.

59. Jan Ciechanowski, *Defeat in Victory* (Garden City, New York: Doubleday, 1947), pp. 5-6. He met with FDR on March 6, 1941.

60. Rosenman, ed., *Public Papers FDR,* 10: 189; on FDR's Bunker Hill comment see Rosenman, *Working with Roosevelt,* p. 286.

61. Press Conferences Nos. 733, 762, May 23, 1941, August 19, 1941, *Complete Press Conferences,* 17: 350-52, 18: 92; and Rosenman, ed., *Public Papers FDR,* 10: 335.

62. See FDR's introductory comments, dated July 17, 1941, to the 1940 collection of his addresses in Rosenman, ed., *Public Papers FDR,* 9: xxix, xxx; and see ibid., 10: 62, 181-83, 440, 443.

63. Press Conferences Nos. 721, 738, 739, 753, February 25, 1941, April 25, 29, 1941, July 8, 1941, *Complete Press Conferences,* 17: 152-53, 288-89, 302, and 18: 17-18.

64. Rosenman, ed., *Public Papers FDR*, 10: 227-30, 385-90, 438-40; Press Conference No. 767, September 5, 1941, *Complete Press Conferences*, 18: 140-54.

65. Phillips to FDR, August 30, 1941, FDR Papers, PSF, DC, Italy, FDRL; FDR to the Secretaries of War and Navy, August 28, 1941, FDR Papers, PSF, DC, Iceland, FDRL. See also Bullitt's memorandum of a conversation with FDR on April 23, 1941 wherein the President mentioned his expectation of an incident as opposed to Stimson's eagerness to go to war now, Bullitt, ed., *For the President*, p. 512. The repeal of Sections 2, 3, and 6 of the 1939 Neutrality Act on November 17, 1941 also increased the possibility of an incident, see *Peace and War*, pp. 787-88 and FDR's comments on repeal, Rosenman, ed., *Public Papers FDR*, 10: 406-11.

66. Mark Watson, *Chief of Staff: Prewar Plans and Preparations* (Washington, D.C.: Historical Division, Department of the Army, 1950), pp. 372-82. Admiral Robert Ghormley headed a naval and military mission to England in July, 1940 which engaged in exploratory conversations concerning aid to Great Britain and coordination of the two nations' military forces if the United States became involved in the war, see ibid., p. 113, and Churchill, *The Grand Alliance*, p. 137.

67. Rosenman, ed., *Public Papers, FDR*, 10: 48-56; *Peace and War*, pp. 627-30; and Sherwood, *Roosevelt and Hopkins*, pp. 267, 270, 271, 309, 311.

68. *FRUS 1941*, 368-69; Sherwood, *Roosevelt and Hopkins*, p. 362; Press Conference No. 762, August 19, 1941, *Complete Press Conferences*, 18: 89; Sumner Welles, *Where Are We Heading?* (New York: Harper and Bros., 1946), p. 17; Joseph Davies, Diary Entry, August 30, 1941, Box 11, Davies Papers, LC. FDR may have also suggested to Churchill an idea he had mentioned to Morgenthau. The British, the President had said, must begin to bomb the small towns in south Germany; towns that had never been bombed before, for that was the only way to break German morale. Morganthau commented "At least you have got to hand it to the British that they stick by their ethical methods of warfare" see Morgenthau, Diary Entry, August 4, 1941, Book 4, Morgenthau Presidential Diaries, FDRL.

69. Press Conference No. 750, June 24, 1941, *Complete Press Conferences*, 17: 408; Stimson to FDR, June 23, 1941 and Knox to FDR, June 23, 1941, FDR Papers, PSF, Departmental Correspondence, Navy FDRL; Carter to FDR, June 25, 1941, FDR Papers, PSF, Subject File, John Carter, FDRL; Obolensky to FDR, June 24, 1941 and FDR to Obolensky, June 30, 1941, FDR Papers, PPF No. 7633, Serge Obolensky, FDRL; FDR to Leahy, June 26, 1941, Diary 6, Box 3, Leahy Papers, LC; and Bohlen, *Witness to History*, pp. 121-22.

70. Unsigned memorandum, War Department to FDR, enclosing London intelligence estimate of Russian resistance, July 9, 1941, FDR Papers, PSF, Safe File, Russia, FDRL; *FRUS 1941*, 1: 788-89; Sherwood, *Roosevelt and Hopkins*, pp. 264, 278, 397-98; Rosenman, ed., *Public Papers FDR*, 10: 481-82; FDR to James Burns, July 21, 1941; FDR to William Knudsen, July 19, 1941; FDR to Stimson, July 21, 1941, and FDR to Knox, July 19, 1941, FDR Papers, PSF, CF, Lend-Lease, FDRL.

71. Sherwood, *Roosevelt and Hopkins*, pp. 318, 322; *FRUS 1941*, 1: 802-14; for Hopkins on Stalin see Joseph Davis, Journal Entry, September 8-10, 1941, Box 11, Davies Papers, LC.

72. Hopkins to FDR, Hull, and Welles, August 1, 1941, *FRUS 1941*, 1: 814; Hull to FDR, enclosing Steinhardt's views of events in Russia, August 6, 1941, FDR Papers, PSF, Safe File, Russia, FDRL; idem, August 8, 1941, ibid.; Unsigned State Department memorandum to FDR enclosing Morris' views on events in Germany, August 8, 1941, FDR Papers, PSF, Safe File, Russia, FDRL; Carter to FDR, August 8, 1941, FDR Papers, PSF, Safe File, John Carter, FDRL; Marshall Field to FDR enclosing portions of Ralph Ingersoll's letter to Field, August 18, 1941, FDR Papers, PPF No. 6095, Marshall Field, FDRL; Morgenthau, Diary Entry, August 4, 1941, Book 4, Morgenthau Presidential Diaries, FDRL.

73. FDR to Coy, August 2, 1941, FDR Papers, PSF, DC, Russia, FDRL; FDR to Stimson and Knox, August 30, 1941, Roosevelt, ed., *FDR Personal Letters*, 4: 1201-03; FDR told Stimson to make all shipments to Russia serviceable and complete, see FDR to Stimson, August 27, 1941, FDR Papers, PSF, CF, Lend-Lease, FDRL; Blum, *From the Morgenthau Diaries*, 2: 264. Berle, upset over the manner in which aid was being given to Russia wrote to Hopkins saying "So for God's sake tell the sentimentalists to watch themselves" see Berle to Hopkins, July 30, 1941, Berle and Jacobs, eds., *Navigating the Rapids*, p. 374; and FDR and Churchill to Stalin, August 15, 1941, Rosenman, ed., *Public Papers, FDR*, 10: 317.

74. FDR to Harriman, September 29, 1941, October 9, 1941, Harriman to FDR, September 30, 1941, October 1, 3, 10, 29, 1941, *FRUS 1941*, 1: 828-29, 836, 838, 839, 841, 844-46, 849-51; FDR to Stalin, October 30, 1941, ibid., p. 851; Stalin to FDR, October 3, 1941, FDR Papers, PSF, DC, Russia, FDRL; FDR to Harriman, October 9, 1941, FDR Papers, PSF, Safe File, Russia, FDRL. On FDR's eagerness to get goods to Stalin see FDR to Stettinius, November 7, 1941, FDR to Morgenthau, December 28, 1941, FDR to Stimson and Knox, December 28, 1941, FDR Papers, PSF, CF, Lend-lease, FDRL.

75. FDR to Taylor, September 1, 1941, FDR to Pope Pius XII, September 3, 1941, FDR Papers, PSF, DC, Myron Taylor, FDRL; and Pope Pius XII to FDR, September 20, 1941, Myron Taylor, ed., *Wartime Correspondence Between President Roosevelt and Pope Pius XII* (New York: Macmillan, 1947), pp. 63-64.

76. Joseph Grew, *Turbulent Era: A Diplomatic Record of Forty Years, 1904-1945*, 2 vols. (Boston: Houghton Mifflin, 1952), 2: 1349.

77. Ickes to FDR, June 20, 23, 30, 1941 and FDR to Ickes, June 18, 25, 1941 and July 1, 1941, Ickes, *Secret Diary*, 3: 553-60, 567-68; Morgenthau, Diary Entry, July 18, 1941, Book 4, Morgenthau Presidential Diaries, FDRL; FDR's views were shared by Navy officials, see Admiral Turner to Stark enclosed in Stark to FDR, July 19, 1941, *Pearl Harbor Hearings*, 5: 2384; Sherwood, *Roosevelt and Hopkins*, p. 319; Hull, *Memoirs*, 2: 1013-15; and *FRUS, Japan 1931-1941*, 2: 529, 549-50.

78. General George Marshall to FDR, July 15, 1941, *Pearl Harbor Hearings*, 20: 4363; Chiang Kai-shek to FDR, July 8, 1941, ibid., 19: 3493; and see MAGIC intercepts, July 2, 14, 1941, ibid., 12: 1-3; Press Conference No. 758, July 25, 1941, *Complete Press Conferences*, 18: 55; FDR to Daniels, July 25, 1941, FDR Papers, PSF, DC, Mexico, FDRL; Sayre to FDR, July 31, 1941, Box 7, Sayre Papers, LC; and Rosenman, ed., *Public Papers FDR*, 10: 281-82.

79. *FRUS 1941*, 1: 354, 357, 358; Hull, *Memoirs*, 2: 1018-19; FDR to Nomura, August 17, 1941, *FRUS Japan 1931-1941*, 2: 556-59.

80. Konoye to FDR, August 27, 1941, *FRUS Japan 1931-1941*, 2: 573; Wallace to FDR, August 29, 1941, Group 62, Box 88, Henry Wallace Papers, FDRL, Hyde Park, New York; Hull, *Memoirs,* 2: 1020-21; Grew, *Turbulent Era,* 2: 1326, 1329, 1334, 1335, 1338, 1340; see also Grew's comments and FDR to Nomura, September 3, 1941, *FRUS Japan 1931-1941,* 2: 565, 590, 645-48; and Grew to FDR, September 22, 1941, *Pearl Harbor Hearings,* 20: 4214.

81. Chiang Kai-shek to FDR, November 2, 1941, and FDR to Chiang Kai-shek, November 11, 1941, *FRUS 1941,* 5: 748-50, 758-60; FDR to Churchill, November 7, 1941, Roosevelt, ed., *FDR Personal Letters,* 4: 1233-34, and Marshall and Stark to FDR, November 5, 1941, *Pearl Harbor Hearings,* 14: 1061-62.

82. Grew to Hull, November 3, 1941, November 17, 1941, 711.94/ 2406, 711.94/2447, Nos. 1736, 1814, FDR Papers, PSF, CF, Japan, FDRL; Marshall and Stark to FDR, November 5, 1941, *Pearl Harbor Hearings,* 14: 1061-62; and Sherwood, *Roosevelt and Hopkins,* p. 420.

83. Donovan to FDR, November 13, 1941, and Hull to FDR, November 21, 1941, *Pearl Harbor Hearings,* 20: 4470-71; *modus vivendi* is in ibid., 14; 1113-15; Chiang Kai-shek on the *modus vivendi,* ibid., 20: 4473; Stimson to FDR, November 24, 1941, ibid., 16: 2014; Marshall and Stark to FDR, November 27, 1941, ibid., 14: 1083; FDR to Sayre, November 26, 1941, ibid., 2: 950; FDR to Churchill, November 24, 1941, Roosevelt, ed., *FDR Personal Letters,* 4: 1245; Churchill to FDR, November 26, 1941, Churchill, *The Grand Alliance,* pp. 596-97; Morgenthau, Diary Entry, November 22, 1941, Book 4, Morgenthau Presidential Dairies, FDRL; and Press Conference No. 787, November 28, 1941, *Complete Press Conferences,* 18: 326.

84. FDR to Hull and Welles, December 1, 1941, Roosevelt, ed., *FDR Personal Letters,* 4: 1247-48; MAGIC intercepts, December 1, 2, 4, 6, 1941, *Pearl Harbor Hearings,* 12: 209, 215, 231, 237; on the British-American war warning see ibid., 11: 5165-66; on the 14 part message see ibid., 12: 238-45; Morgenthau, Diary Entries, December 1, 3, 1941, Book 4, Morgenthau Presidential Diaries, FDRL; Sherwood, *Roosevelt and Hopkins,* pp. 426-27; FDR to Emperor Hirohito, December 6, 1941, *FRUS Japan 1931-1941,* 2: 785-86.

85. MAGIC intercepts, November 29, 1941 from Berlin, December 3, 1941 from Rome, *Pearl Harbor Hearings,* 12: 200-02, 228-29; and the rough draft of the message to Congress submitted by Secretary Knox on November 29, 1941, is in *Pearl Harbor Hearings,* 19: 3508-19.

BIBLIOGRAPHY

PRIMARY SOURCES: UNPUBLISHED MATERIALS

Manuscripts

Hyde Park, New York. Franklin D. Roosevelt Library.
  John M. Carmody Papers
  Wayne Coy Papers
  Stephen Early Papers
  William Hassett Papers
  Leon Henderson Papers
  Harry Hopkins Papers
  Lowell Mellett Papers
  Henry H. Morgenthau, Jr. Papers
  R. Walton Moore Papers
  Herbert C. Pell Papers
  Franklin D. Roosevelt Papers:
    Papers Pertaining to Family, Business, and Personal Affairs
    Papers as Assistant Secretary of the Navy
    Papers as President: Official File
    Papers as President: President's Personal File
    Papers as President: President's Secretary's File
  Henry A. Wallace Papers
  Louis Brandeis Wehle Papers

Washington, D.C. Library of Congress.
  Josephus Daniels Papers
  Joseph Davies Papers
  Norman H. Davis Papers
  William Dodd Papers
  Herbert Feis Papers
  Robert La Follette, Jr. Papers
  Felix Frankfurter Papers
  Cordell Hull Papers
  Nelson Johnson Papers
  Jesse Jones Papers
  William Leahy Papers

Breckinridge Long Papers
Key Pittman Papers
Francis Sayre Papers
Laurence Steinhardt Papers
Arthur Sweetzer Papers
William A. White Papers

Washington, D.C. National Archives. Diplomatic Division. Record Group 59: General Records of the Department of State. Decimal File, 1937-1941.

PRIMARY SOURCES: PUBLISHED MATERIALS

Official Diplomatic Documents

Ministere des Affaires Etrangeres, Commission de Publication des Documents Relatifs aux Origines de la Guerre, 1939-1945. *Documents Diplomatiques Francais, 1932-1939.* Ire Serie, 1932-1935. 6 vols. Paris: Imprimerie Nationale, 1966-1972.

————. *Documents Diplomatiques Francais, 1932-1939.* 2e Serie, 1936-1939. 7 vols. Paris: Imprimerie Nationale, 1966-1972.

U.S., Department of State. *Documents on German Foreign Policy, 1918-1945.* Series C. 5 vols. Washington: Government Printing Office, 1957-1964.

————. *Documents on German Foreign Policy, 1918-1945.* Series D. 13 vols. Washington: Government Printing Office, 1949-1964.

————. *Foreign Relations of the United States, Japan, 1931-1941.* 2 vols. Washington: Government Printing Office, 1943.

————. *Foreign Relations of the United States, The Soviet Union, 1933-1939.* Washington: Government Printing Office, 1952.

————. *Foreign Relations of the United States, 1922.* 2 vols. Washington: Government Printing Office, 1938.

————. *Foreign Relations of the United States, 1928.* 3 vols. Washington: Government Printing Office,1942-1943.

————. *Foreign Relations of the United States, 1930.* 3 vols. Washington: Government Printing Office, 1945.

U.S. Department of State. *Foreign Relations of the United States, 1933.* 5 vols. Washington: Government Printing Office, 1949-1950.

————. *Foreign Relations of the United States, 1934.* 5 vols. Washington: Government Printing Office, 1950-1951.

————. *Foreign Relations of the United States, 1935.* 4 vols. Washington: Government Printing Office, 1953.

————. *Foreign Relations of the United States, 1936.* 5 vols. Washington: Government Printing Office, 1953-1954.

————. *Foreign Relations of the United States, 1937.* 5 vols. Washington: Government Printing Office, 1954.

————. *Foreign Relations of the United States, 1938.* 5 vols. Washington: Government Printing Office, 1955.

————. *Foreign Relations of the United States, 1939.* 5 vols. Washington: Government Printing Office, 1956-1957.

————. *Foreign Relations of the United States, 1940.* 5 vols. Washington: Government Printing Office, 1959-1961.

————. *Foreign Relations of the United States, 1941.* 7 vols. Washington: Government Printing Office, 1958-1962.

————. *Peace and War: United States Foreign Policy, 1931-1941.* Washington: Government Printing Office, 1943.

Woodward, E., and Butler, R., eds. *Documents on British Foreign Policy, 1919-1939.* Second Series. 9 vols. London: His Majesty's Stationery Office, 1946-1965.

————. *Documents on British Foreign Policy, 1919-1399.* Third Series. 9 vols. London: His Majesty's Stationery Office, 1949-1955.

Speeches, Press Conference, and Public Records

Complete Press Conferences of Franklin D. Roosevelt. 25 vols. New York: Da Capo Press, 1972.

Rosenman, Samuel, ed. *The Public Papers and Addresses of Franklin D. Roosevelt.* 13 vols. New York: Random House, 1938-1950.

U.S. Congress, House. *Hearings Before the Committee on Naval Affairs on Estimates Submitted by the Secretary of the Navy.* 63rd Cong., 2nd Sess., 1915.

————. *Hearings Before the Committee on Naval Affairs on Estimates Submitted by the Secretary of the Navy.* 3 vols. 64th Cong., 1st Sess., 1916.

————. Joint Committee on the Investigation of the Pearl Harbor Attack. *Hearings Before the Joint Committee on the Investigation of the Pearl Harbor Attack.* 39 vols. 79th Cong., 1946. Washington: Government Printing Office, 1946.

Letters and Diaries

Berle, Beatrice B., and Jacobs, Travis. *Navigating the Rapids, 1918-1971.* New York: Harcourt, Brace, Jovanovich, 1973.

Bullitt, Orville, H., ed. *For the President Personal and Secret: Correspondence Between Franklin D. Roosevelt and William Bullitt.* Boston: Houghton Mifflin Co., 1972.

Blum, John M., ed. *From the Morgenthau Diaries.* 3 vols. Boston: Houghton Mifflin Co., 1950-'65.

Freedman, Max, ed. *Roosevelt and Frankfurter: Their Correspondence, 1928-1945.* Boston: Little, Brown and Co., 1967.

Hooker, Nancy H., ed. *The Moffat Papers, Selections from the Diplomatic Journals of Jay Pierrepont Moffat, 1919-1943.* Cambridge: Harvard University Press, 1956.

Ickes, Harold L. *The Secret Diary of Harold L. Ickes.* 3 vols. New York: Simon and Schuster, 1953-'54.

Israel, Fred L., ed. *The War Diary of Breckinridge Long.* Lincoln: University of Nebarska Press, 1966.

Loewenheim, Francis, Langley, Harold, and Jonas, Manfred, eds. *Roosevelt and Churchill, Their Secret Wartime Correspondence.* New York: E. P. Dutton and Co., 1975.

Nixon, Edgar B., ed. *Franklin D. Roosevelt and Foreign Affairs.* 3 vols. Cambridge: Belknap Press of Harvard University Press, 1969.

Roosevelt, Elliot, ed. *FDR: His Personal Letters.* 4 vols. New York: Duell, Sloan, and Pearce, 1947-'50.

Wartime Correspondence between Roosevelt and Pope Pius XII. New York: Macmillan Co., 1947.

SECONDARY SOURCES

BOOKS

Biographical Studies

Asbell, Bernard. *The F.D.R. Memoirs.* New York: Doubleday and Co., 1973.

Burns, James MacGregor. *Roosevelt: The Lion and the Fox.* New York: Harcourt, Brace, and World, 1956.

————. *The Soldier of Freedom.* New York: Harcourt, Brace, and Jovanovich, Inc., 1970.

Busch, Noel. *What Manner of Man?* New York: Harper and Bros., 1944.

Davis, Kenneth S. *FDR, The Beckoning of Destiny, 1882-1928.* G. P. Putnam's Sons,1 971.

Einaudi, Mario. *The Roosevelt Revolution.* New York: Harcourt, Brace, and Co., 1959.

Flynn, John T. *The Roosevelt Myth.* New York: Devin-Adair Co., 1948.

Freidel, Frank. *Franklin D. Roosevelt.* 3 vols. Boston: Little, Brown and Co., 1952-'73.

Greer, Thomas H. *What Roosevelt Thought.* East Lansing: Michigan State University Press, 1958.

Gunther, John. *Roosevelt in Retrospect, A Profile in History.* New York: Harper and Bros., 1950.

Halasz, Nicholas. *Roosevelt Through Foreign Eyes.* New York: D. Van Nostrand Co., 1961.

Hatch, Alden. *Franklin D. Roosevelt. An Informal Biography.* New York: Henry Holt and Co., 1947.

Leuchtenburg, William. *Franklin D. Roosevelt and the New Deal, 1932-1940.* New York: Harper and Row, 1963.

Lindley, Ernest K. *Half Way with Roosevelt. New York*s Viking Press, 1937.

————. *Franklin D. Roosevelt: A Career in Progressive Democracy.* New York: Blue Ribbon Books, 1934.

————. *The Roosevelt Revolution.* New York: Viking Press, 1933.

Ludwig, Emil. *Roosevelt: A Study in Fortune and Power.* New York: Viking Press, 1938.

Perkins, Dexter. *The New Age of Franklin Roosevelt, 1932-1945.* Chicago: University of Chicago Press, 1959.

Robinson, Edgar. *The Roosevelt Leadership, 1933-1945.* New York: J. B. Lippincott Co., 1955.

Rollins, Alfred B., Jr. *Roosevelt and Howe.* New York: Alfred A. Knopf, 1962.

Ross, Leland and Grobin, Allan. *The Life Story of F.D. — An Authentic Biography.* New York: E. P. Dutton, 1932.

Schlesinger, Arthur M., Jr. *The Age of Roosevelt.* 3 vols. Boston: Houghton Mifflin Co., 1956-'58.

Talbot, Hugh. *Franklin Roosevelt.* London: SCM Press, 1950.

Tugwell, Rexford. *The Democratic Roosevelt.* Garden City, New York: Doubleday and Co., 1957.

————. *In Search of Roosevelt*. Cambridge: Harvard University Press, 1972.

Venkataramani, M. S. *The Sunny Side of FDR*. Columbus: Ohio University Press, 1973.

White, William S. *Majesty and Mischief, A Mixed Tribute to FDR*. New York: McGraw-Hill Book Co., 1961.

Personal Reminiscenes

Bohlen, Charles E. *Witness to History, 1929-1969*. New York: Norton and Co., 1973.

————. *The Transformation of American Foreign Policy*. New York: W. W. Norton, 1969.

Bowers, Claude G. *My Mission to Spain*. New York: Simon and Schuster, 1954.

Churchill, Winston. *Their Finest Hour*. Boston: Houghton Mifflin Co., 1949.

————. *The Grand Alliance*. Boston: Houghton Mifflin Co., 1951.

Daniels, Josephus. *The Wilson Era*. 2 vols. Chapel Hill: University of North Carolina Press, 1944-'46.

Davies, Joseph E. *Mission to Moscow*. New York: Simon and Schuster, 1941.

Dodd, William E., ed. *Ambassador Dodd's Diary, 1933-1938*. New York: Harcourt, Brace, Jovanovich, 1941.

Farley, James A. *Behind the Ballots*. New York: Harcourt, Brace and Co., 1938.

————. *Jim Farley's Story, The Roosevelt Years*. New York: McGraw-Hill Book Co., 1948.

Feis, Herbert. *1933: Characters in Crisis*. New York: Little, Brown and Co., 1966.

Grew, Joseph. *Turbulent Era: A Diplomatic Record of Forty Years, 1904-1945*. 2 vols. Boston: Houghton Mifflin Co., 1952.

Hull, Cordell. *The Memoirs of Cordell Hull*. 2 vols. New York: Macmillan Co., 1948.

Kennan, George. *Memoirs, 1925-1950*. Boston: Little, Brown and Co., 1967.

Leahy, William. *I Was There*. New York: McGraw-Hill Book Co., 1950.

McIntire, Ross. *White House Physician*. New York: G. P. Putnams Sons, 1946.

Moley, Raymond. *After Seven Years*. New York: Harper and Bros., 1939.

Murphy, Robert. *Diplomat Among Warriors*. Garden City, New York: Doubleday and Co., 1964.

Perkins, Frances. *The Roosevelt I Knew*. New York: Viking Press, 1946.

Phillips, William. *Ventures in Diplomacy*. Portland, Maine: Anthoensen Press, 1952.

Roosevelt, Eleanor. *This I Remember*. New York: Harper and Bros., 1949.

————. *The Autobiography of Eleanor Roosevelt*. London: Hutchinson and Co., 1947.

Roosevelt, Elliot. *As He Saw It*. New York: Duell, Sloan, and Pearce, 1946.

Roosevelt, Franklin. *On Our Way*. New York: John Day Co., 1934.

Roosevelt, Mrs. James. *My Boy Franklin*. New York: Ray Long and Richard R. Smith, Inc., 1933.

Roosevelt, James and Shalett, Sidney. *Affectionately, FDR.* New York: Harcourt, Brace, and Co., 1959.

Rosenman, Samuel. *Working with Roosevelt.* New York: Harper and Bros., 1952.

Sherwood, Robert H. *Roosevelt and Hopkins, An Intimate History.* New York: Harper and Bros., 1948.

Smith, A. Merriman. *Thank You, Mr. President.* New York: Harper and Bros., 1946.

Stimson, Henry L. and Bundy, McGeorge. *On Active Service in Peace and War.* New York: Harper and Bros., 1947.

Tully, Grace. *FDR, My Boss.* New York: Charles Scribner's Sons, 1949.

Wehle, Louis B. *Hidden Threads of History, Wilson through Roosevelt.* New York: Macmillan Co., 1953.

Welles, Sumner. *The Time for Decision.* New York: Harper and Row, 1944.

————. *Where Are We Heading?* New York: Harper and Row, 1946.

————. *Seven Decisions that Shaped History.* New York: Harper and Row, 1951.

Subject Area Studies
Germany, Japan, Italy

Baker, Leonard. *Roosevelt and Pearl Harbor.* London: Macmillan Co., 1970.

Bisson, T. A. *America's Far Eastern Policy.* New York: Macmillan Co., 1945.

Borg Dorothy. *The United States and the Far Eastern Crisis of 1933-1938.* Cambridge: Harvard University Press, 1964.

Compton, James V. *The Swastika and the Eagle.* Boston: Houghton Mifflin Co., 1967.

Duggan, Laurence. *The Americas: The Search for Hemispheric Security.* New York: Henry Holt and Co., 1949.

Farago, Ladislas. *The Broken Seal.* New York: Random House, 1967.

Feis, Herbert. *The Road to Pearl Harbor: The Coming of the War Between the United States and Japan.* Princeton: Princeton University Press, 1950.

Freidlander, Saul. *Prelude to Downfall: Hitler and the United States, 1939-1941.* New York: Alfred A. Knopf, 1967.

Frye, Alton. *Nazi Germany and the American Hemisphere, 1933-1941.* New Haven: Yale University Press, 1967.

Griswold, A. Whitney. *The Far Eastern Policy of the United States.* New York: Harcourt, Brace and Co., 1938.

Guerrant, Edward O. *Roosevelt's Good Neighbor Policy.* Albuquerque: University of New Mexico Press, 1950.

Guttman, Allen. *The Wound in the Heart, America and the Spanish Civil War.* New York: Free Press of Glencoe, 1962.

Harris, Brice. *The United States and the Italo-Ethiopian Crisis.* Stanford: Stanford University Press, 1964.

Heinrichs, Waldo H. *American Ambassador: Joseph C. Grew and the Development of the United States Diplomatic Tradition.* Boston: Little, Brown and Co., 1966.

Johnstone, William C. *The United States and Japan's New Order.* New York: Oxford University Press, 1941.

Koginos, Manny. *The Panay Incident: Prelude to War.* Lafayette: Purdue University Studies, 1967.

Millis, Walter. *This Is Pearl! The United States and Japan, 1941.* New York: William Morrow and Co., 1947.

Morgenstern, George. *Pearl Harbor: The Story of the Secret War.* Old Greenwich, Conn.: Devin-Adair Co., 1947.

Morison, Samuel E. *The Rising Sun in the Pacific, 1931–April 1942.* Boston: Little, Brown and Co., 1948.

Neumann, William L. *America Encounters Japan.* Baltimore: John Hopkins Press, 1963.

Offner, Arnold. *American Appeasement, United States Foreign Policy and Germany, 1933-1938.* Cambridge: Harvard University Press, 1969.

Puzzo, Dante. *The Spanish Civil War.* New York: Van Nostrand Reinhold Co., 1969.

Schroeder, Paul. *The Axis-Alliance and Japanese-American Relations, 1941.* Ithaca: Cornell University Press, 1958.

Taylor, A. J. P. *The Origins of the Second World War.* New York: Atheneum, 1962.

Taylor, F. Jay. *The United States and the Spanish Civil War.* New York: Bookman Associates, 1956.

Traina, Richard P. *American Diplomacy and the Spanish Civil War.* Bloomington: Indiana University Press, 1968.

Trefousse, H. P. *Germany and American Neutrality, 1939-1941.* New York: Bookman Associates, 1951.

Waller, George M., ed. *Pearl Harbor, Roosevelt and the Coming of the War.* Boston: D. C. Heath, 1965.

Wheeler-Bennett, John W. *Munich, Prologue to Tragedy.* New York: Duell, Sloan, and Pearce, 1943.

Wohlstetter, Roberta. *Pearl Harbor: Warning and Decision.* Stanford: Stanford University Press, 1962.

The Soviet Union

Bailey, Thomas A. *America Faces Russia.* Ithaca: Cornell University Press, 1950.

Bishop, Donald G. *The Roosevelt-Litvinov Agreements.* Syracuse: Syracuse University Press, 1965.

Browder, Robert P. *The Origins of Soviet-American Diplomacy.* Princeton: Princeton University Press, 1953.

Bullitt, William C. *The Great Globe Itself, A Preface to World Affairs.* New York: Charles Scribners Sons, 1946.

Crocker, George. *Roosevelt's Road to Russia.* Chicago: Henry Regnery Co., 1959.

Dawson, R. H. *The Decision to Aid Russia, 1941.* Chapel Hill: University of North Carolina Press, 1959.

Dean, Vera. *The United States and Russia.* Cambridge: Harvard University Press, 1947.

Dulles, Foster R. *The Road to Teheran.* Princeton: Princeton University Press, 1944.

Farnsworth, Beatrice. *William C. Bullitt and the Soviet Union.* Bloomington: Indiana University Press, 1967.

Fisher, Harold. *America and Russia in the World Community.* Claremont: Claremont College Press, 1946.

Harriman, W. Averell. *America and Russia in a Changing World.* New York: Doubleday and Co., 1971.

Ierring, George C. *Aid to Russia, 1941-1946.* New York: Columbia University Press, 1973.

Kennan, George. *Russia and the West under Lenin and Stalin*. Boston: Little, Brown & Co., 1960.

Kimball, Warren F. *The most unsordid act, Lend Lease 1939-1941*. Baltimore: John Hopkins University Press, 1969.

McClelland, Robert C. *President Roosevelt's Recognition of the Soviet Union*. Norfolk: College of William and Mary, General Publication Series, 1956.

Morris, Bernard. *International Communism and American Policy*. New York: Atherton Press, 1966.

Schwartz, Andrew J. *America and the Russo-Finnish War*. Washington: Public Affairs Press, 1960.

Sobel, Robert. *The Origins of Interventionism*. New York: Bookman Associates, 1960.

Williams, William A. *American-Russian Relations, 1781-1947*. New York: Rinehart Co., 1952.

Franklin D. Roosevelt and American Foreign Policy

Adler, Selig. *The Isolationist Impulse — Its Twentieth Century Reaction*. New York: Abelard-Schuman, 1957.

————, *The Uncertain Giant, 1921-1941*. New York: Macmillan Co., 1965.

Alsop, J. and Kintner, R. *American White Paper*. New York: Simon and Schuster, 1940.

Barnes, Harry E. *Selected Revisionist Pamphlets*. New York: Arno Press, 1972.

Barron, Gloria. *Leadership in Crisis: FDR and the Path to Intervention*. Port Washington, New York: Kennikat Press, 1973.

Beard, Charles A. *American Foreign Policy in the Making, 1932-1940*. New Haven: Yale University Press, 1946.

————. *President Roosevelt and the Coming of the War, 1941*. New Haven: Yale University Press, 1948.

Brogan, Dennis. *The Era of Franklin D. Roosevelt: A Chronicle of the New Deal and Global War*. New York: United States Publishers Assoc., 1950.

Chadwin, Mark L. *The Hawks of World War II*. Kingsport, Tennessee: University of North Carolina Press, 1968.

Chamberlin, William H. *America's Second Crusade*. Chicago: Henry Regnery Co., 1950.

Cole, Wayne. *America First, The Battle Against Intervention, 1940-1941*. Madison: University of Wisconsin Press, 1953.

Dallek, Robert, ed. *The Roosevelt Diplomacy and World War II*. New York: Holt, Rinehart, and Winston, 1970.

Davids, Jules. *America and the World of Our Time: United States Diplomacy in the Twentieth Century*. 3rd ed. New York: Random House, 1970.

DeConde, Alexander, ed. *Isolation and Security*. Durham: Duke University Press, 1957.

Divine, Robert. *Roosevelt and World War II*. Baltimore: John Hopkins Press, 1969.

————. *Second Chance, The Triumph of Interventionism in America During World War II*. New York: Atheneum, 1967.

————. *The Reluctant Belligerent, America's Entry into World War II*. New York: John Wiley and Sons, 1965.

Drummond, Donald. *The Passing of American Neutrality, 1937-1941*. Ann Arbor: University of Michigan Press, 1955.

Duroselle, Jean-Baptiste. *From Wilson to Roosevelt*. Trans. Nancy Roelker. Cambridge: Harvard University Press, 1963.

Fehrenbach, T. R. *FDR's Undeclared War*. New York: David McKay Co., 1967.

Gardner, Lloyd. *Economic Aspects of New Deal Diplomacy*. Boston: Beacon Press, 1964.

Graebner, Norman, ed. *An American Tradition: American Secretaries of State in the Twentieth Century*. New York: McGraw-Hill, 1961.

Haight, John M. *American Aid to France, 1938-1940*. New York: Atheneum, 1970.

Hoehling, A. A. *America's Road to War, 1939-1941*. New York: Abelard-Schuman, 1970.

Holbo, Paul S. *Isolationism, Interventionism, 1932-1941*. Chicago: Rand McNally, 1967.

Jonas, Manfred. *Isolationism in America, 1935-1941*. Ithaca: Cornell University Press, 1966.

Langer, William and Gleason, S. Everett. *The Challenge to Isolation, 1937-1940*. New York: Harper and Bros., 1952.

————. *The Undeclared War, 1940-1941*. New York: Harper and Bros., 1953.

Lindley, Ernest K., and Davis, Forrest. *How War Came*. New York: Simon and Schuster, 1942.

Martin, James J. *American Liberalism and World Politics, 1931-1941*. 2 vols. New York: Devin-Adair Co., 1964.

Matloff, Maurice. *Mr. Roosevelt's Three Wars: FDR as War Leader*. Colorado: U.S. Air Force Academy, 1964.

Nevins, Allan. *The New Deal and World Affairs*. New Haven: Yale University Press, 1950.

Offner, Arnold, ed. *America and the Origins of World War II, 1933-1941*. Boston: Houghton Mifflin Co., 1971.

Osgood, Robert E. *Ideals and Self-Interest in America's Foreign Relations*. Chicago: University of Chicago Press, 1953.

Range, Willard. *Franklin D. Roosevelt's World Order*. Athens: University of Georgia Press, 1959.

Rauch, Basil. *Roosevelt from Munich to Pearl Harbor*. New York: Creative Age Press, 1950.

Sanborn, Fredeick R. *Design for War*. New York: Devin-Adair Co., 1951.

Sargent, Porter. *Getting Us into War*. Boston: Privately Printed, 1941.

Stromberg, Roland N. *Collective Security and American Foreign Policy*. New York, Frederick A. Praeger, 1963.

Tansill, Charles C. *Back Door to War*. Chicago: Henry Regnery Co., 1952.

Wiltz, John E. *From Isolation to War, 1931-1941*. New York: Thomas Y. Crowell, 1968.

UNPUBLISHED DISSERTATIONS

Abbazia, Patrick. "Mr. Roosevelt's Navy: The Little War of the United States Atlantic Fleet, 1939-1942." Ph.D. dissertation, Columbia University.

Aldred, Francis. "The Brussels Conference." Ph.D. dissertation, University of Virginia, 1967.

Bauer, Wolfred. "The Shipment of American Strategic Raw Materials to Nazi Germany: A Study in United States Economic Foregin Policy, 1933-1939." Ph.D. dissertation, University of Washington, 1964.

Bennett, Edward M. "Franklin D. Roosevelt and Russian-American Relations, 1933-1939." Ph.D. dissertation, University of Washington, 1964.

Boswell, G. "Buddha Bill: The Roller-Coaster Career of William C. Bullitt." Ph.D. dissertation, Texas Christian University, 1972.

Braddick, Henderson. "The United States and Italy, International Politics, 1937-1941." Ph.D. dissertation, University of Washington, 1957.

Brown, Robert J. "Emergence from Isolation, 1937-1941." Ph.D. dissertation, Syracuse University, 1968.

Burke, Robert L. "Franklin D. Roosevelt and the Far East: 1913-1941." Ph.D. dissertation, Michigan State University, 1969.

Costi, Robert. "To Stop a War: Efforts by the League of Nations and the United States to Place Economic Restrictions on Italy During the Italo-Ethiopian War, 1935-1936." Ph.D. dissertation, University of Idaho, 1972.

DeCola, Thomas G. "Roosevelt and Mussolini: The Critical Years, 1938-1941." Ph.D. dissertation, Kent State University, 1967.

Eagles, Keith. "Ambassador Joseph E. Davies and American-Soviet Relations, 1937-1941." Ph.D. dissertation, University of Washington, 1966.

Etzold, Thomas. "Fair Play: American Principles and Practice in Relations with Germany, 1933-1939." Ph.D. dissertation, Yale University, 1970.

Everen, Brooks Van. "Franklin D. Roosevelt and the German Problem, 1914-1945." Ph.D. dissertation, University of Colorado, 1970.

Gerberding, William P. "Franklin D. Roosevelt's Conceptions of the Soviet Union in World Politics." Ph.D. dissertation, University of Chicago, 1959.

Handen, Ella. "Neutrality Legislation and Presidential Discretion: A Study of the 1930s." Ph.D. dissertation, Rutgers University, 1968.

Henson, Edward L. "Britain, America, and the European Crisis, 1937-1938." Ph.D. dissertation, University of Virginia, 1969.

Holland, Caroline. "The Foreign Contacts Made by the German Opposition to Hitler." Ph.D. dissertation, University of Pennsylvania, 1967.

Kunert, Dirk. "German-American Relations and the Soviet Union." Ph.D. dissertation, Georgetown University, 1972.

Lane, Peter. "The United States and the Balkan Crisis of 1940-1941." Ph.D. dissertation, University of Washington, 1972.

Leutze, James R. "If Britain Should Fall: Roosevelt and Churchill and British American Naval Relations, 1938-1940." Ph.D. dissertation, Duke University, 1968.

Lindley, Christopher. "Franklin D. Roosevelt and the Politics of Isolationism, 1932-1936." Ph.D. dissertation, Cornell University, 1963.

Maddux, Thomas R. "American Relations with the Soviet Union, 1933-1941." Ph.D. dissertation, University of Michigan, 1969.

McCarty, Kenneth. "Stanley K. Hornbeck and the Far East, 1931-1941." Ph.D. dissertation, Duke University, 1970.

Millsap, Mary. "Mussolini and the United States: Italo-American Relations, 1935-1941." Ph.D. dissertation, University of California, 1972.

Moore, James W. "The Logic of Isolation and Neutrality, American Foreign Policy, 1933-1935." Ph.D. dissertation, University of North Carolina, 1970.

Notaro, Carmen. "Franklin D. Roosevelt and the American Communists." Ph.D. dissertation, University of New York, 1969.

O'Connor, Joseph E. "Laurence A. Steinhardt and American Policy Toward the Soviet Union, 1939-1941." Ph.D. dissertation, University of Virginia, 1968.

Ostrower, Gary. "The United States, the League of Nations, and Collective Security, 1931-1934." Ph.D. dissertation, University of Rochester, 1970.

Papachristou, Judith. "American-Soviet Relations anad United States Policy in the Pacific, 1933-1941." Ph.D. dissertation, University of Colorado, 1968.

Ragland, James. "Franklin D. Roosevelt and Public Opinion, 1933-1940." Ph.D. dissertation, Stanford University, 1954.

Reitzes, Robert. "Marxist-Leninist Ideology and Soviet Policies Toward the United States, 1919-1939." Ph.D. dissertation, Georgetown University, 1973.

Remak, Joachim. "Germany and the United States, 1933-1939." Ph.D. dissertation, Stanford University, 1955.

Viault, B. "The Peace Issue, 1939-1940." Ph.D. dissertation, Duke University, 1963.

Whitehead, Donald. "Foreign Policy During President Roosevelt's First Term." Ph.D. dissertation, University of Chicago, 1951.

ARTICLES

Abjerg, Victor. "Isolationism and the Early New Deal, 1932-1937." Current History 35 (October 1958): 204-10.

Ballantine, Joseph W. "From Mukden to Pearl Harbor: The Foreign Policies of Japan." Foreign Affairs 27 (July 1949): 651-64.

Bemis, Samuel F. "First Gun of a Revisionist Historiography for the Second World War." Journal of Modern History 19 (March 1947): 55-59.

Boller, Paul F. "The 'Great Conspiracy' of 1933: A Study in Short Memories." Southwest Review 39 (Spring 1954): 97-112.

Borg, Dorothy. "Notes on Roosevelt's 'Quarantine' Speech." Political Science Quarterly 72 (September 1957): 405-33.

Bowers, Robert E. "Senator Arthur Robinson of Indiana Vindicated: William Bullitt's Secret Mission to Europe." Indiana Magazine of History 61 (September 1965): 189-204.

Boyle, John H. "The Drought-Walsh Mission to Japan." Pacific Historical Review 34 (May 1965): 141-61.

Browder, Robert P. "Soviet Far Eastern Policy and American Recognition, 1932-1934." Pacific Historical Review 21 (August 1952): 263-73.

———. "The United States, the Soviet Union and the Comintern." Russian Review 12 (January 1953): 25-39.

———. "The First Encounter: Roosevelt and the Russians, 1933." United States Naval Institute Proceedings 83 (May 1957): 523-31.

Butow, Robert. "The Hull-Nomura Conversations: A Fundamental Misconception." American Historical Review 65 (July 1960): 822-36.

Clauss, Errol. "The Roosevelt Administration and Manchukuo, 1933-1941." Historian 32 (August 1970): 595-611.

Clyde, Paul H. "Historical Reflections on American Relations with the Far East." *Sou*th *Atlantic Quarterly* 61 (Autumn 1962): 437-49.

Cole, Wayne S. "The America First Committee." *Journal of the Illinois State Histo*ica¹ *Society* 64 (Winter 1951): 305-22.

————. "America First and the South 1940-1941." *Journal of Southern History* 22 (February 1956): 36-47.

————. "Senator Key Pittman and American Neutrality Policies, 1933-1940." *Mississippi Valley Historical Review* 46 (March 1960): 644-62.

————. "American Entry into World War II: A Historiographical Appraisal." *Mississippi Valley Historical Review* 43 (March 1957): 595-617.

Conn, Stetson. "Changing Concepts of National Defense in the United States, 1937-1941." *Military Affairs* 28 (Spring 1964): 1-7.

Craig, Gordon A. "High Tide of Appeasement: The Road to Munich, 1937-1938." *Political Science Quarterly* 65 (March 1950): 20-37.

Current, Richard N. "How Stimson Meant to 'Maneuver' the Japanese." *Mississippi Valley Historical Review* 60 (June 1953): 67-74.

Deac, W. P. "America's Undeclared Naval War." *United States Naval Institute Proceedings* 87 (October 1961): 70-9.

Divine, Robert. "Franklin D. Roosevelt and Collective Security, 1933." *Mississippi Va*ley *Historical Review* 68 (June 1961): 42-59.

Donovan, John C. "Congressional Isolationists and the Roosevelt Foreign Policy." *World Politics* 3 (April 1951); 299-316.

Dupuy, T. N. "Pearl Harbor: Who Blundered?" *American Heritage* 13 (February 1962): 64-81.

Esthus, Raymond. "President Roosevelt's Commitment to Britain to Intervene in a Pacific War." *Mississippi Valley Historical Review* 50 (June 1963): 28-38.

Fagan, George V. "F.D.R. and Naval Limitation." *United States Naval Institute Proceedings* 81 (April 1955): 411-18.

Feis, Herbert. "War Came at Pearl Harbor: Suspicions Considered." *Yale Review* 45 (Spring 1956): 379-90.

Ferrell, Robert H. "Pearl Harbor and the Revisionists." *Historian* 17 (Spring 1955): 215-33.

Fischer, George. "Genesis of U.S.-Soviet Relations in World War II." *Review of Politics* 12 (July 1950): 363-78.

Freidel, Frank. "World War II: Before Pearl Harbor." *Current History* 35 (October 1958): 211-15.

Greenberg, Daniel S. "U.S. Destroyers for British Bases — Fifty Old Ships Go to War." *United States Naval Institute Proceedings* 88 (November 1962): 70-83.

Greaves, Percy and Barnes, Harry E. "Mystery of Pearl Harbor." *National Review* 13 December 1966, pp. 1260-72.

Haight, John McV. "France and the Aftermath of Roosevelt's "Quarantine" Speech." *World Politics* 14 (January 1962): 283-306.

———— "Roosevelt and the Aftermath of the Quarantine Speech." *Review of Politics* 24 (April 1962): 233-59.

————. "France's First War Mission to the United States." *Air Power Historian* 11 (January 1964): 11-15.

————. "France, the United States, and the Munich Crisis." *Journal of Modern History* 32 (December, 1930): 340-58.

———— " Roosevelt as Friend of France." *Foreign Affairs* 44 (April 1966): 518-26.

————. "Franklin D. Roosevelt and A Naval Quarantine of Japan." *Pacific Historical Review* 40 (May 1971): 203-26.

Hammond, Mary K. "Revolution in Foreign Policy: 1932-1952." *Current History* 28 (January 1955): 1-6.

Haslip, Harvey. "Summit Meeting." *United States Naval Institute Proceedings* 89 (November 1963): 76-80.

Herzog, James H. "Influence of the United States Navy in the Embargo of Oil to Japan, 1940-1941." *Pacific Historical Review* 35 (August 1966): 317-28.

Hill, Norman. "Was There an Ultimatum before Pearl Harbor?" *American Journal of International Law* 42 (April 1948): 355-67

Hoehling, A. A. "New Clues to the Pearl Harbor Puzzle." *True* March, 1963, pp. 115-29.

Howard, Michael. "Military Intelligence and Surprise Attack; The 'Lessons' of Pearl Harbor." *World Politics* 15 (July 1963): 701-11.

Hsu, Immanuel. "Kurusu's Mission to the United States and the Abortive Modus Vivendi." *Journal of Modern History* 24 (September 1952): 301-07.

Jablon, Howard. "Franklin D. Roosevelt and the Spanish Civil War." *Social Studies* 56 (February 1965): 59-69.

Jacobs, Travis. "Roosevelt's Quarantine Speech.' ". *Historian* 24 (August 1962): 483-502.

Jonas, Manfred. "Prophet Without Honor: Hans Heinrich Dieckhoff's Reports from Washington." *Mid-America* 47 (July 1965): 222-33.

Kahn, Herman. "World War II and Its Background: Research Materials at the Franklin D. Roosevelt Library and Policies Concerning Their Use." *The American Archivist* 17 (April 1954): 149-62.

Kennedy, Thomas C. "Charles A. Beard and the 'Court Historians'." *Historian* 25 (August 1963): 439-50.

Kimball, Warren F. "Dieckhoff and America: A German's View of German-American Relations, 1937-1941." *Historian* 27 (February 1965): 218-43.

Kittredge, T. B. "The Muddle before Pearl Harbor." *U.S. News*, December 3, 1954, pp. 52-63, 110-39.

Lukas, Richard C. "The Impact of 'Barbarossa' on the Soviet Air Force and the Resulting Commitment of United States Aircraft, June-October, 1941." *Historian* 29 (November 1966): 60-80.

Matloff, Maurice. "Prewar Military Plans and Preparations, 1939-1941." *United States Naval Institute Proceedings* 79 (July 1953): 741-48.

Miles, Sherman. "Pearl Harbor in Retrospect," *Atlantic,* July, 1948, pp. 65-72.

Morgenthau, Henry. "The Morgenthau Diaries," *Colliers,* September 27, October 4, 11, 18, 25, November 1, 1947, pp. 11-13, 20-1, 20-1, 16-17, 24-5, 22-3.

Morison, Samuel E. "Did Roosevelt Start the War? History Through a Beard." *Atlantic,* August, 1948, pp. 91-7.

Morris, Robert L. "A Reassessment of Russian Recognition." *Historian* 24 (August 1962): 470-82.

Morton, Louis. "Pearl Harbor in Perspective: A Bibliographical Survey." *United States Naval Institute Proceedings* 81 (April 1955): 461-8.

Namier, Sir Lewis. "Diplomacy in the Interwar Period." *World Politics* 7 (October 1954): 102-18.

Neumann, William L. "Franklin D. Roosevelt and Japan, 1913-1933." *Pacific Historical Review* 22 (May 1953): 143-53.

Nomura, Kichisaburo. "Stepping Stones to War." *United States Naval Institute Proceedings* 77 (September 1951): 927-31.

Offner, Arnold A. "William E. Dodd: Romantic Historian and Diplomatic Cassandra." *Historian* 24 (August 1962): 451-69.

Perkins, Dexter. "American Wars and Critical Historians." *Yale Review* 40 (Summer, 1951): 682-95.

Pratt, Julius. "The Ordeal of Cordell Hull," *Review of Politics* 28 (January 1966): 76-98.

Ragland, James. "Franklin D. Roosevelt and the Spanish Civil War." *American Philosophical Year Book* 1960: 415-21.

Roosevelt, Franklin D. "On Your Own Heads." *Scribners Magazine,* January-June 1917, pp. 413-16.

————. "What the Navy Can Do For Your Boy." *The Ladies Home Journal,* June 1917, pp. 25, 88.

Rothfels, Hans. "The German Resistance in Its International Aspects." *International Affairs* 34 (October 1958): 477-89.

Schlesinger, Jr., Arthur M. "Roosevelt and His Detractors," *Harpers,* June 1950, pp 62-8.

Sherwood, Robert E. "Secret Papers of Harry L. Hopkins." *Colliers,* May 29, June 5, 12, 19, 26, 1948, pp. 13-5, 14-5, 26-7, 22-3, 18-9; July 3, 10, 17, 24, 31, August 7, 14, 21, 28, September 4, 11, 18, 1948, pp. 18-9, 27, 23, 20, 22, 25-6, 24-5, 18-9, 18, 28, 28-9, 28.

Sontag, Raymond. "The Origins of the Second World War." *Review of Politics* 25 (October 1963): 497-508.

Sternsher, Bernard. "The Stimson Doctrine: F.D.R. versus Moley and Tugwell." *Pacific Historical Review* 31 (August 1962): 281-9.

Theobold, R. A. "Final Secret of Pearl Harbor." *U.S. News,* April 2, 1954, pp. 48-93.

Thompson, Kenneth W. "Collective Security Reexamined." *American Political Science Review.* 47 (September 1953): 753-72.

Trefousse, H. L. "Germany and Pearl Harbor." *Far Eastern Quarterly* 11 (November 1951): 35-50.

Uhlig, Frank and Mathews, William R. "Franklin Delano Roosevelt: A Discipline of Mahan." *United States Naval Institute Proceedings* 79 (May 1953): 561-62.

Ullman, Richard. "The Davies Mission and United States-Soviet Relations, 1937-1941." *World Politics* 9 (January 1957): 220-39.

Van Alstyne, Richard W. "Before Pearl Harbor." *Current History.* 20 (February 1951): 70-6.

Vogel, Bertram. "Diplomatic Prelude to Pearl Harbor." *United States Naval Institute Procedings* 75 (April 1949): 415-21.

Wallace, William V. "Roosevelt and British Appeasement, 1938." *The Bulletin of the British Association for American Studies* 5 (December 1962): 4-30.

Wasserman, Benno. "The Failure of Intelligence Prediction." *Political Studies* 8(June 1960): 156-69.

Watson, Mark S. "First Vigorous Steps in Re-Arming, 1938-'39." *Military Affairs* 12 (Summer 1948): 65-78.

Welles, Sumner. "Roosevelt and the Far East." *Harpers,* February-March, 1951, pp. 27-38, 70-80.

Wiltz, John E. "The Nye Committee Revisited." *Historian* 23 (February 1961): 211-33.

Wright, Gordon. "Ambassador Bullitt and the Fall of France," *World Politics* 10 (October 1957): 63-90.

Wylie, J. C. "Reflections on the War in the Pacific." *United States Naval Institute Proceedings* 78 (April 1952): 350-61.

Zimmerman, John L. "Force in Readiness." *United States Naval Institute Proceedings* 83 (February 1957): 165-71.

INDEX